Another Day in
PARADISE

W9-AZA-213

Other Books by Jim Toomey

Sherman's Lagoon: Ate That, What's Next?

Poodle: The Other White Meat

An Illustrated Guide to Shark Etiquette

Another Day in PARADISE

The Fourth Sherman's Lagoon Collection
by Jim Toomey

**Andrews McMeel
Publishing**

Kansas City

Sherman's Lagoon is distributed internationally by King Features Syndicate, Inc. For information, write King Features Syndicate, Inc., 888 Seventh Avenue, New York, New York 10019.

Another Day in Paradise copyright © 2001 by J.P. Toomey. All rights reserved. Printed in the United States of America. No part of this book may be used or reproduced in any manner whatsoever without written permission except in the case of reprints in the context of reviews. For information, write Andrews McMeel Publishing, an Andrews McMeel Universal company, 4520 Main Street, Kansas City, Missouri 64111.

01 02 03 04 05 BAH 10 9 8 7 6 5 4 3 2 1

ISBN: 0-7407-2012-0

Library of Congress Catalog Card Number: 2001088695

Sherman's Lagoon may be viewed on the Internet at:
www.slagoon.com

ATTENTION: SCHOOLS AND BUSINESSES

Andrews McMeel books are available at quantity discounts with bulk purchase for educational, business, or sales promotional use. For information, please write to: Special Sales Department, Andrews McMeel Publishing, 4520 Main Street, Kansas City, Missouri 64111.

"Joy to the fishes in the deep blue sea . . ."

—Three Dog Night

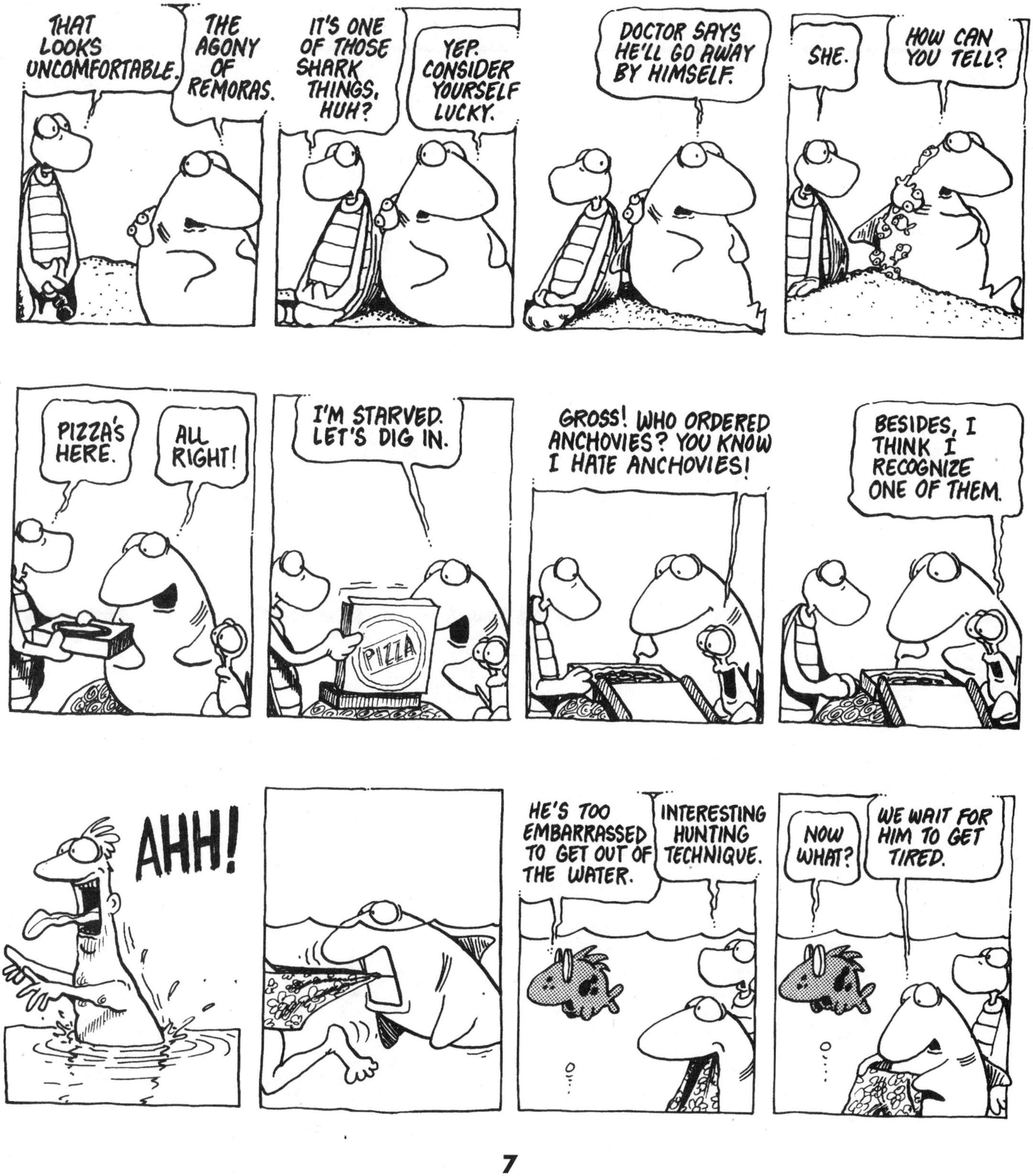

THAT LOOKS UNCOMFORTABLE.
THE AGONY OF REMORAS.
IT'S ONE OF THOSE SHARK THINGS, HUH?
YEP. CONSIDER YOURSELF LUCKY.
DOCTOR SAYS HE'LL GO AWAY BY HIMSELF.
SHE.
HOW CAN YOU TELL?
PIZZA'S HERE.
ALL RIGHT!
I'M STARVED. LET'S DIG IN.
PIZZA
GROSS! WHO ORDERED ANCHOVIES? YOU KNOW I HATE ANCHOVIES!
BESIDES, I THINK I RECOGNIZE ONE OF THEM.
AHH!
HE'S TOO EMBARRASSED TO GET OUT OF THE WATER.
INTERESTING HUNTING TECHNIQUE.
NOW WHAT?
WE WAIT FOR HIM TO GET TIRED.

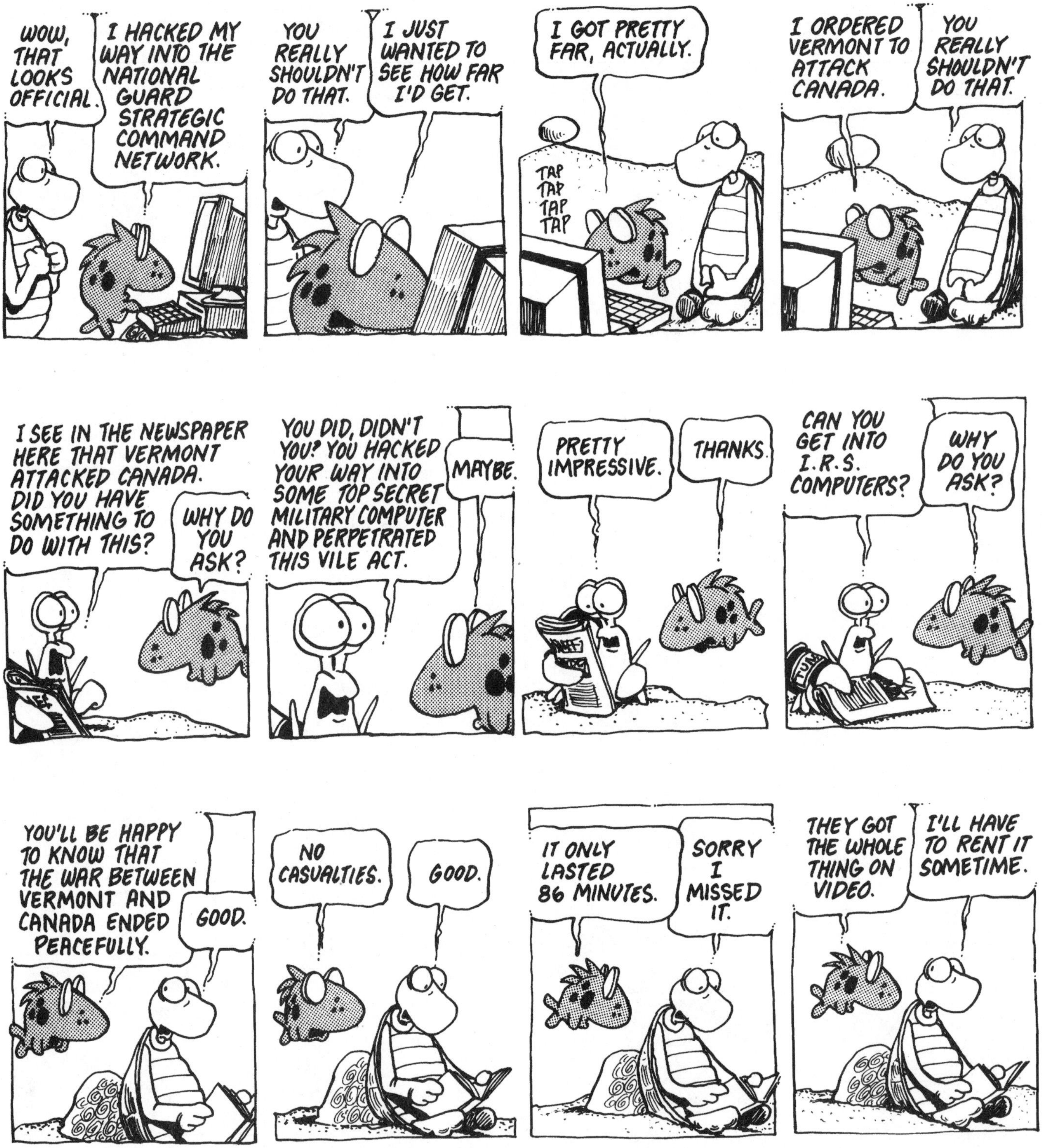
WOW, THAT LOOKS OFFICIAL.
I HACKED MY WAY INTO THE NATIONAL GUARD STRATEGIC COMMAND NETWORK.
YOU REALLY SHOULDN'T DO THAT.
I JUST WANTED TO SEE HOW FAR I'D GET.
I GOT PRETTY FAR, ACTUALLY.
TAP TAP TAP TAP
I ORDERED VERMONT TO ATTACK CANADA.
YOU REALLY SHOULDN'T DO THAT.
I SEE IN THE NEWSPAPER HERE THAT VERMONT ATTACKED CANADA. DID YOU HAVE SOMETHING TO DO WITH THIS?
WHY DO YOU ASK?
YOU DID, DIDN'T YOU? YOU HACKED YOUR WAY INTO SOME TOP SECRET MILITARY COMPUTER AND PERPETRATED THIS VILE ACT.
MAYBE.
PRETTY IMPRESSIVE.
THANKS.
CAN YOU GET INTO I.R.S. COMPUTERS?
WHY DO YOU ASK?
YOU'LL BE HAPPY TO KNOW THAT THE WAR BETWEEN VERMONT AND CANADA ENDED PEACEFULLY.
GOOD.
NO CASUALTIES.
GOOD.
IT ONLY LASTED 86 MINUTES.
SORRY I MISSED IT.
THEY GOT THE WHOLE THING ON VIDEO.
I'LL HAVE TO RENT IT SOMETIME.

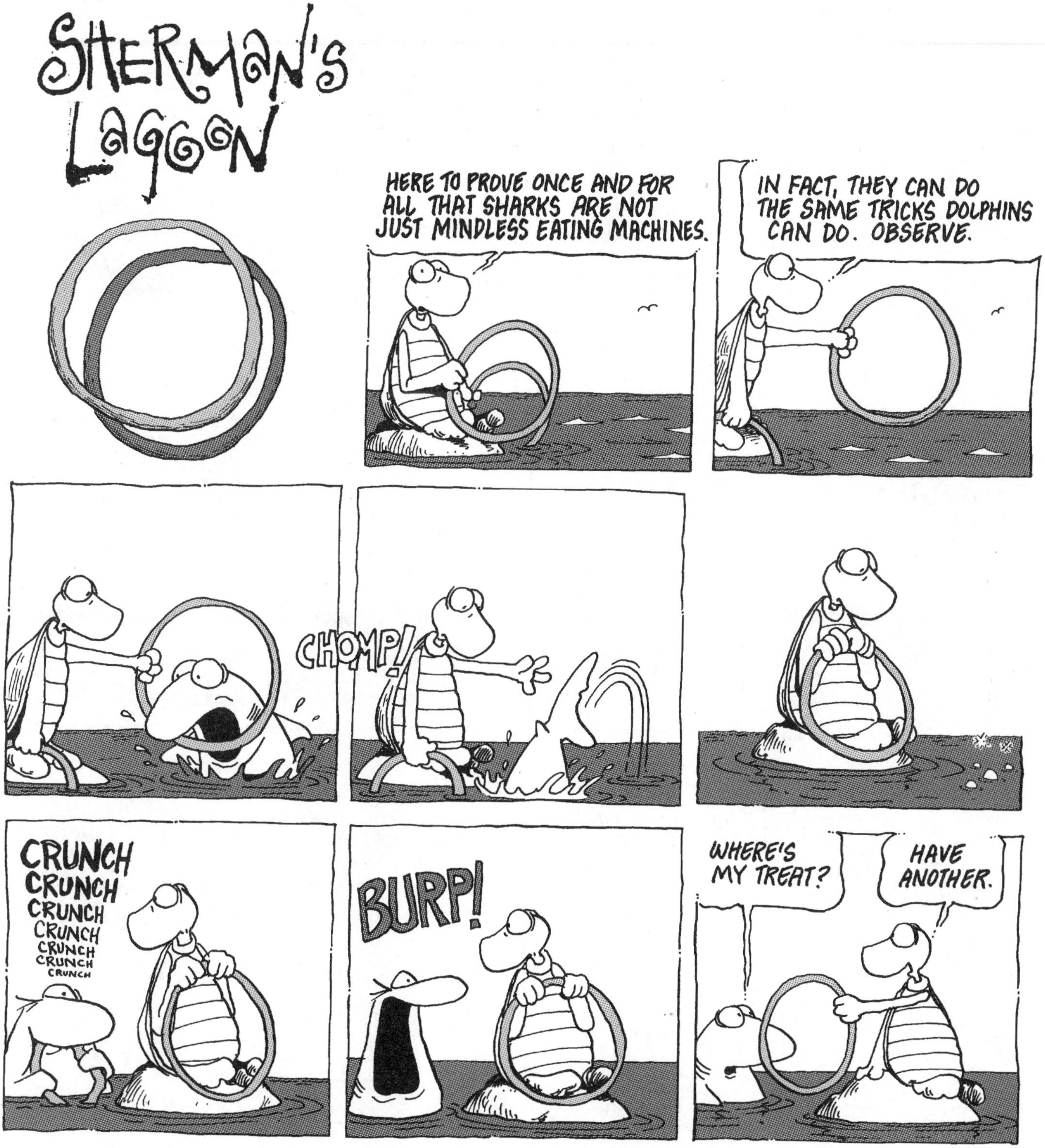
SHERMAN'S LAGOON
HERE TO PROVE ONCE AND FOR ALL THAT SHARKS ARE NOT JUST MINDLESS EATING MACHINES.
IN FACT, THEY CAN DO THE SAME TRICKS DOLPHINS CAN DO. OBSERVE.
CHOMP!
CRUNCH CRUNCH CRUNCH CRUNCH CRUNCH CRUNCH CRUNCH
BURP!
WHERE'S MY TREAT?
HAVE ANOTHER.

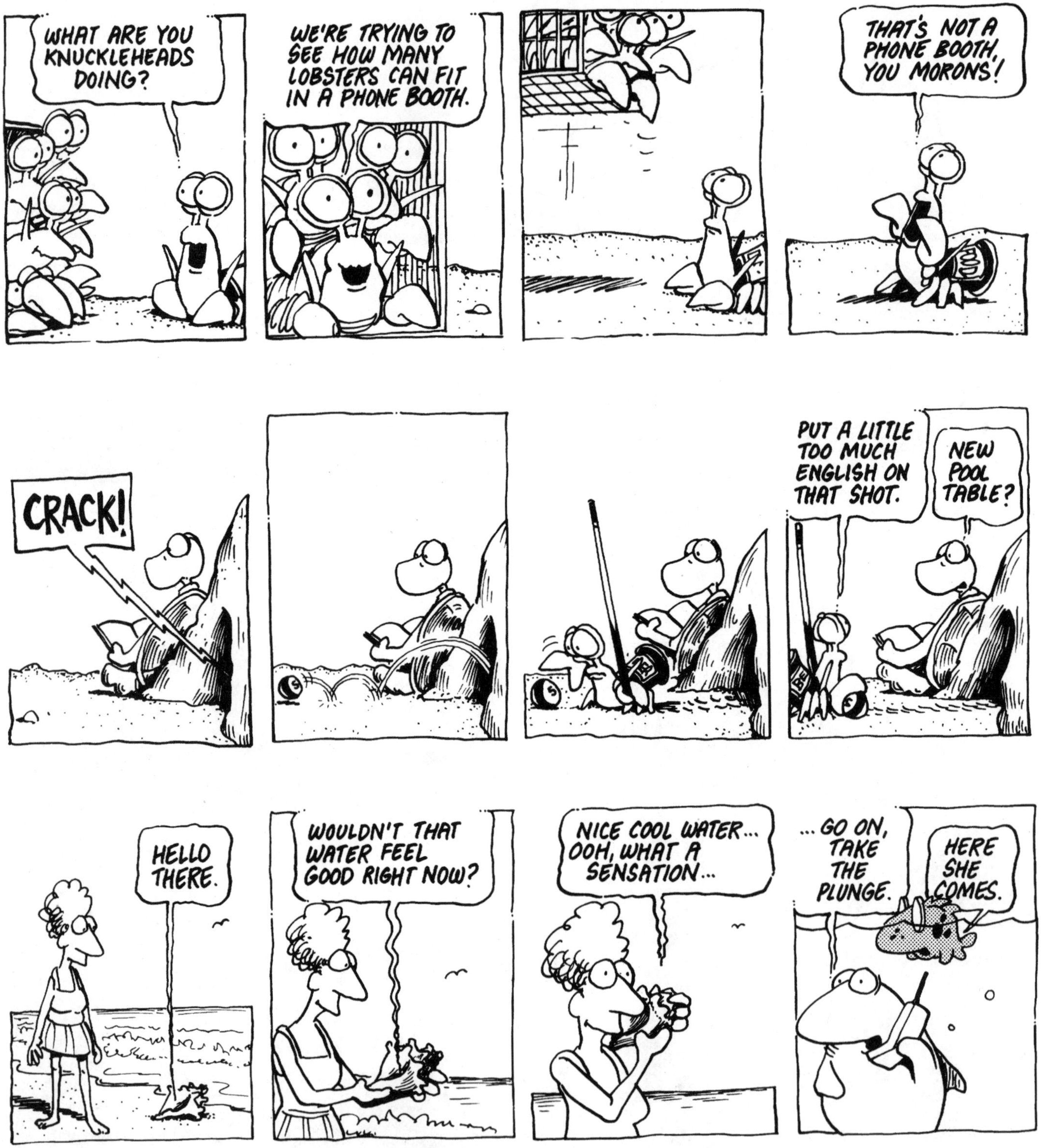
WHAT ARE YOU KNUCKLEHEADS DOING?
WE'RE TRYING TO SEE HOW MANY LOBSTERS CAN FIT IN A PHONE BOOTH.
THAT'S NOT A PHONE BOOTH, YOU MORONS!
CRACK!
PUT A LITTLE TOO MUCH ENGLISH ON THAT SHOT.
NEW POOL TABLE?
HELLO THERE.
WOULDN'T THAT WATER FEEL GOOD RIGHT NOW?
NICE COOL WATER... OOH, WHAT A SENSATION...
...GO ON, TAKE THE PLUNGE.
HERE SHE COMES.

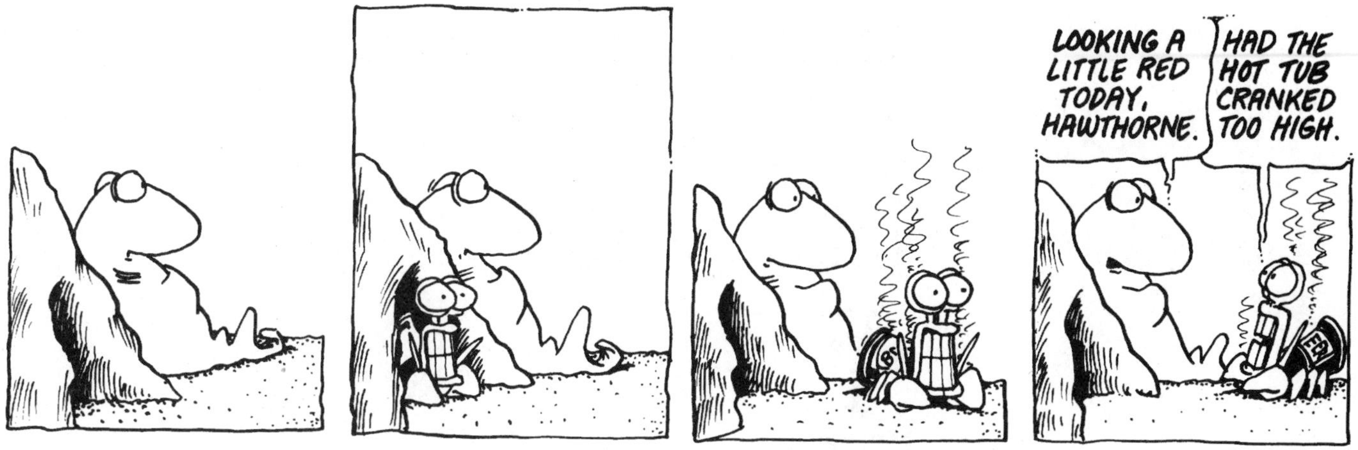
LOOKING A LITTLE RED TODAY, HAWTHORNE.
HAD THE HOT TUB CRANKED TOO HIGH.

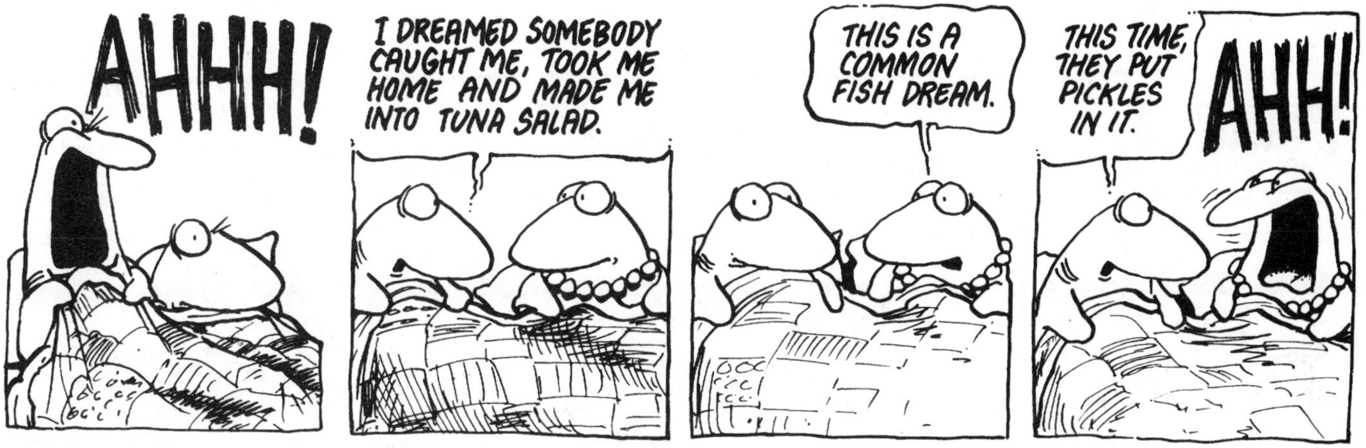
AHHH!
I DREAMED SOMEBODY CAUGHT ME, TOOK ME HOME AND MADE ME INTO TUNA SALAD.
THIS IS A COMMON FISH DREAM.
THIS TIME, THEY PUT PICKLES IN IT.
AHH!

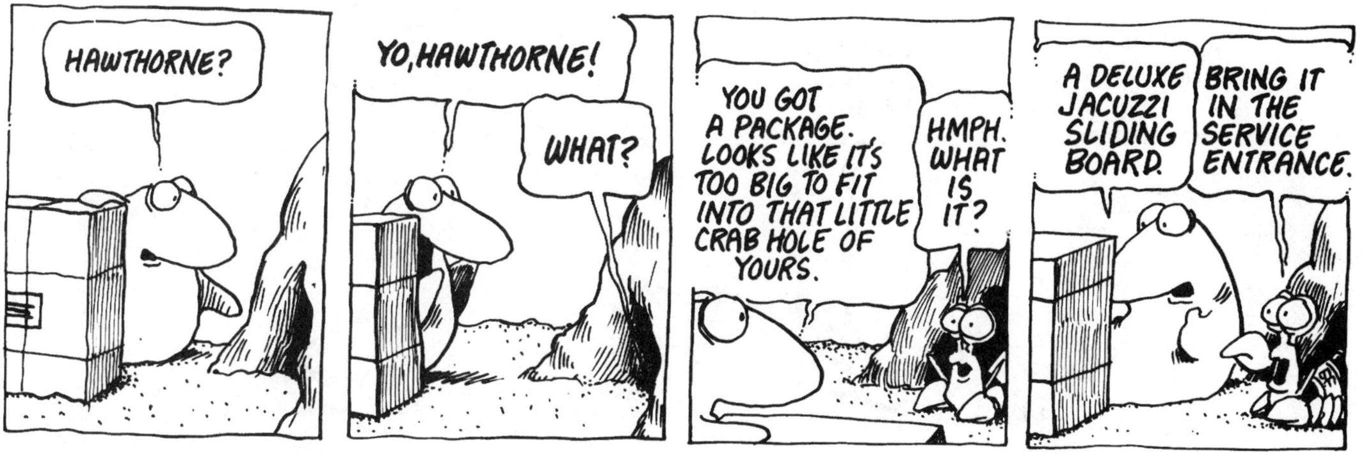
HAWTHORNE?
YO, HAWTHORNE!
WHAT?
YOU GOT A PACKAGE. LOOKS LIKE IT'S TOO BIG TO FIT INTO THAT LITTLE CRAB HOLE OF YOURS.
HMPH. WHAT IS IT?
A DELUXE JACUZZI SLIDING BOARD.
BRING IT IN THE SERVICE ENTRANCE.

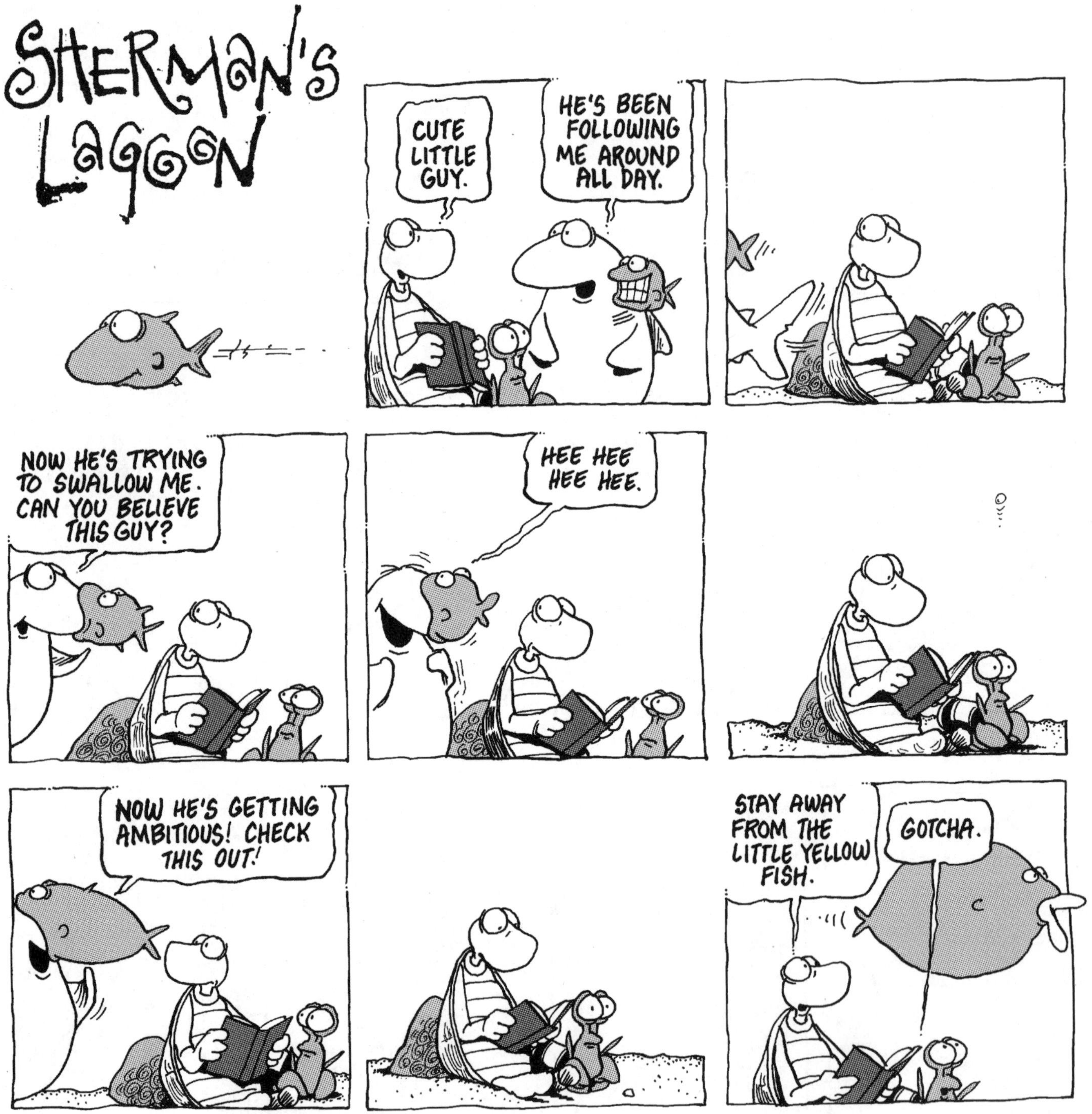
SHERMAN'S LAGOON
CUTE LITTLE GUY.
HE'S BEEN FOLLOWING ME AROUND ALL DAY.
NOW HE'S TRYING TO SWALLOW ME. CAN YOU BELIEVE THIS GUY?
HEE HEE HEE HEE.
NOW HE'S GETTING AMBITIOUS! CHECK THIS OUT!
STAY AWAY FROM THE LITTLE YELLOW FISH.
GOTCHA.

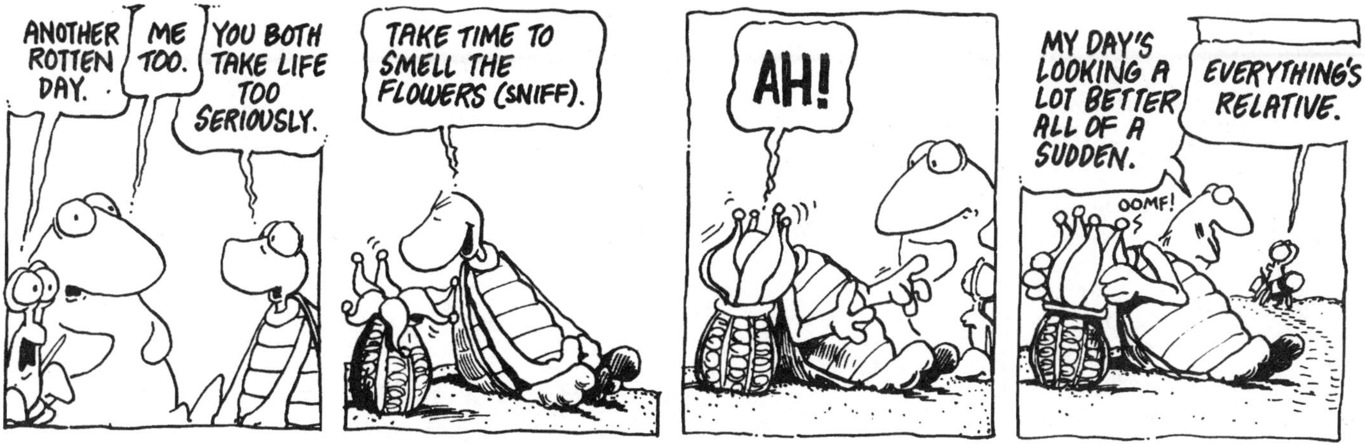
ANOTHER ROTTEN DAY.
ME TOO.
YOU BOTH TAKE LIFE TOO SERIOUSLY.
TAKE TIME TO SMELL THE FLOWERS (SNIFF).
AH!
MY DAY'S LOOKING A LOT BETTER ALL OF A SUDDEN.
OOMF!
EVERYTHING'S RELATIVE.

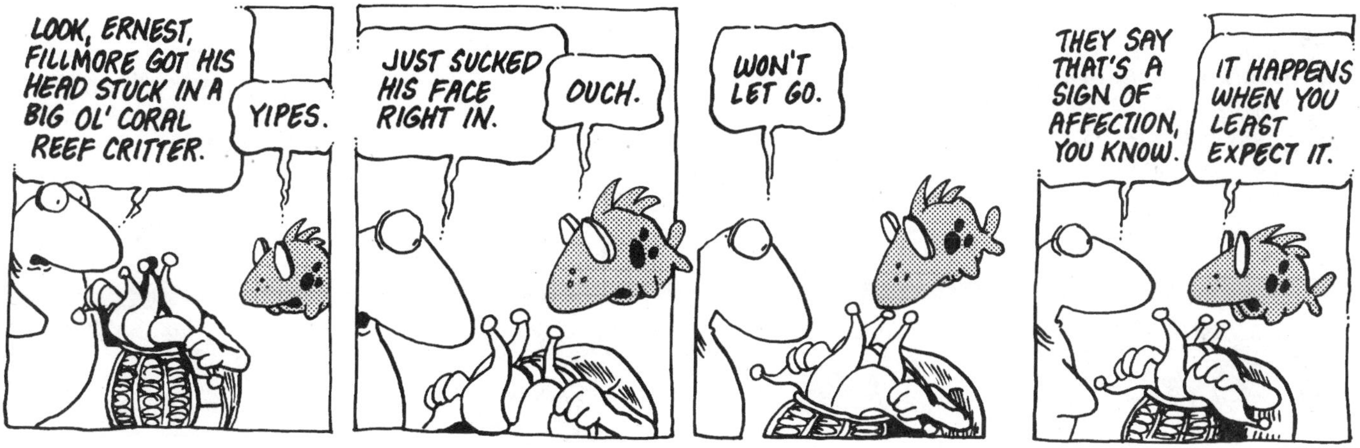
LOOK, ERNEST, FILLMORE GOT HIS HEAD STUCK IN A BIG OL' CORAL REEF CRITTER.
YIPES.
JUST SUCKED HIS FACE RIGHT IN.
OUCH.
WON'T LET GO.
THEY SAY THAT'S A SIGN OF AFFECTION, YOU KNOW.
IT HAPPENS WHEN YOU LEAST EXPECT IT.

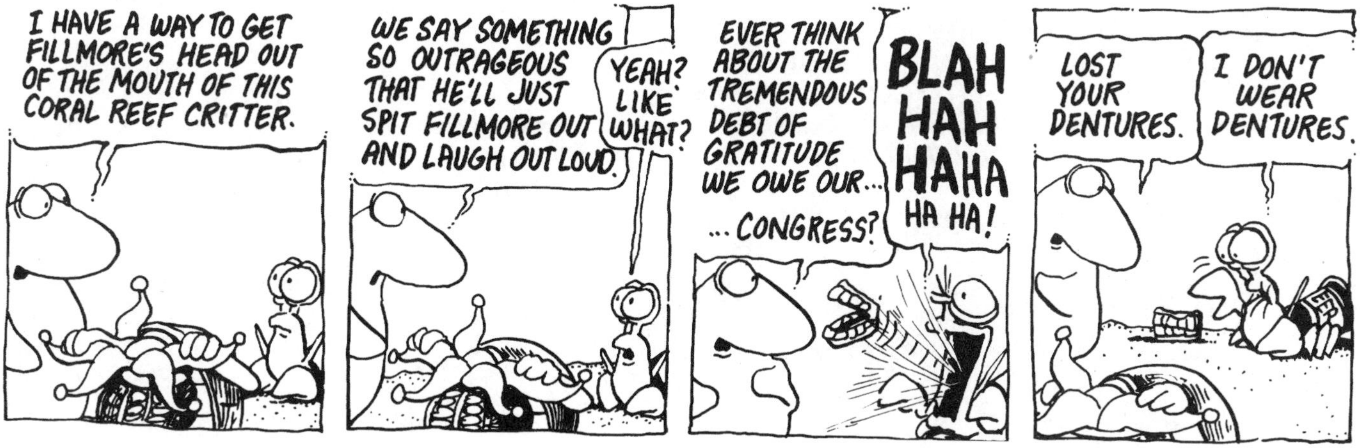
I HAVE A WAY TO GET FILLMORE'S HEAD OUT OF THE MOUTH OF THIS CORAL REEF CRITTER.
WE SAY SOMETHING SO OUTRAGEOUS THAT HE'LL JUST SPIT FILLMORE OUT AND LAUGH OUT LOUD.
YEAH? LIKE WHAT?
EVER THINK ABOUT THE TREMENDOUS DEBT OF GRATITUDE WE OWE OUR...
... CONGRESS?
BLAH HAH HAHA HA HA!
LOST YOUR DENTURES.
I DON'T WEAR DENTURES.

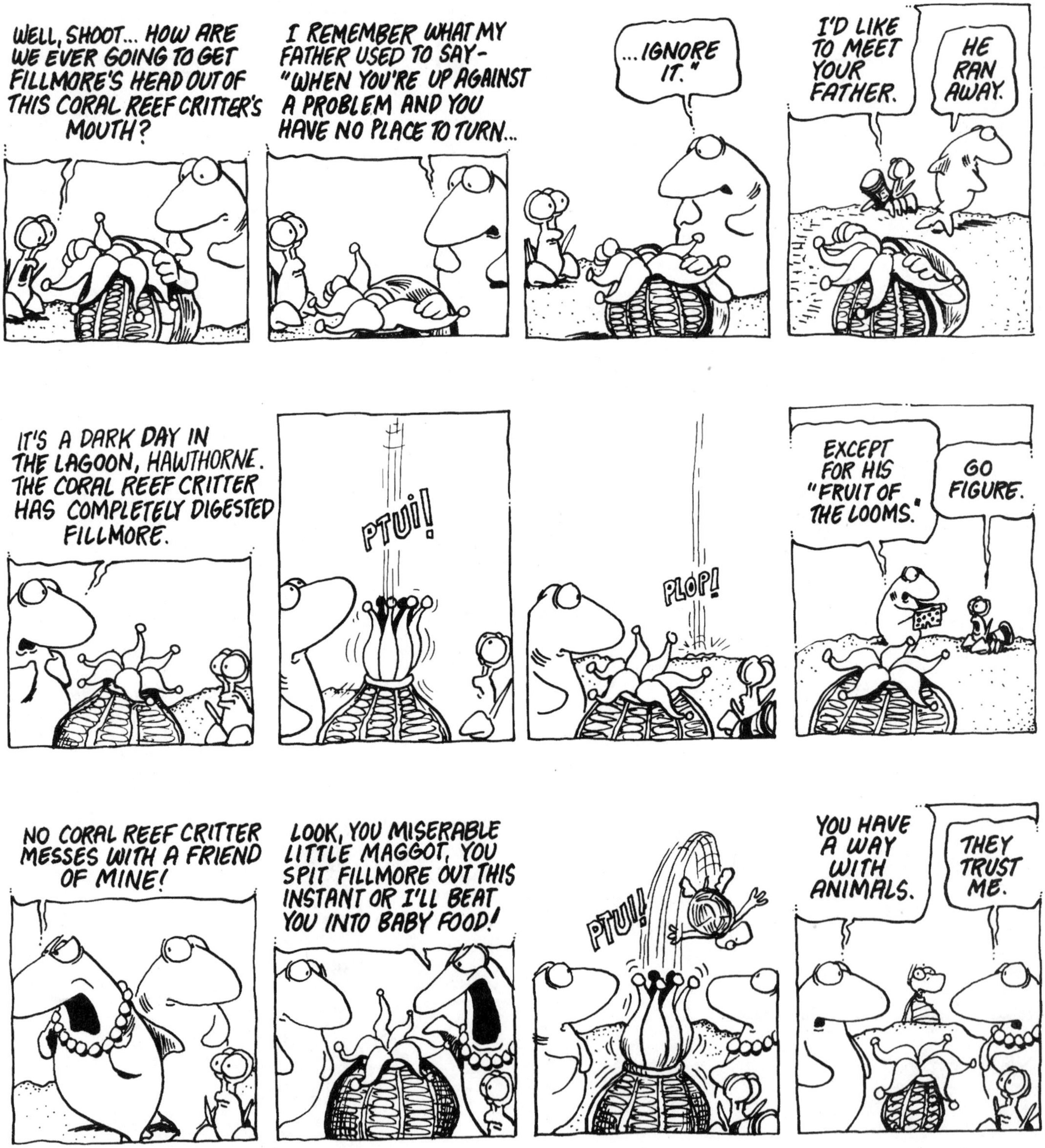
WELL, SHOOT... HOW ARE WE EVER GOING TO GET FILLMORE'S HEAD OUT OF THIS CORAL REEF CRITTER'S MOUTH?
I REMEMBER WHAT MY FATHER USED TO SAY- "WHEN YOU'RE UP AGAINST A PROBLEM AND YOU HAVE NO PLACE TO TURN...
...IGNORE IT."
I'D LIKE TO MEET YOUR FATHER.
HE RAN AWAY.
IT'S A DARK DAY IN THE LAGOON, HAWTHORNE. THE CORAL REEF CRITTER HAS COMPLETELY DIGESTED FILLMORE.
PTUI!
PLOP!
EXCEPT FOR HIS "FRUIT OF THE LOOMS."
GO FIGURE.
NO CORAL REEF CRITTER MESSES WITH A FRIEND OF MINE!
LOOK, YOU MISERABLE LITTLE MAGGOT, YOU SPIT FILLMORE OUT THIS INSTANT OR I'LL BEAT YOU INTO BABY FOOD!
PTUI!
YOU HAVE A WAY WITH ANIMALS.
THEY TRUST ME.

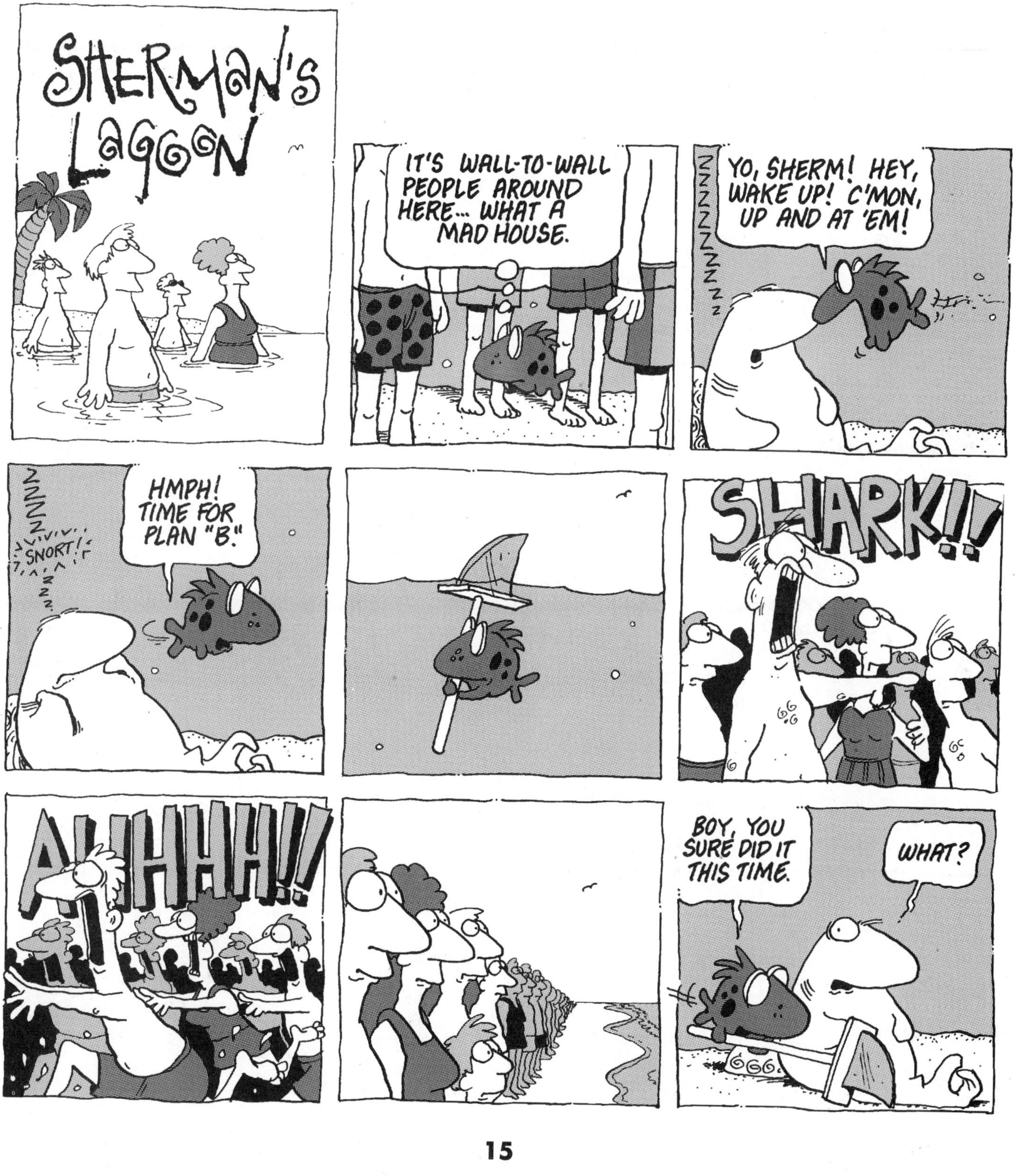
SHERMAN'S LAGOON
IT'S WALL-TO-WALL PEOPLE AROUND HERE... WHAT A MAD HOUSE.
ZZZZZZZZZ
YO, SHERM! HEY, WAKE UP! C'MON, UP AND AT 'EM!
SNORT!
HMPH! TIME FOR PLAN "B."
SHARK!!
AHHHHH!!
BOY, YOU SURE DID IT THIS TIME.
WHAT?

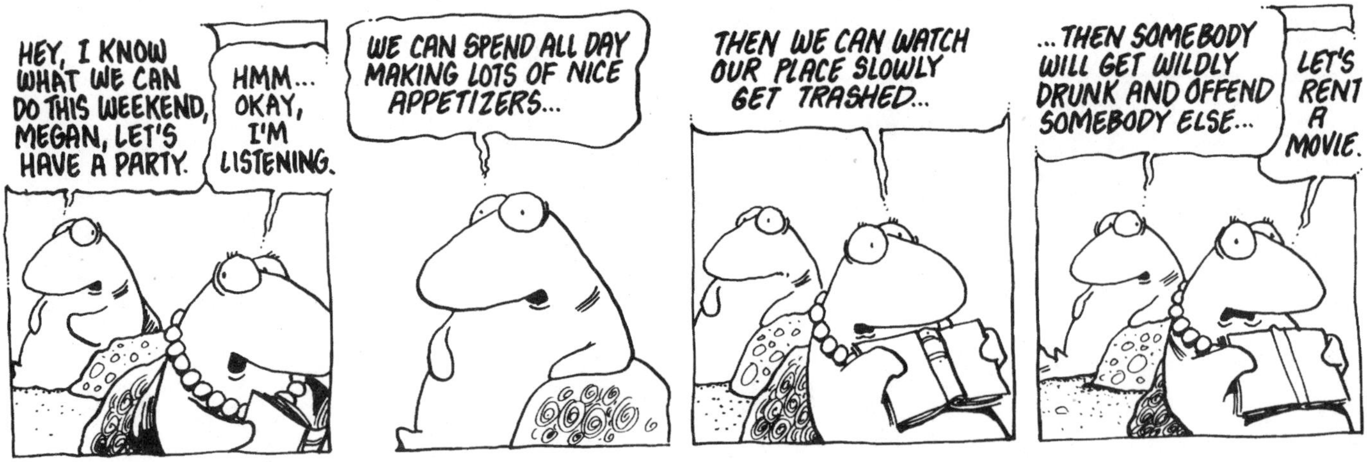
HEY, I KNOW WHAT WE CAN DO THIS WEEKEND, MEGAN, LET'S HAVE A PARTY.
HMM... OKAY, I'M LISTENING.
WE CAN SPEND ALL DAY MAKING LOTS OF NICE APPETIZERS...
THEN WE CAN WATCH OUR PLACE SLOWLY GET TRASHED...
...THEN SOMEBODY WILL GET WILDLY DRUNK AND OFFEND SOMEBODY ELSE...
LET'S RENT A MOVIE.

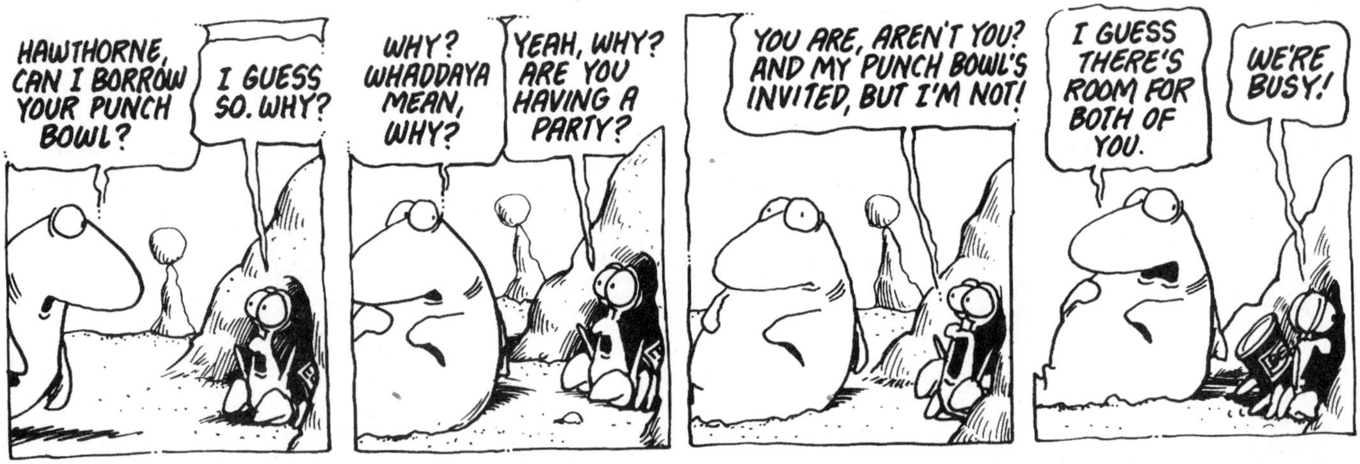
HAWTHORNE, CAN I BORROW YOUR PUNCH BOWL?
I GUESS SO. WHY?
WHY? WHADDAYA MEAN, WHY?
YEAH, WHY? ARE YOU HAVING A PARTY?
YOU ARE, AREN'T YOU? AND MY PUNCH BOWL'S INVITED, BUT I'M NOT!
I GUESS THERE'S ROOM FOR BOTH OF YOU.
WE'RE BUSY!

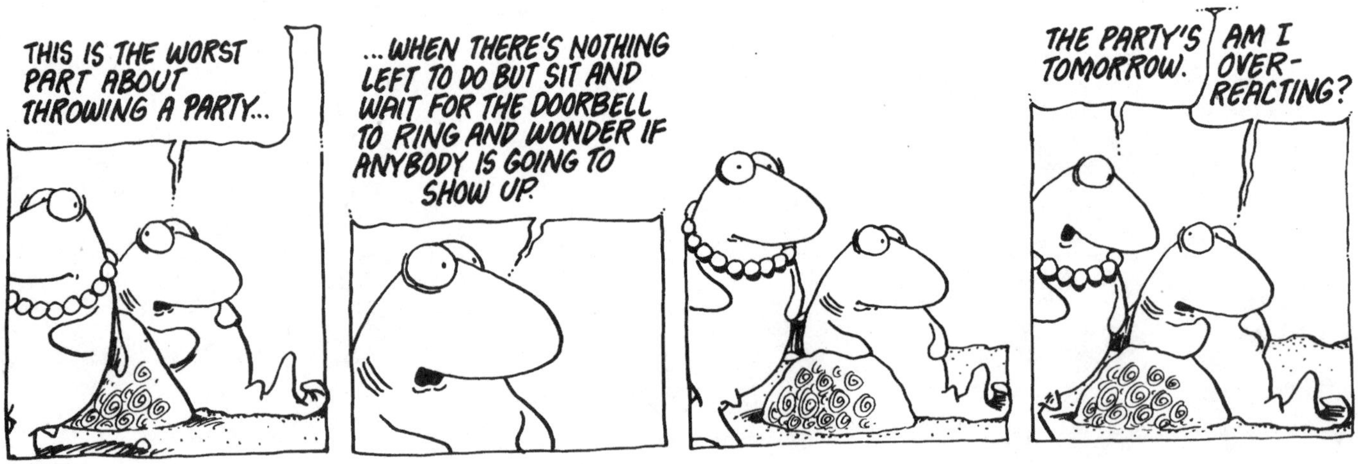
THIS IS THE WORST PART ABOUT THROWING A PARTY...
...WHEN THERE'S NOTHING LEFT TO DO BUT SIT AND WAIT FOR THE DOORBELL TO RING AND WONDER IF ANYBODY IS GOING TO SHOW UP.
THE PARTY'S TOMORROW.
AM I OVER-REACTING?

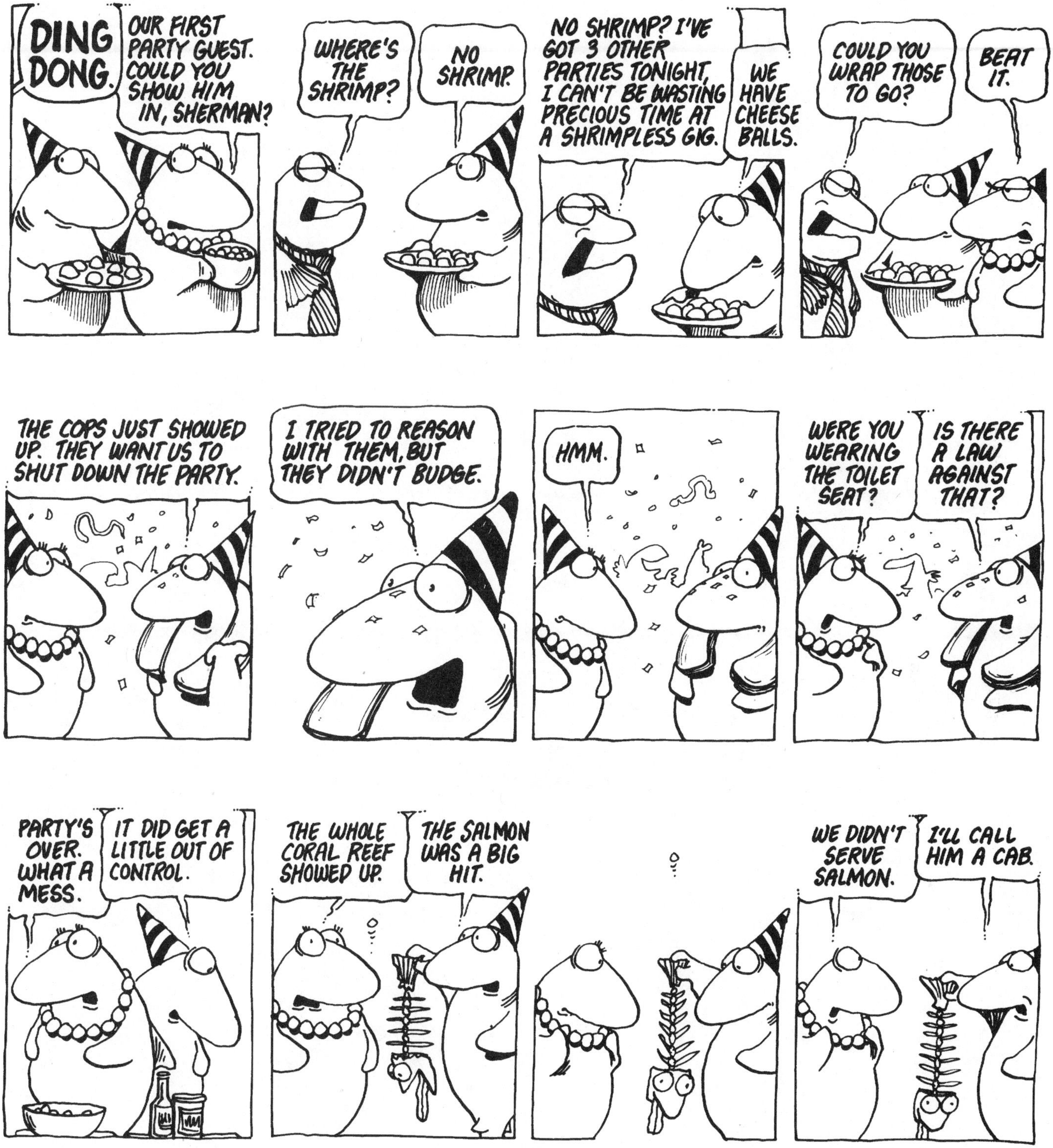
DING DONG.
OUR FIRST PARTY GUEST. COULD YOU SHOW HIM IN, SHERMAN?
WHERE'S THE SHRIMP?
NO SHRIMP.
NO SHRIMP? I'VE GOT 3 OTHER PARTIES TONIGHT, I CAN'T BE WASTING PRECIOUS TIME AT A SHRIMPLESS GIG.
WE HAVE CHEESE BALLS.
COULD YOU WRAP THOSE TO GO?
BEAT IT.
THE COPS JUST SHOWED UP. THEY WANT US TO SHUT DOWN THE PARTY.
I TRIED TO REASON WITH THEM, BUT THEY DIDN'T BUDGE.
HMM.
WERE YOU WEARING THE TOILET SEAT?
IS THERE A LAW AGAINST THAT?
PARTY'S OVER. WHAT A MESS.
IT DID GET A LITTLE OUT OF CONTROL.
THE WHOLE CORAL REEF SHOWED UP.
THE SALMON WAS A BIG HIT.
WE DIDN'T SERVE SALMON.
I'LL CALL HIM A CAB.

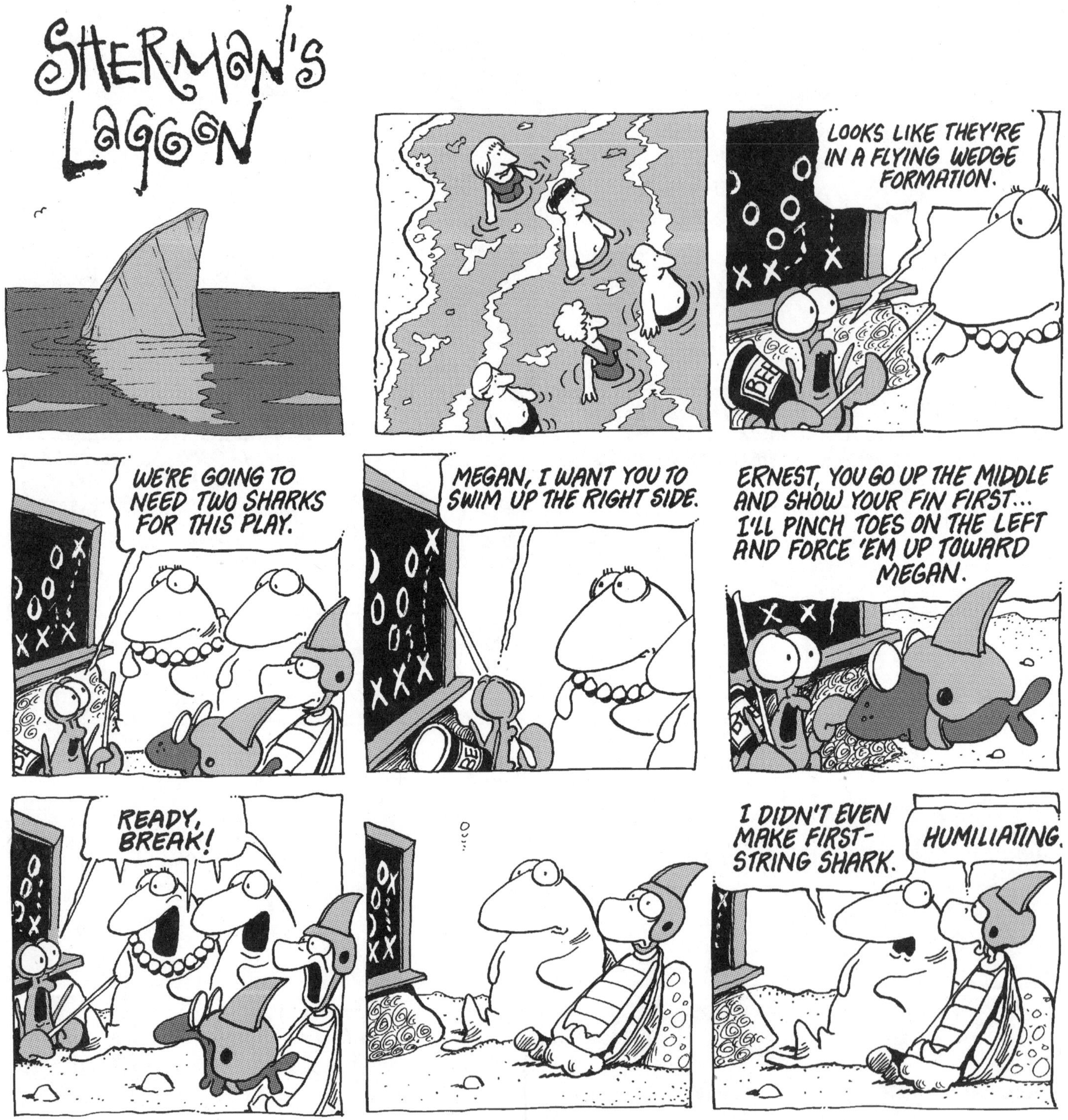
SHERMAN'S LAGOON
LOOKS LIKE THEY'RE IN A FLYING WEDGE FORMATION.
WE'RE GOING TO NEED TWO SHARKS FOR THIS PLAY.
MEGAN, I WANT YOU TO SWIM UP THE RIGHT SIDE.
ERNEST, YOU GO UP THE MIDDLE AND SHOW YOUR FIN FIRST... I'LL PINCH TOES ON THE LEFT AND FORCE 'EM UP TOWARD MEGAN.
READY, BREAK!
I DIDN'T EVEN MAKE FIRST-STRING SHARK.
HUMILIATING.

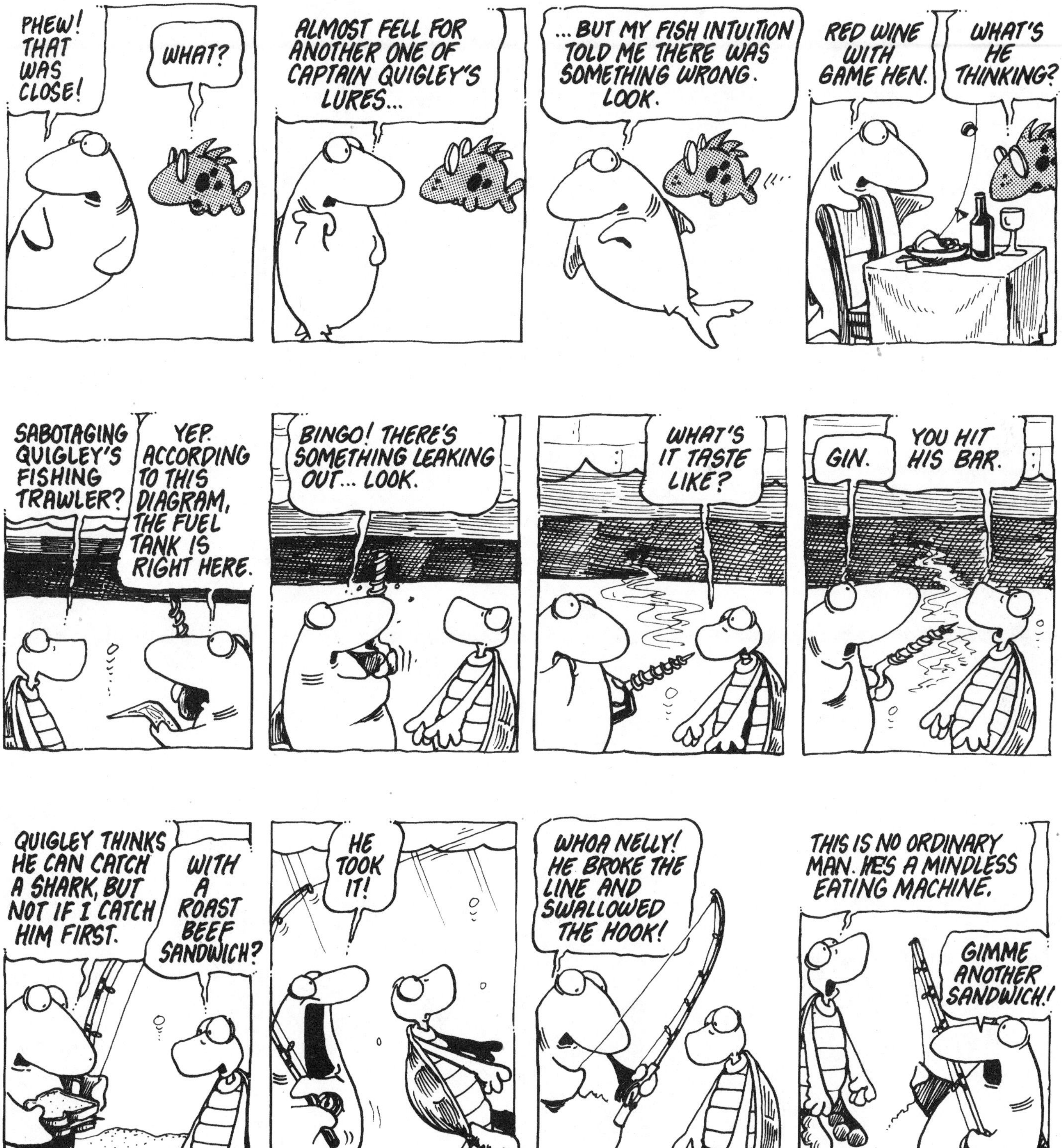
PHEW! THAT WAS CLOSE!
WHAT?
ALMOST FELL FOR ANOTHER ONE OF CAPTAIN QUIGLEY'S LURES...
...BUT MY FISH INTUITION TOLD ME THERE WAS SOMETHING WRONG. LOOK.
RED WINE WITH GAME HEN.
WHAT'S HE THINKING?
SABOTAGING QUIGLEY'S FISHING TRAWLER?
YEP. ACCORDING TO THIS DIAGRAM, THE FUEL TANK IS RIGHT HERE.
BINGO! THERE'S SOMETHING LEAKING OUT... LOOK.
WHAT'S IT TASTE LIKE?
GIN.
YOU HIT HIS BAR.
QUIGLEY THINKS HE CAN CATCH A SHARK, BUT NOT IF I CATCH HIM FIRST.
WITH A ROAST BEEF SANDWICH?
HE TOOK IT!
WHOA NELLY! HE BROKE THE LINE AND SWALLOWED THE HOOK!
THIS IS NO ORDINARY MAN. HE'S A MINDLESS EATING MACHINE.
GIMME ANOTHER SANDWICH!

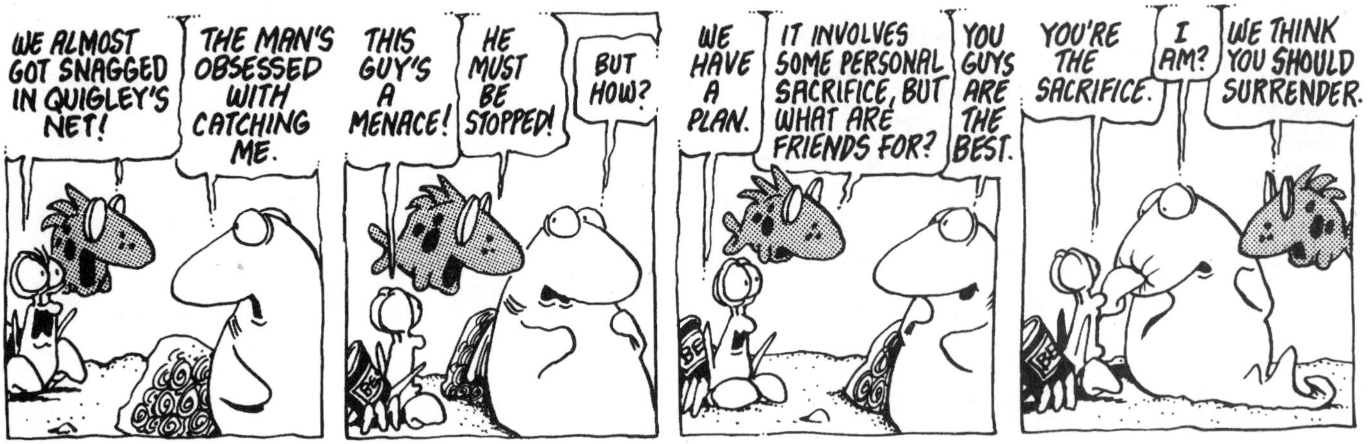
WE ALMOST GOT SNAGGED IN QUIGLEY'S NET!
THE MAN'S OBSESSED WITH CATCHING ME.
THIS GUY'S A MENACE!
HE MUST BE STOPPED!
BUT HOW?
WE HAVE A PLAN.
IT INVOLVES SOME PERSONAL SACRIFICE, BUT WHAT ARE FRIENDS FOR?
YOU GUYS ARE THE BEST.
YOU'RE THE SACRIFICE.
I AM?
WE THINK YOU SHOULD SURRENDER.

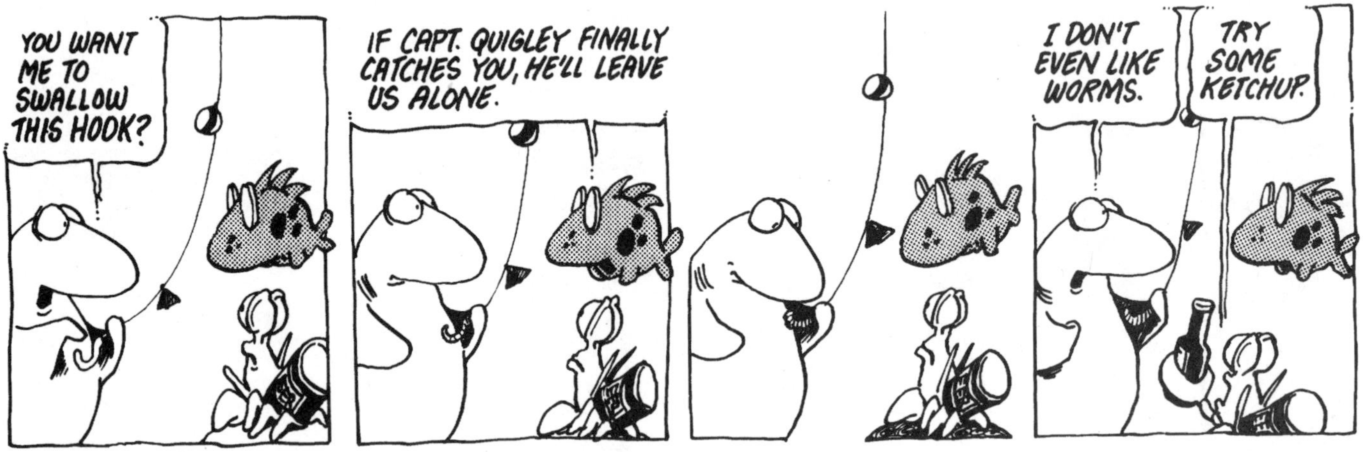
YOU WANT ME TO SWALLOW THIS HOOK?
IF CAPT. QUIGLEY FINALLY CATCHES YOU, HE'LL LEAVE US ALONE.
I DON'T EVEN LIKE WORMS.
TRY SOME KETCHUP.

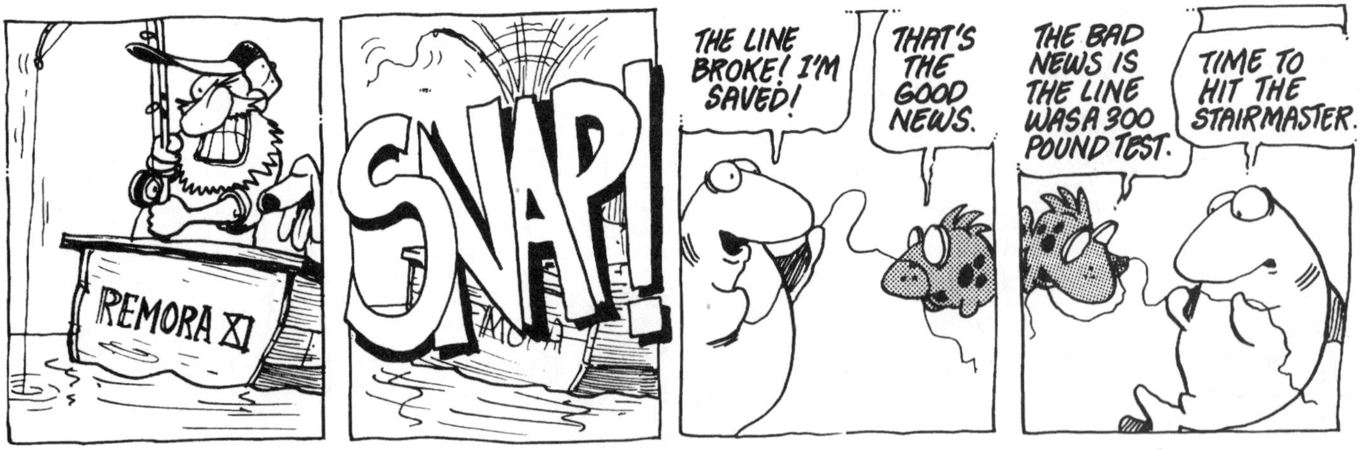
REMORA XI
SNAP!
THE LINE BROKE! I'M SAVED!
THAT'S THE GOOD NEWS.
THE BAD NEWS IS THE LINE WAS A 300 POUND TEST.
TIME TO HIT THE STAIRMASTER.

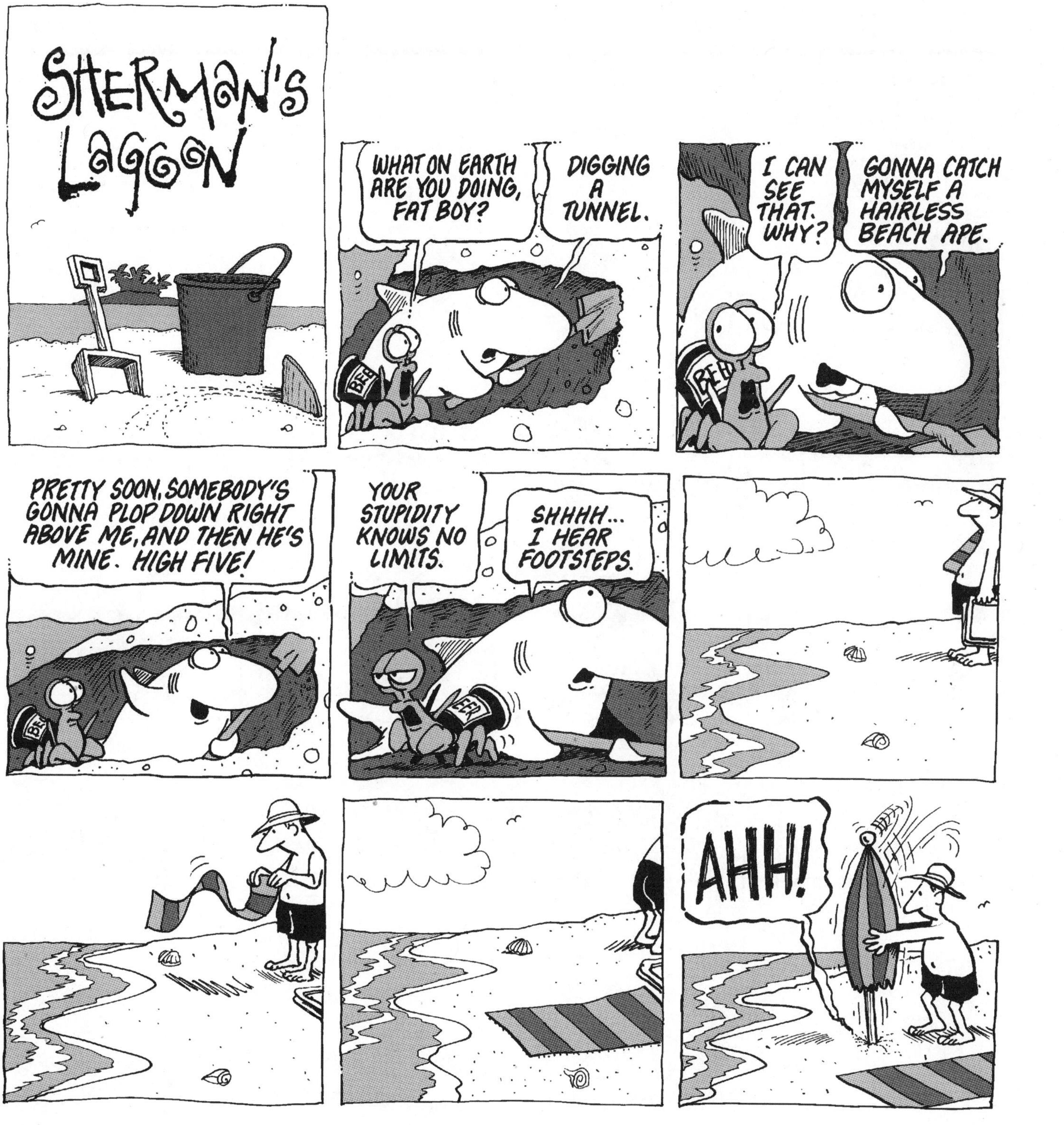
SHERMAN'S LAGOON
WHAT ON EARTH ARE YOU DOING, FAT BOY?
DIGGING A TUNNEL.
I CAN SEE THAT. WHY?
GONNA CATCH MYSELF A HAIRLESS BEACH APE.
PRETTY SOON, SOMEBODY'S GONNA PLOP DOWN RIGHT ABOVE ME, AND THEN HE'S MINE. HIGH FIVE!
YOUR STUPIDITY KNOWS NO LIMITS.
SHHHH... I HEAR FOOTSTEPS.
AHH!

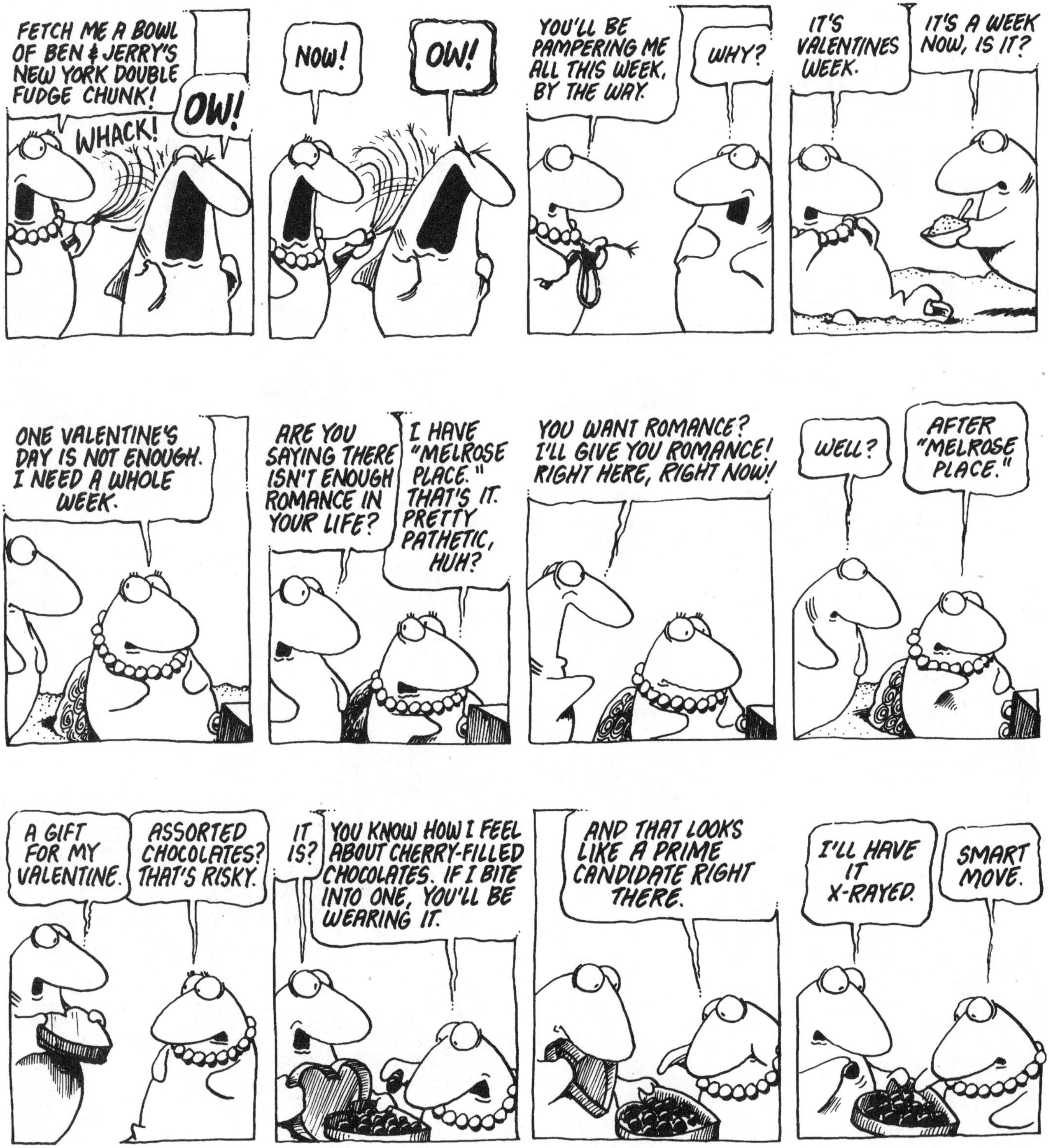
FETCH ME A BOWL OF BEN & JERRY'S NEW YORK DOUBLE FUDGE CHUNK!
WHACK!
OW!
NOW!
OW!
YOU'LL BE PAMPERING ME ALL THIS WEEK, BY THE WAY.
WHY?
IT'S VALENTINES WEEK.
IT'S A WEEK NOW, IS IT?
ONE VALENTINE'S DAY IS NOT ENOUGH. I NEED A WHOLE WEEK.
ARE YOU SAYING THERE ISN'T ENOUGH ROMANCE IN YOUR LIFE?
I HAVE "MELROSE PLACE." THAT'S IT. PRETTY PATHETIC, HUH?
YOU WANT ROMANCE? I'LL GIVE YOU ROMANCE! RIGHT HERE, RIGHT NOW!
WELL?
AFTER "MELROSE PLACE."
A GIFT FOR MY VALENTINE.
ASSORTED CHOCOLATES? THAT'S RISKY.
IT IS?
YOU KNOW HOW I FEEL ABOUT CHERRY-FILLED CHOCOLATES. IF I BITE INTO ONE, YOU'LL BE WEARING IT.
AND THAT LOOKS LIKE A PRIME CANDIDATE RIGHT THERE.
I'LL HAVE IT X-RAYED.
SMART MOVE.

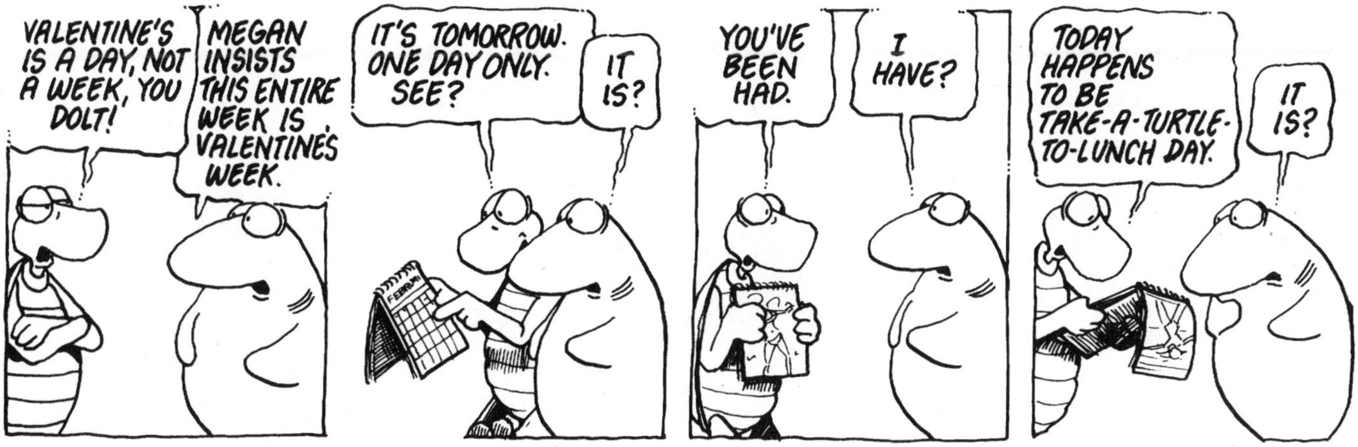
VALENTINE'S IS A DAY, NOT A WEEK, YOU DOLT!
MEGAN INSISTS THIS ENTIRE WEEK IS VALENTINE'S WEEK.
IT'S TOMORROW. ONE DAY ONLY. SEE?
IT IS?
YOU'VE BEEN HAD.
I HAVE?
TODAY HAPPENS TO BE TAKE-A-TURTLE-TO-LUNCH DAY.
IT IS?

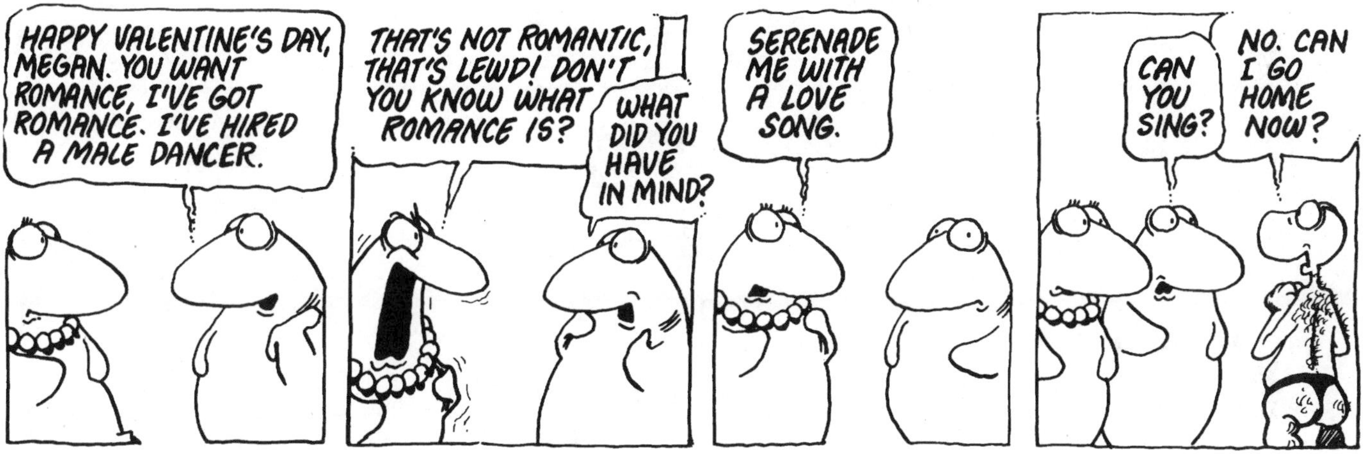
HAPPY VALENTINE'S DAY, MEGAN. YOU WANT ROMANCE, I'VE GOT ROMANCE. I'VE HIRED A MALE DANCER.
THAT'S NOT ROMANTIC, THAT'S LEWD! DON'T YOU KNOW WHAT ROMANCE IS?
WHAT DID YOU HAVE IN MIND?
SERENADE ME WITH A LOVE SONG.
CAN YOU SING?
NO. CAN I GO HOME NOW?

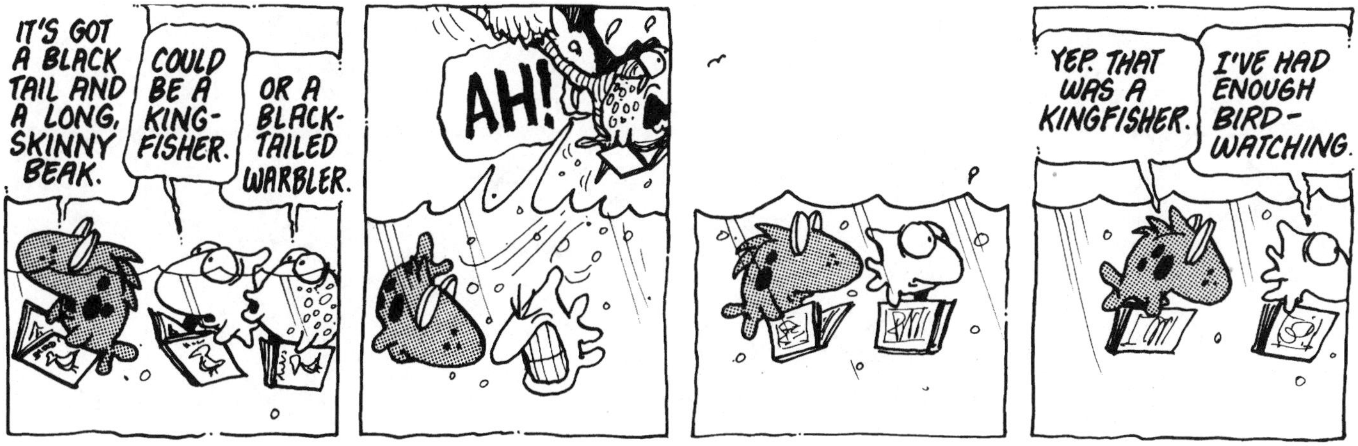
IT'S GOT A BLACK TAIL AND A LONG, SKINNY BEAK.
COULD BE A KING-FISHER.
OR A BLACK-TAILED WARBLER.
AH!
YEP. THAT WAS A KINGFISHER.
I'VE HAD ENOUGH BIRD-WATCHING.

SHERMAN'S LAGOON

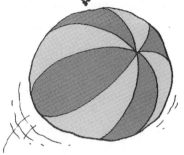

BONK!

LOOKS LIKE YOU'VE MADE A COUPLE OF HUMAN FRIENDS.

THEY THINK I'M A DOLPHIN.

HEADS UP!

BONK!

THIS DOLPHIN MASK HAS OPENED A NEW DOOR IN MY LIFE, FILLMORE.

I'VE DISCOVERED A PLAYFUL SIDE I NEVER KNEW I HAD.

THEY'RE GETTING IN THE WATER.

FOOLS.

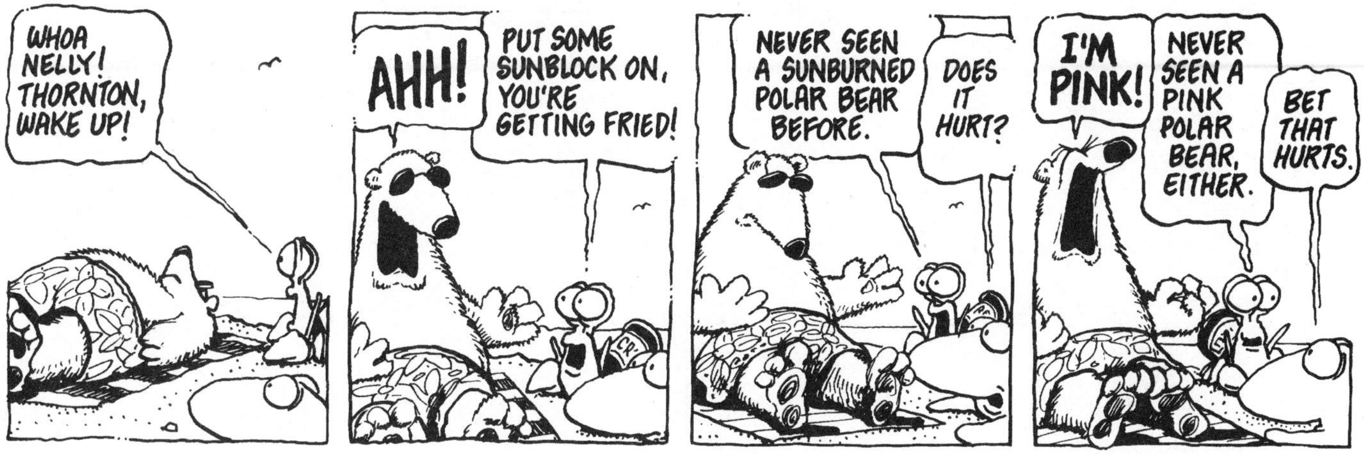
WHOA NELLY! THORNTON, WAKE UP!
AHH!
PUT SOME SUNBLOCK ON, YOU'RE GETTING FRIED!
NEVER SEEN A SUNBURNED POLAR BEAR BEFORE.
DOES IT HURT?
I'M PINK!
NEVER SEEN A PINK POLAR BEAR, EITHER.
BET THAT HURTS.

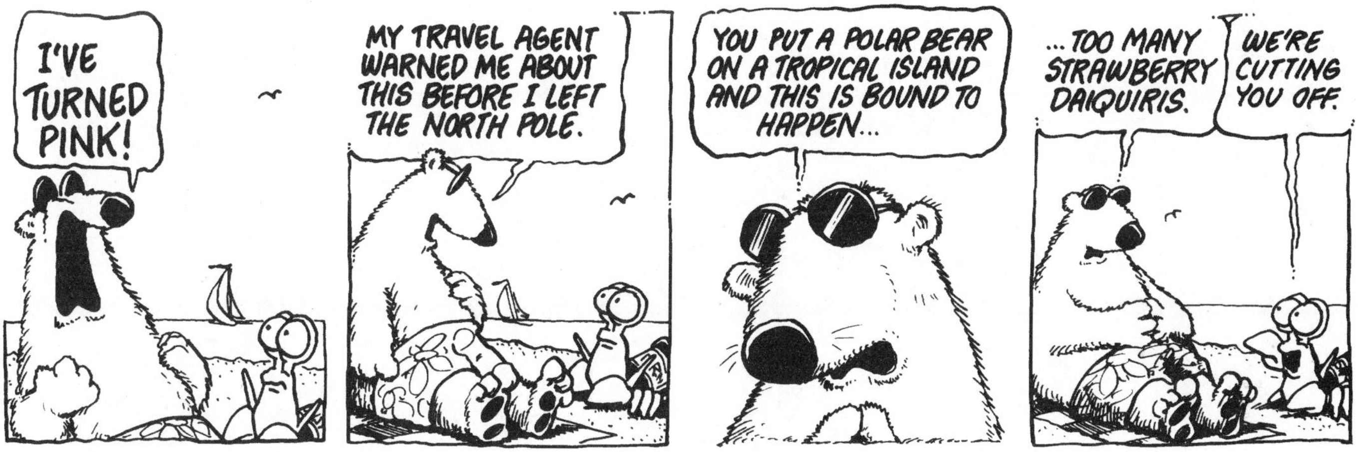
I'VE TURNED PINK!
MY TRAVEL AGENT WARNED ME ABOUT THIS BEFORE I LEFT THE NORTH POLE.
YOU PUT A POLAR BEAR ON A TROPICAL ISLAND AND THIS IS BOUND TO HAPPEN...
...TOO MANY STRAWBERRY DAIQUIRIS.
WE'RE CUTTING YOU OFF.

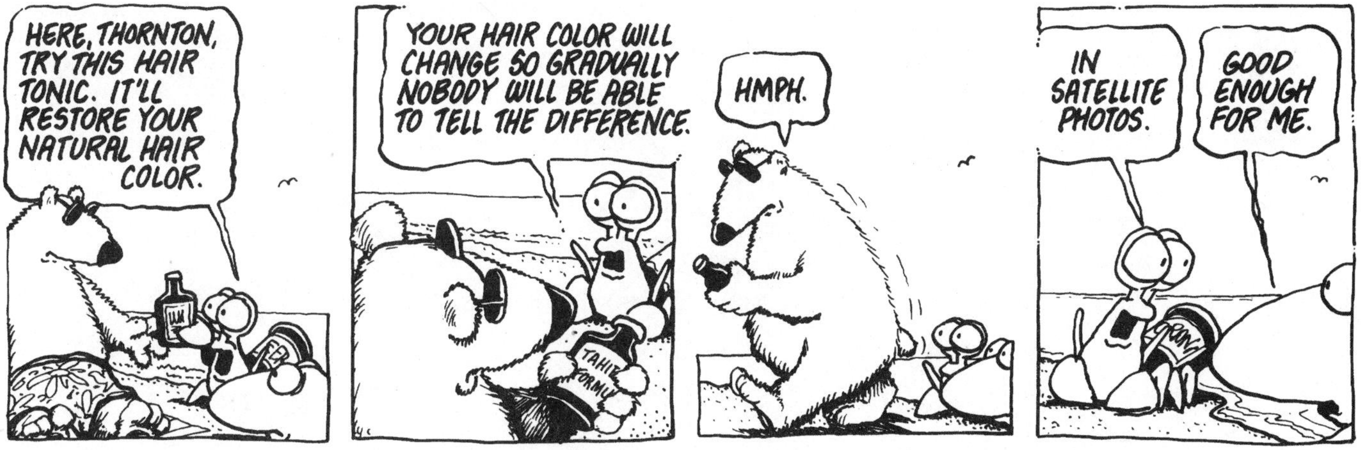
HERE, THORNTON, TRY THIS HAIR TONIC. IT'LL RESTORE YOUR NATURAL HAIR COLOR.
YOUR HAIR COLOR WILL CHANGE SO GRADUALLY NOBODY WILL BE ABLE TO TELL THE DIFFERENCE.
HMPH.
IN SATELLITE PHOTOS.
GOOD ENOUGH FOR ME.

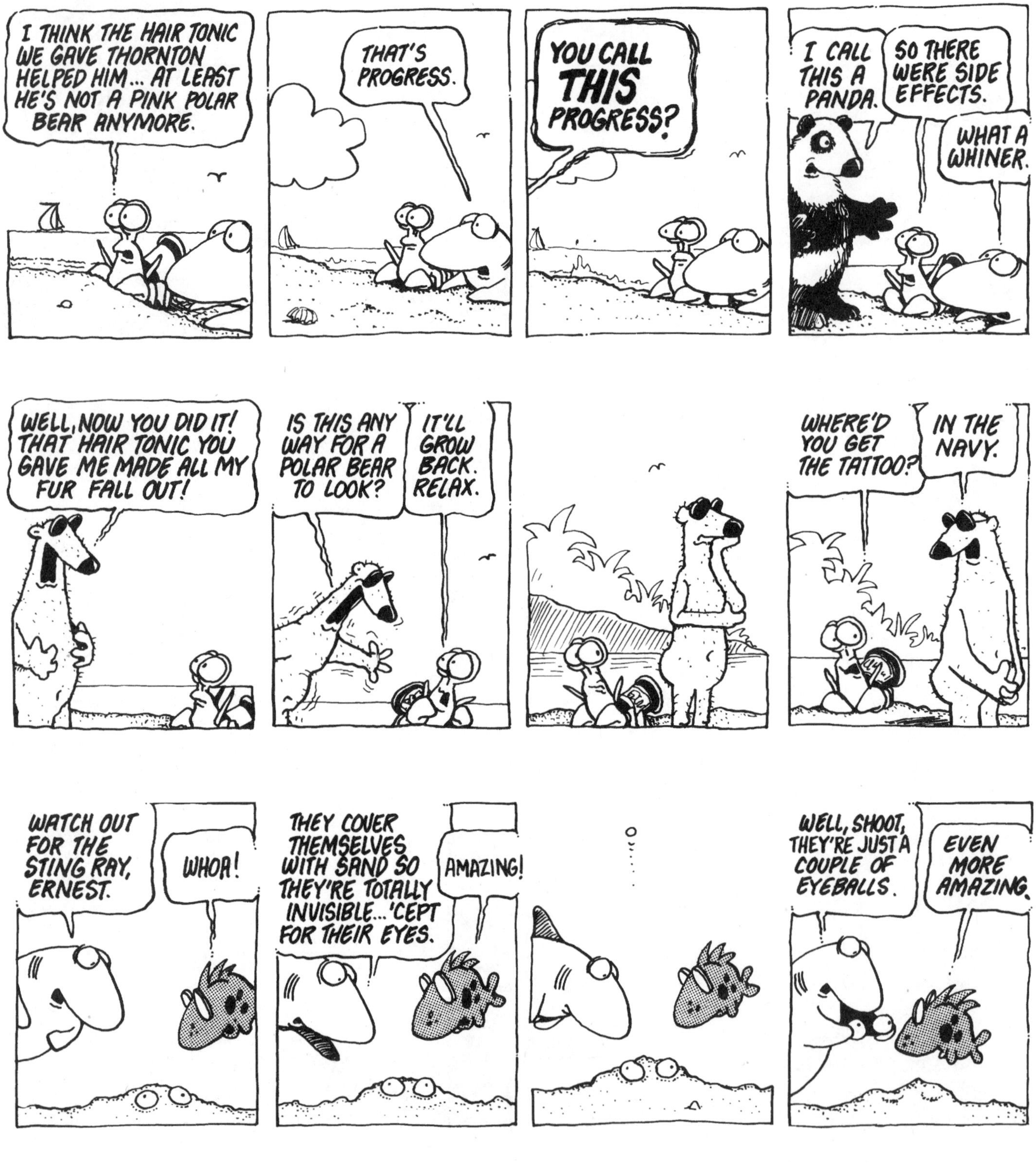
I THINK THE HAIR TONIC WE GAVE THORNTON HELPED HIM... AT LEAST HE'S NOT A PINK POLAR BEAR ANYMORE.
THAT'S PROGRESS.
YOU CALL THIS PROGRESS?
I CALL THIS A PANDA.
SO THERE WERE SIDE EFFECTS.
WHAT A WHINER.
WELL, NOW YOU DID IT! THAT HAIR TONIC YOU GAVE ME MADE ALL MY FUR FALL OUT!
IS THIS ANY WAY FOR A POLAR BEAR TO LOOK?
IT'LL GROW BACK. RELAX.
WHERE'D YOU GET THE TATTOO?
IN THE NAVY.
WATCH OUT FOR THE STING RAY, ERNEST.
WHOA!
THEY COVER THEMSELVES WITH SAND SO THEY'RE TOTALLY INVISIBLE...'CEPT FOR THEIR EYES.
AMAZING!
WELL, SHOOT, THEY'RE JUST A COUPLE OF EYEBALLS.
EVEN MORE AMAZING.

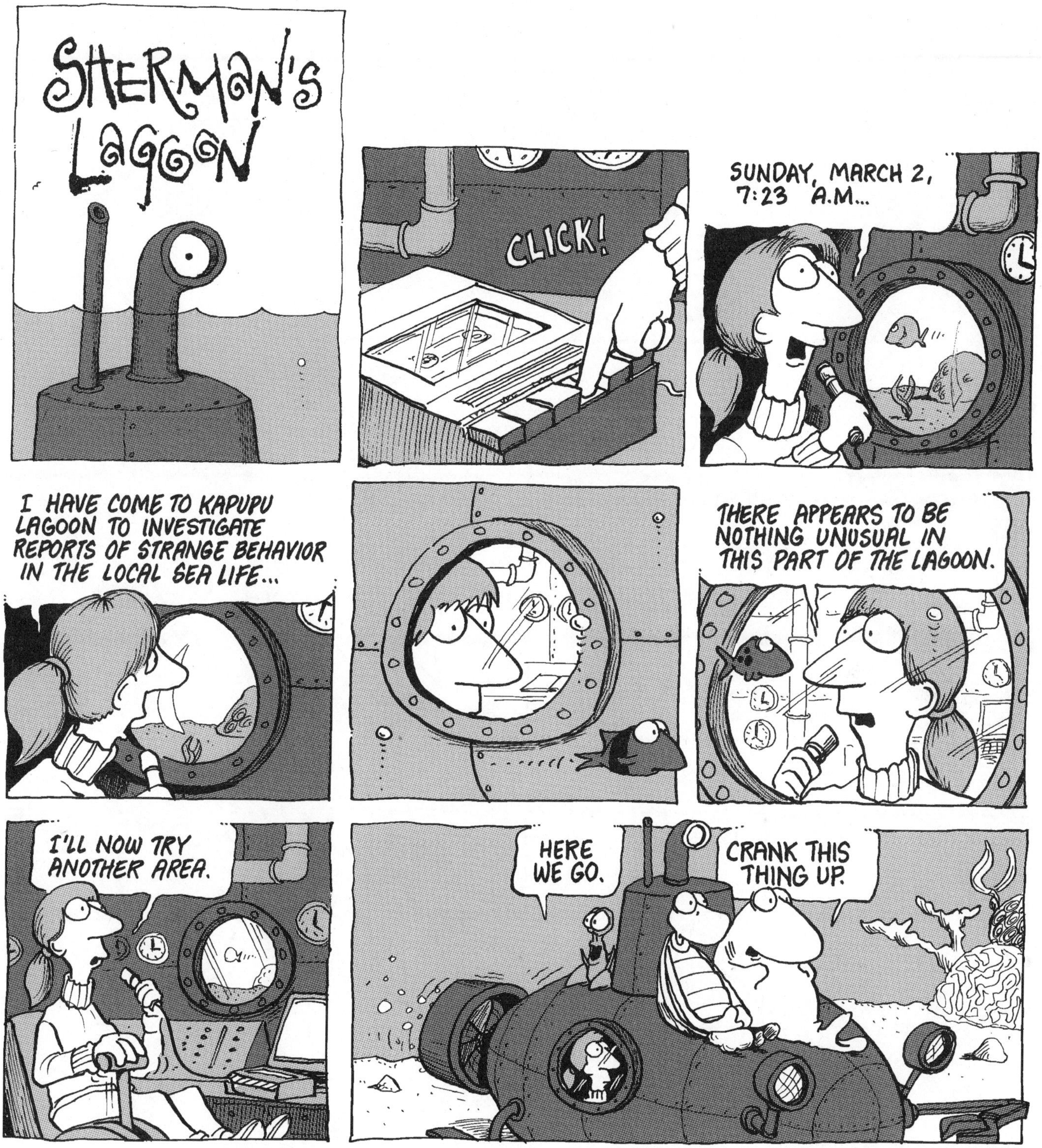
SHERMAN'S LAGOON
CLICK!
SUNDAY, MARCH 2, 7:23 A.M...
I HAVE COME TO KAPUPU LAGOON TO INVESTIGATE REPORTS OF STRANGE BEHAVIOR IN THE LOCAL SEA LIFE...
THERE APPEARS TO BE NOTHING UNUSUAL IN THIS PART OF THE LAGOON.
I'LL NOW TRY ANOTHER AREA.
HERE WE GO.
CRANK THIS THING UP.

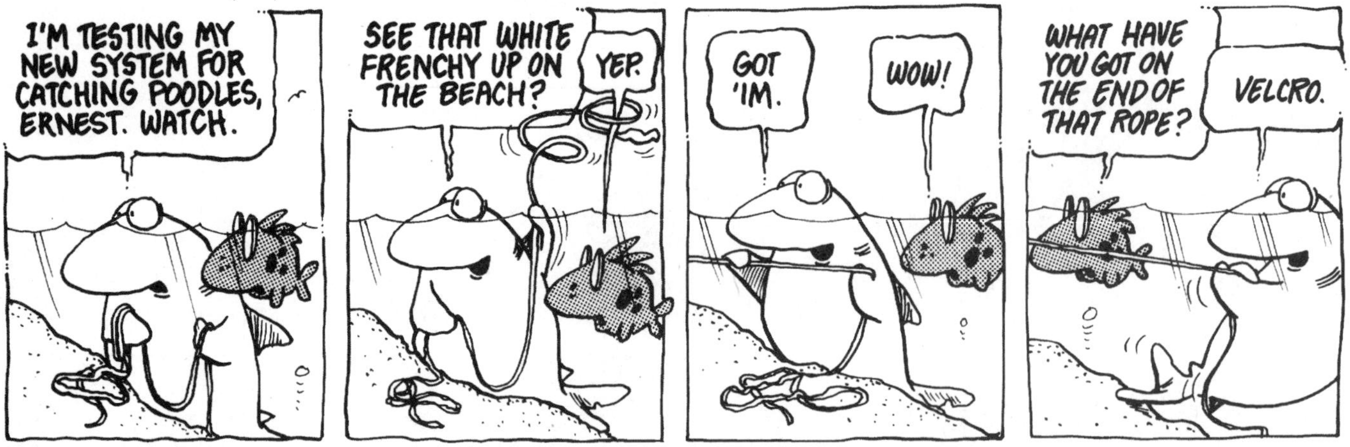
I'M TESTING MY NEW SYSTEM FOR CATCHING POODLES, ERNEST. WATCH.
SEE THAT WHITE FRENCHY UP ON THE BEACH?
YEP.
GOT 'IM.
WOW!
WHAT HAVE YOU GOT ON THE END OF THAT ROPE?
VELCRO.

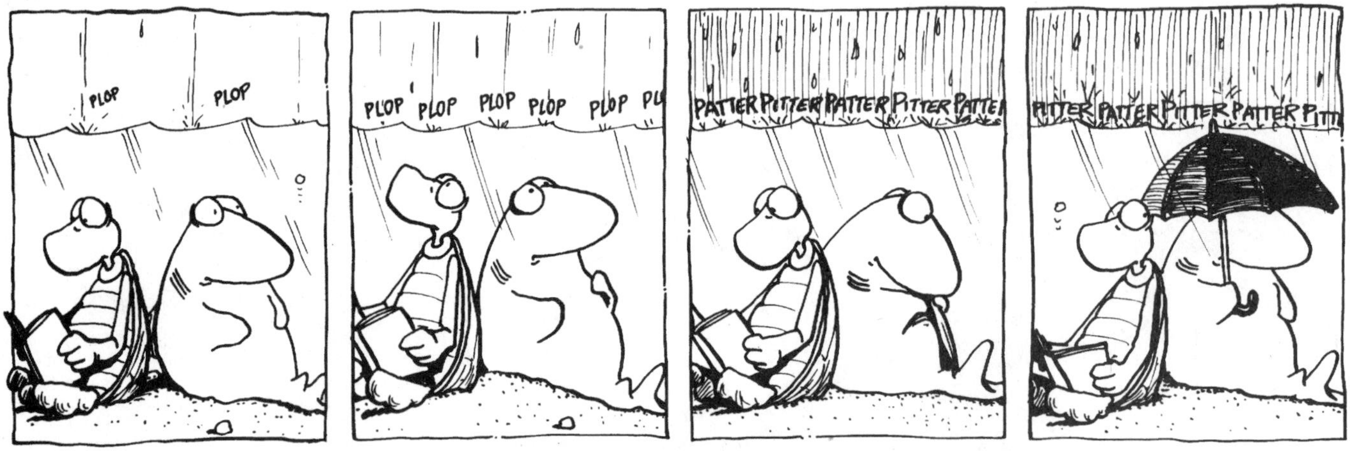
PLOP
PLOP
PLOP PLOP PLOP PLOP PLOP
PATTER PITTER PATTER PITTER
PITTER PATTER PITTER PATTER

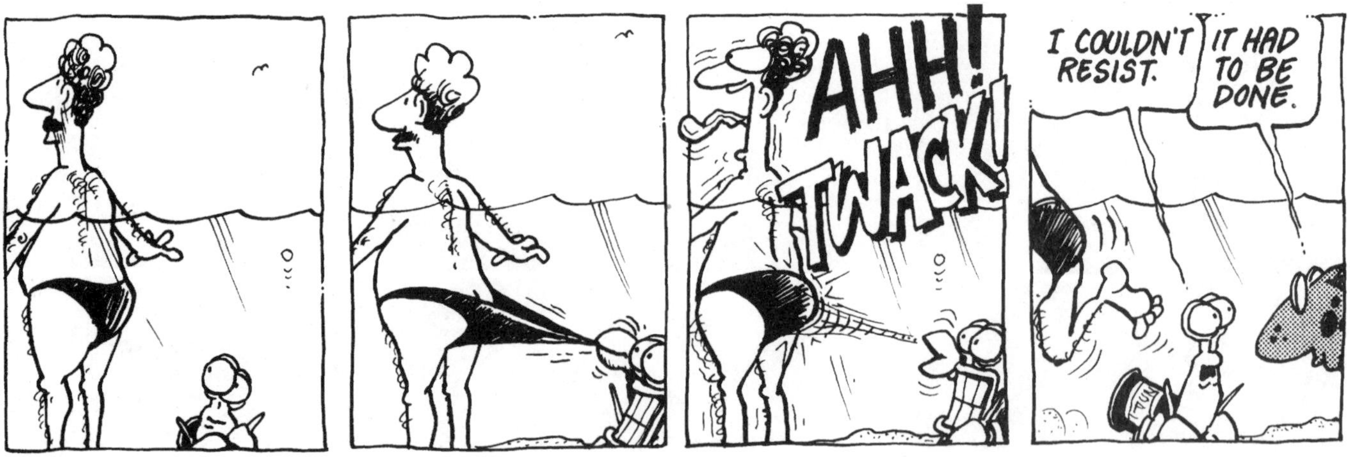
AHH!
TWACK!
I COULDN'T RESIST.
IT HAD TO BE DONE.

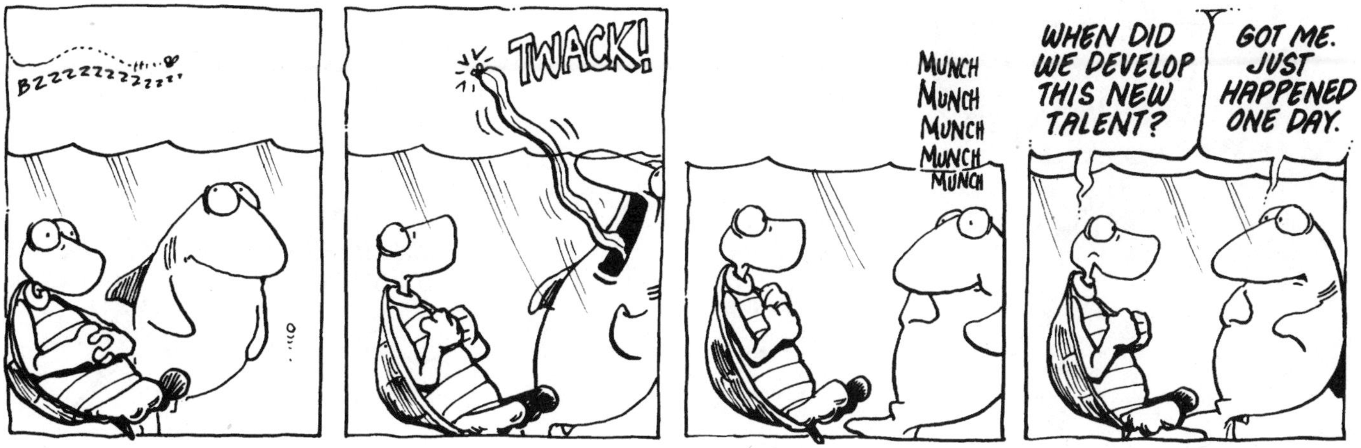
BZZZZZZZZZZZZZ
TWACK!
MUNCH MUNCH MUNCH MUNCH MUNCH
WHEN DID WE DEVELOP THIS NEW TALENT?
GOT ME. JUST HAPPENED ONE DAY.

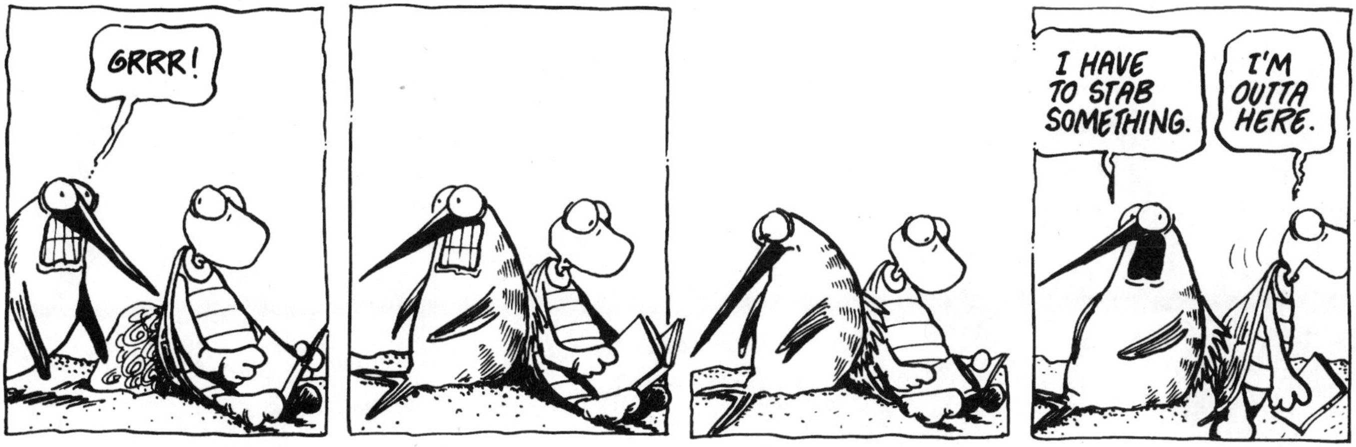
GRRR!
I HAVE TO STAB SOMETHING.
I'M OUTTA HERE.

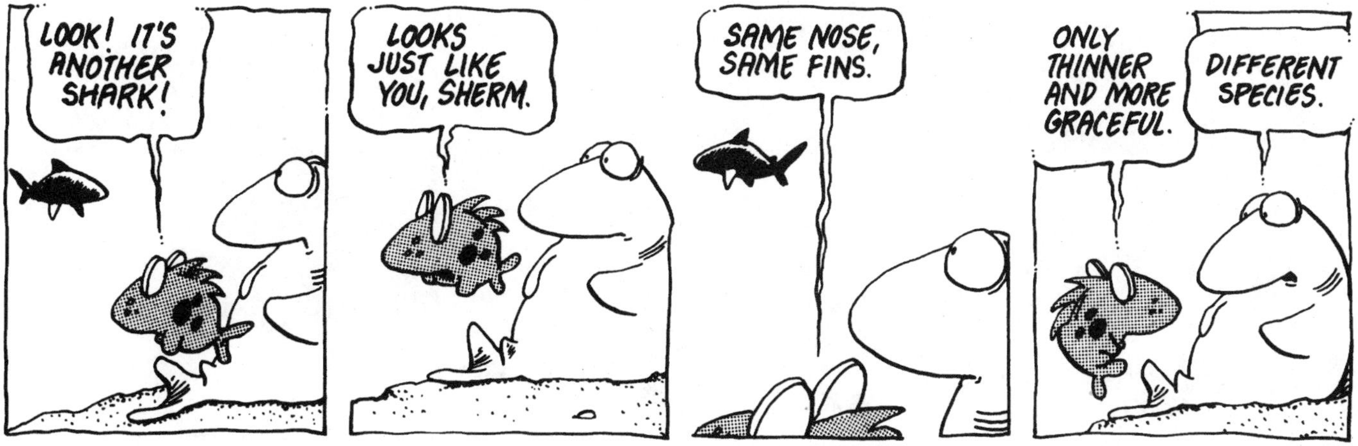
LOOK! IT'S ANOTHER SHARK!
LOOKS JUST LIKE YOU, SHERM.
SAME NOSE, SAME FINS.
ONLY THINNER AND MORE GRACEFUL.
DIFFERENT SPECIES.

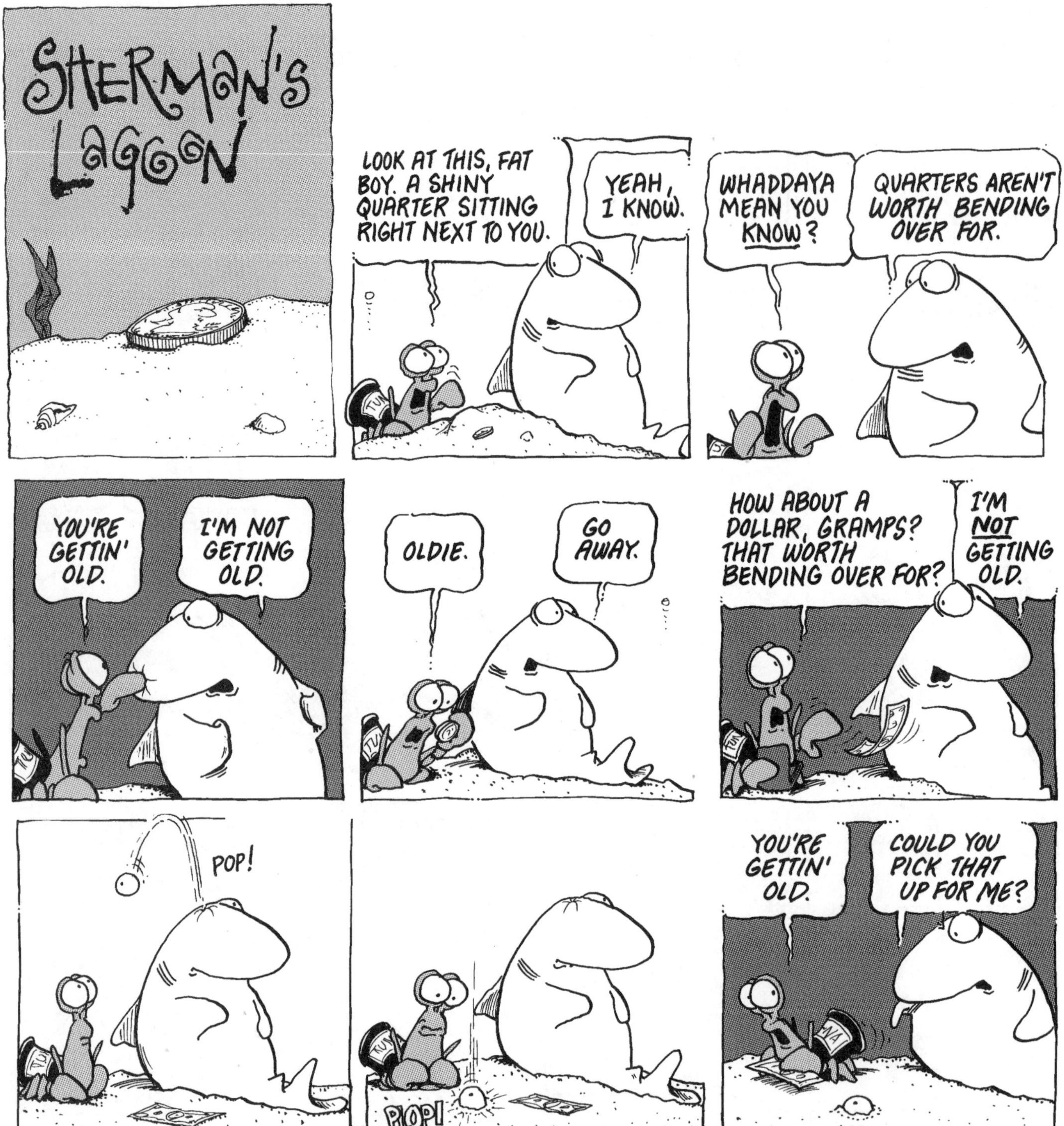
SHERMAN'S LAGOON
LOOK AT THIS, FAT BOY. A SHINY QUARTER SITTING RIGHT NEXT TO YOU.
YEAH, I KNOW.
WHADDAYA MEAN YOU KNOW?
QUARTERS AREN'T WORTH BENDING OVER FOR.
YOU'RE GETTIN' OLD.
I'M NOT GETTING OLD.
OLDIE.
GO AWAY.
HOW ABOUT A DOLLAR, GRAMPS? THAT WORTH BENDING OVER FOR?
I'M NOT GETTING OLD.
POP!
PLOP!
YOU'RE GETTIN' OLD.
COULD YOU PICK THAT UP FOR ME?

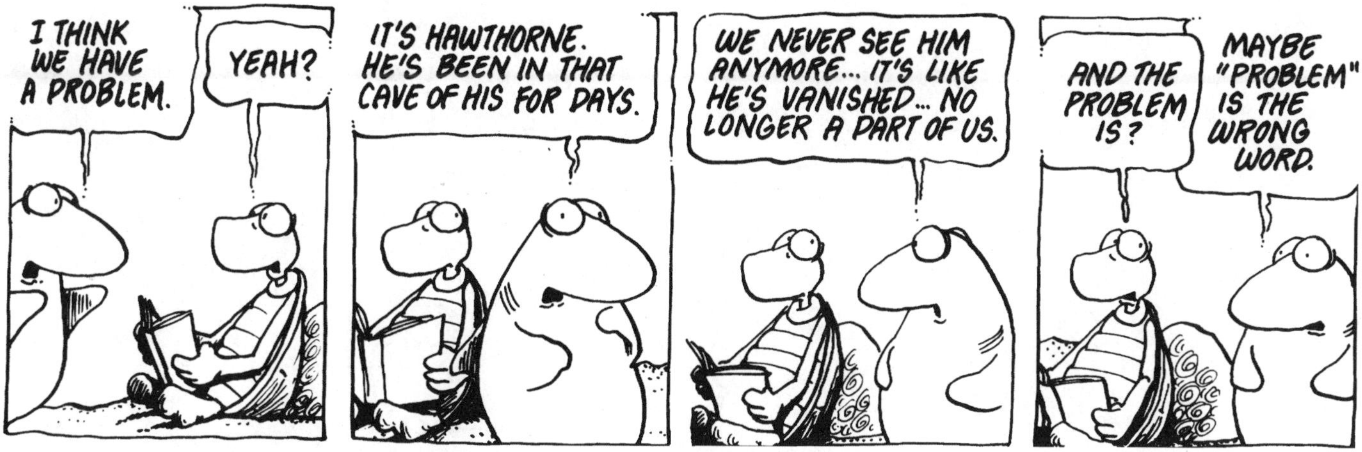
I THINK WE HAVE A PROBLEM.
YEAH?
IT'S HAWTHORNE. HE'S BEEN IN THAT CAVE OF HIS FOR DAYS.
WE NEVER SEE HIM ANYMORE... IT'S LIKE HE'S VANISHED... NO LONGER A PART OF US.
AND THE PROBLEM IS?
MAYBE "PROBLEM" IS THE WRONG WORD.

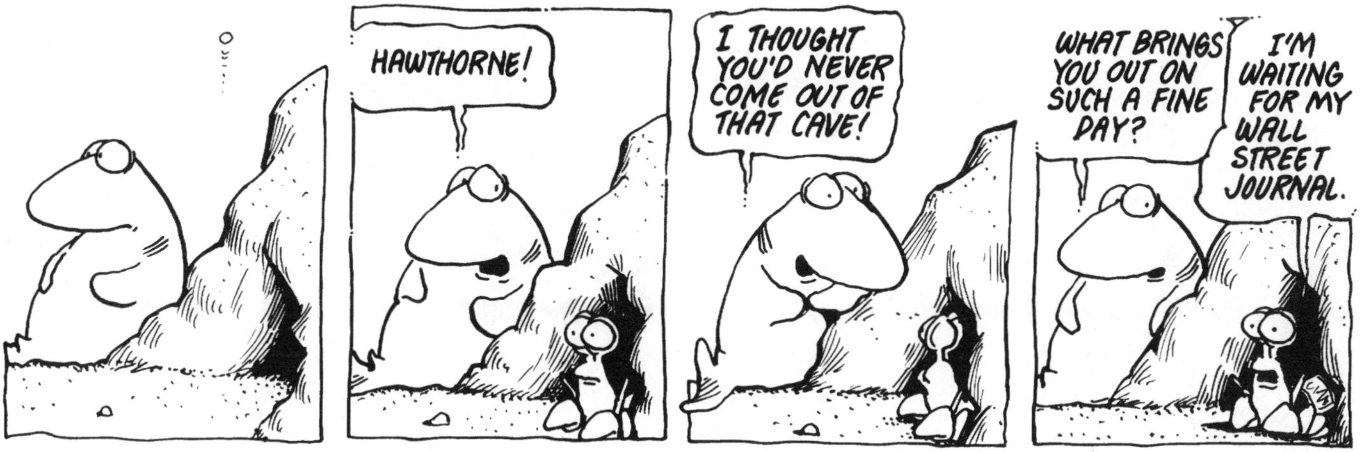
HAWTHORNE!
I THOUGHT YOU'D NEVER COME OUT OF THAT CAVE!
WHAT BRINGS YOU OUT ON SUCH A FINE DAY?
I'M WAITING FOR MY WALL STREET JOURNAL.

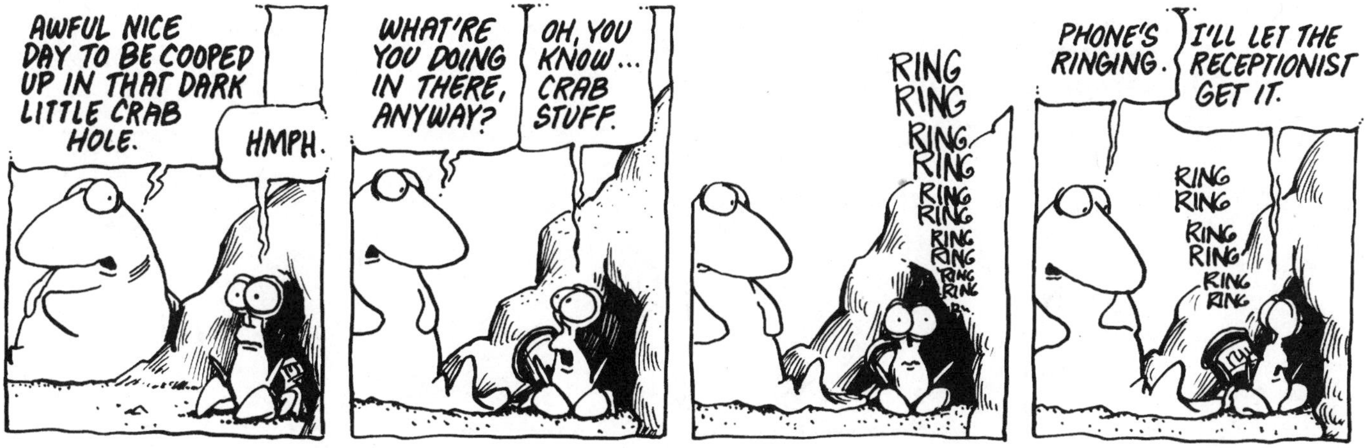
AWFUL NICE DAY TO BE COOPED UP IN THAT DARK LITTLE CRAB HOLE.
HMPH.
WHAT'RE YOU DOING IN THERE, ANYWAY?
OH, YOU KNOW... CRAB STUFF.
RING RING RING RING RING RING
PHONE'S RINGING.
I'LL LET THE RECEPTIONIST GET IT.
RING RING RING RING RING RING

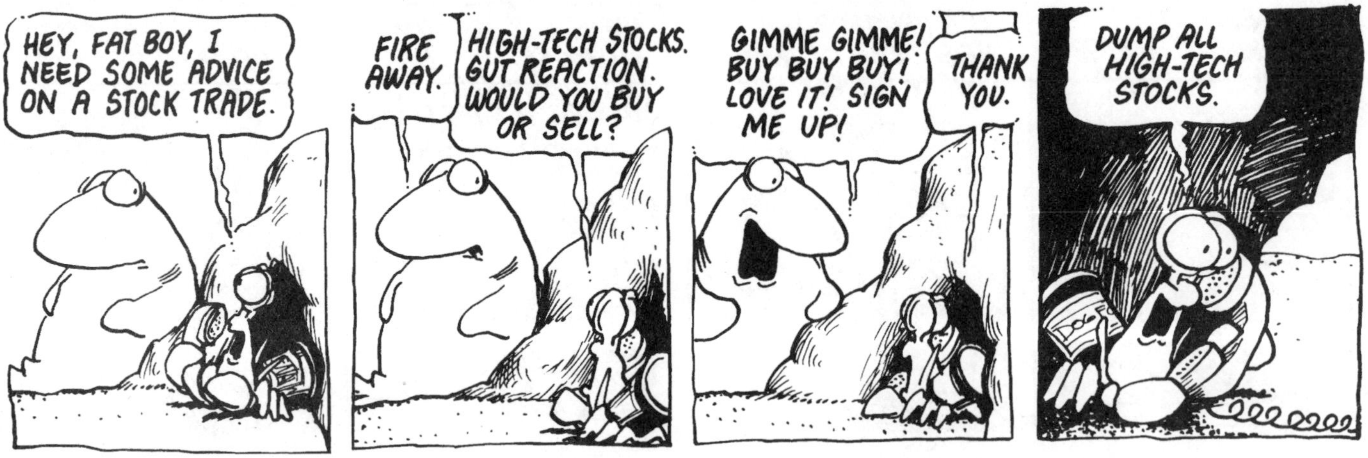
HEY, FAT BOY, I NEED SOME ADVICE ON A STOCK TRADE.
FIRE AWAY.
HIGH-TECH STOCKS. GUT REACTION. WOULD YOU BUY OR SELL?
GIMME GIMME! BUY BUY BUY! LOVE IT! SIGN ME UP!
THANK YOU.
DUMP ALL HIGH-TECH STOCKS.

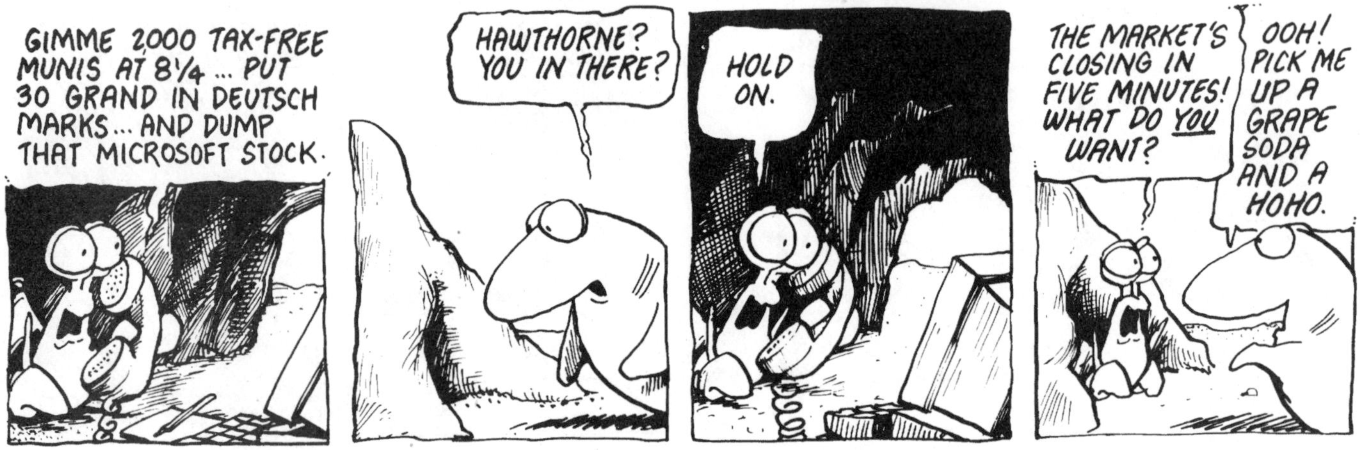
GIMME 2,000 TAX-FREE MUNIS AT 8¼ ... PUT 30 GRAND IN DEUTSCH MARKS... AND DUMP THAT MICROSOFT STOCK.
HAWTHORNE? YOU IN THERE?
HOLD ON.
THE MARKET'S CLOSING IN FIVE MINUTES! WHAT DO YOU WANT?
OOH! PICK ME UP A GRAPE SODA AND A HOHO.

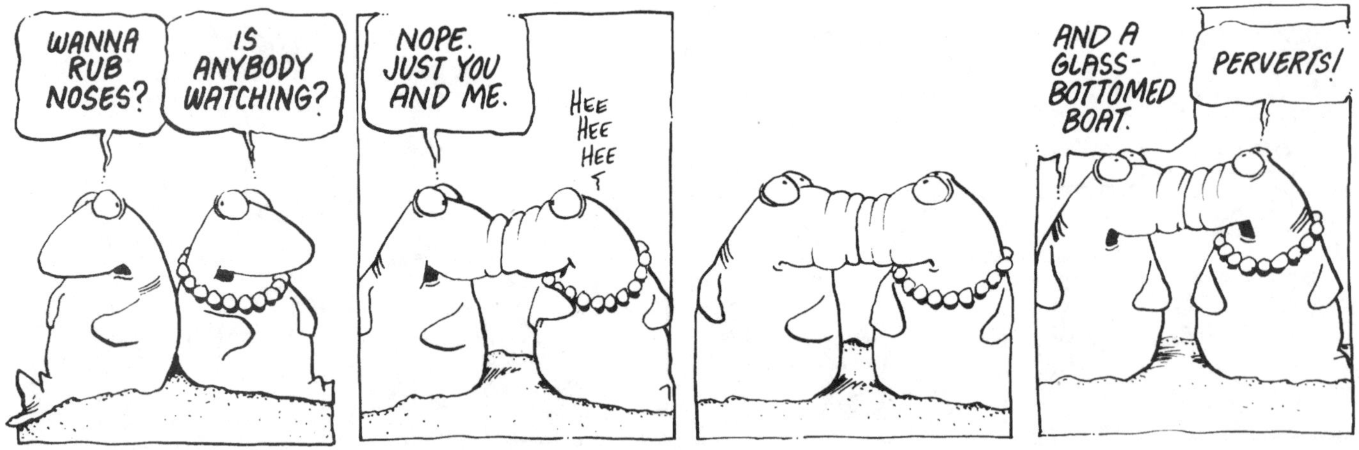
WANNA RUB NOSES?
IS ANYBODY WATCHING?
NOPE. JUST YOU AND ME.
HEE HEE HEE
AND A GLASS-BOTTOMED BOAT.
PERVERTS!

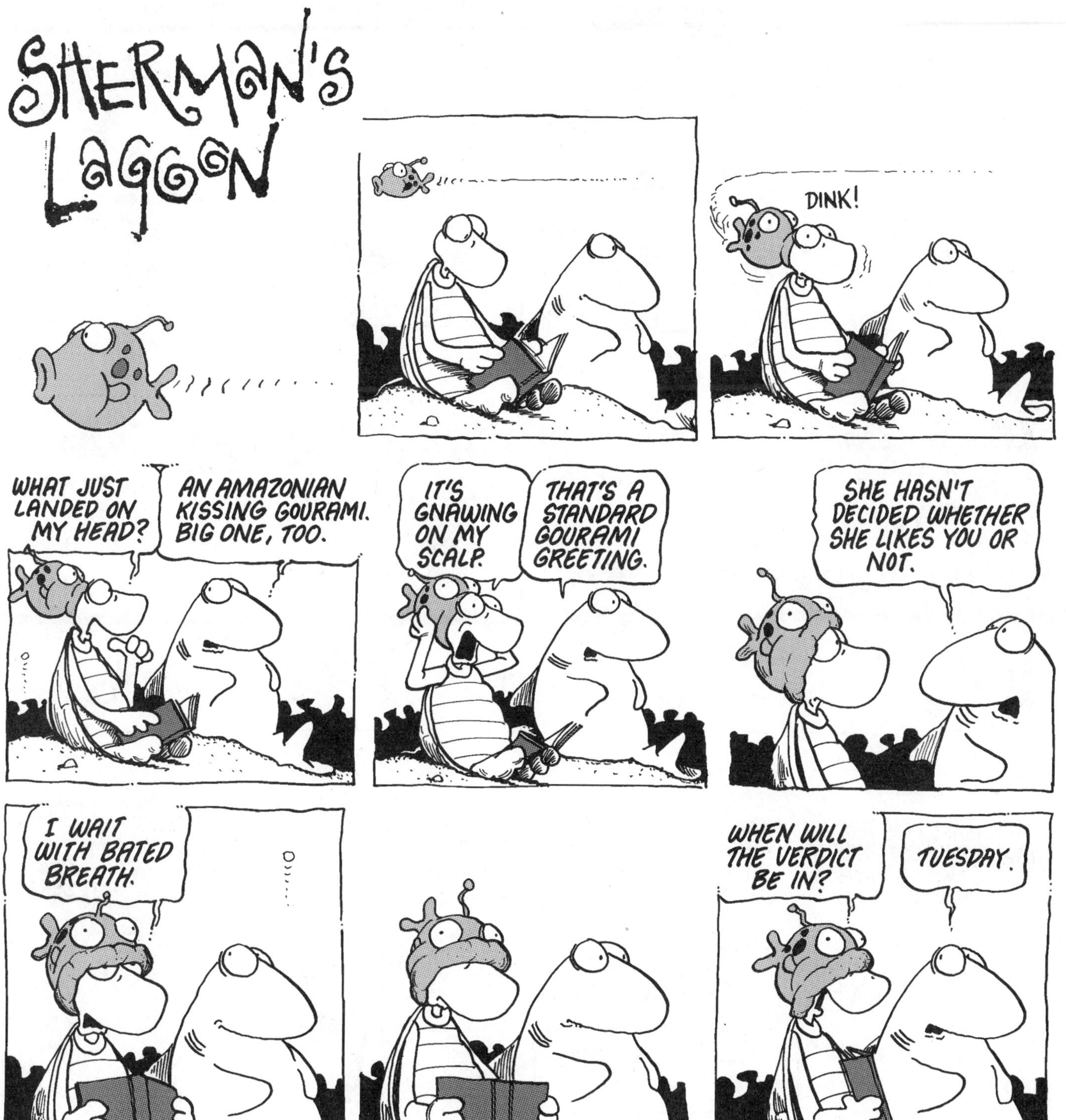
SHERMAN'S LAGOON
DINK!
WHAT JUST LANDED ON MY HEAD?
AN AMAZONIAN KISSING GOURAMI. BIG ONE, TOO.
IT'S GNAWING ON MY SCALP.
THAT'S A STANDARD GOURAMI GREETING.
SHE HASN'T DECIDED WHETHER SHE LIKES YOU OR NOT.
I WAIT WITH BATED BREATH.
WHEN WILL THE VERDICT BE IN?
TUESDAY.

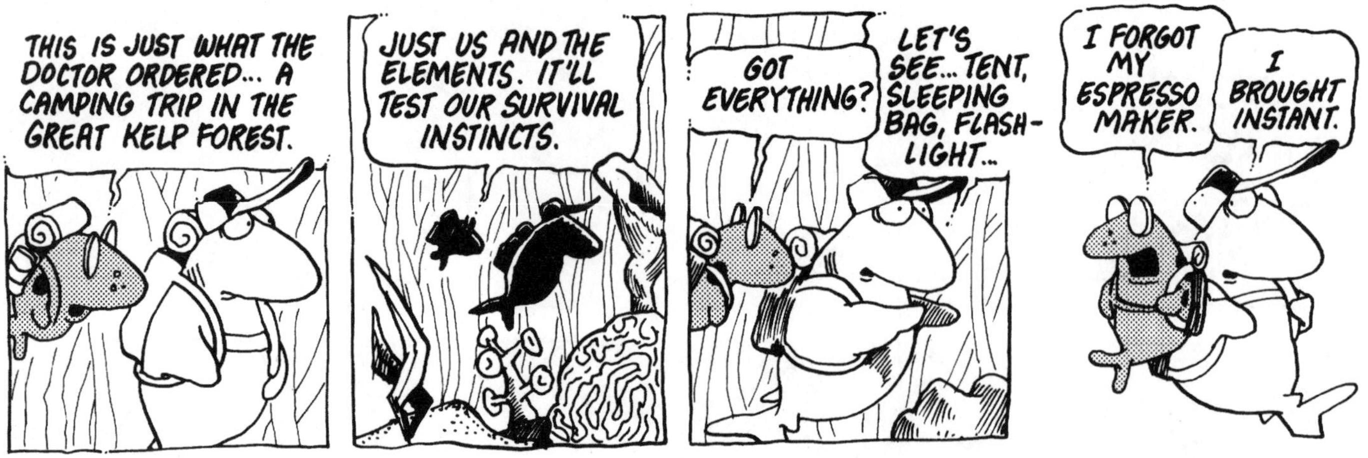
THIS IS JUST WHAT THE DOCTOR ORDERED... A CAMPING TRIP IN THE GREAT KELP FOREST.
JUST US AND THE ELEMENTS. IT'LL TEST OUR SURVIVAL INSTINCTS.
GOT EVERYTHING?
LET'S SEE... TENT, SLEEPING BAG, FLASH-LIGHT...
I FORGOT MY ESPRESSO MAKER.
I BROUGHT INSTANT.

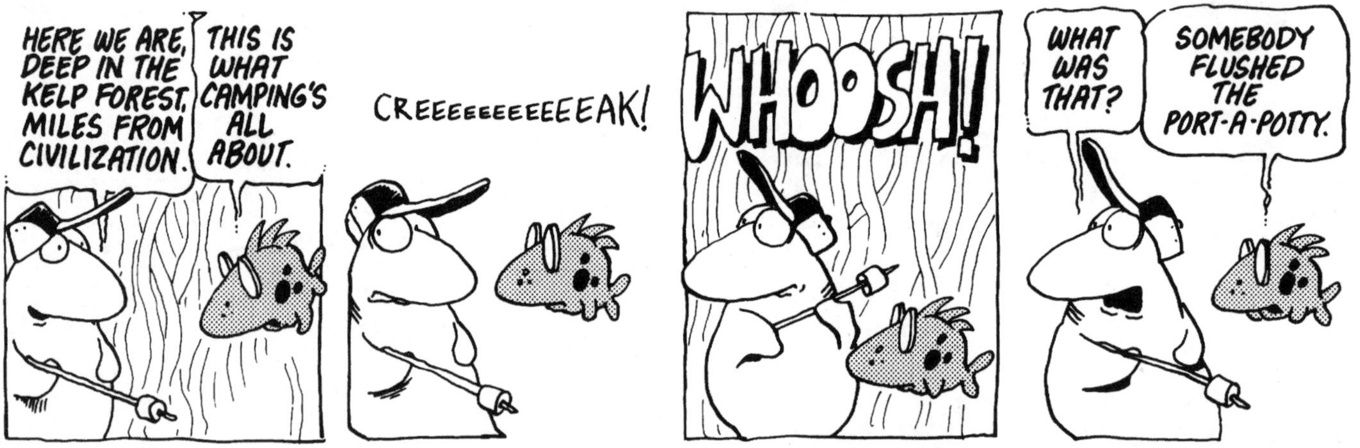
HERE WE ARE, DEEP IN THE KELP FOREST, MILES FROM CIVILIZATION.
THIS IS WHAT CAMPING'S ALL ABOUT.
CREEEEEEEEEEEAK!
WHOOSH!
WHAT WAS THAT?
SOMEBODY FLUSHED THE PORT-A-POTTY.

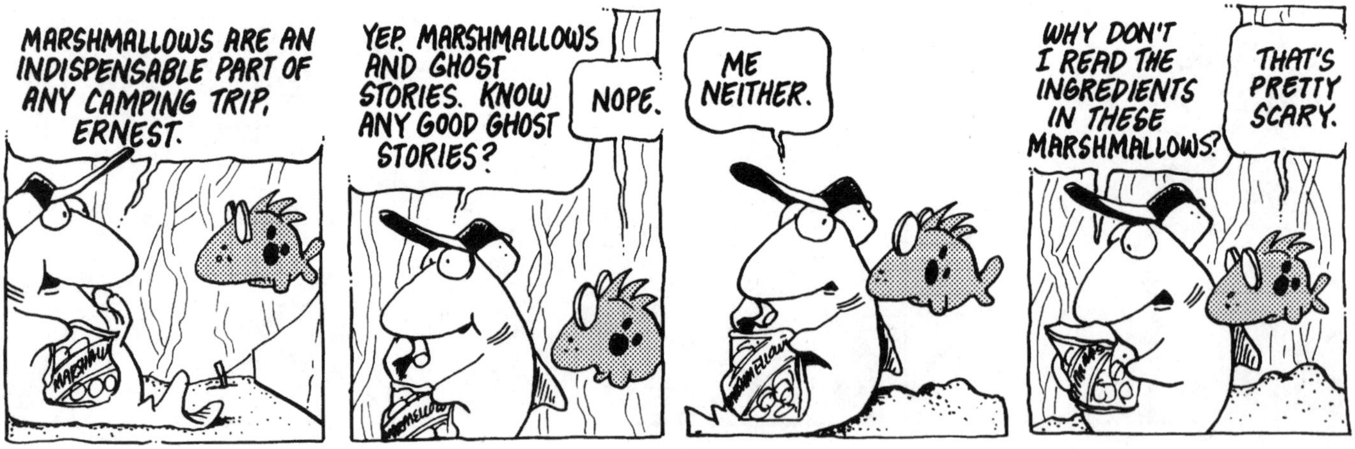
MARSHMALLOWS ARE AN INDISPENSABLE PART OF ANY CAMPING TRIP, ERNEST.
YEP. MARSHMALLOWS AND GHOST STORIES. KNOW ANY GOOD GHOST STORIES?
NOPE.
ME NEITHER.
WHY DON'T I READ THE INGREDIENTS IN THESE MARSHMALLOWS?
THAT'S PRETTY SCARY.

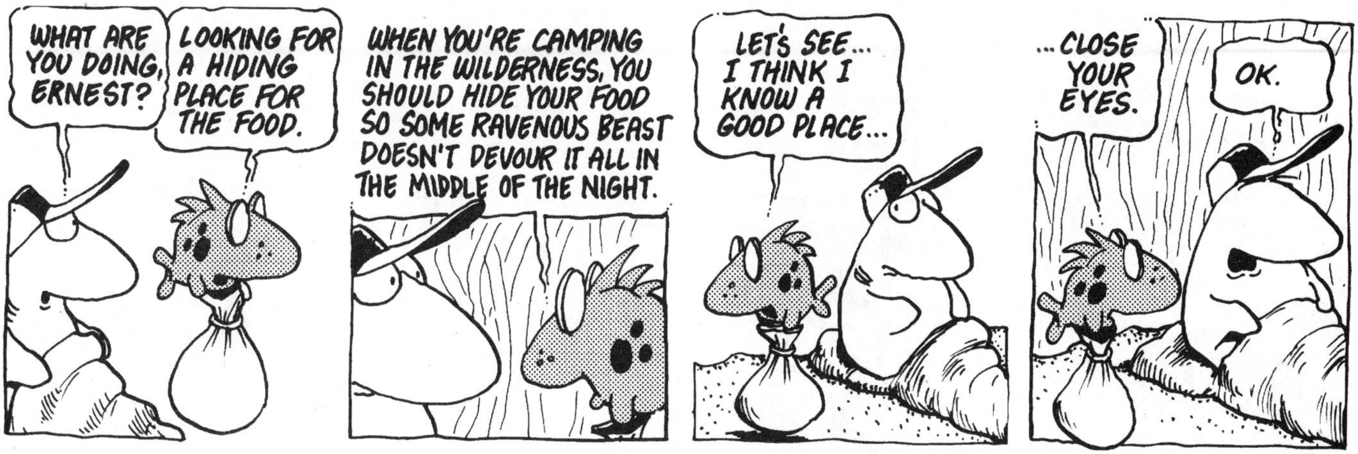
WHAT ARE YOU DOING, ERNEST?
LOOKING FOR A HIDING PLACE FOR THE FOOD.
WHEN YOU'RE CAMPING IN THE WILDERNESS, YOU SHOULD HIDE YOUR FOOD SO SOME RAVENOUS BEAST DOESN'T DEVOUR IT ALL IN THE MIDDLE OF THE NIGHT.
LET'S SEE... I THINK I KNOW A GOOD PLACE...
...CLOSE YOUR EYES.
OK.

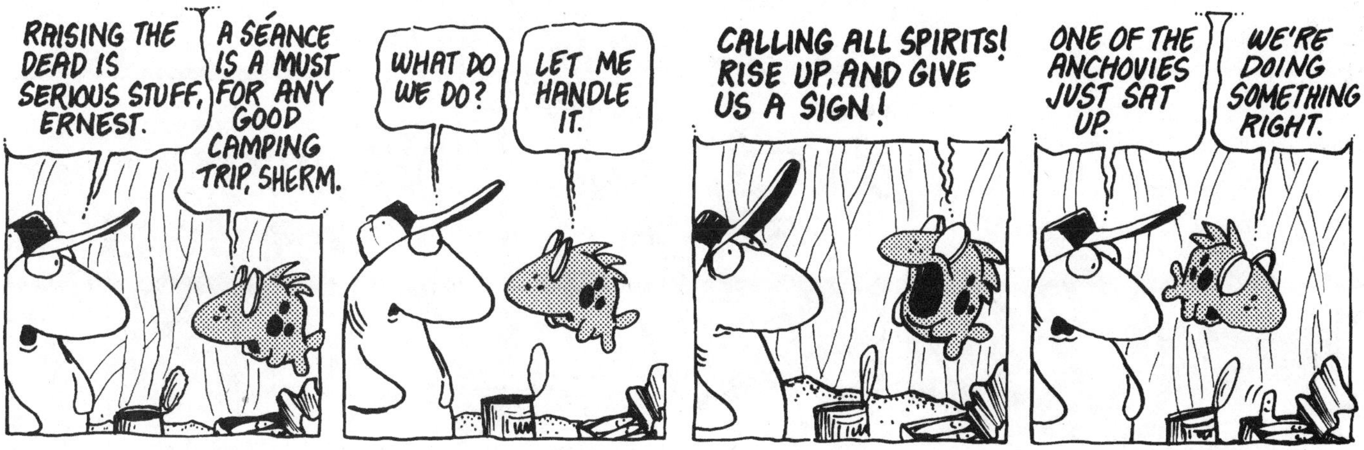
RAISING THE DEAD IS SERIOUS STUFF, ERNEST.
A SÉANCE IS A MUST FOR ANY GOOD CAMPING TRIP, SHERM.
WHAT DO WE DO?
LET ME HANDLE IT.
CALLING ALL SPIRITS! RISE UP, AND GIVE US A SIGN!
ONE OF THE ANCHOVIES JUST SAT UP.
WE'RE DOING SOMETHING RIGHT.

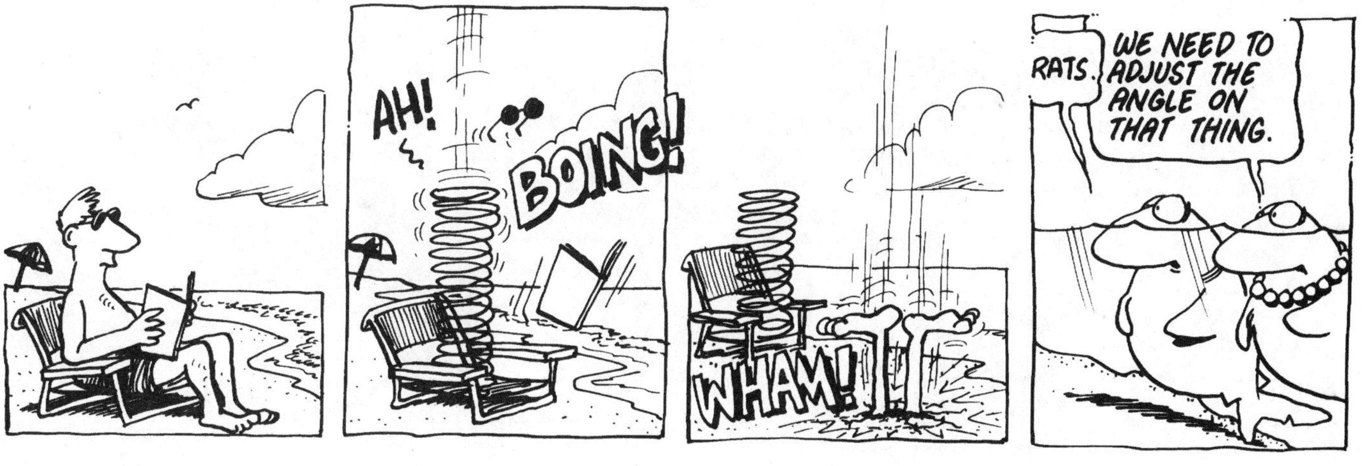
AH!
BOING!
WHAM!
RATS.
WE NEED TO ADJUST THE ANGLE ON THAT THING.

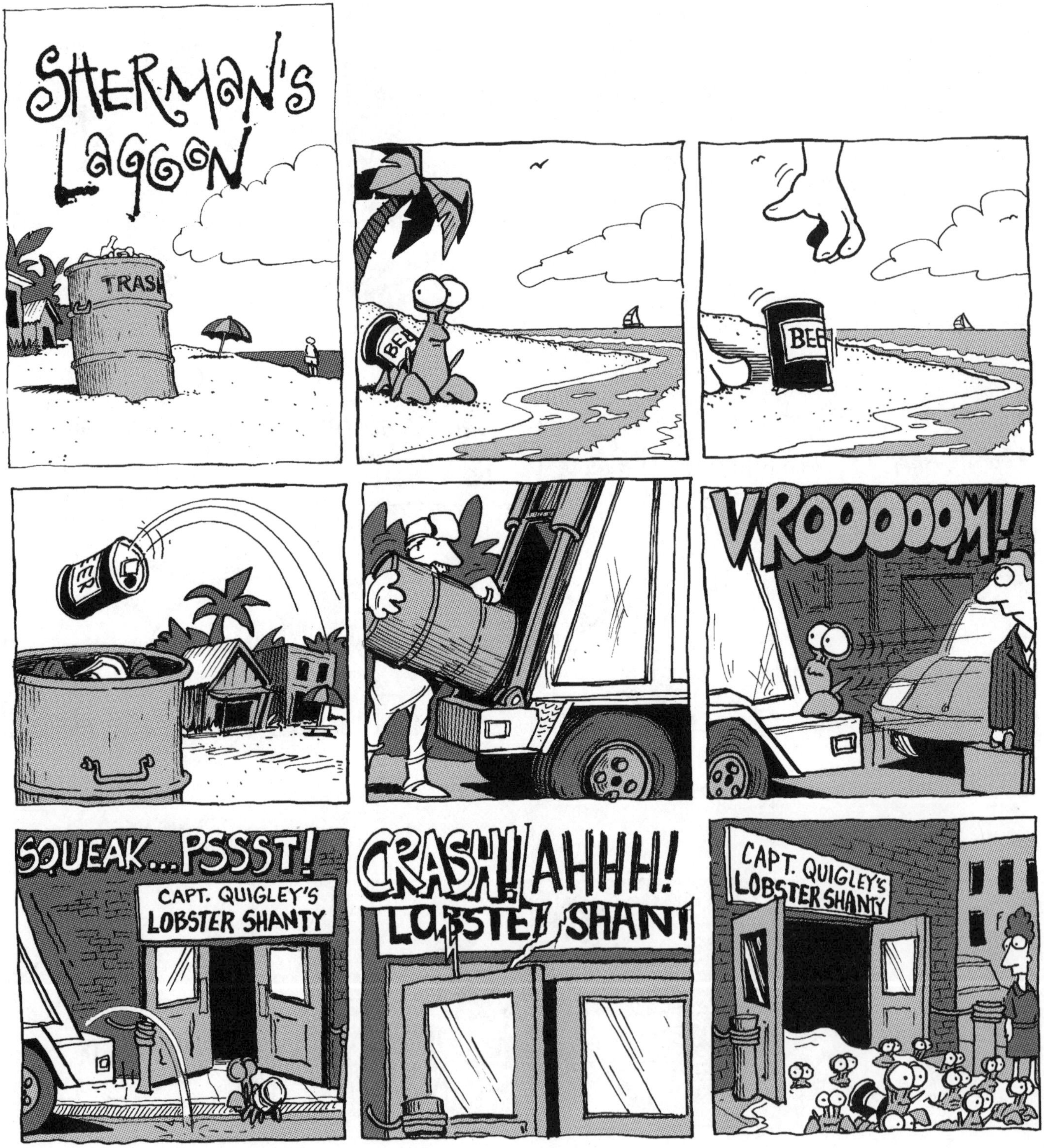
SHERMAN'S LAGOON
TRASH
BEE
BEE
ER
VROOOOOM!
SQUEAK... PSSST!
CAPT. QUIGLEY'S LOBSTER SHANTY
CRASH! AHHH!
LOBSTE SHANT
CAPT. QUIGLEY'S LOBSTER SHANTY

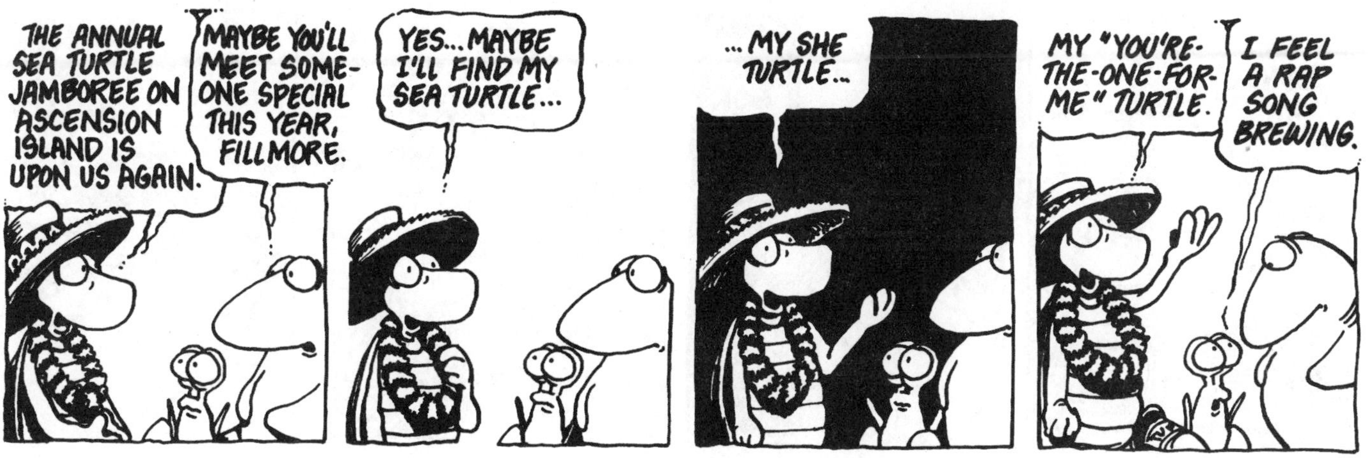
THE ANNUAL SEA TURTLE JAMBOREE ON ASCENSION ISLAND IS UPON US AGAIN.
MAYBE YOU'LL MEET SOMEONE SPECIAL THIS YEAR, FILLMORE.
YES... MAYBE I'LL FIND MY SEA TURTLE...
... MY SHE TURTLE...
MY "YOU'RE-THE-ONE-FOR-ME" TURTLE.
I FEEL A RAP SONG BREWING.

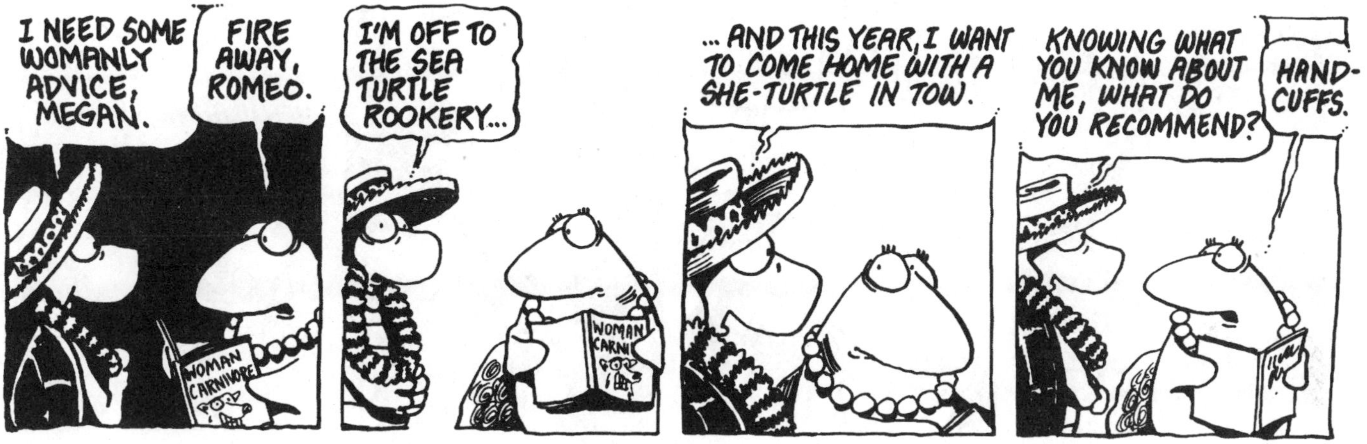
I NEED SOME WOMANLY ADVICE, MEGAN.
FIRE AWAY, ROMEO.
WOMAN CARNIVORE
I'M OFF TO THE SEA TURTLE ROOKERY...
... AND THIS YEAR, I WANT TO COME HOME WITH A SHE-TURTLE IN TOW.
KNOWING WHAT YOU KNOW ABOUT ME, WHAT DO YOU RECOMMEND?
HANDCUFFS.

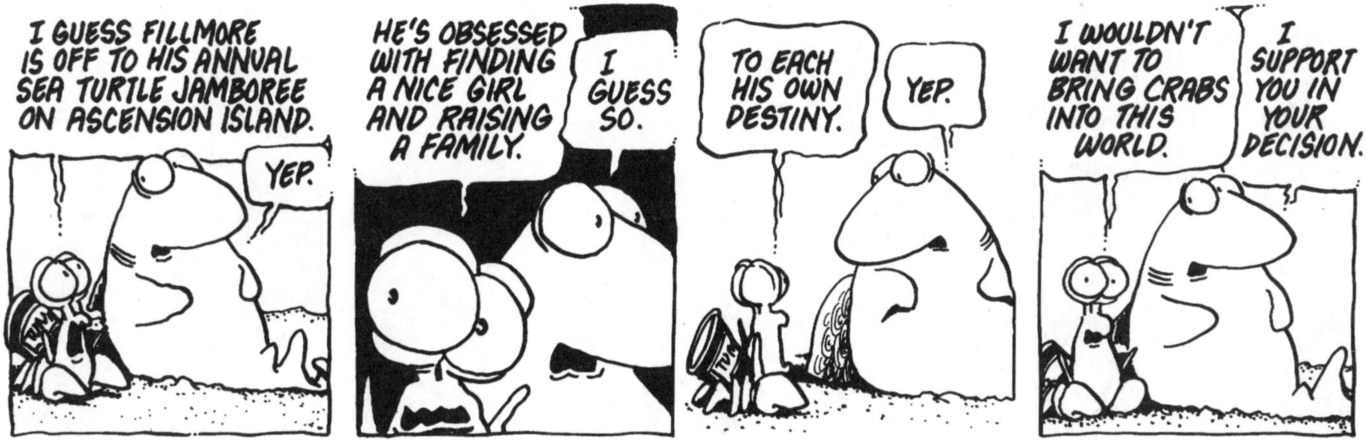
I GUESS FILLMORE IS OFF TO HIS ANNUAL SEA TURTLE JAMBOREE ON ASCENSION ISLAND.
YEP.
HE'S OBSESSED WITH FINDING A NICE GIRL AND RAISING A FAMILY.
I GUESS SO.
TO EACH HIS OWN DESTINY.
YEP.
I WOULDN'T WANT TO BRING CRABS INTO THIS WORLD.
I SUPPORT YOU IN YOUR DECISION.

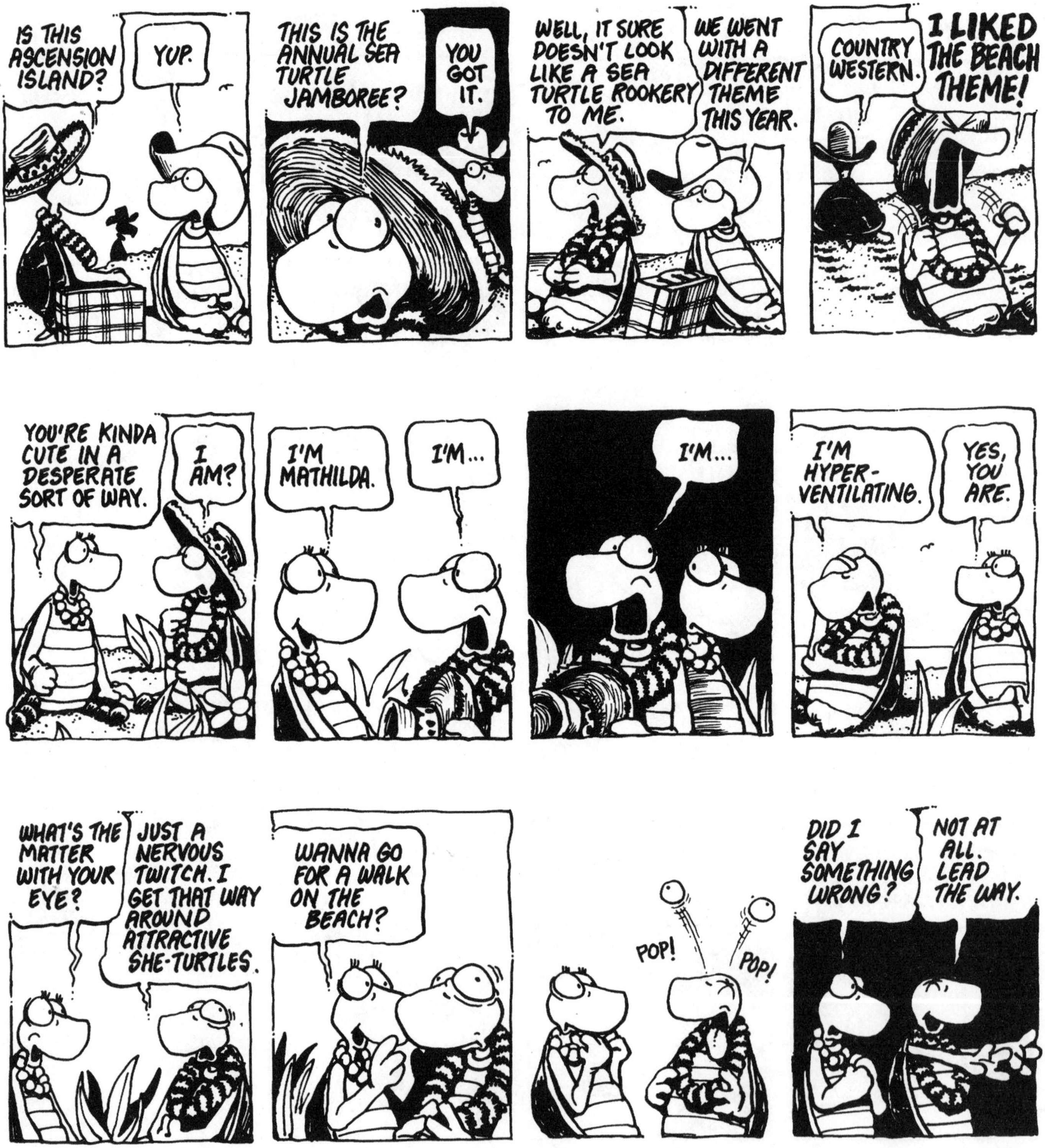
IS THIS ASCENSION ISLAND?
YUP.
THIS IS THE ANNUAL SEA TURTLE JAMBOREE?
YOU GOT IT.
WELL, IT SURE DOESN'T LOOK LIKE A SEA TURTLE ROOKERY TO ME.
WE WENT WITH A DIFFERENT THEME THIS YEAR.
COUNTRY WESTERN.
I LIKED THE BEACH THEME!
YOU'RE KINDA CUTE IN A DESPERATE SORT OF WAY.
I AM?
I'M MATHILDA.
I'M...
I'M...
I'M HYPER-VENTILATING.
YES, YOU ARE.
WHAT'S THE MATTER WITH YOUR EYE?
JUST A NERVOUS TWITCH. I GET THAT WAY AROUND ATTRACTIVE SHE-TURTLES.
WANNA GO FOR A WALK ON THE BEACH?
POP!
POP!
DID I SAY SOMETHING WRONG?
NOT AT ALL. LEAD THE WAY.

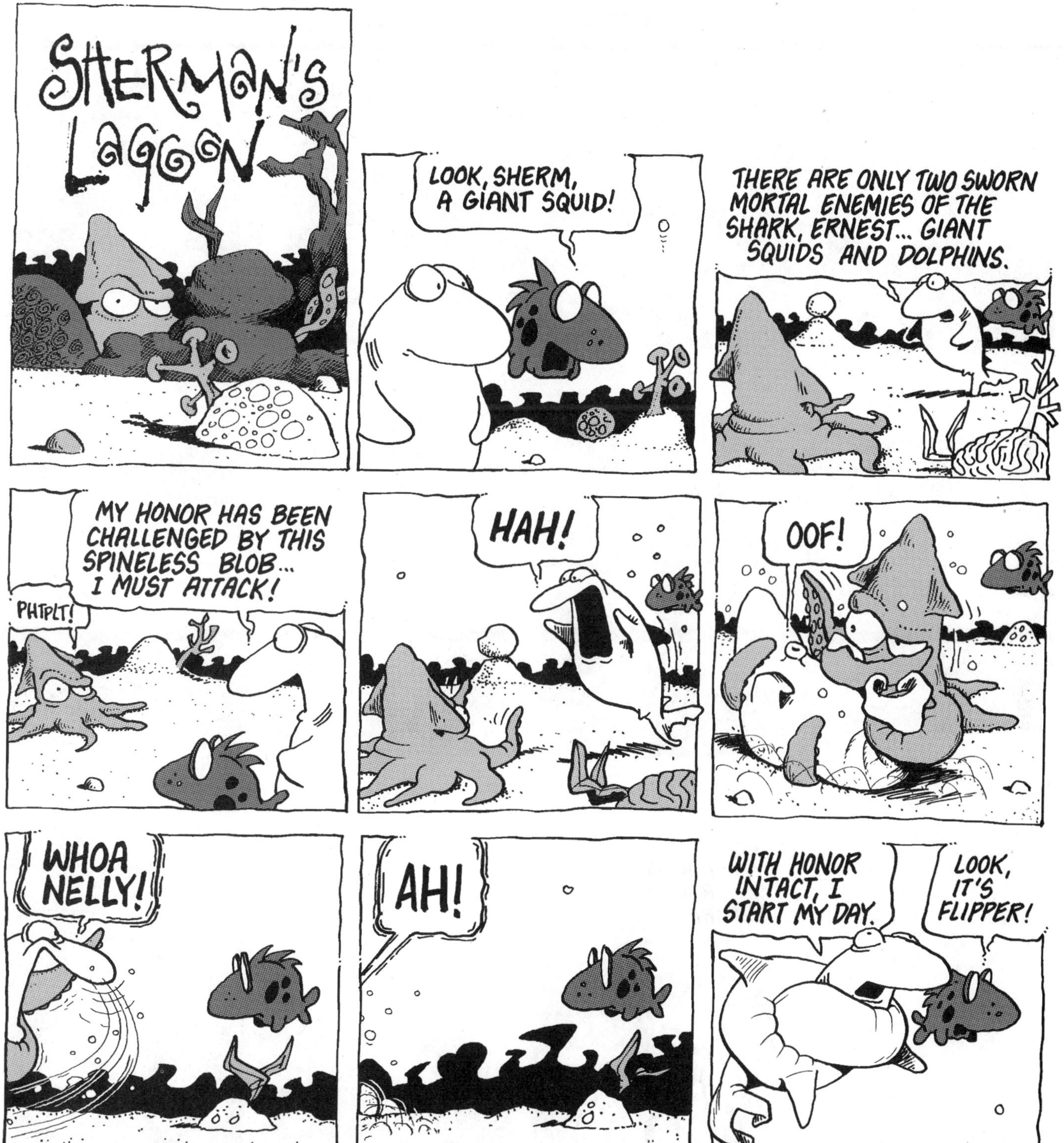
SHERMAN'S LAGOON
LOOK, SHERM, A GIANT SQUID!
THERE ARE ONLY TWO SWORN MORTAL ENEMIES OF THE SHARK, ERNEST... GIANT SQUIDS AND DOLPHINS.
PHTPLT!
MY HONOR HAS BEEN CHALLENGED BY THIS SPINELESS BLOB... I MUST ATTACK!
HAH!
OOF!
WHOA NELLY!
AH!
WITH HONOR INTACT, I START MY DAY.
LOOK, IT'S FLIPPER!

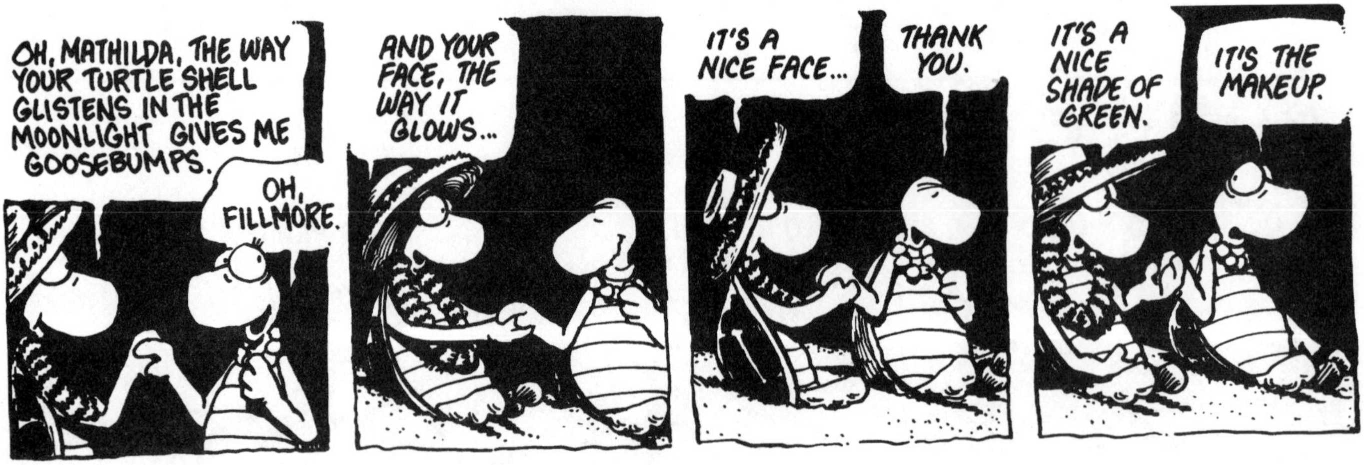
OH, MATHILDA, THE WAY YOUR TURTLE SHELL GLISTENS IN THE MOONLIGHT GIVES ME GOOSEBUMPS.
OH, FILLMORE.
AND YOUR FACE, THE WAY IT GLOWS...
IT'S A NICE FACE...
THANK YOU.
IT'S A NICE SHADE OF GREEN.
IT'S THE MAKEUP.

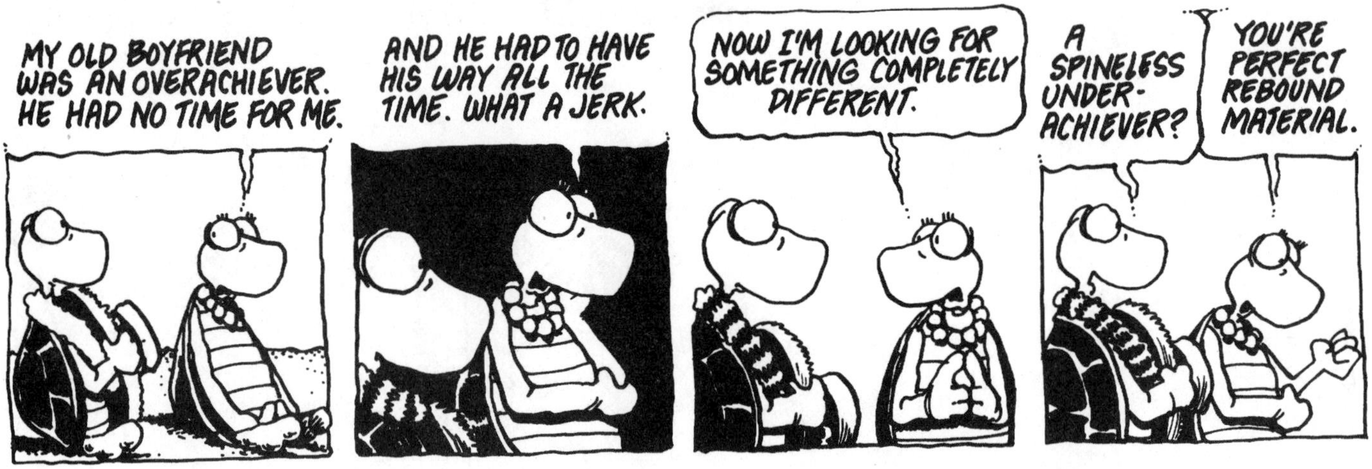
MY OLD BOYFRIEND WAS AN OVERACHIEVER. HE HAD NO TIME FOR ME.
AND HE HAD TO HAVE HIS WAY ALL THE TIME. WHAT A JERK.
NOW I'M LOOKING FOR SOMETHING COMPLETELY DIFFERENT.
A SPINELESS UNDER-ACHIEVER?
YOU'RE PERFECT REBOUND MATERIAL.

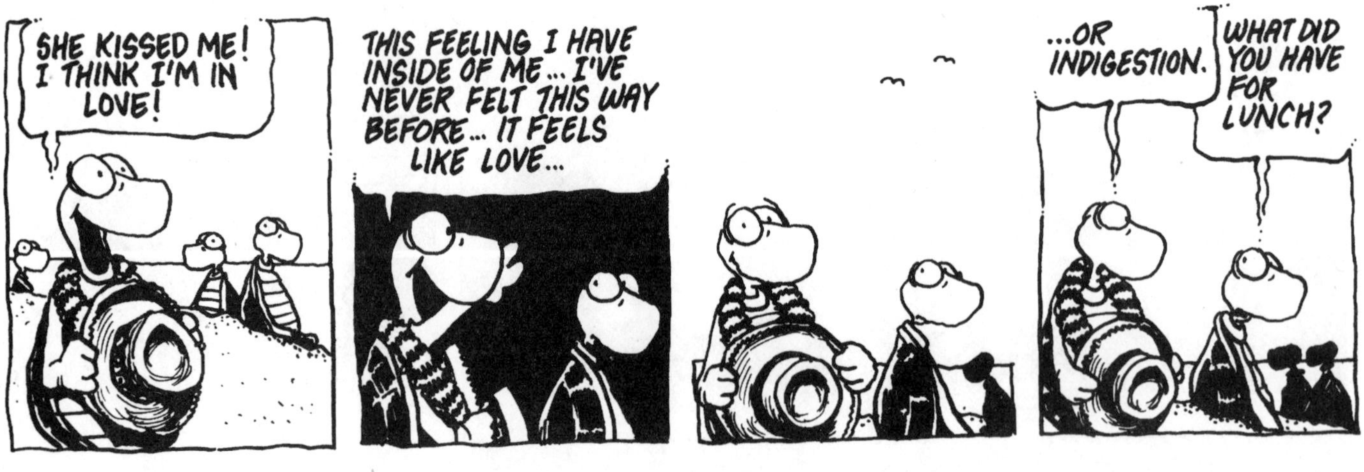
SHE KISSED ME! I THINK I'M IN LOVE!
THIS FEELING I HAVE INSIDE OF ME... I'VE NEVER FELT THIS WAY BEFORE... IT FEELS LIKE LOVE...
...OR INDIGESTION.
WHAT DID YOU HAVE FOR LUNCH?

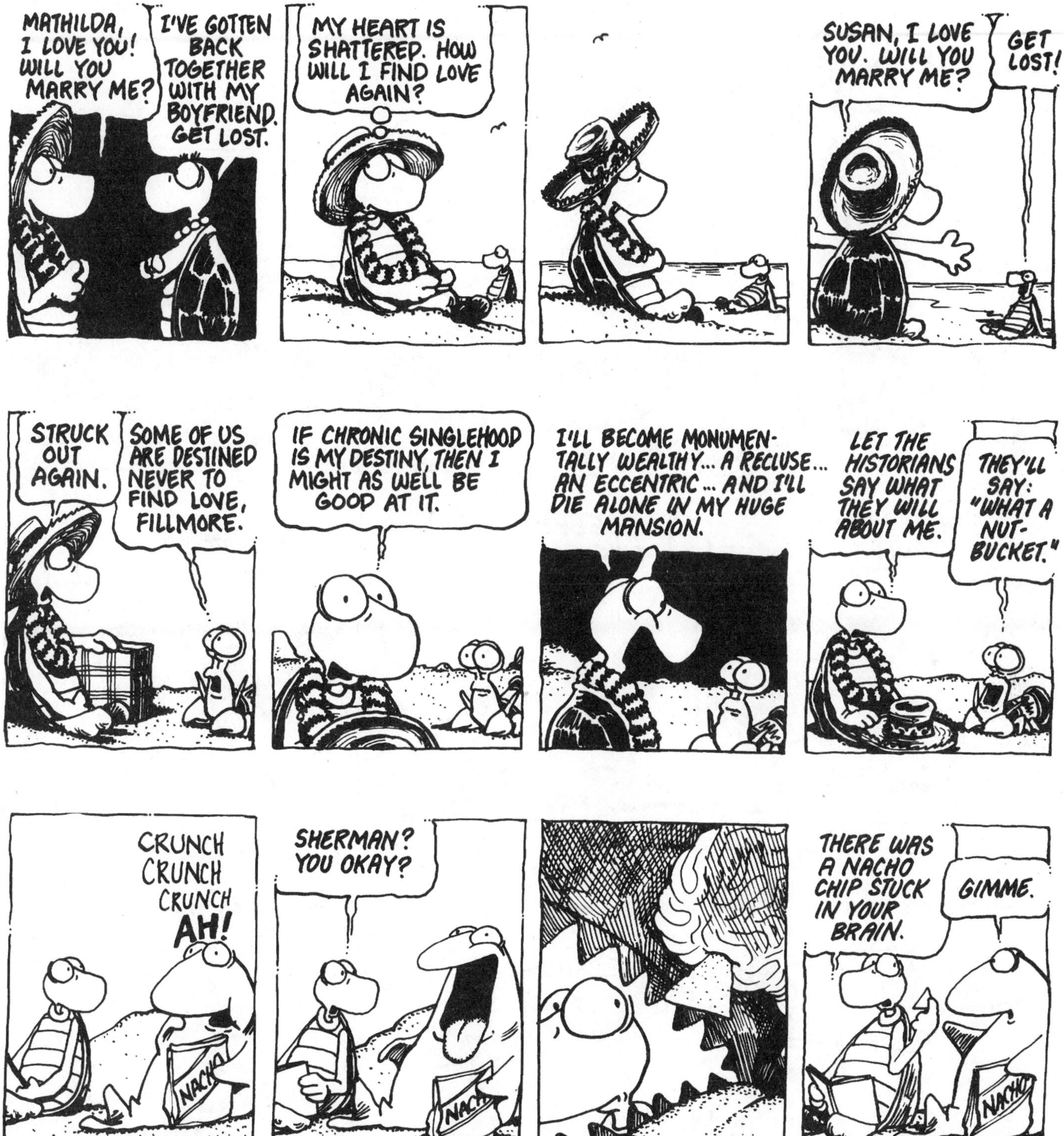
MATHILDA, I LOVE YOU! WILL YOU MARRY ME?
I'VE GOTTEN BACK TOGETHER WITH MY BOYFRIEND. GET LOST.
MY HEART IS SHATTERED. HOW WILL I FIND LOVE AGAIN?
SUSAN, I LOVE YOU. WILL YOU MARRY ME?
GET LOST!
STRUCK OUT AGAIN.
SOME OF US ARE DESTINED NEVER TO FIND LOVE, FILLMORE.
IF CHRONIC SINGLEHOOD IS MY DESTINY, THEN I MIGHT AS WELL BE GOOD AT IT.
I'LL BECOME MONUMENTALLY WEALTHY... A RECLUSE... AN ECCENTRIC... AND I'LL DIE ALONE IN MY HUGE MANSION.
LET THE HISTORIANS SAY WHAT THEY WILL ABOUT ME.
THEY'LL SAY: "WHAT A NUT-BUCKET."
CRUNCH
CRUNCH
CRUNCH
AH!
NACHO
SHERMAN? YOU OKAY?
NACHO
THERE WAS A NACHO CHIP STUCK IN YOUR BRAIN.
GIMME.
NACHO

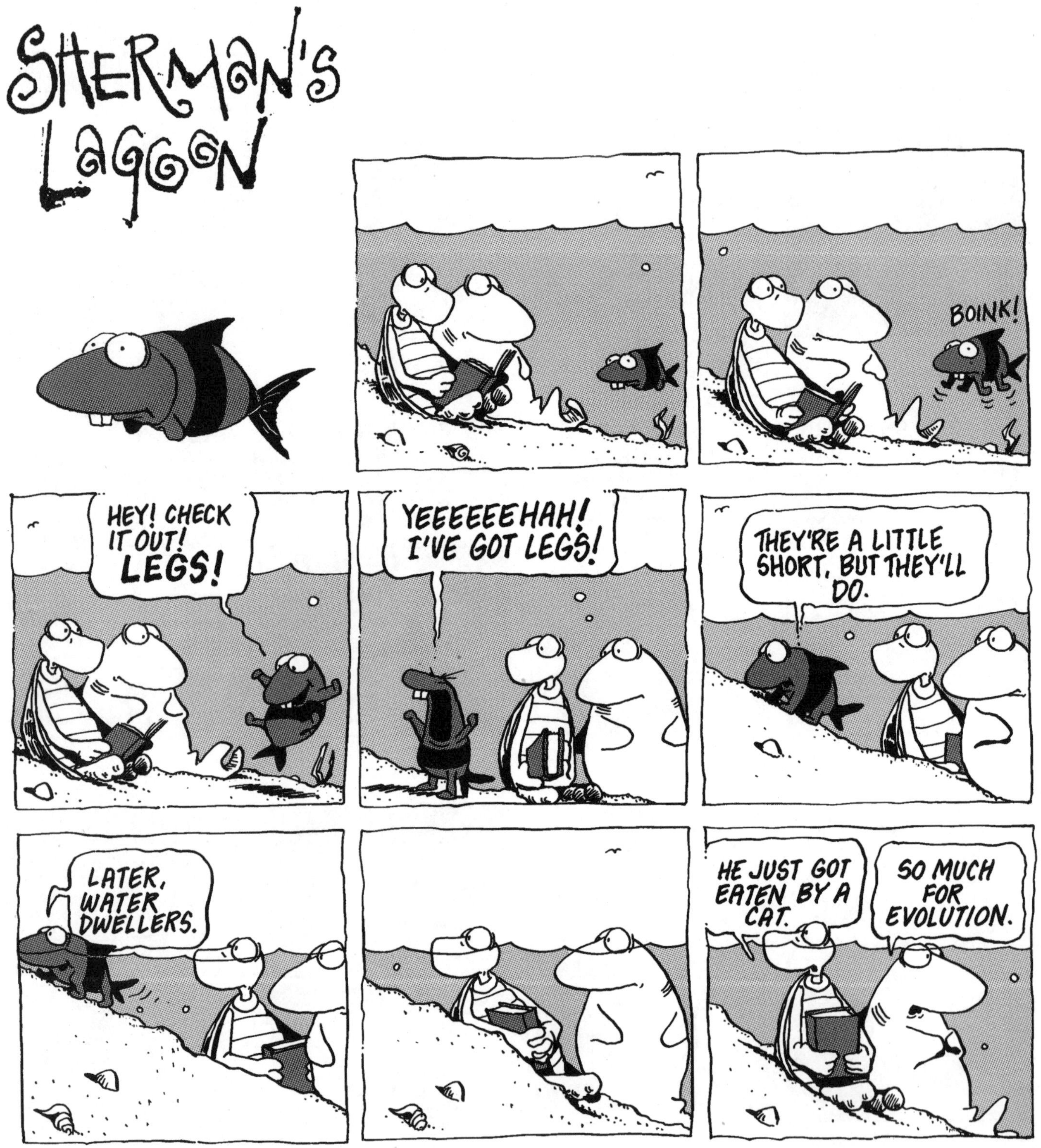
SHERMAN'S LAGOON
BOINK!
HEY! CHECK IT OUT! LEGS!
YEEEEEEHAH! I'VE GOT LEGS!
THEY'RE A LITTLE SHORT, BUT THEY'LL DO.
LATER, WATER DWELLERS.
HE JUST GOT EATEN BY A CAT.
SO MUCH FOR EVOLUTION.

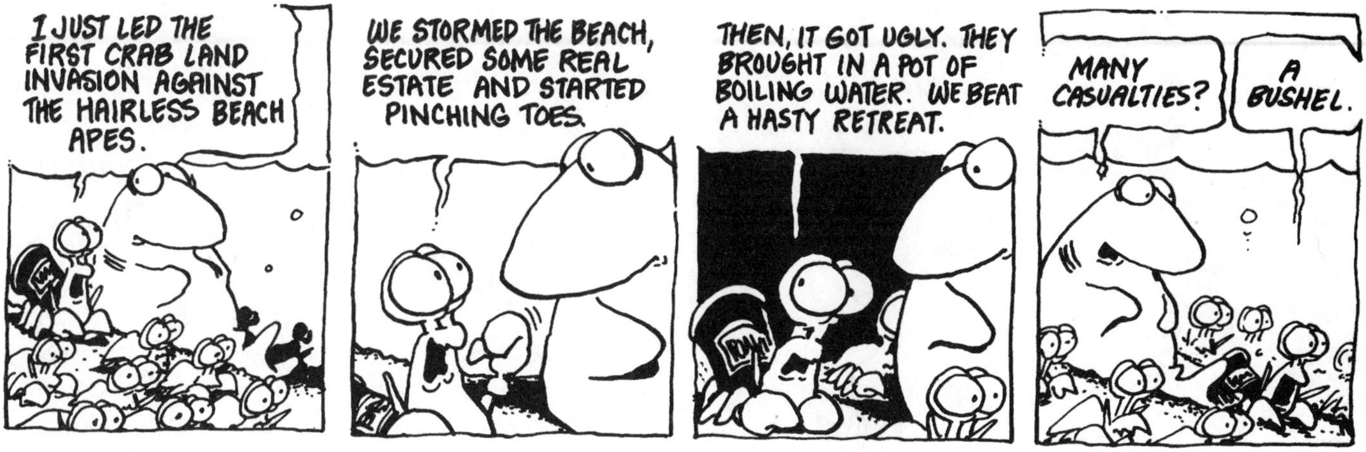
I JUST LED THE FIRST CRAB LAND INVASION AGAINST THE HAIRLESS BEACH APES.
WE STORMED THE BEACH, SECURED SOME REAL ESTATE AND STARTED PINCHING TOES.
THEN, IT GOT UGLY. THEY BROUGHT IN A POT OF BOILING WATER. WE BEAT A HASTY RETREAT.
MANY CASUALTIES?
A BUSHEL.

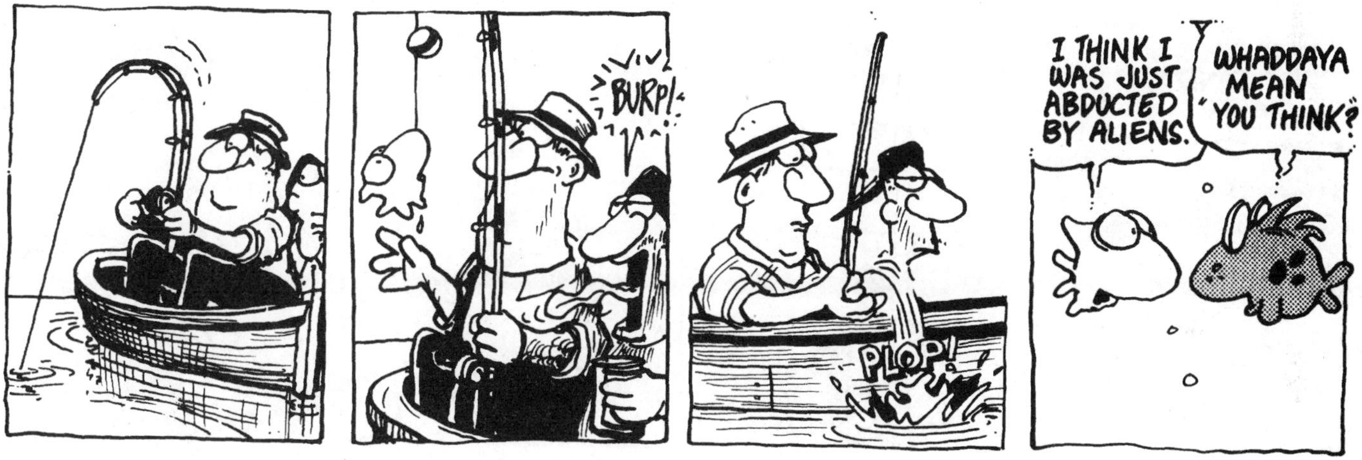
BURP!
PLOP!
I THINK I WAS JUST ABDUCTED BY ALIENS.
WHADDAYA MEAN "YOU THINK"?

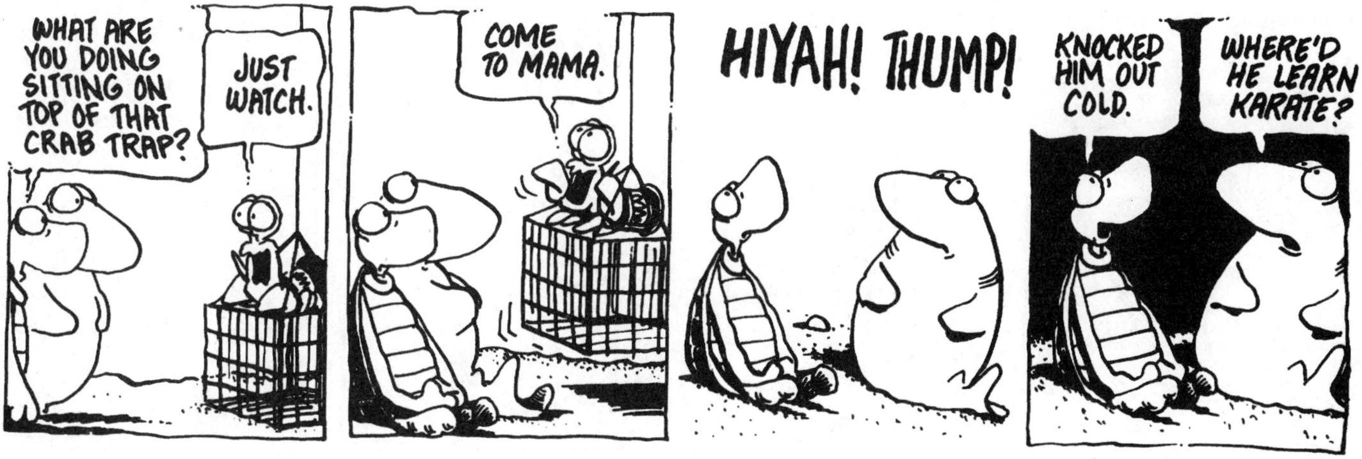
WHAT ARE YOU DOING SITTING ON TOP OF THAT CRAB TRAP?
JUST WATCH.
COME TO MAMA.
HIYAH! THUMP!
KNOCKED HIM OUT COLD.
WHERE'D HE LEARN KARATE?

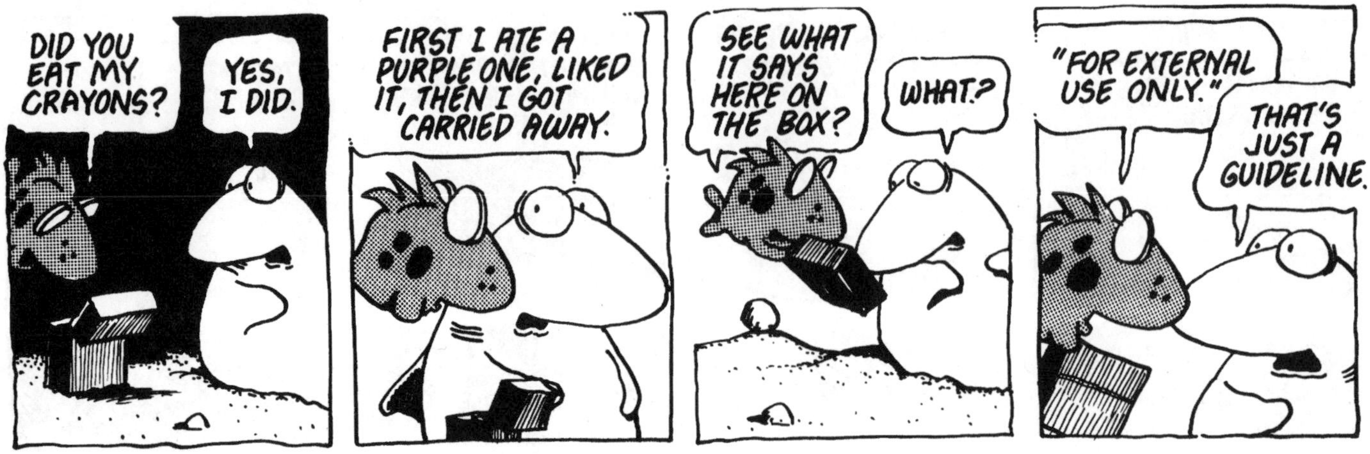
DID YOU EAT MY CRAYONS?
YES, I DID.
FIRST I ATE A PURPLE ONE, LIKED IT, THEN I GOT CARRIED AWAY.
SEE WHAT IT SAYS HERE ON THE BOX?
WHAT?
"FOR EXTERNAL USE ONLY."
THAT'S JUST A GUIDELINE.

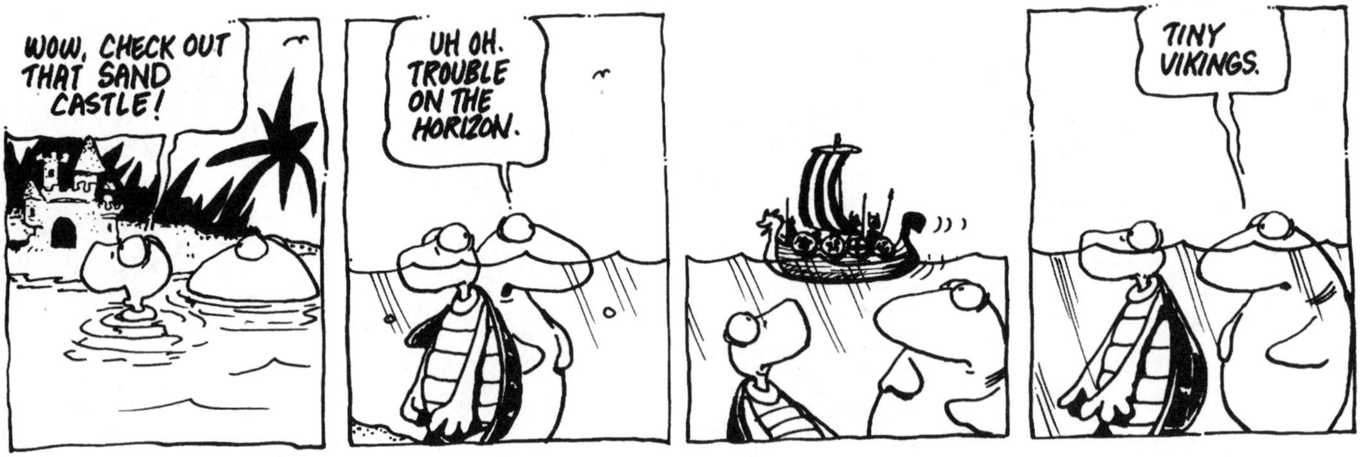
WOW, CHECK OUT THAT SAND CASTLE!
UH OH. TROUBLE ON THE HORIZON.
TINY VIKINGS.

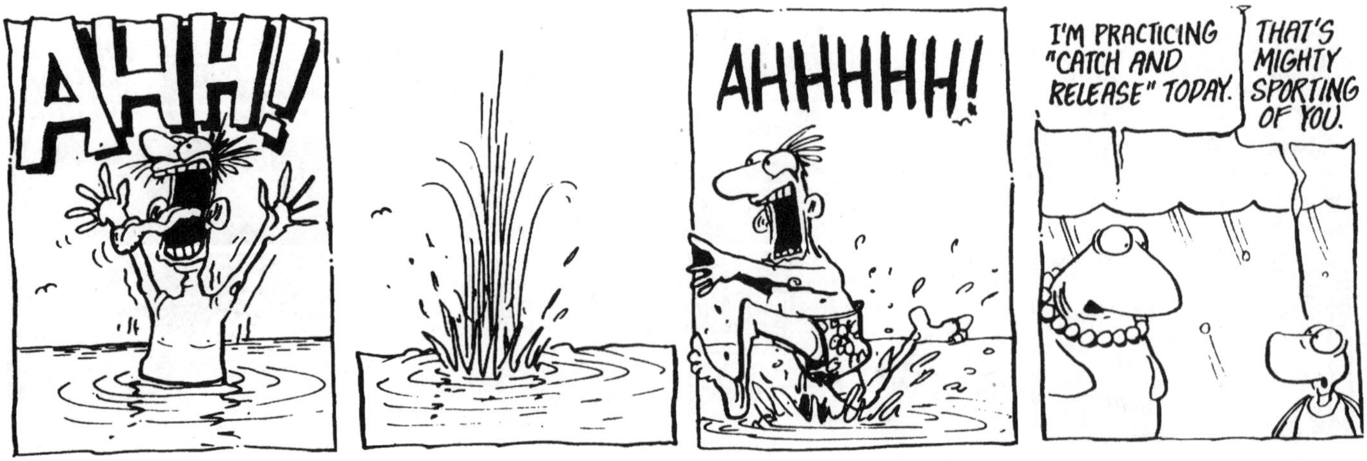
AHH!
AHHHHH!
I'M PRACTICING "CATCH AND RELEASE" TODAY.
THAT'S MIGHTY SPORTING OF YOU.

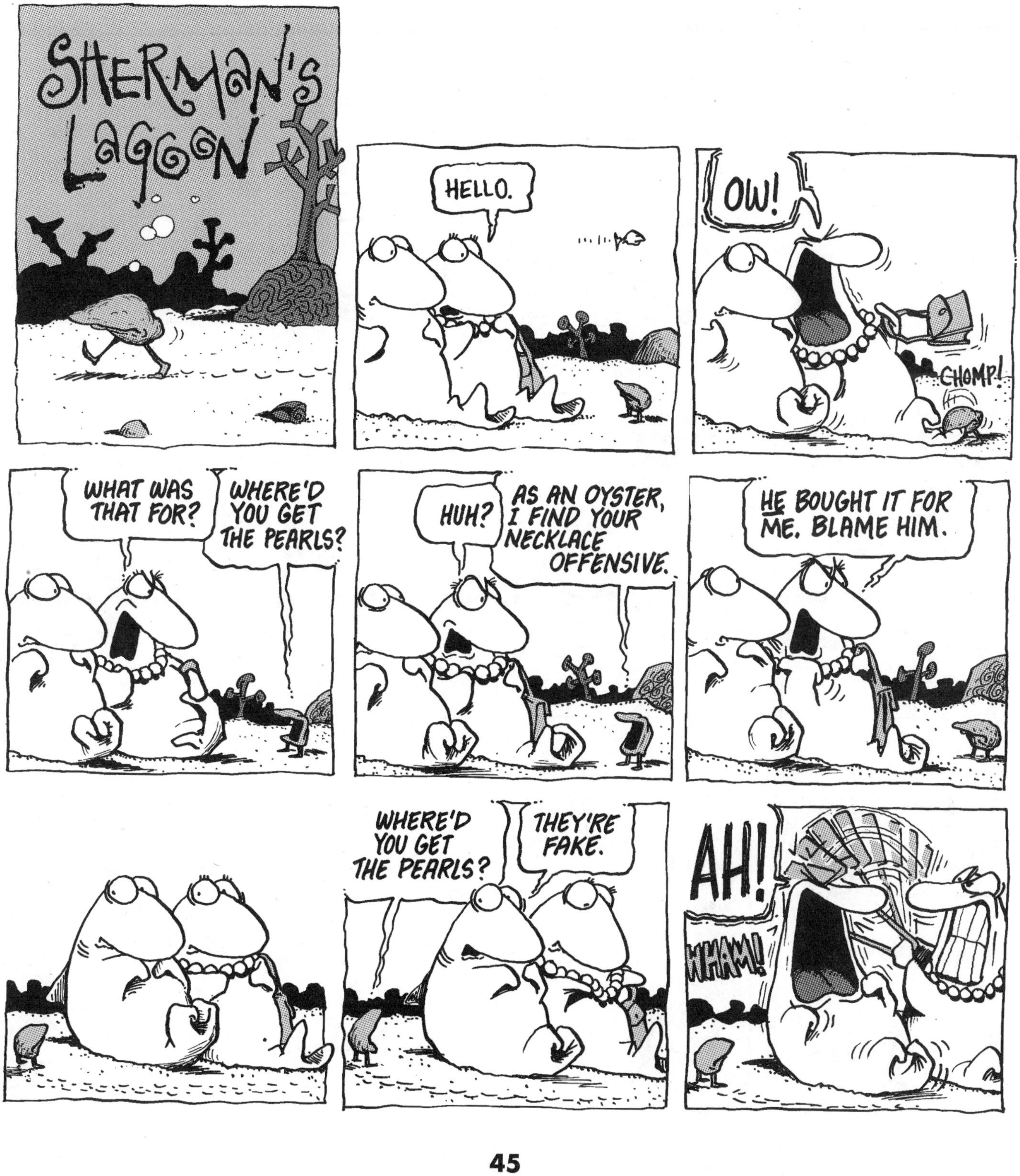
SHERMAN'S LAGOON
HELLO.
OW!
CHOMP!
WHAT WAS THAT FOR?
WHERE'D YOU GET THE PEARLS?
HUH?
AS AN OYSTER, I FIND YOUR NECKLACE OFFENSIVE.
HE BOUGHT IT FOR ME. BLAME HIM.
WHERE'D YOU GET THE PEARLS?
THEY'RE FAKE.
AH!
WHAM!

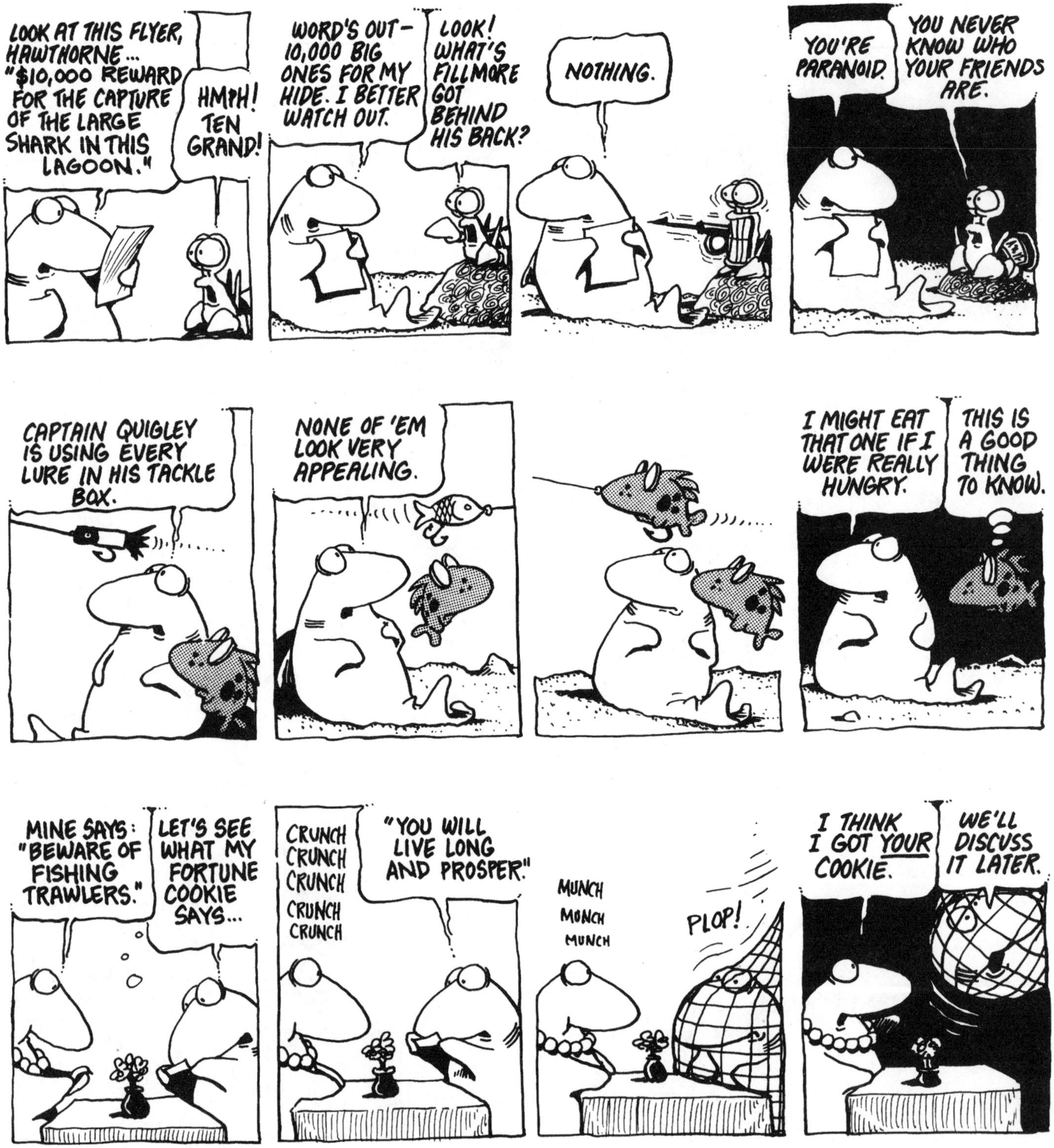
LOOK AT THIS FLYER, HAWTHORNE... "$10,000 REWARD FOR THE CAPTURE OF THE LARGE SHARK IN THIS LAGOON."
HMPH! TEN GRAND!
WORD'S OUT- 10,000 BIG ONES FOR MY HIDE. I BETTER WATCH OUT.
LOOK! WHAT'S FILLMORE GOT BEHIND HIS BACK?
NOTHING.
YOU'RE PARANOID.
YOU NEVER KNOW WHO YOUR FRIENDS ARE.
CAPTAIN QUIGLEY IS USING EVERY LURE IN HIS TACKLE BOX.
NONE OF 'EM LOOK VERY APPEALING.
I MIGHT EAT THAT ONE IF I WERE REALLY HUNGRY.
THIS IS A GOOD THING TO KNOW.
MINE SAYS: "BEWARE OF FISHING TRAWLERS."
LET'S SEE WHAT MY FORTUNE COOKIE SAYS...
CRUNCH
CRUNCH
CRUNCH
CRUNCH
CRUNCH
"YOU WILL LIVE LONG AND PROSPER."
MUNCH
MONCH
MUNCH
PLOP!
I THINK I GOT YOUR COOKIE.
WE'LL DISCUSS IT LATER.

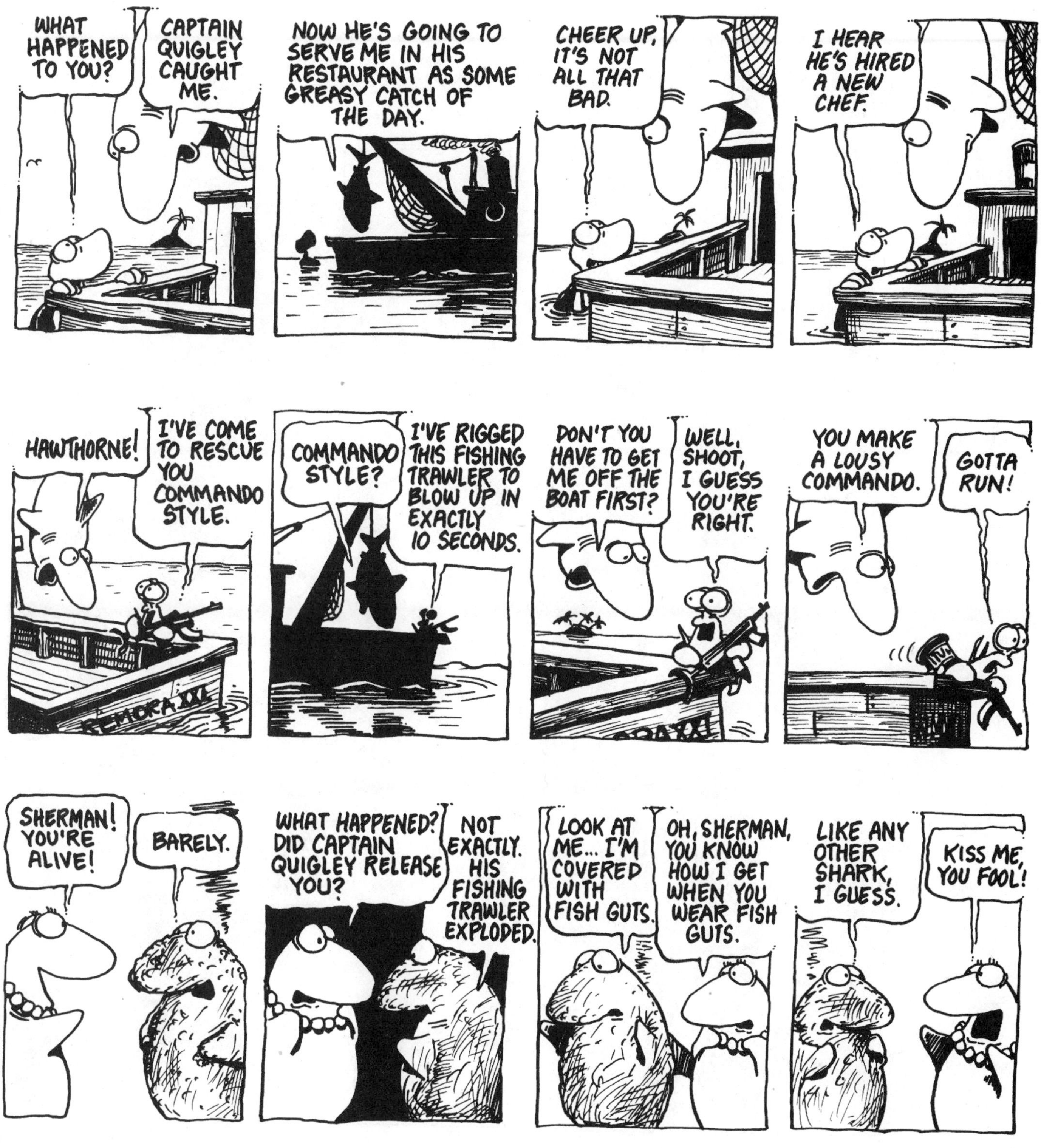
WHAT HAPPENED TO YOU?
CAPTAIN QUIGLEY CAUGHT ME.
NOW HE'S GOING TO SERVE ME IN HIS RESTAURANT AS SOME GREASY CATCH OF THE DAY.
CHEER UP, IT'S NOT ALL THAT BAD.
I HEAR HE'S HIRED A NEW CHEF.
HAWTHORNE!
I'VE COME TO RESCUE YOU COMMANDO STYLE.
COMMANDO STYLE?
I'VE RIGGED THIS FISHING TRAWLER TO BLOW UP IN EXACTLY 10 SECONDS.
DON'T YOU HAVE TO GET ME OFF THE BOAT FIRST?
WELL, SHOOT, I GUESS YOU'RE RIGHT.
YOU MAKE A LOUSY COMMANDO.
GOTTA RUN!
REMORA XXI
SHERMAN! YOU'RE ALIVE!
BARELY.
WHAT HAPPENED? DID CAPTAIN QUIGLEY RELEASE YOU?
NOT EXACTLY. HIS FISHING TRAWLER EXPLODED.
LOOK AT ME... I'M COVERED WITH FISH GUTS.
OH, SHERMAN, YOU KNOW HOW I GET WHEN YOU WEAR FISH GUTS.
LIKE ANY OTHER SHARK, I GUESS.
KISS ME, YOU FOOL!

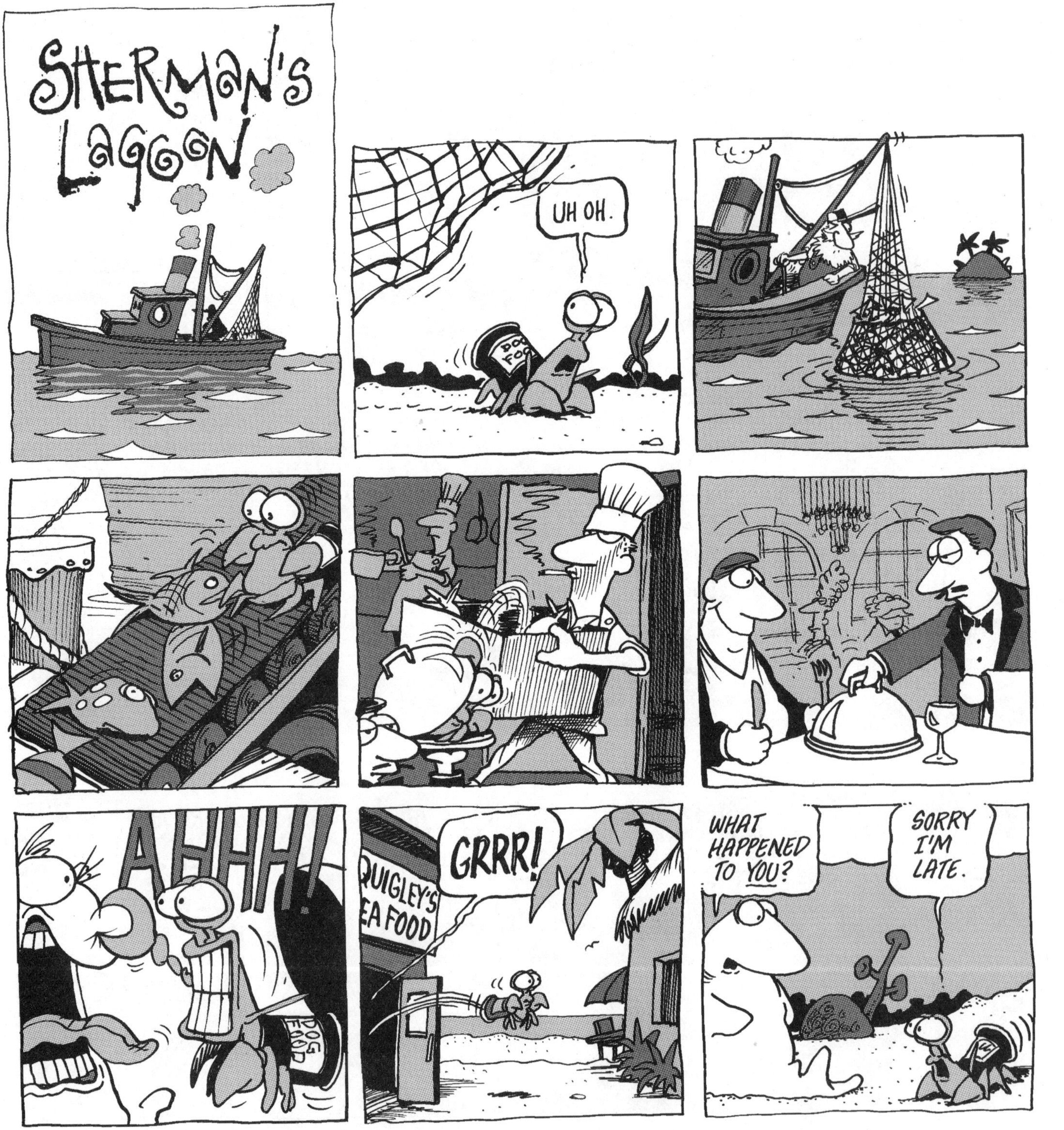
SHERMAN'S LAGOON
UH OH.
DOG FOOD
AHHH!!
DOG FOOD
QUIGLEY'S EA FOOD
GRRR!
WHAT HAPPENED TO YOU?
SORRY I'M LATE.

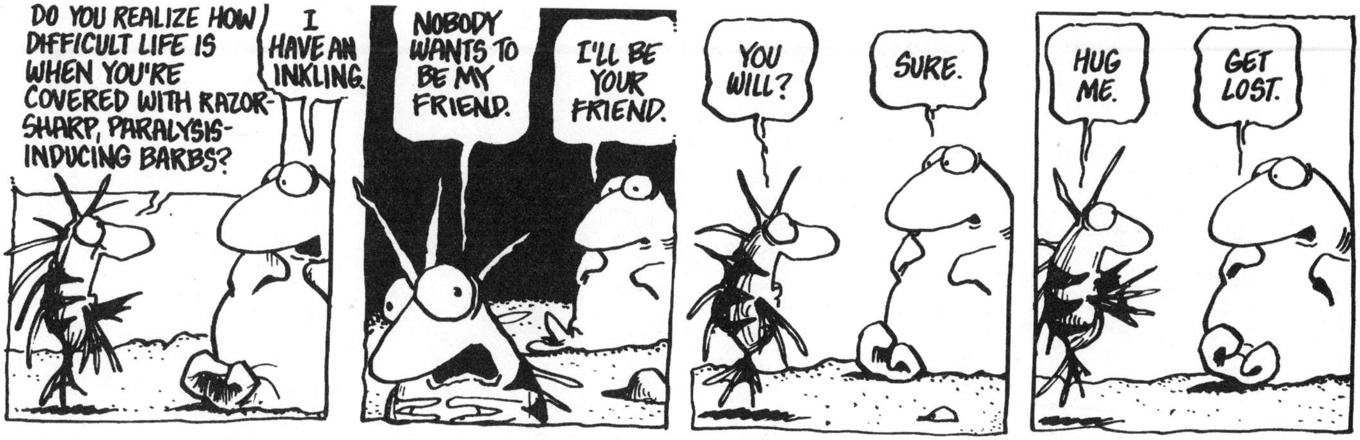
DO YOU REALIZE HOW DIFFICULT LIFE IS WHEN YOU'RE COVERED WITH RAZOR-SHARP, PARALYSIS-INDUCING BARBS?
I HAVE AN INKLING.
NOBODY WANTS TO BE MY FRIEND.
I'LL BE YOUR FRIEND.
YOU WILL?
SURE.
HUG ME.
GET LOST.

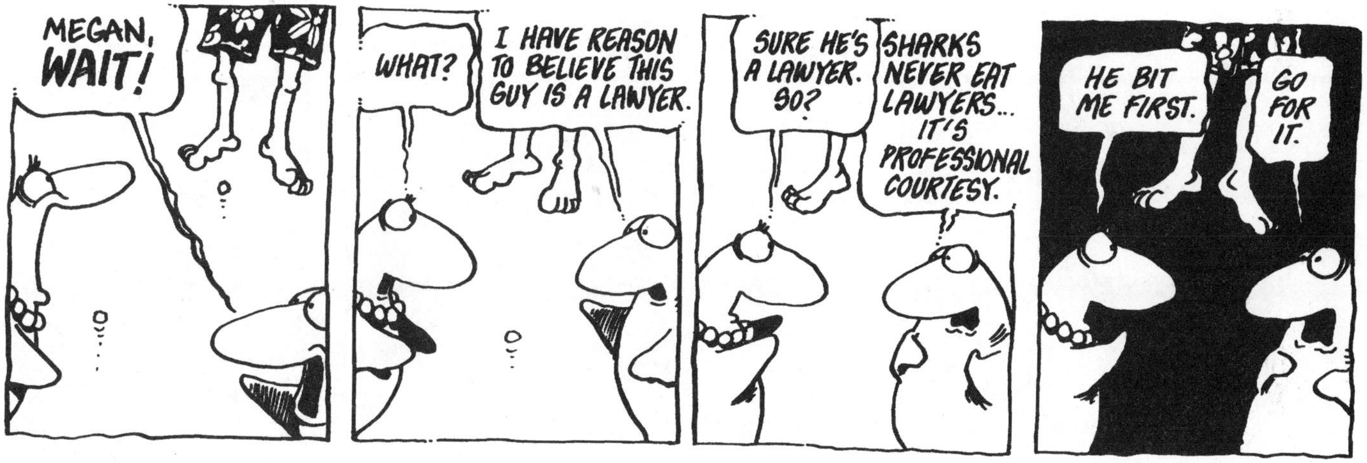
MEGAN, WAIT!
WHAT?
I HAVE REASON TO BELIEVE THIS GUY IS A LAWYER.
SURE HE'S A LAWYER. SO?
SHARKS NEVER EAT LAWYERS... IT'S PROFESSIONAL COURTESY.
HE BIT ME FIRST.
GO FOR IT.

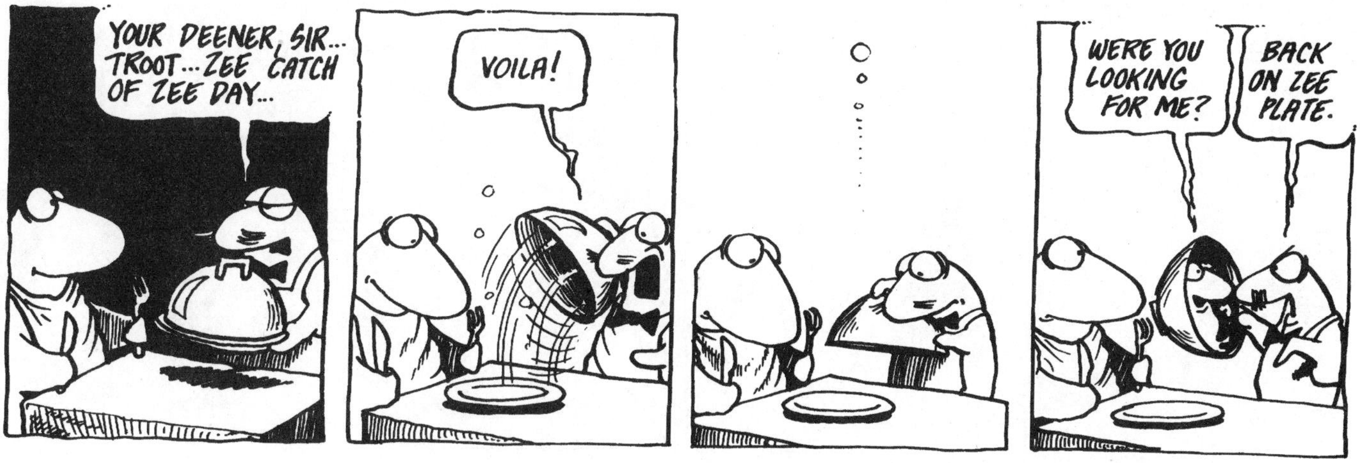
YOUR DEENER, SIR... TROOT... ZEE CATCH OF ZEE DAY...
VOILA!
WERE YOU LOOKING FOR ME?
BACK ON ZEE PLATE.

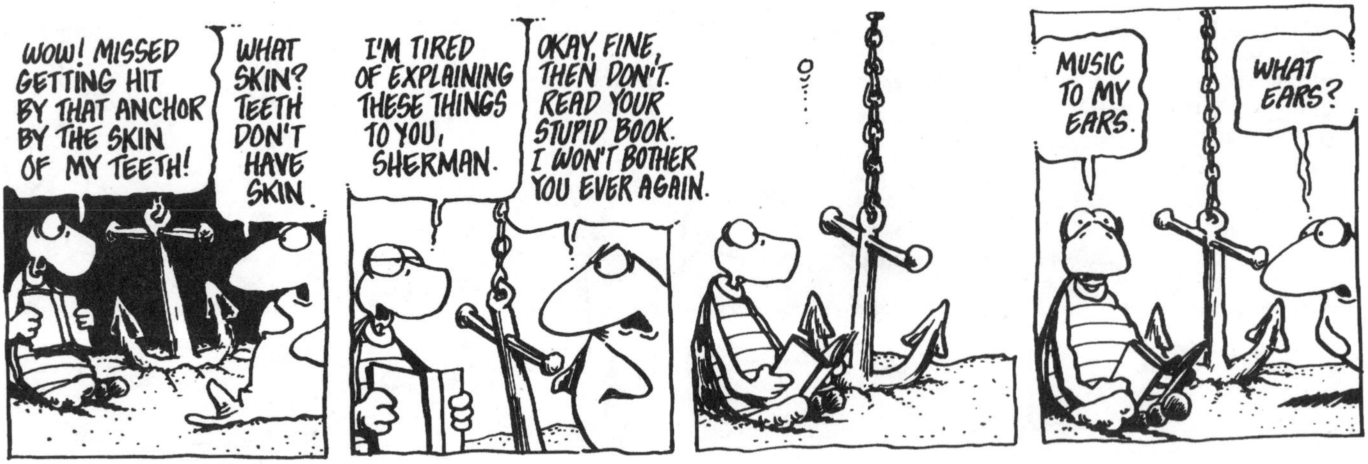
WOW! MISSED GETTING HIT BY THAT ANCHOR BY THE SKIN OF MY TEETH!
WHAT SKIN? TEETH DON'T HAVE SKIN.
I'M TIRED OF EXPLAINING THESE THINGS TO YOU, SHERMAN.
OKAY, FINE, THEN DON'T. READ YOUR STUPID BOOK. I WON'T BOTHER YOU EVER AGAIN.
MUSIC TO MY EARS.
WHAT EARS?

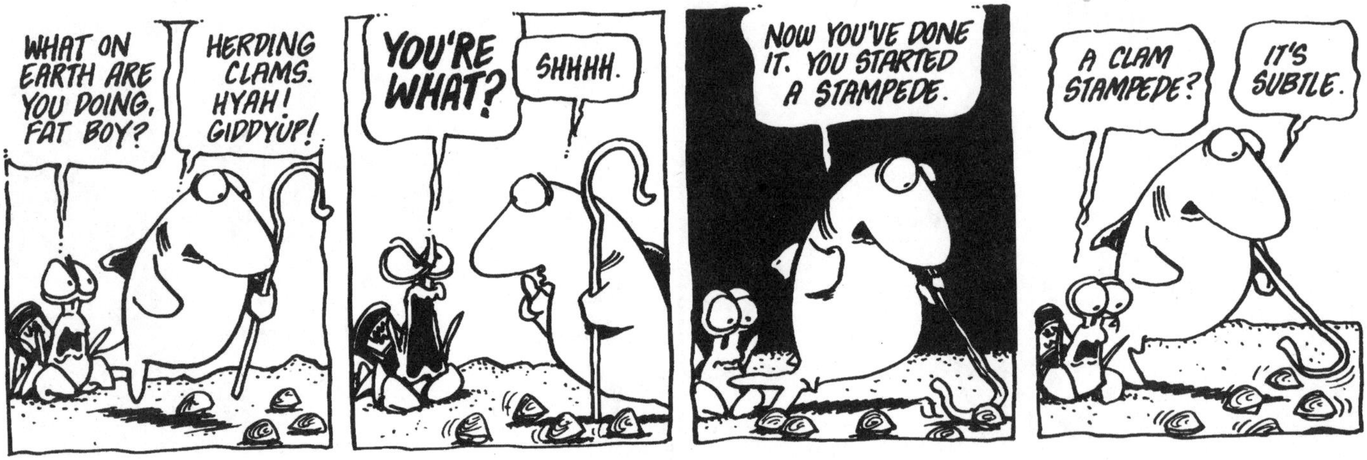
WHAT ON EARTH ARE YOU DOING, FAT BOY?
HERDING CLAMS. HYAH! GIDDYUP!
YOU'RE WHAT?
SHHHH.
NOW YOU'VE DONE IT. YOU STARTED A STAMPEDE.
A CLAM STAMPEDE?
IT'S SUBTLE.

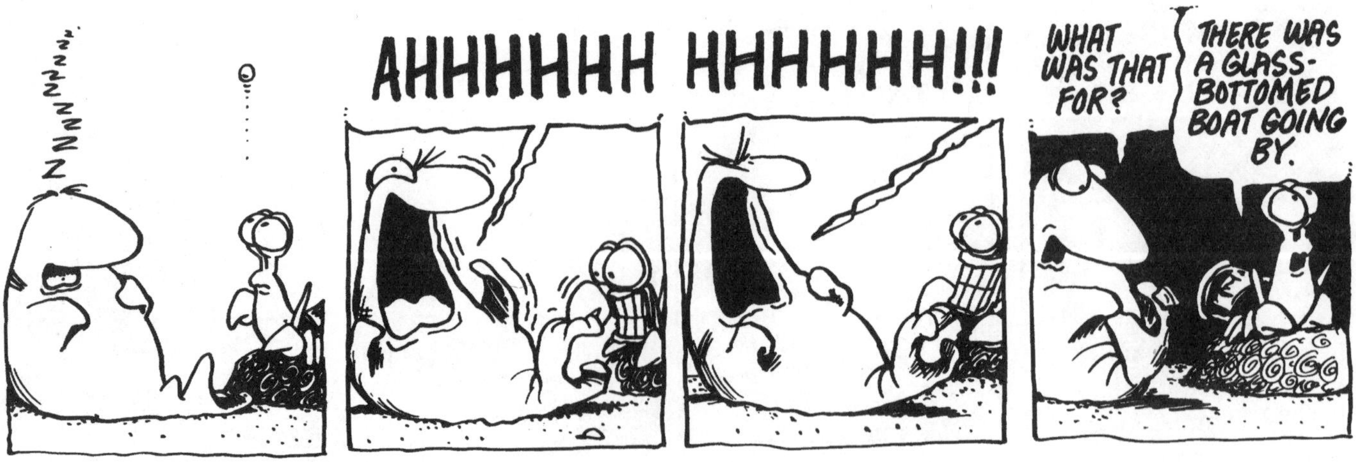
AHHHHHH HHHHHHH!!!
WHAT WAS THAT FOR?
THERE WAS A GLASS-BOTTOMED BOAT GOING BY.

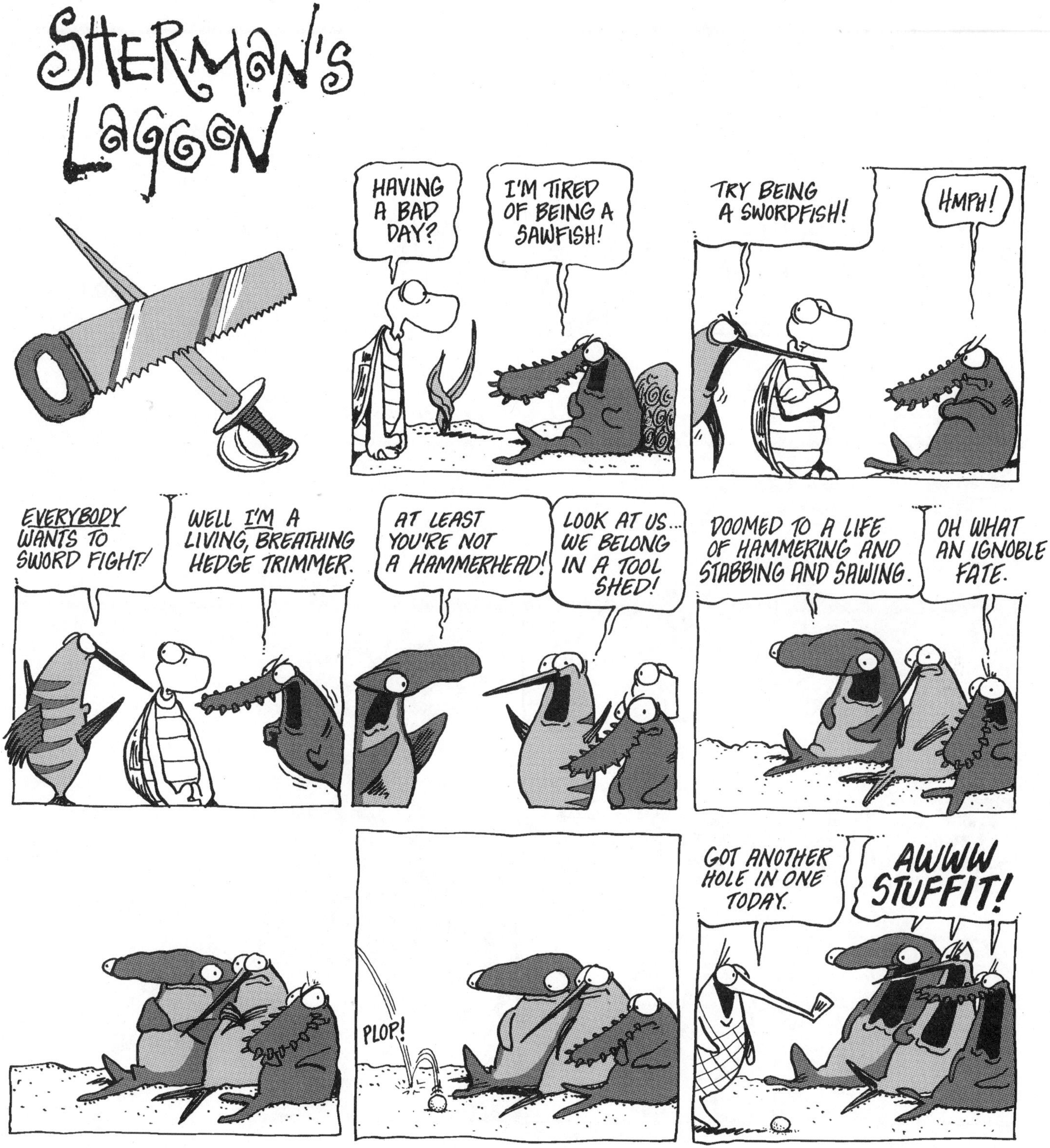
SHERMAN'S LAGOON
HAVING A BAD DAY?
I'M TIRED OF BEING A SAWFISH!
TRY BEING A SWORDFISH!
HMPH!
EVERYBODY WANTS TO SWORD FIGHT!
WELL I'M A LIVING, BREATHING HEDGE TRIMMER.
AT LEAST YOU'RE NOT A HAMMERHEAD!
LOOK AT US... WE BELONG IN A TOOL SHED!
DOOMED TO A LIFE OF HAMMERING AND STABBING AND SAWING.
OH WHAT AN IGNOBLE FATE.
PLOP!
GOT ANOTHER HOLE IN ONE TODAY.
AWWW STUFFIT!

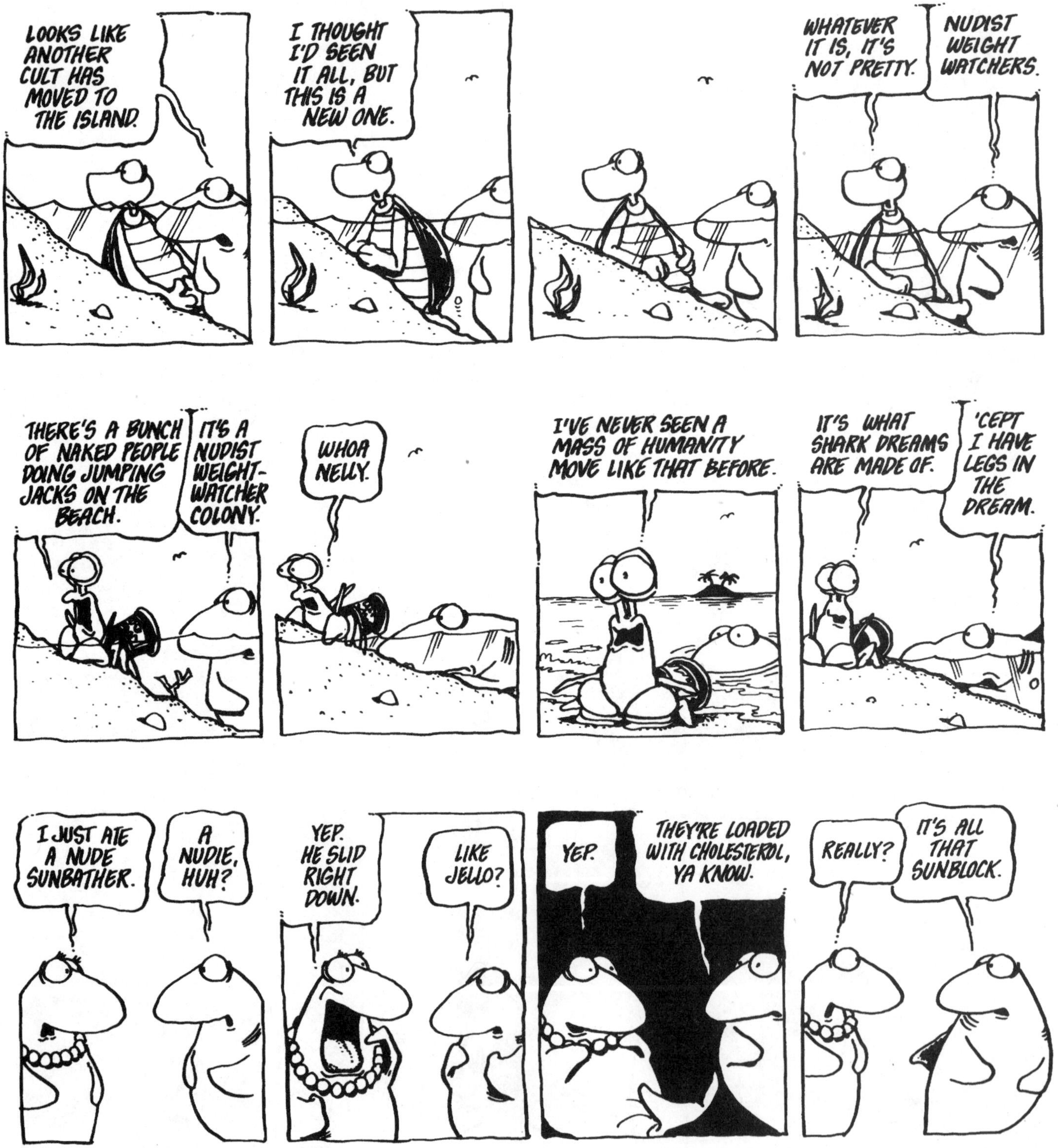
LOOKS LIKE ANOTHER CULT HAS MOVED TO THE ISLAND.
I THOUGHT I'D SEEN IT ALL, BUT THIS IS A NEW ONE.
WHATEVER IT IS, IT'S NOT PRETTY.
NUDIST WEIGHT WATCHERS.
THERE'S A BUNCH OF NAKED PEOPLE DOING JUMPING JACKS ON THE BEACH.
IT'S A NUDIST WEIGHT-WATCHER COLONY.
WHOA NELLY.
I'VE NEVER SEEN A MASS OF HUMANITY MOVE LIKE THAT BEFORE.
IT'S WHAT SHARK DREAMS ARE MADE OF.
'CEPT I HAVE LEGS IN THE DREAM.
I JUST ATE A NUDE SUNBATHER.
A NUDIE, HUH?
YEP. HE SLID RIGHT DOWN.
LIKE JELLO?
YEP.
THEY'RE LOADED WITH CHOLESTEROL, YA KNOW.
REALLY?
IT'S ALL THAT SUNBLOCK.

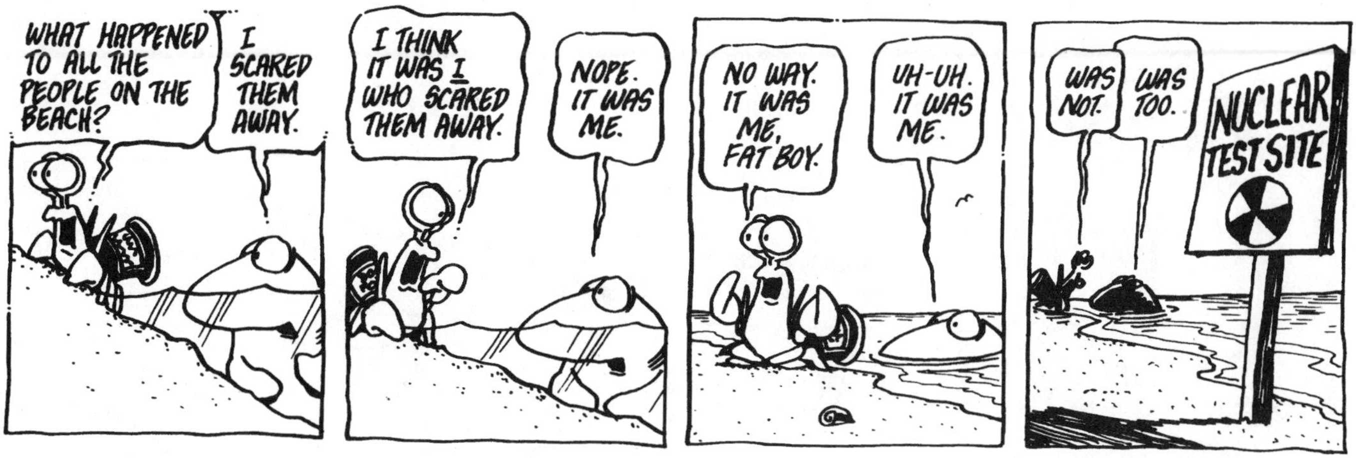
WHAT HAPPENED TO ALL THE PEOPLE ON THE BEACH?
I SCARED THEM AWAY.
I THINK IT WAS I WHO SCARED THEM AWAY.
NOPE. IT WAS ME.
NO WAY. IT WAS ME, FAT BOY.
UH-UH. IT WAS ME.
WAS NOT.
WAS TOO.
NUCLEAR TEST SITE

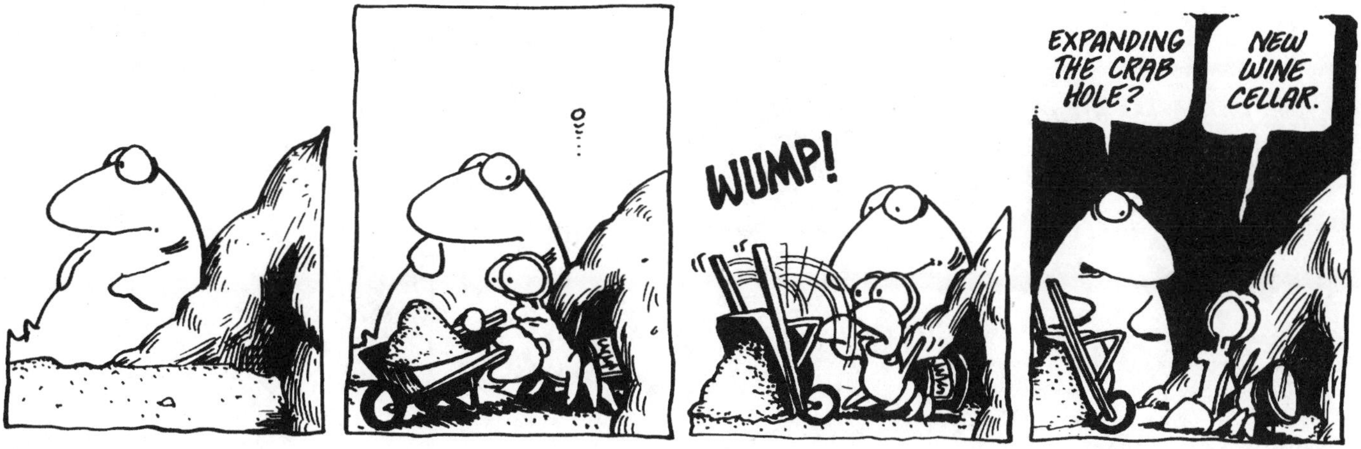
WUMP!
EXPANDING THE CRAB HOLE?
NEW WINE CELLAR.

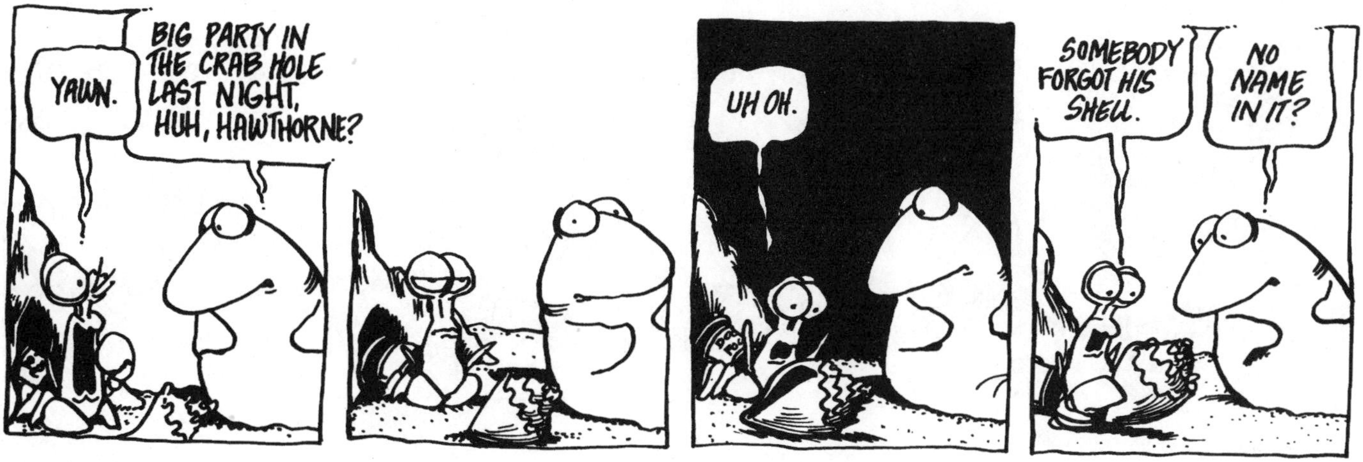
YAWN.
BIG PARTY IN THE CRAB HOLE LAST NIGHT, HUH, HAWTHORNE?
UH OH.
SOMEBODY FORGOT HIS SHELL.
NO NAME IN IT?

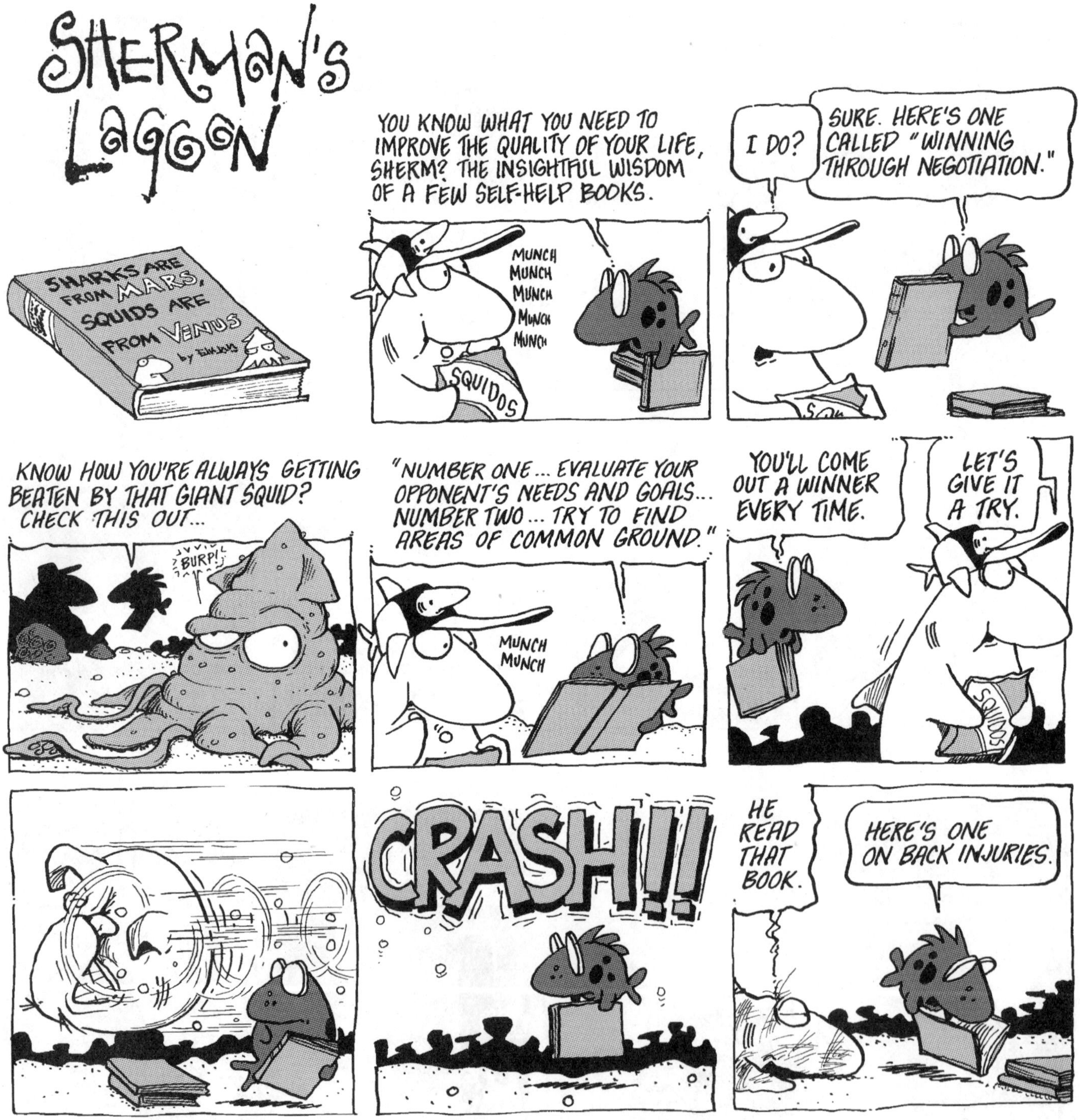

SHERMAN'S LAGOON
SHARKS ARE FROM MARS, SQUIDS ARE FROM VENUS
YOU KNOW WHAT YOU NEED TO IMPROVE THE QUALITY OF YOUR LIFE, SHERM? THE INSIGHTFUL WISDOM OF A FEW SELF-HELP BOOKS.
MUNCH MUNCH MUNCH MUNCH MUNCH
SQUIDOS
I DO?
SURE. HERE'S ONE CALLED "WINNING THROUGH NEGOTIATION."
KNOW HOW YOU'RE ALWAYS GETTING BEATEN BY THAT GIANT SQUID? CHECK THIS OUT...
BURP!
"NUMBER ONE... EVALUATE YOUR OPPONENT'S NEEDS AND GOALS... NUMBER TWO... TRY TO FIND AREAS OF COMMON GROUND."
MUNCH MUNCH
YOU'LL COME OUT A WINNER EVERY TIME.
LET'S GIVE IT A TRY.
SQUIDOS
CRASH!!
HE READ THAT BOOK.
HERE'S ONE ON BACK INJURIES.

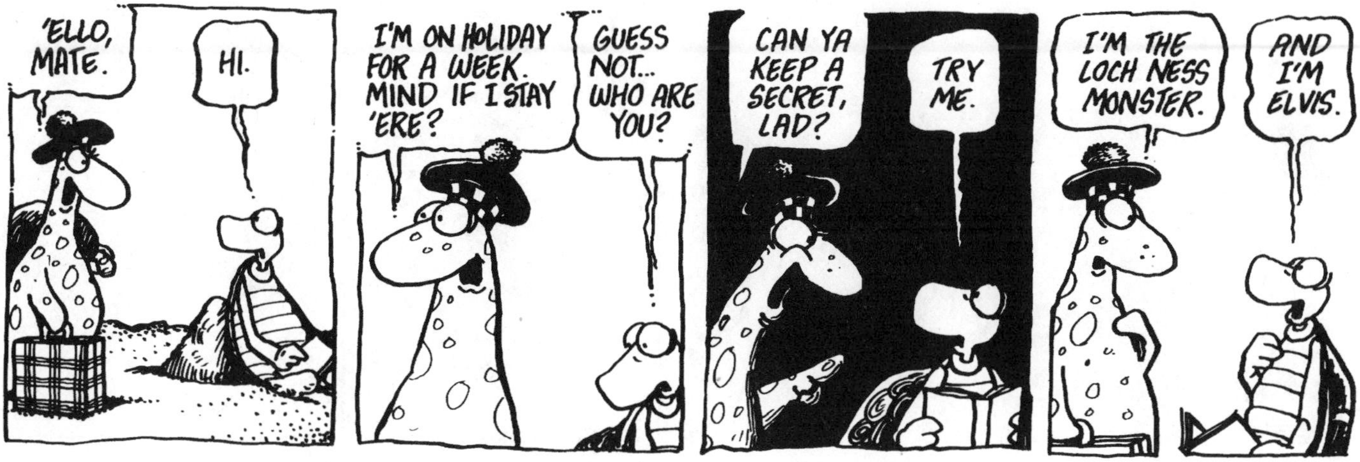
'ELLO, MATE.
HI.
I'M ON HOLIDAY FOR A WEEK. MIND IF I STAY 'ERE?
GUESS NOT... WHO ARE YOU?
CAN YA KEEP A SECRET, LAD?
TRY ME.
I'M THE LOCH NESS MONSTER.
AND I'M ELVIS.

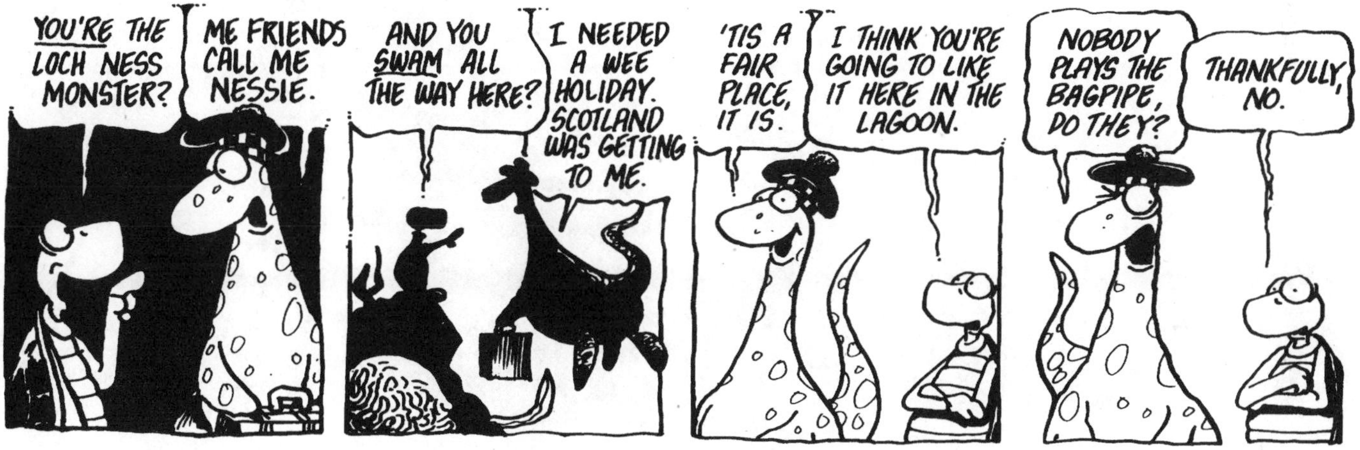
YOU'RE THE LOCH NESS MONSTER?
ME FRIENDS CALL ME NESSIE.
AND YOU SWAM ALL THE WAY HERE?
I NEEDED A WEE HOLIDAY. SCOTLAND WAS GETTING TO ME.
'TIS A FAIR PLACE, IT IS.
I THINK YOU'RE GOING TO LIKE IT HERE IN THE LAGOON.
NOBODY PLAYS THE BAGPIPE, DO THEY?
THANKFULLY, NO.

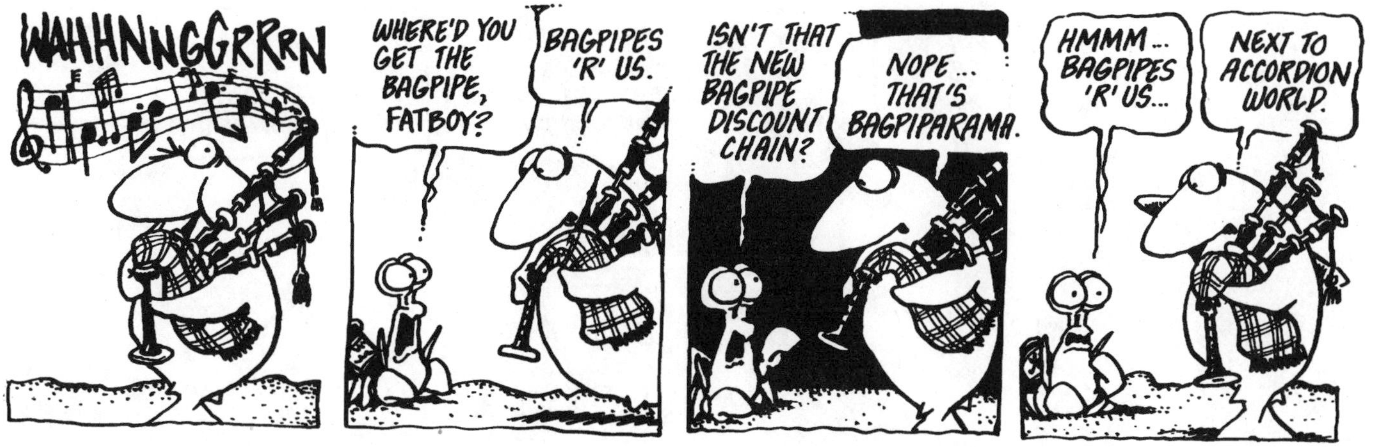
WAHHNNGGRRRN
WHERE'D YOU GET THE BAGPIPE, FATBOY?
BAGPIPES 'R' US.
ISN'T THAT THE NEW BAGPIPE DISCOUNT CHAIN?
NOPE... THAT'S BAGPIPARAMA.
HMMM... BAGPIPES 'R' US...
NEXT TO ACCORDION WORLD.

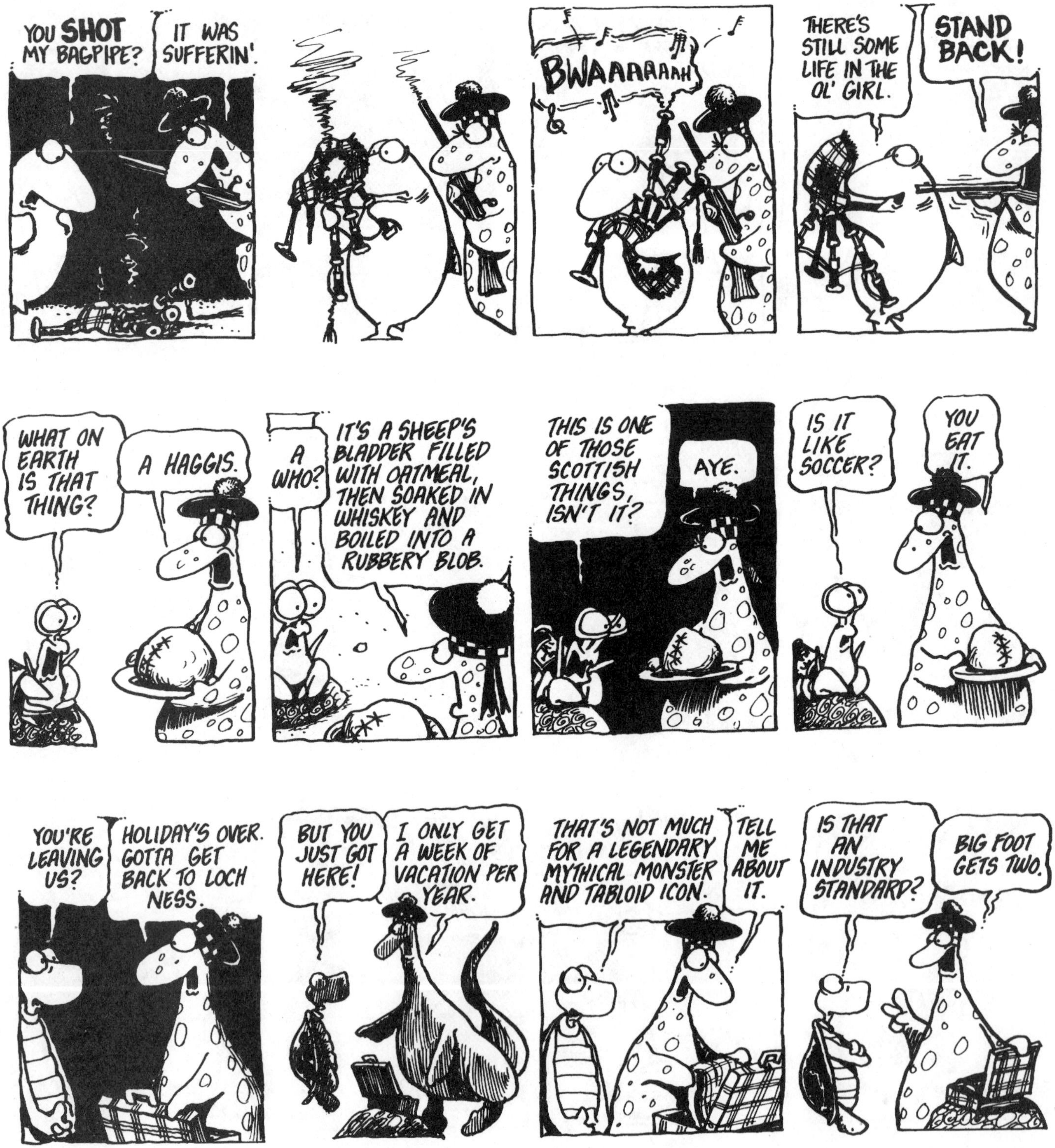
YOU SHOT MY BAGPIPE?
IT WAS SUFFERIN'.
BWAAAAAAH
THERE'S STILL SOME LIFE IN THE OL' GIRL.
STAND BACK!
WHAT ON EARTH IS THAT THING?
A HAGGIS.
A WHO?
IT'S A SHEEP'S BLADDER FILLED WITH OATMEAL, THEN SOAKED IN WHISKEY AND BOILED INTO A RUBBERY BLOB.
THIS IS ONE OF THOSE SCOTTISH THINGS, ISN'T IT?
AYE.
IS IT LIKE SOCCER?
YOU EAT IT.
YOU'RE LEAVING US?
HOLIDAY'S OVER. GOTTA GET BACK TO LOCH NESS.
BUT YOU JUST GOT HERE!
I ONLY GET A WEEK OF VACATION PER YEAR.
THAT'S NOT MUCH FOR A LEGENDARY MYTHICAL MONSTER AND TABLOID ICON.
TELL ME ABOUT IT.
IS THAT AN INDUSTRY STANDARD?
BIG FOOT GETS TWO.

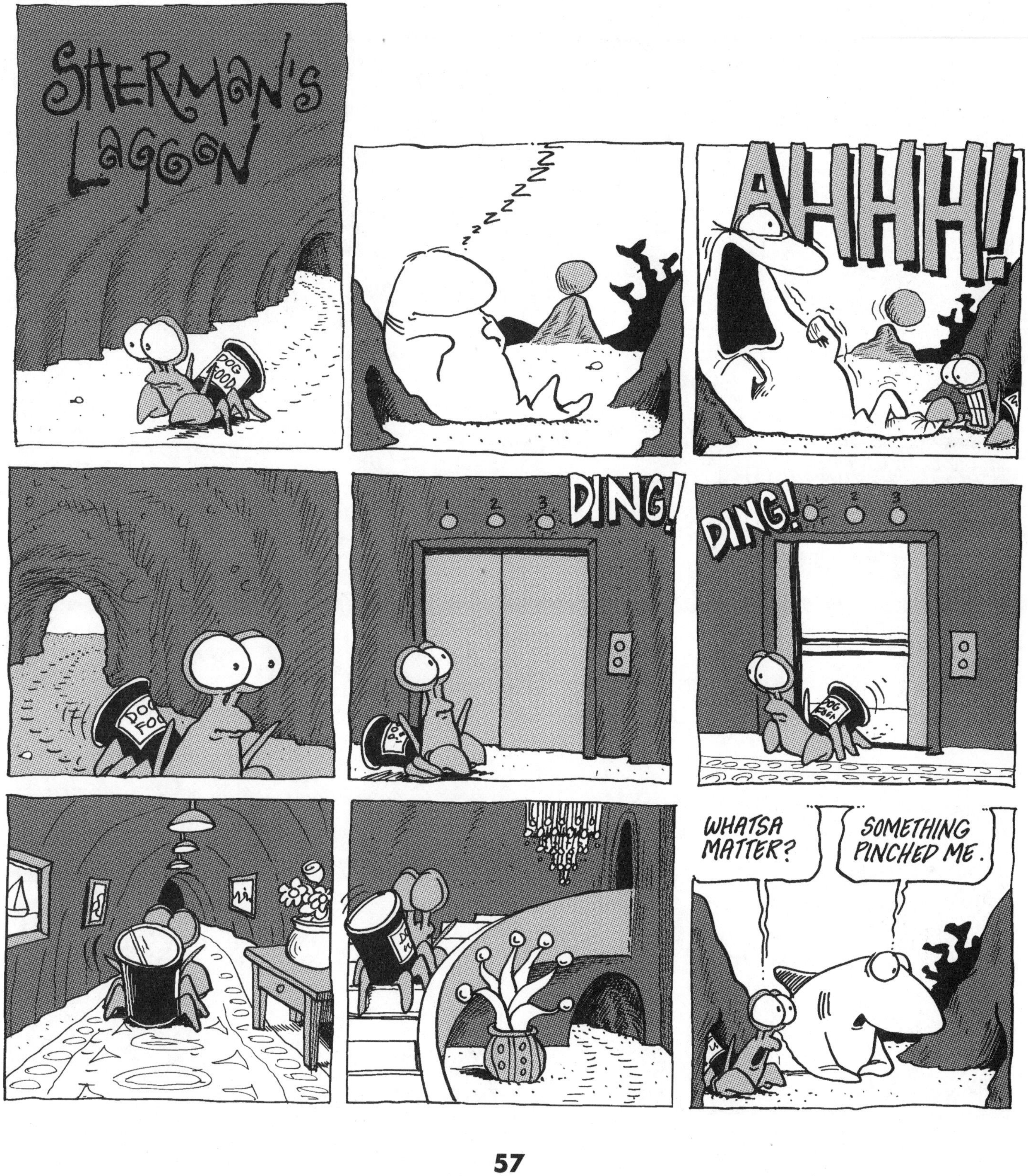
SHERMAN'S LAGOON
DOG FOOD
ZZZZZZZZZ
AHHHH!
DOG FOOD
1 2 3
DING!
1 2 3
DING!
DOG FOOD
WHATSA MATTER?
SOMETHING PINCHED ME.

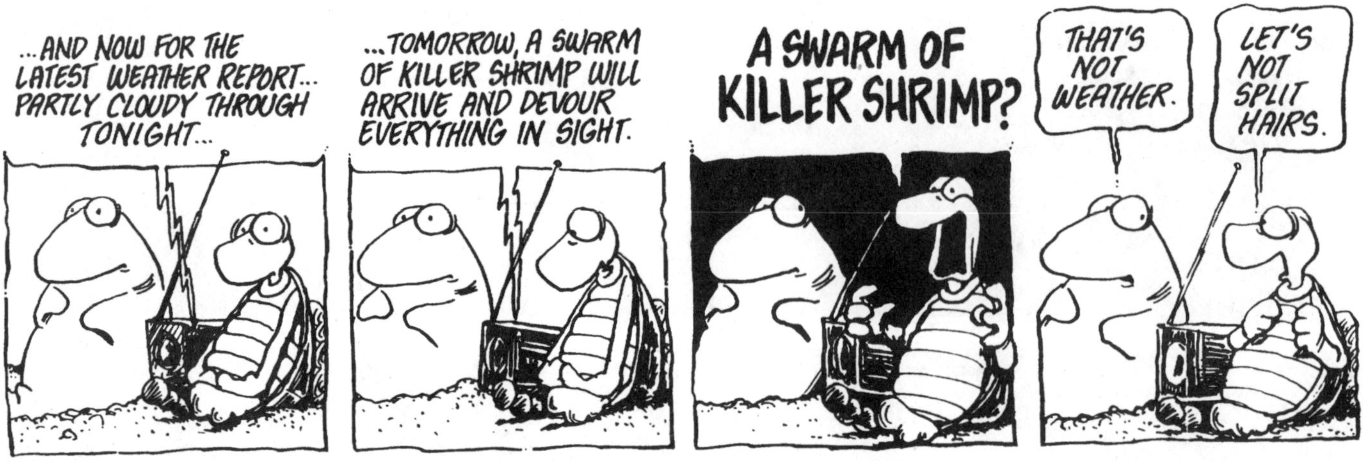
...AND NOW FOR THE LATEST WEATHER REPORT... PARTLY CLOUDY THROUGH TONIGHT...
...TOMORROW, A SWARM OF KILLER SHRIMP WILL ARRIVE AND DEVOUR EVERYTHING IN SIGHT.
A SWARM OF KILLER SHRIMP?
THAT'S NOT WEATHER.
LET'S NOT SPLIT HAIRS.

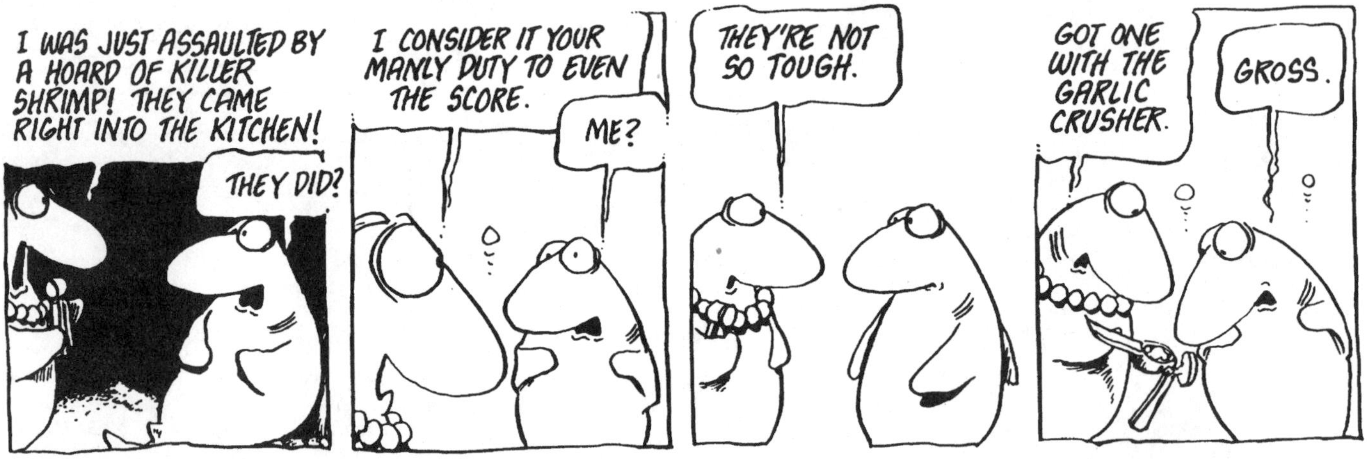
I WAS JUST ASSAULTED BY A HOARD OF KILLER SHRIMP! THEY CAME RIGHT INTO THE KITCHEN!
THEY DID?
I CONSIDER IT YOUR MANLY DUTY TO EVEN THE SCORE.
ME?
THEY'RE NOT SO TOUGH.
GOT ONE WITH THE GARLIC CRUSHER.
GROSS.

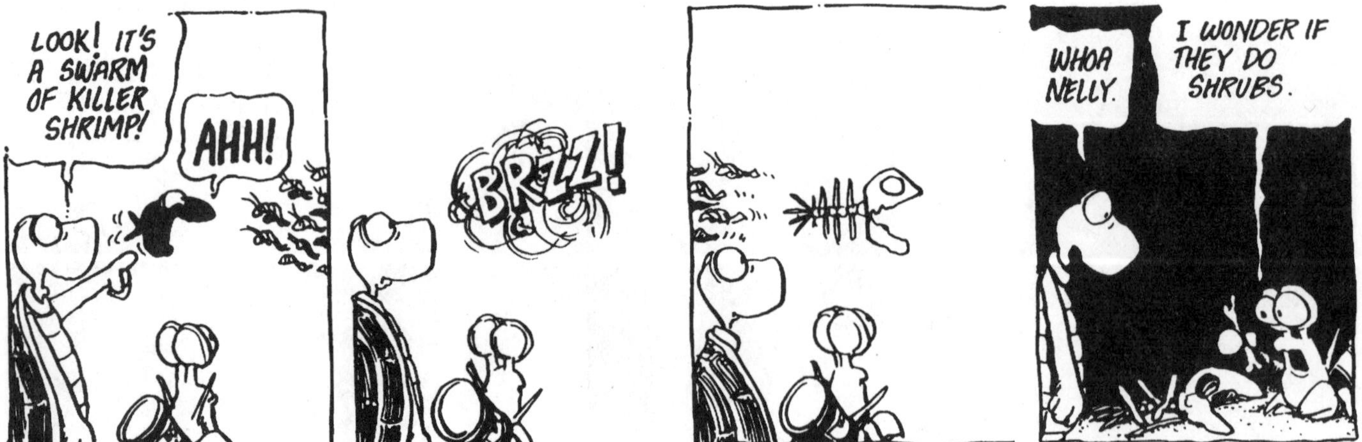
LOOK! IT'S A SWARM OF KILLER SHRIMP!
AHH!
BRZZZ!
WHOA NELLY.
I WONDER IF THEY DO SHRUBS.

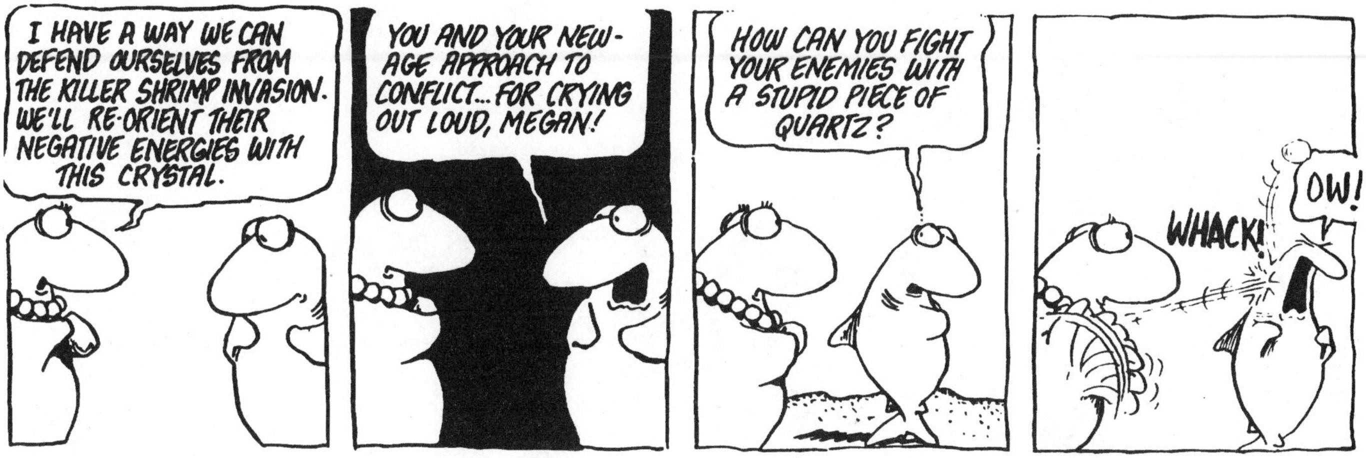
I HAVE A WAY WE CAN DEFEND OURSELVES FROM THE KILLER SHRIMP INVASION. WE'LL RE-ORIENT THEIR NEGATIVE ENERGIES WITH THIS CRYSTAL.
YOU AND YOUR NEW-AGE APPROACH TO CONFLICT... FOR CRYING OUT LOUD, MEGAN!
HOW CAN YOU FIGHT YOUR ENEMIES WITH A STUPID PIECE OF QUARTZ?
WHACK!
OW!

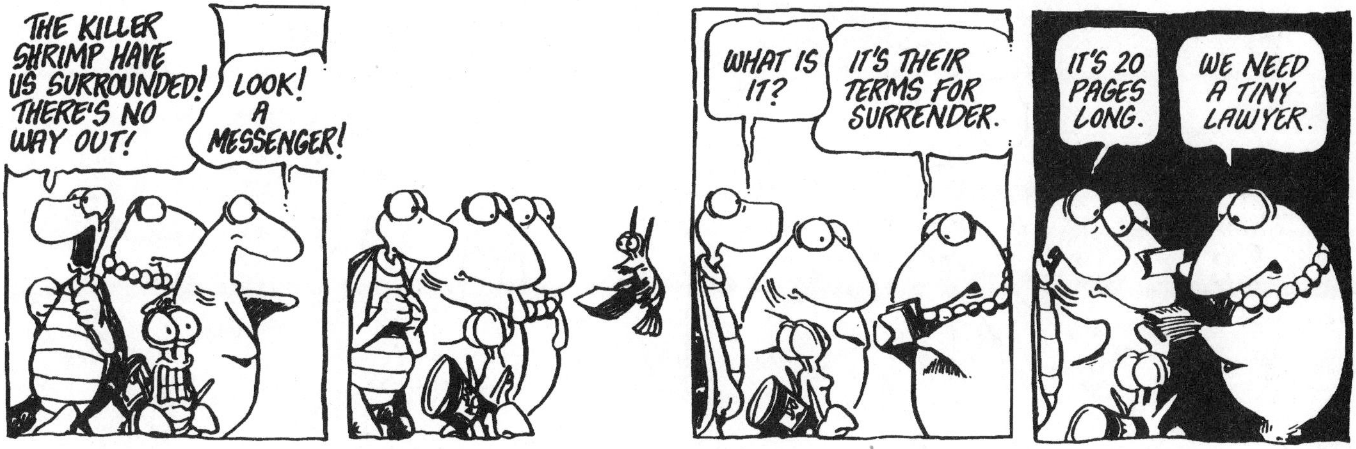
THE KILLER SHRIMP HAVE US SURROUNDED! THERE'S NO WAY OUT!
LOOK! A MESSENGER!
WHAT IS IT?
IT'S THEIR TERMS FOR SURRENDER.
IT'S 20 PAGES LONG.
WE NEED A TINY LAWYER.

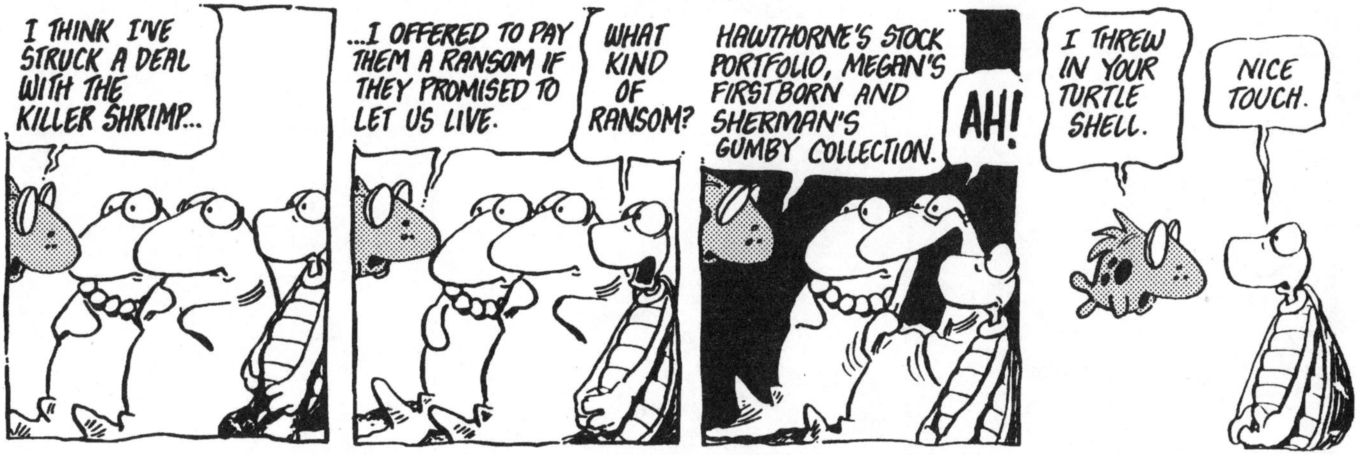
I THINK I'VE STRUCK A DEAL WITH THE KILLER SHRIMP...
...I OFFERED TO PAY THEM A RANSOM IF THEY PROMISED TO LET US LIVE.
WHAT KIND OF RANSOM?
HAWTHORNE'S STOCK PORTFOLIO, MEGAN'S FIRSTBORN AND SHERMAN'S GUMBY COLLECTION.
AH!
I THREW IN YOUR TURTLE SHELL.
NICE TOUCH.

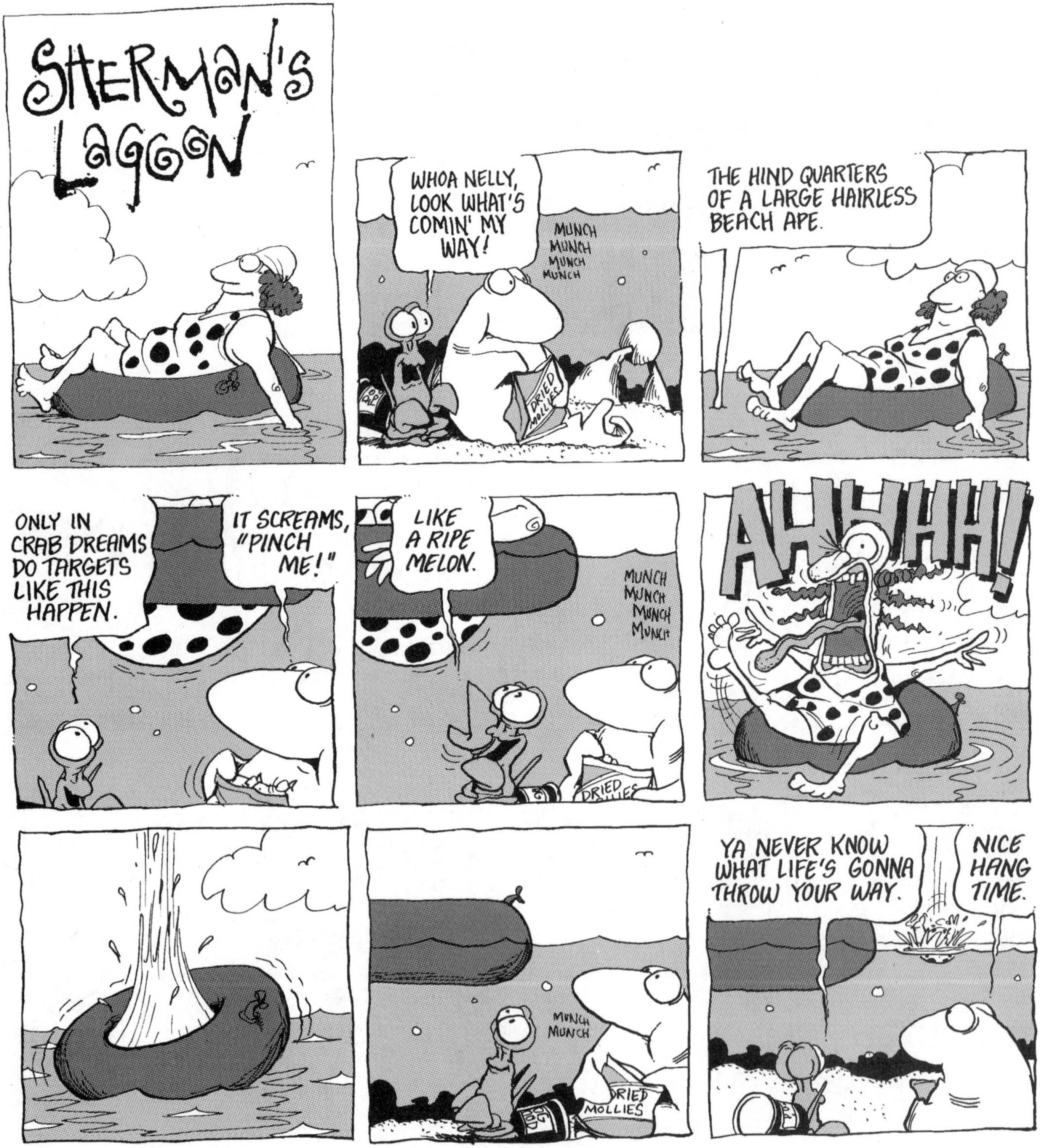
SHERMAN'S LAGOON
WHOA NELLY, LOOK WHAT'S COMIN' MY WAY!
MUNCH MUNCH MUNCH MUNCH
DRIED MOLLIES
THE HIND QUARTERS OF A LARGE HAIRLESS BEACH APE.
ONLY IN CRAB DREAMS DO TARGETS LIKE THIS HAPPEN.
IT SCREAMS, "PINCH ME!"
LIKE A RIPE MELON.
MUNCH MUNCH MUNCH MUNCH
DRIED
AHHHH!
MUNCH MUNCH
DRIED MOLLIES
YA NEVER KNOW WHAT LIFE'S GONNA THROW YOUR WAY.
NICE HANG TIME.

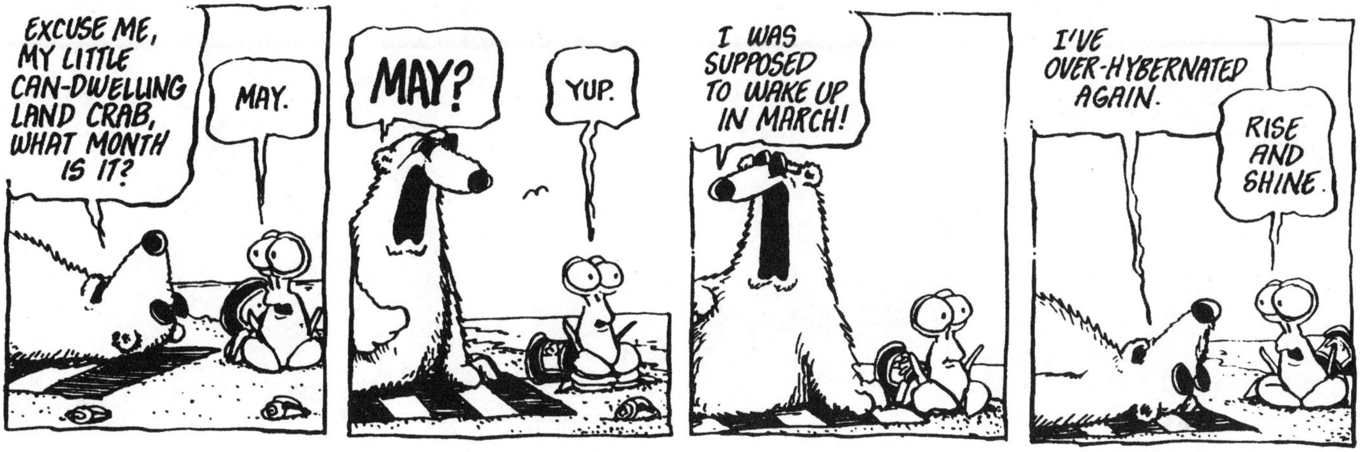
EXCUSE ME, MY LITTLE CAN-DWELLING LAND CRAB, WHAT MONTH IS IT?
MAY.
MAY?
YUP.
I WAS SUPPOSED TO WAKE UP IN MARCH!
I'VE OVER-HYBERNATED AGAIN.
RISE AND SHINE.

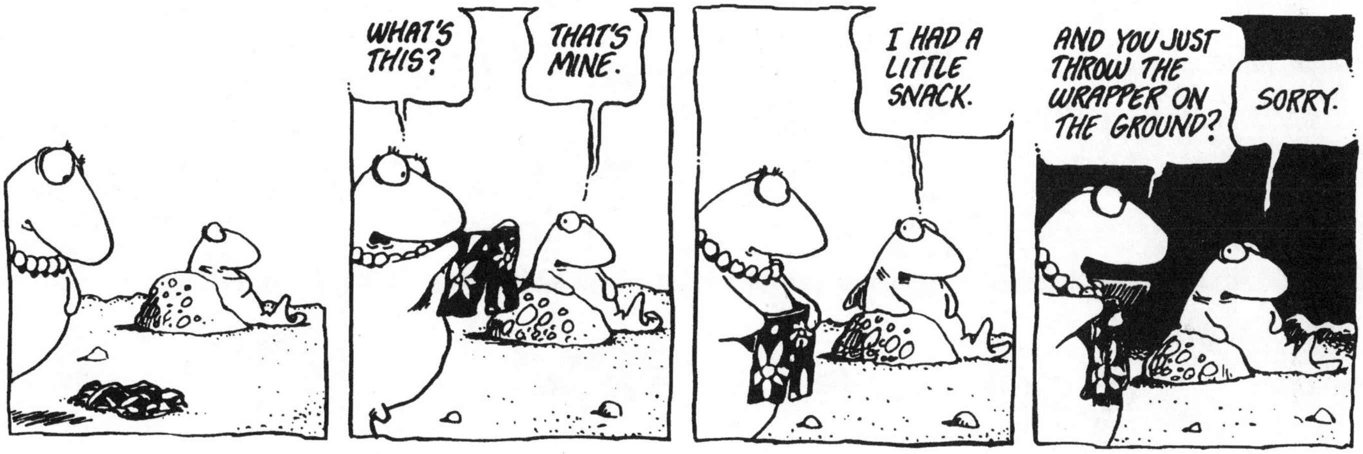
WHAT'S THIS?
THAT'S MINE.
I HAD A LITTLE SNACK.
AND YOU JUST THROW THE WRAPPER ON THE GROUND?
SORRY.

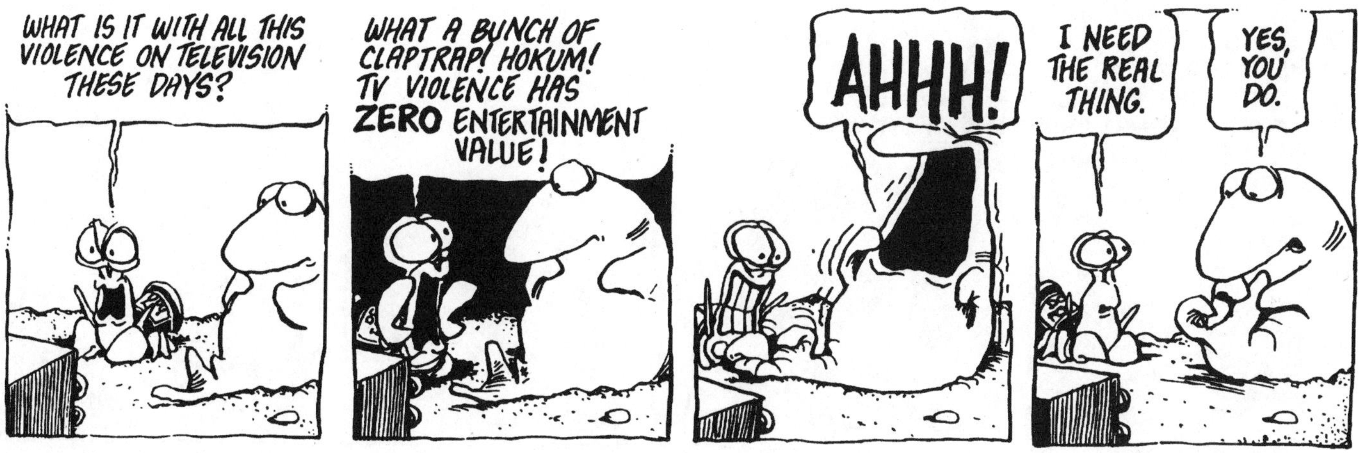
WHAT IS IT WITH ALL THIS VIOLENCE ON TELEVISION THESE DAYS?
WHAT A BUNCH OF CLAPTRAP! HOKUM! TV VIOLENCE HAS ZERO ENTERTAINMENT VALUE!
AHHH!
I NEED THE REAL THING.
YES, YOU DO.

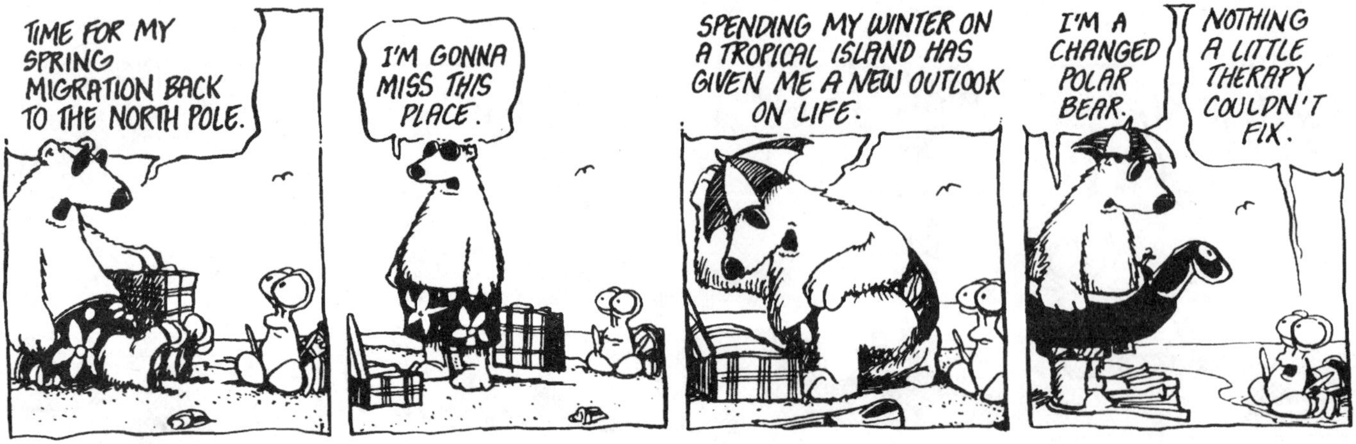
TIME FOR MY SPRING MIGRATION BACK TO THE NORTH POLE.
I'M GONNA MISS THIS PLACE.
SPENDING MY WINTER ON A TROPICAL ISLAND HAS GIVEN ME A NEW OUTLOOK ON LIFE.
I'M A CHANGED POLAR BEAR.
NOTHING A LITTLE THERAPY COULDN'T FIX.

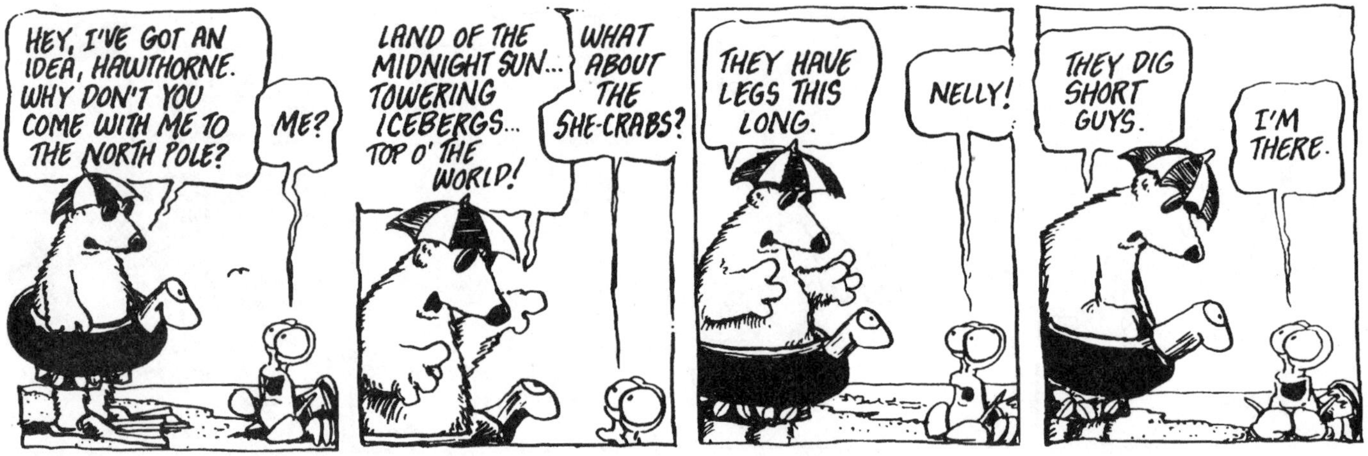
HEY, I'VE GOT AN IDEA, HAWTHORNE. WHY DON'T YOU COME WITH ME TO THE NORTH POLE?
ME?
LAND OF THE MIDNIGHT SUN... TOWERING ICEBERGS... TOP O' THE WORLD!
WHAT ABOUT THE SHE-CRABS?
THEY HAVE LEGS THIS LONG.
NELLY!
THEY DIG SHORT GUYS.
I'M THERE.

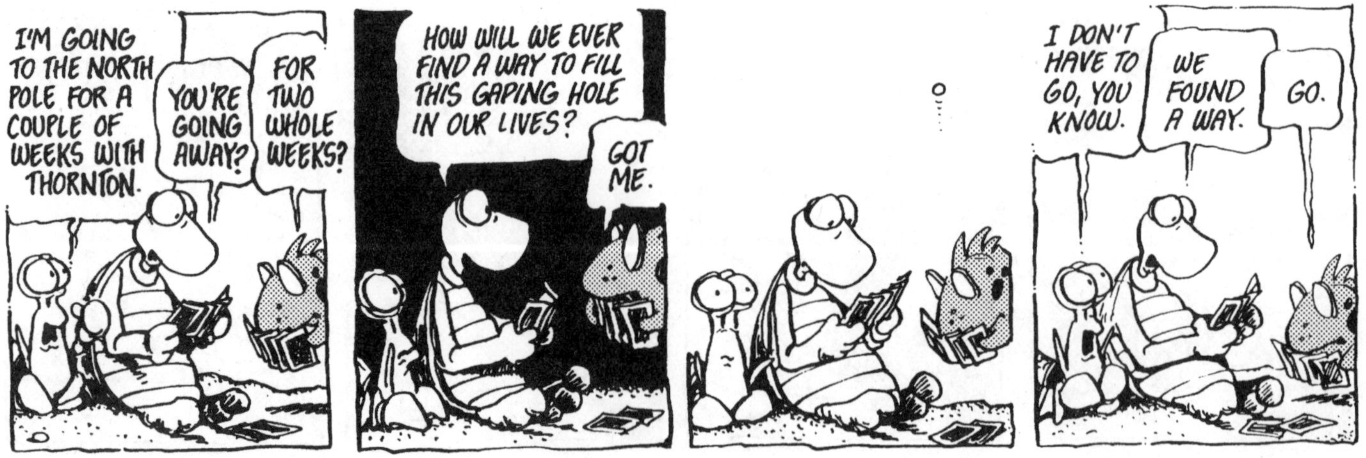
I'M GOING TO THE NORTH POLE FOR A COUPLE OF WEEKS WITH THORNTON.
YOU'RE GOING AWAY?
FOR TWO WHOLE WEEKS?
HOW WILL WE EVER FIND A WAY TO FILL THIS GAPING HOLE IN OUR LIVES?
GOT ME.
I DON'T HAVE TO GO, YOU KNOW.
WE FOUND A WAY.
GO.

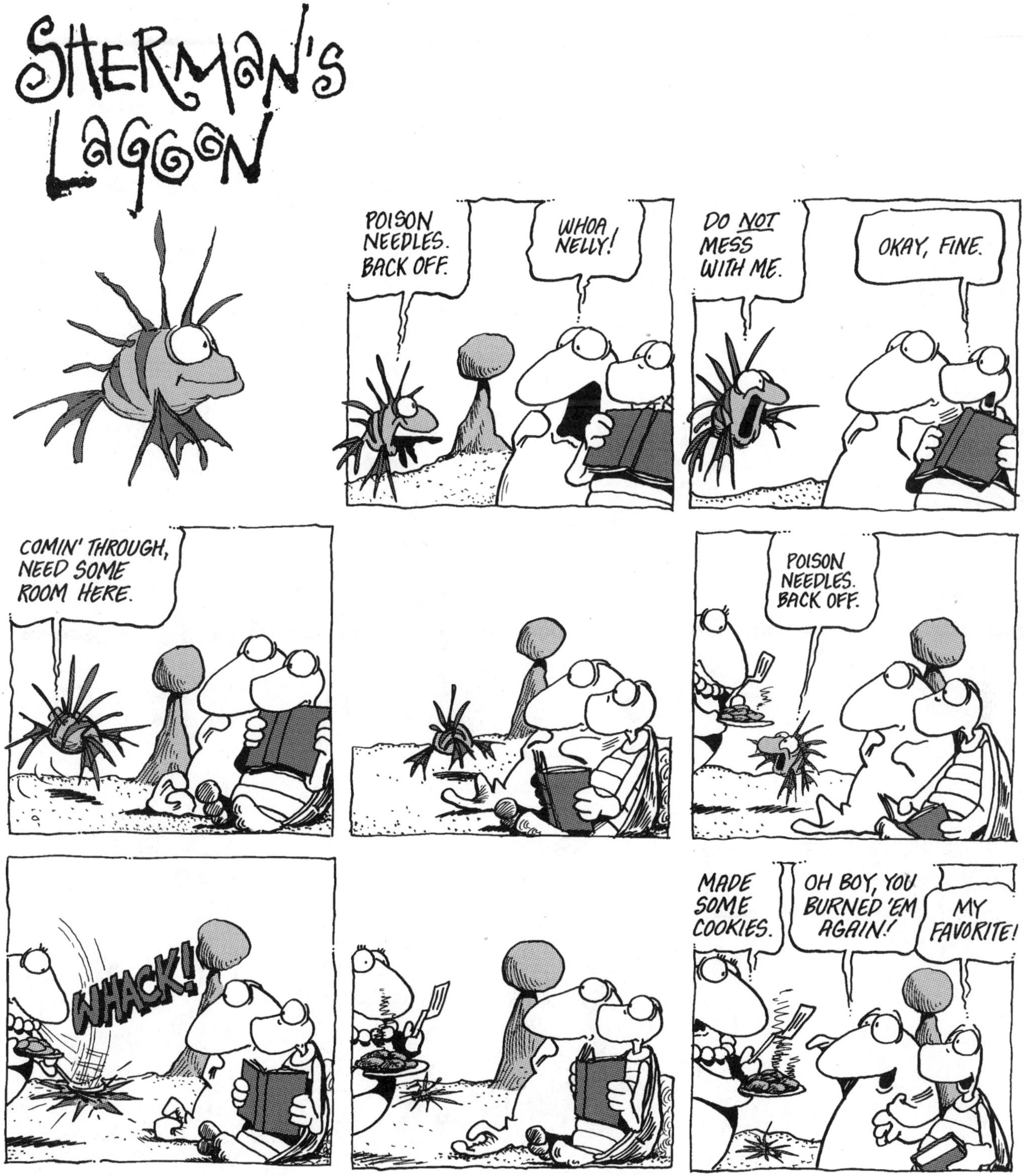
SHERMAN'S LAGOON
POISON NEEDLES. BACK OFF.
WHOA NELLY!
DO NOT MESS WITH ME.
OKAY, FINE.
COMIN' THROUGH, NEED SOME ROOM HERE.
POISON NEEDLES. BACK OFF.
WHACK!
MADE SOME COOKIES.
OH BOY, YOU BURNED 'EM AGAIN!
MY FAVORITE!

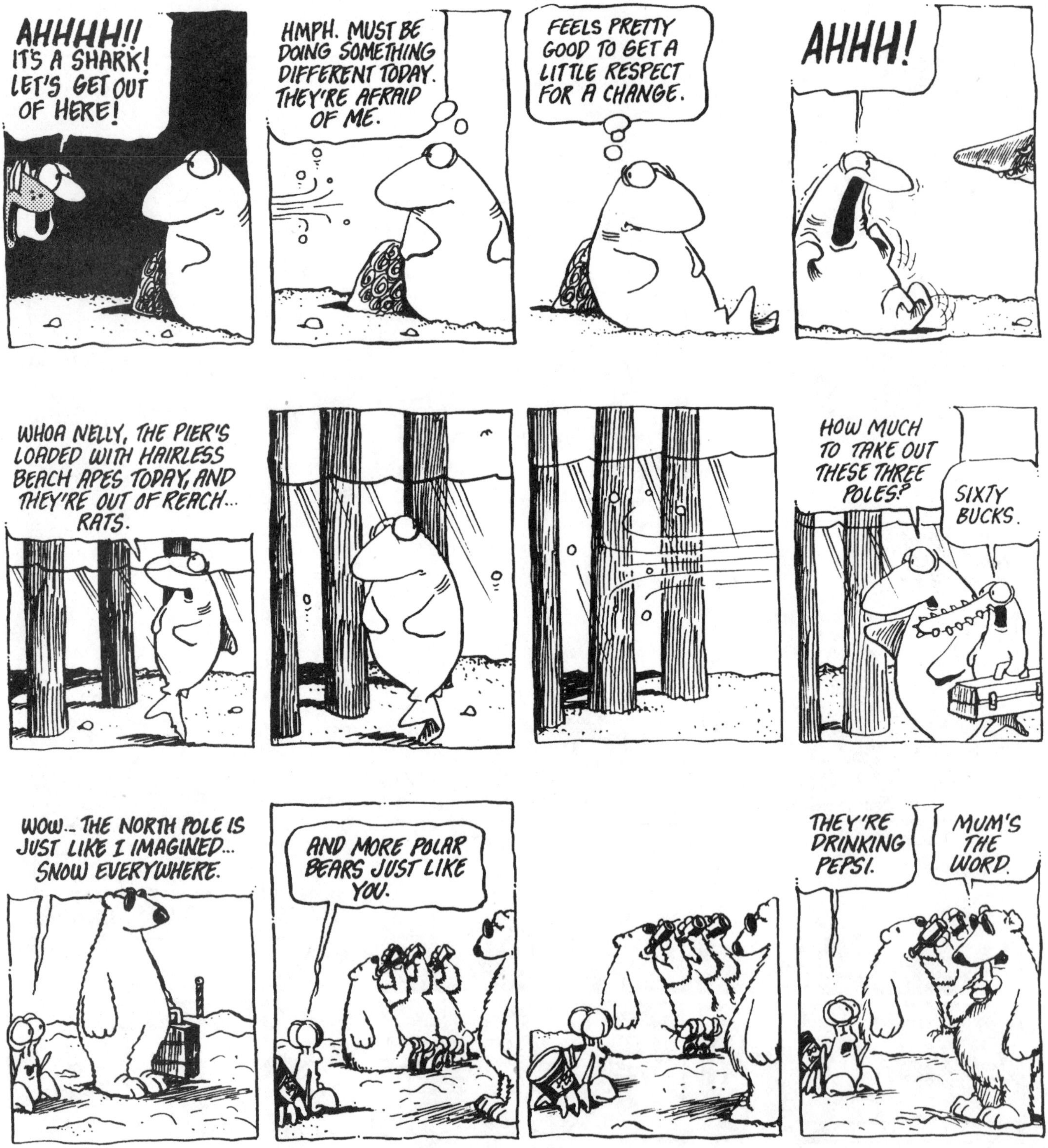
AHHHH!! IT'S A SHARK! LET'S GET OUT OF HERE!
HMPH. MUST BE DOING SOMETHING DIFFERENT TODAY. THEY'RE AFRAID OF ME.
FEELS PRETTY GOOD TO GET A LITTLE RESPECT FOR A CHANGE.
AHHH!
WHOA NELLY, THE PIER'S LOADED WITH HAIRLESS BEACH APES TODAY, AND THEY'RE OUT OF REACH... RATS.
HOW MUCH TO TAKE OUT THESE THREE POLES?
SIXTY BUCKS.
WOW... THE NORTH POLE IS JUST LIKE I IMAGINED... SNOW EVERYWHERE.
AND MORE POLAR BEARS JUST LIKE YOU.
THEY'RE DRINKING PEPSI.
MUM'S THE WORD.

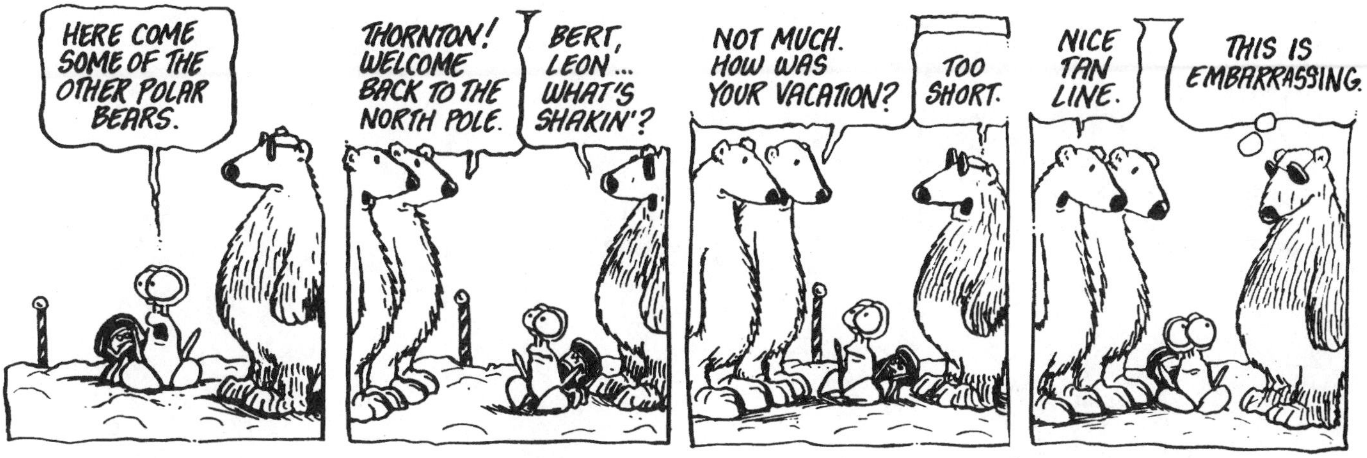
HERE COME SOME OF THE OTHER POLAR BEARS.
THORNTON! WELCOME BACK TO THE NORTH POLE.
BERT, LEON... WHAT'S SHAKIN'?
NOT MUCH. HOW WAS YOUR VACATION?
TOO SHORT.
NICE TAN LINE.
THIS IS EMBARRASSING.

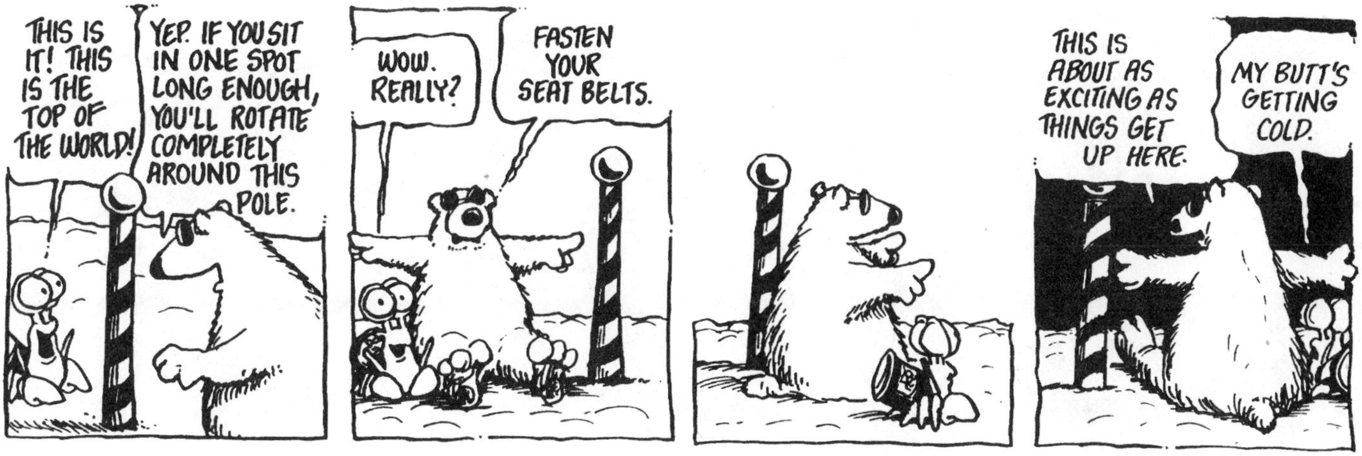
THIS IS IT! THIS IS THE TOP OF THE WORLD!
YEP. IF YOU SIT IN ONE SPOT LONG ENOUGH, YOU'LL ROTATE COMPLETELY AROUND THIS POLE.
WOW. REALLY?
FASTEN YOUR SEAT BELTS.
THIS IS ABOUT AS EXCITING AS THINGS GET UP HERE.
MY BUTT'S GETTING COLD.

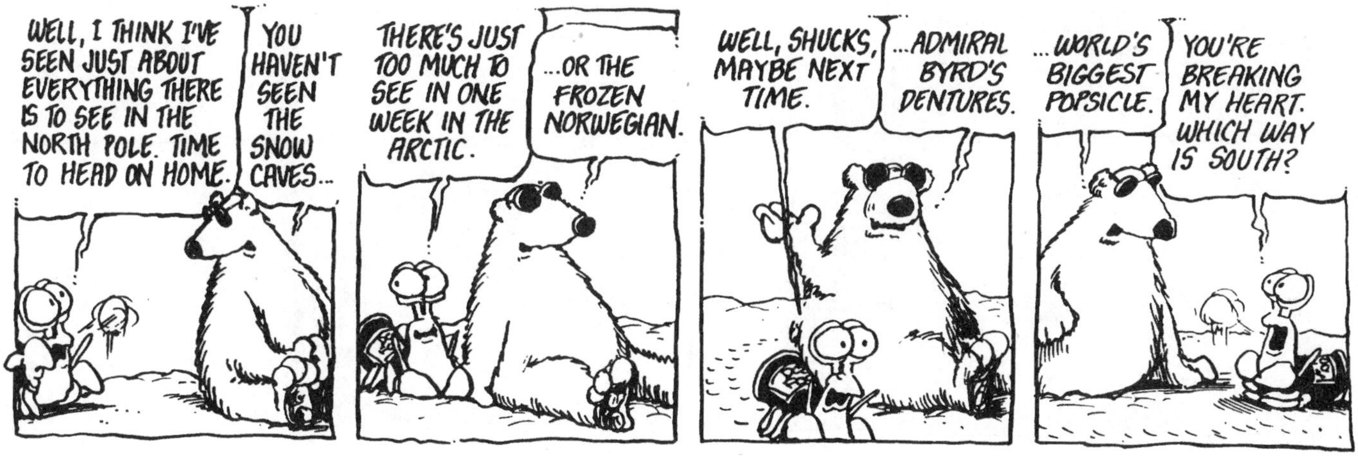
WELL, I THINK I'VE SEEN JUST ABOUT EVERYTHING THERE IS TO SEE IN THE NORTH POLE. TIME TO HEAD ON HOME.
YOU HAVEN'T SEEN THE SNOW CAVES...
THERE'S JUST TOO MUCH TO SEE IN ONE WEEK IN THE ARCTIC.
...OR THE FROZEN NORWEGIAN.
WELL, SHUCKS, MAYBE NEXT TIME.
...ADMIRAL BYRD'S DENTURES.
...WORLD'S BIGGEST POPSICLE.
YOU'RE BREAKING MY HEART. WHICH WAY IS SOUTH?

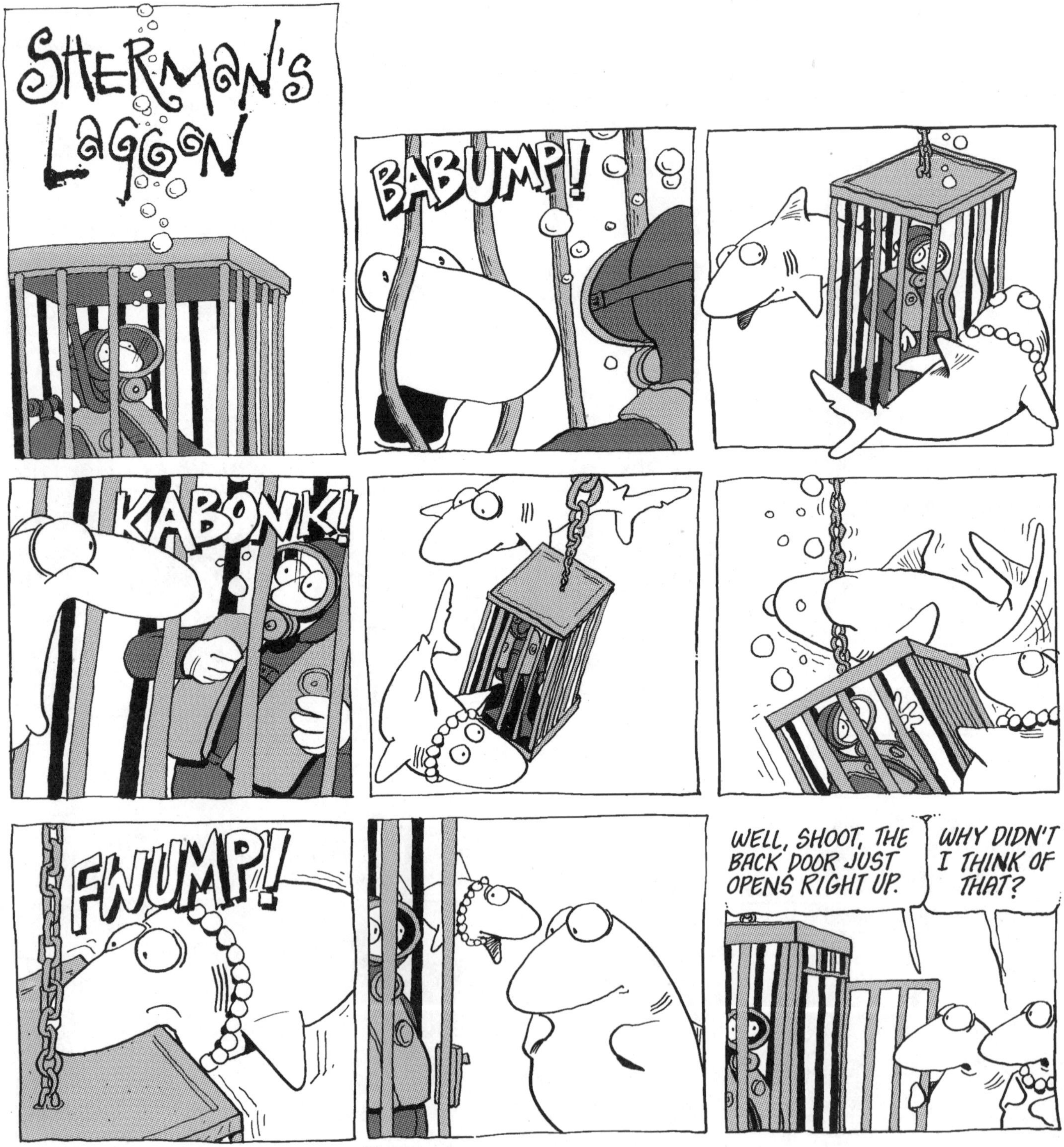
SHERMAN'S LAGOON
BABUMP!
KABONK!
FWUMP!
WELL, SHOOT, THE BACK DOOR JUST OPENS RIGHT UP.
WHY DIDN'T I THINK OF THAT?

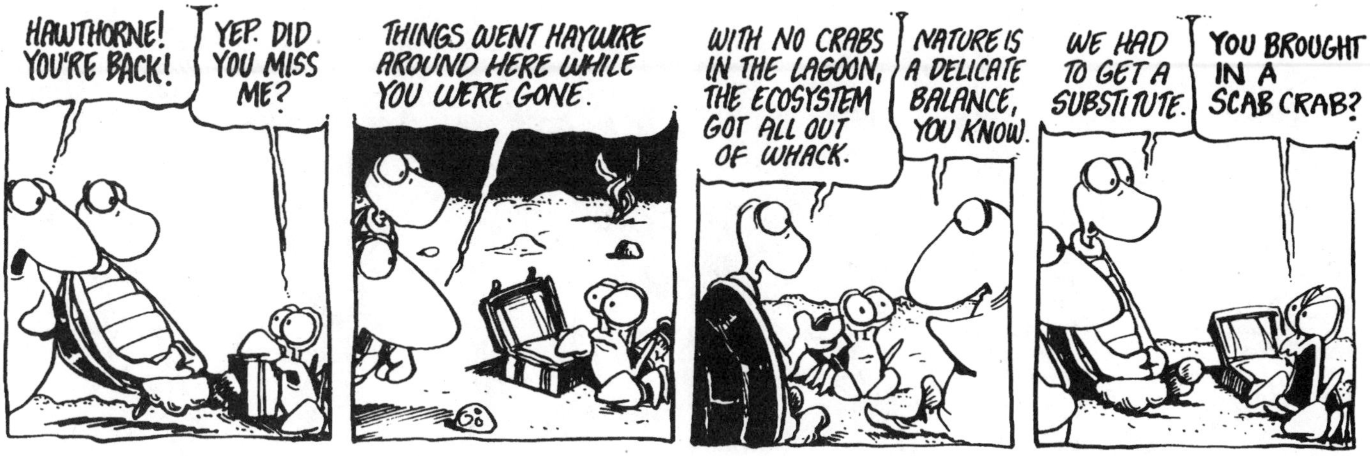
HAWTHORNE! YOU'RE BACK!
YEP. DID YOU MISS ME?
THINGS WENT HAYWIRE AROUND HERE WHILE YOU WERE GONE.
WITH NO CRABS IN THE LAGOON, THE ECOSYSTEM GOT ALL OUT OF WHACK.
NATURE IS A DELICATE BALANCE, YOU KNOW.
WE HAD TO GET A SUBSTITUTE.
YOU BROUGHT IN A SCAB CRAB?

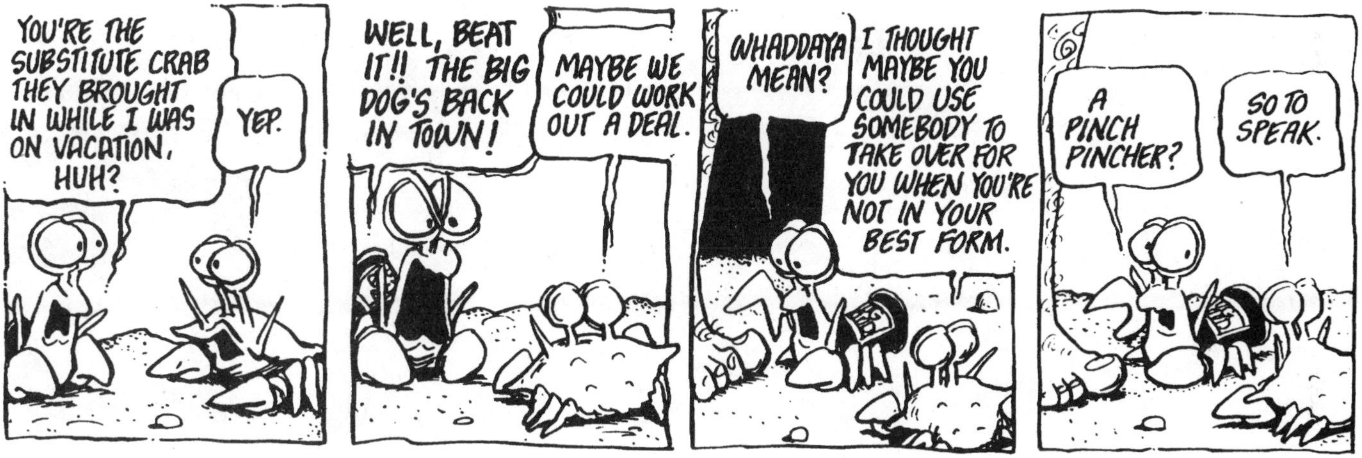
YOU'RE THE SUBSTITUTE CRAB THEY BROUGHT IN WHILE I WAS ON VACATION, HUH?
YEP.
WELL, BEAT IT!! THE BIG DOG'S BACK IN TOWN!
MAYBE WE COULD WORK OUT A DEAL.
WHADDAYA MEAN?
I THOUGHT MAYBE YOU COULD USE SOMEBODY TO TAKE OVER FOR YOU WHEN YOU'RE NOT IN YOUR BEST FORM.
A PINCH PINCHER?
SO TO SPEAK.

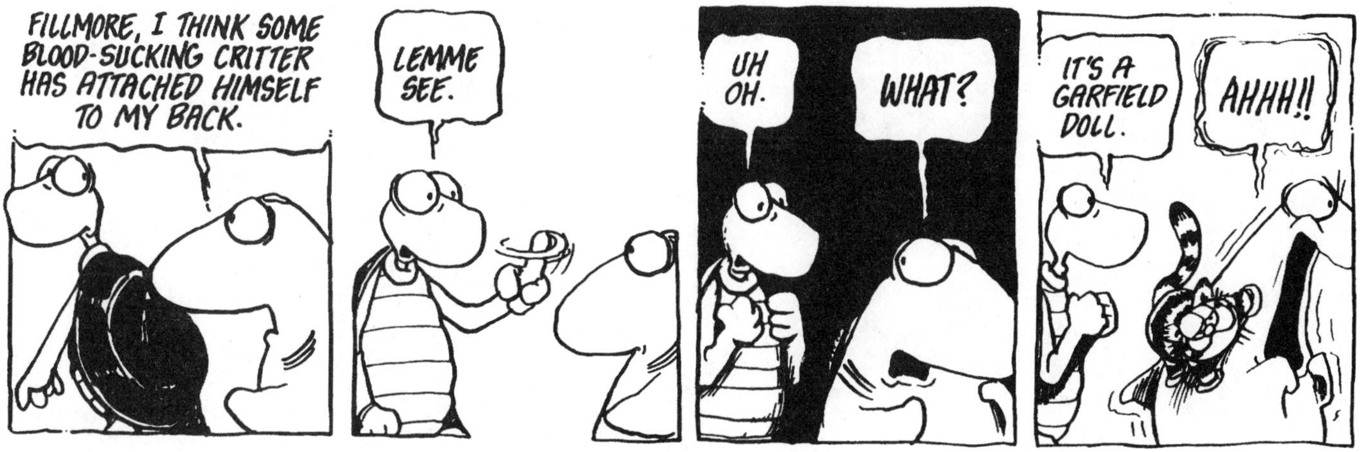
FILLMORE, I THINK SOME BLOOD-SUCKING CRITTER HAS ATTACHED HIMSELF TO MY BACK.
LEMME SEE.
UH OH.
WHAT?
IT'S A GARFIELD DOLL.
AHHH!!

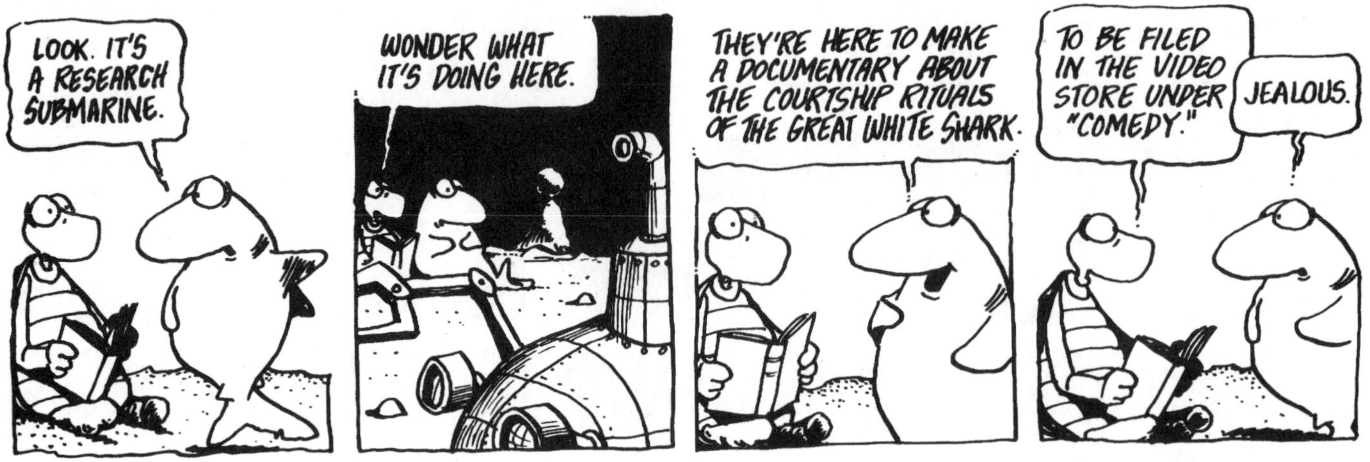
LOOK. IT'S A RESEARCH SUBMARINE.
WONDER WHAT IT'S DOING HERE.
THEY'RE HERE TO MAKE A DOCUMENTARY ABOUT THE COURTSHIP RITUALS OF THE GREAT WHITE SHARK.
TO BE FILED IN THE VIDEO STORE UNDER "COMEDY."
JEALOUS.

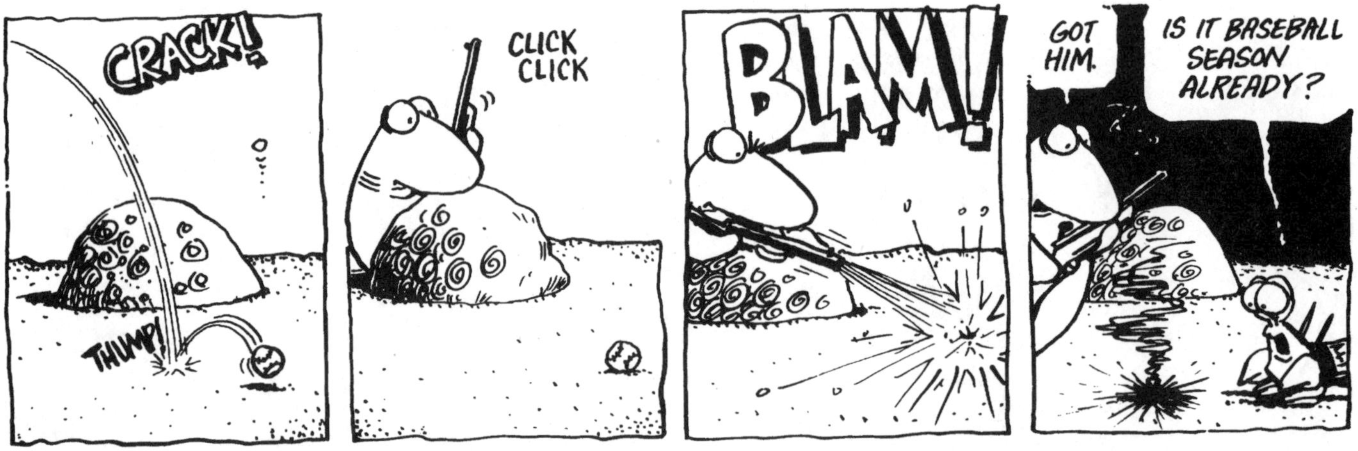
CRACK!
THUMP!
CLICK CLICK
BLAM!!
GOT HIM.
IS IT BASEBALL SEASON ALREADY?

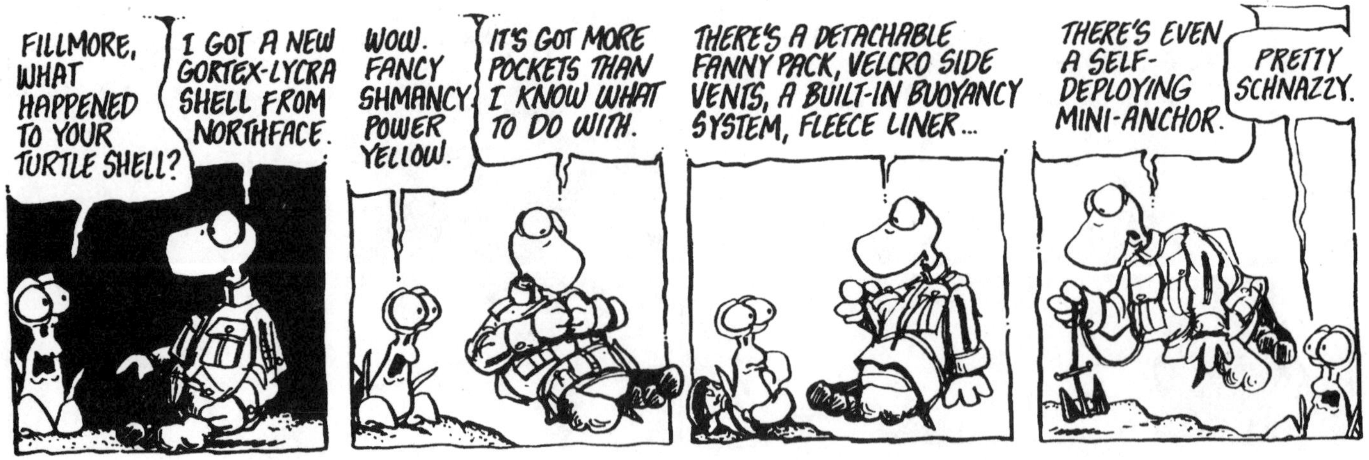
FILLMORE, WHAT HAPPENED TO YOUR TURTLE SHELL?
I GOT A NEW GORTEX-LYCRA SHELL FROM NORTHFACE.
WOW. FANCY SHMANCY POWER YELLOW.
IT'S GOT MORE POCKETS THAN I KNOW WHAT TO DO WITH.
THERE'S A DETACHABLE FANNY PACK, VELCRO SIDE VENTS, A BUILT-IN BUOYANCY SYSTEM, FLEECE LINER...
THERE'S EVEN A SELF-DEPLOYING MINI-ANCHOR.
PRETTY SCHNAZZY.

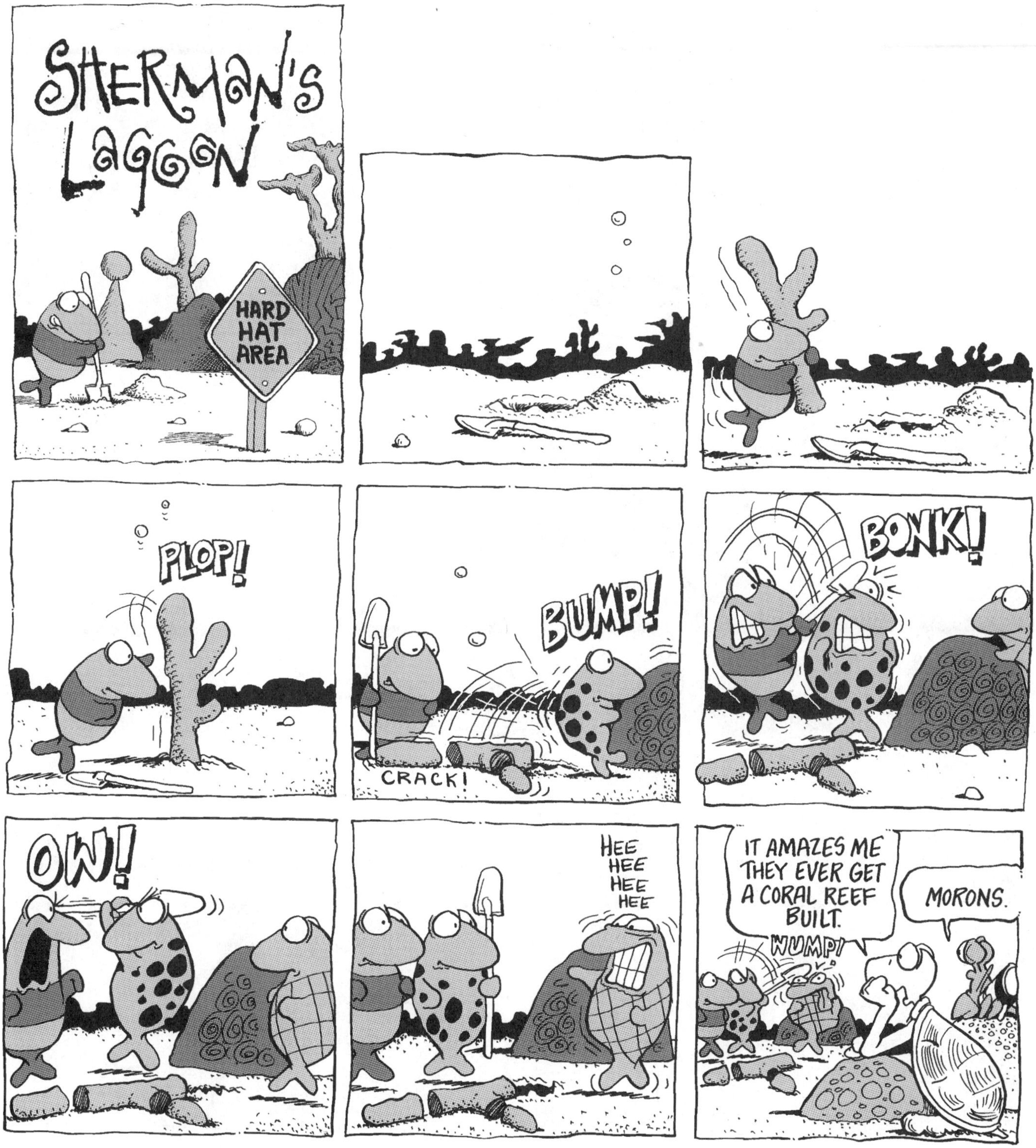
SHERMAN'S LAGOON
HARD HAT AREA
PLOP!
BUMP!
CRACK!
BONK!
OW!
HEE HEE HEE HEE
IT AMAZES ME THEY EVER GET A CORAL REEF BUILT.
WUMP!
MORONS.

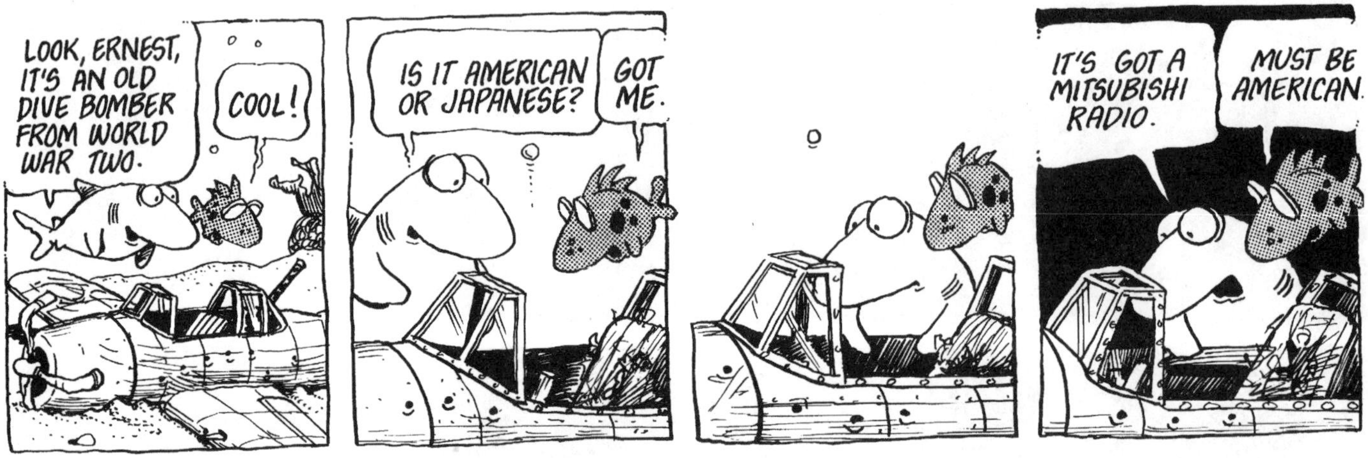
LOOK, ERNEST, IT'S AN OLD DIVE BOMBER FROM WORLD WAR TWO.
COOL!
IS IT AMERICAN OR JAPANESE?
GOT ME.
IT'S GOT A MITSUBISHI RADIO.
MUST BE AMERICAN.

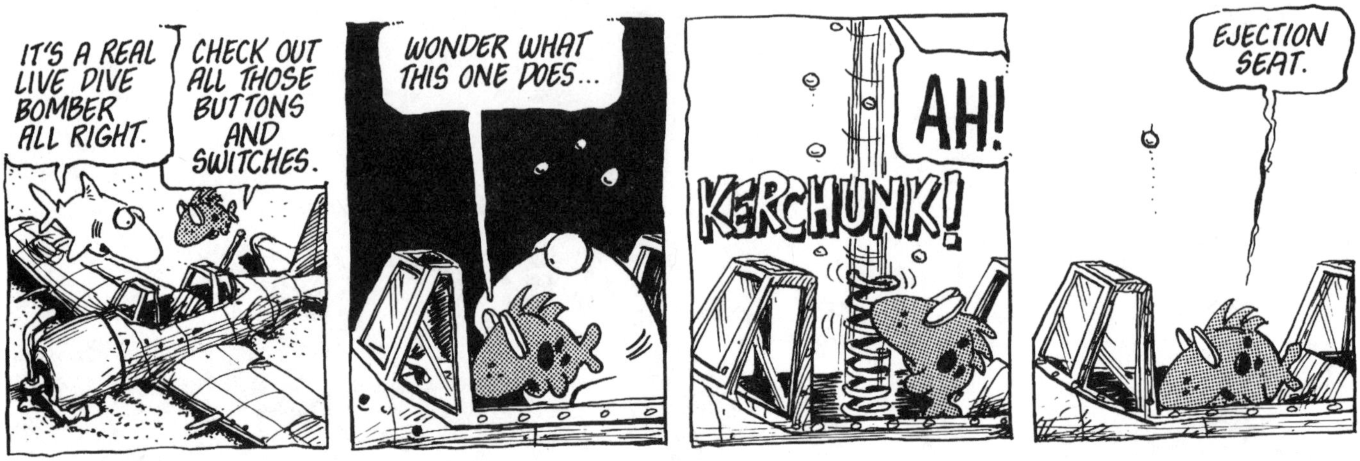
IT'S A REAL LIVE DIVE BOMBER ALL RIGHT.
CHECK OUT ALL THOSE BUTTONS AND SWITCHES.
WONDER WHAT THIS ONE DOES...
AH!
KERCHUNK!
EJECTION SEAT.

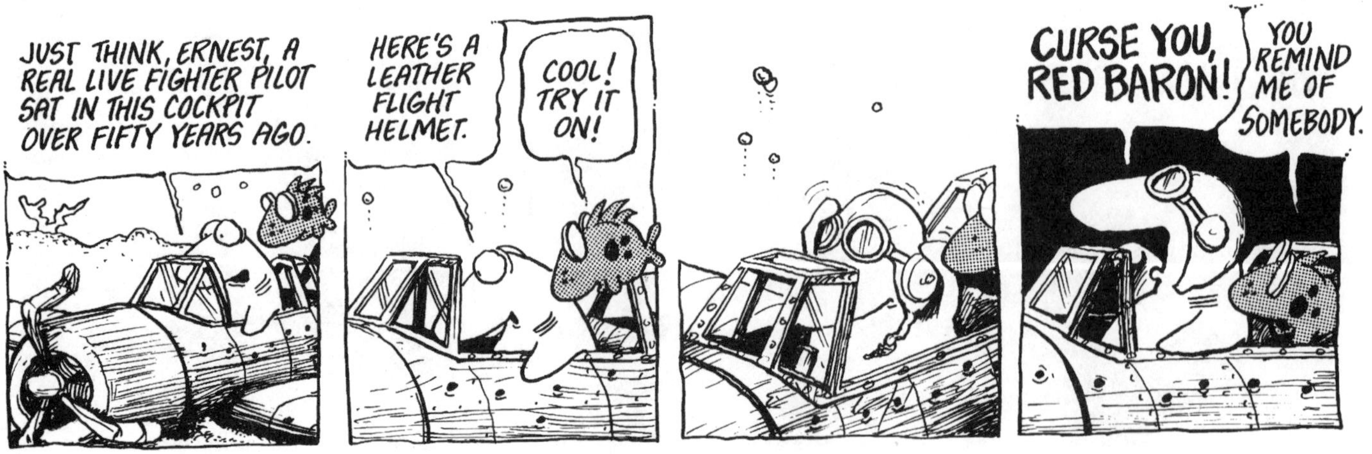
JUST THINK, ERNEST, A REAL LIVE FIGHTER PILOT SAT IN THIS COCKPIT OVER FIFTY YEARS AGO.
HERE'S A LEATHER FLIGHT HELMET.
COOL! TRY IT ON!
CURSE YOU, RED BARON!
YOU REMIND ME OF SOMEBODY.

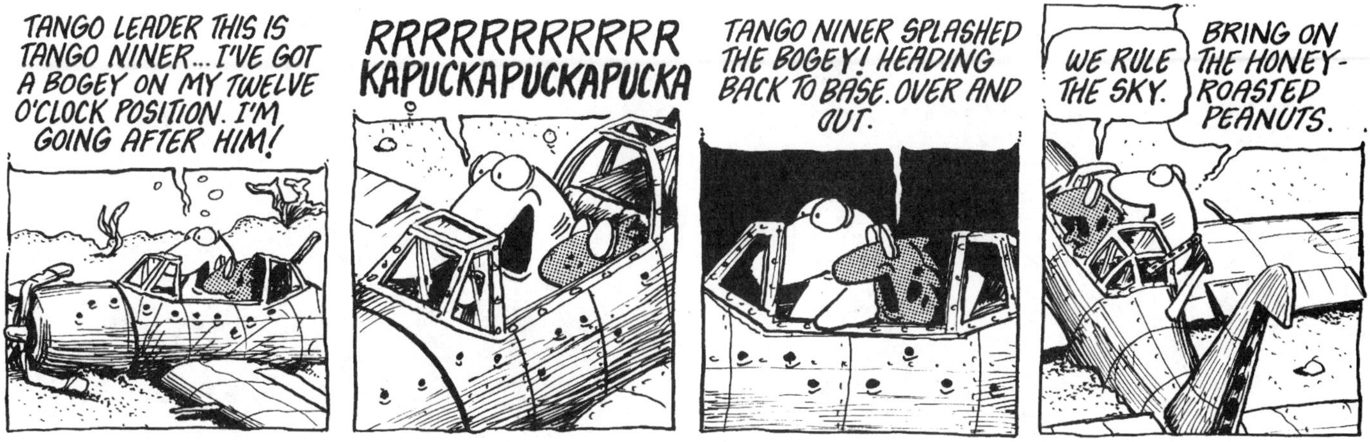
TANGO LEADER THIS IS TANGO NINER... I'VE GOT A BOGEY ON MY TWELVE O'CLOCK POSITION. I'M GOING AFTER HIM!
RRRRRRRRRRRR KAPUCKAPUCKAPUCKA
TANGO NINER SPLASHED THE BOGEY! HEADING BACK TO BASE. OVER AND OUT.
WE RULE THE SKY.
BRING ON THE HONEY-ROASTED PEANUTS.

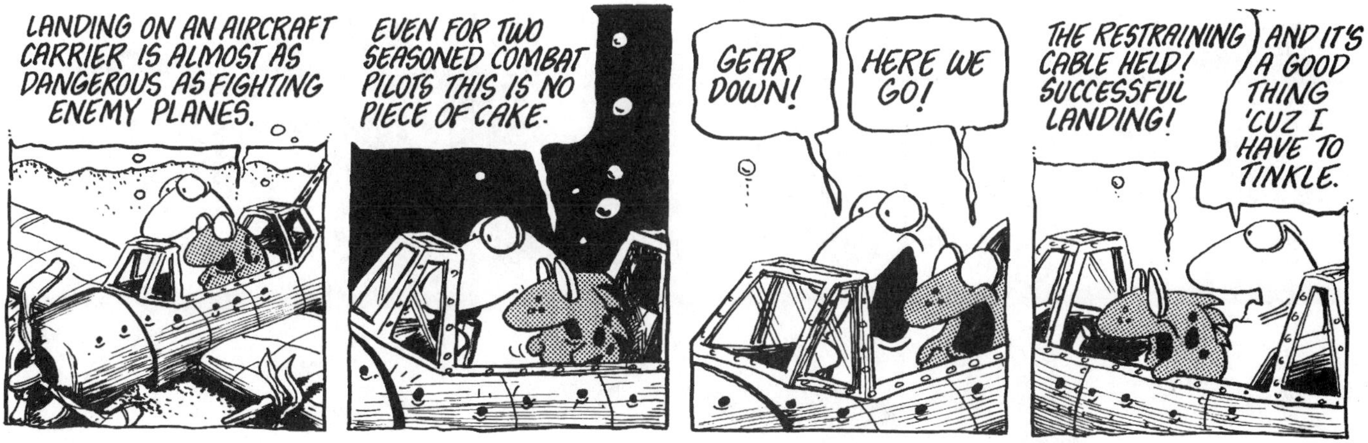
LANDING ON AN AIRCRAFT CARRIER IS ALMOST AS DANGEROUS AS FIGHTING ENEMY PLANES.
EVEN FOR TWO SEASONED COMBAT PILOTS THIS IS NO PIECE OF CAKE.
GEAR DOWN!
HERE WE GO!
THE RESTRAINING CABLE HELD! SUCCESSFUL LANDING!
AND IT'S A GOOD THING 'CUZ I HAVE TO TINKLE.

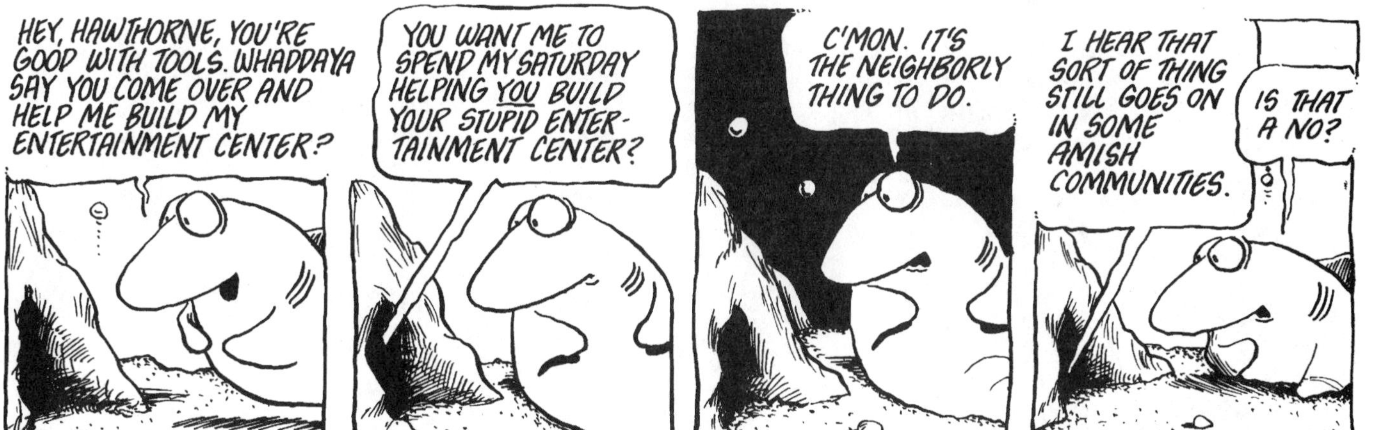
HEY, HAWTHORNE, YOU'RE GOOD WITH TOOLS. WHADDAYA SAY YOU COME OVER AND HELP ME BUILD MY ENTERTAINMENT CENTER?
YOU WANT ME TO SPEND MY SATURDAY HELPING YOU BUILD YOUR STUPID ENTER-TAINMENT CENTER?
C'MON. IT'S THE NEIGHBORLY THING TO DO.
I HEAR THAT SORT OF THING STILL GOES ON IN SOME AMISH COMMUNITIES.
IS THAT A NO?

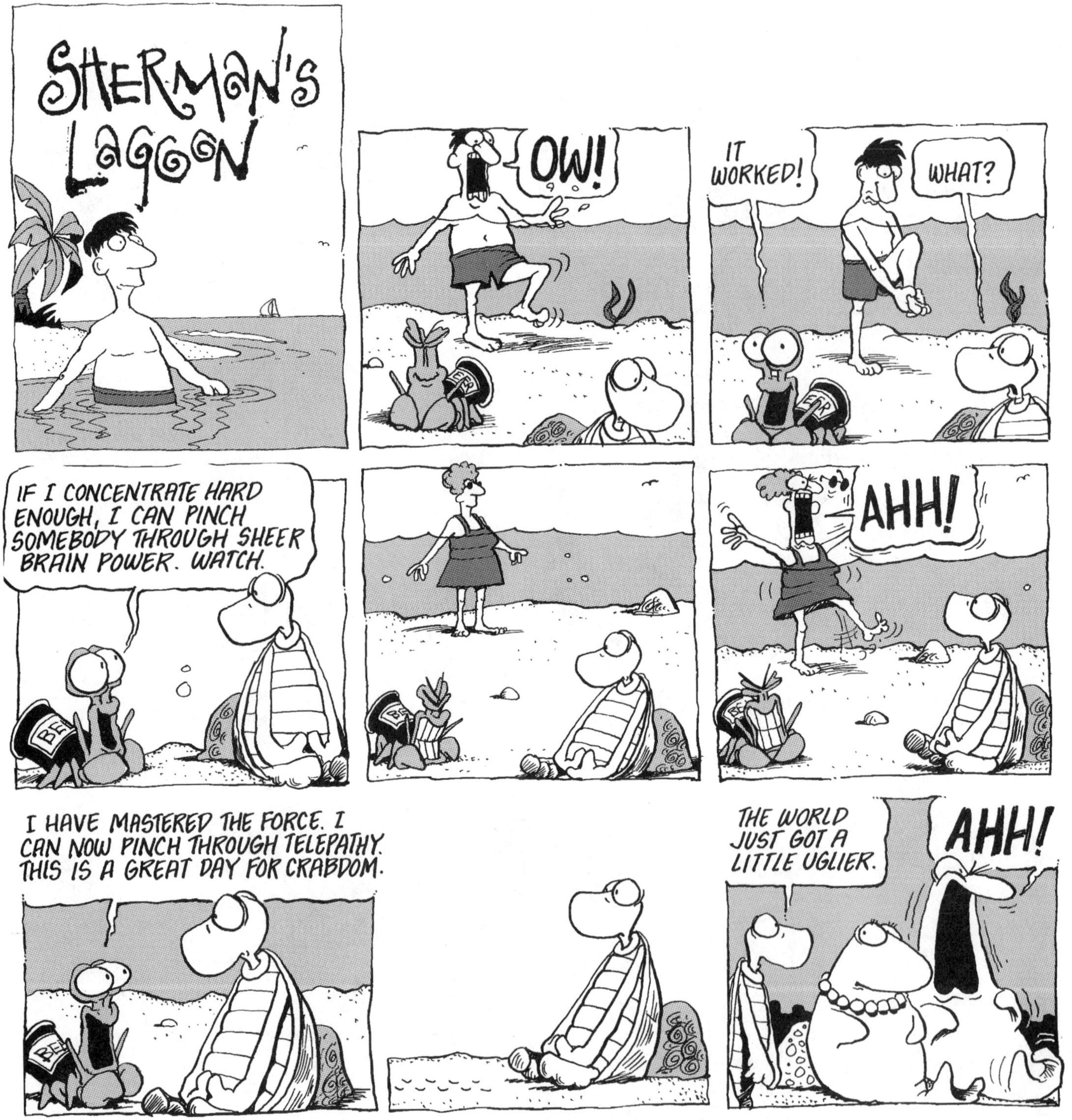
SHERMAN'S LAGOON
OW!
IT WORKED!
WHAT?
IF I CONCENTRATE HARD ENOUGH, I CAN PINCH SOMEBODY THROUGH SHEER BRAIN POWER. WATCH.
AHH!
I HAVE MASTERED THE FORCE. I CAN NOW PINCH THROUGH TELEPATHY. THIS IS A GREAT DAY FOR CRABDOM.
THE WORLD JUST GOT A LITTLE UGLIER.
AHH!

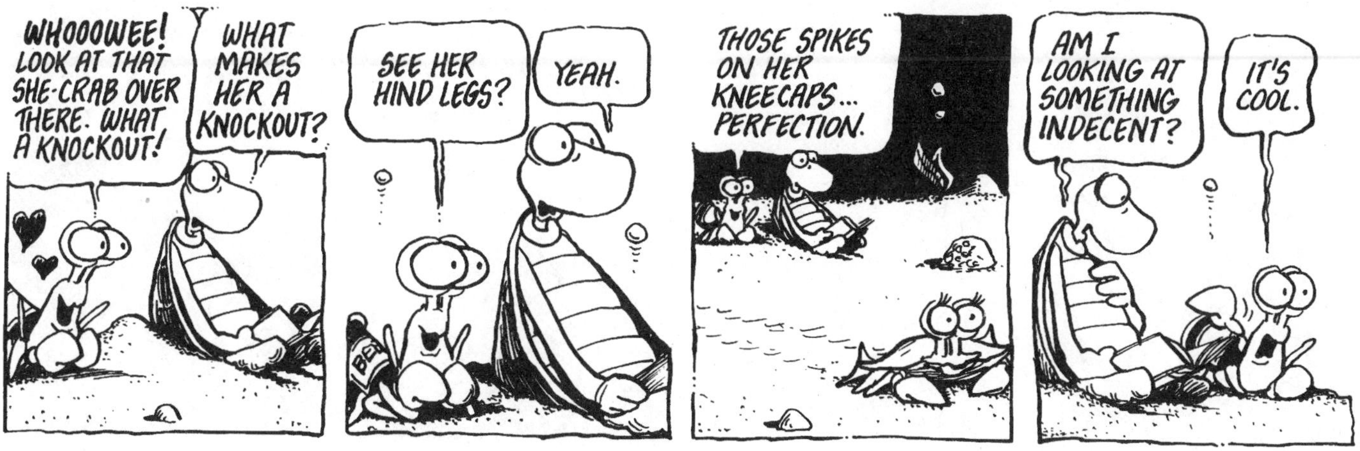
WHOOOWEE! LOOK AT THAT SHE-CRAB OVER THERE. WHAT A KNOCKOUT!
WHAT MAKES HER A KNOCKOUT?
SEE HER HIND LEGS?
YEAH.
THOSE SPIKES ON HER KNEECAPS... PERFECTION.
AM I LOOKING AT SOMETHING INDECENT?
IT'S COOL.

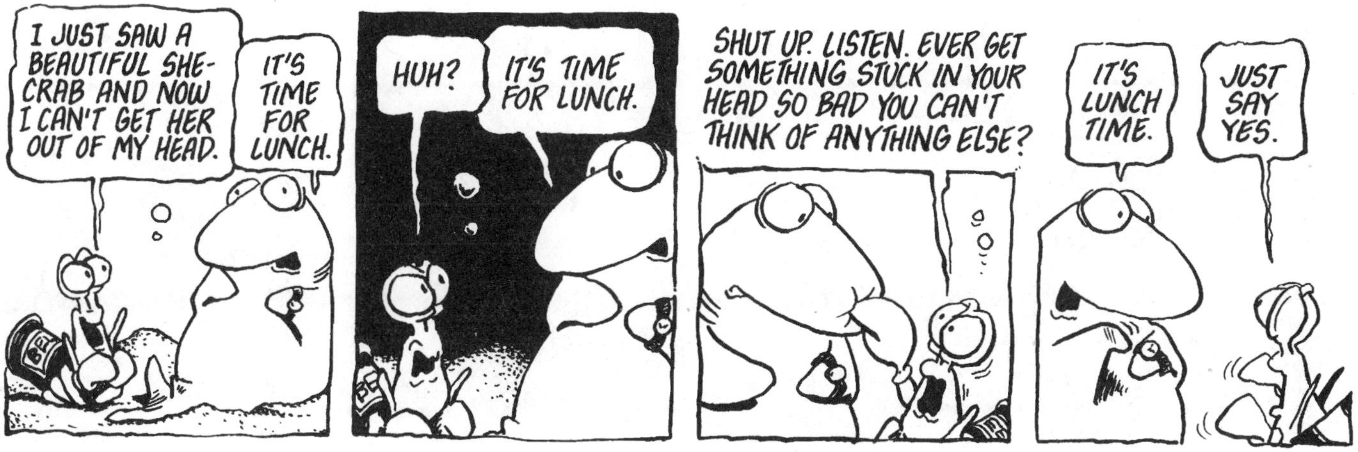
I JUST SAW A BEAUTIFUL SHE-CRAB AND NOW I CAN'T GET HER OUT OF MY HEAD.
IT'S TIME FOR LUNCH.
HUH?
IT'S TIME FOR LUNCH.
SHUT UP. LISTEN. EVER GET SOMETHING STUCK IN YOUR HEAD SO BAD YOU CAN'T THINK OF ANYTHING ELSE?
IT'S LUNCH TIME.
JUST SAY YES.

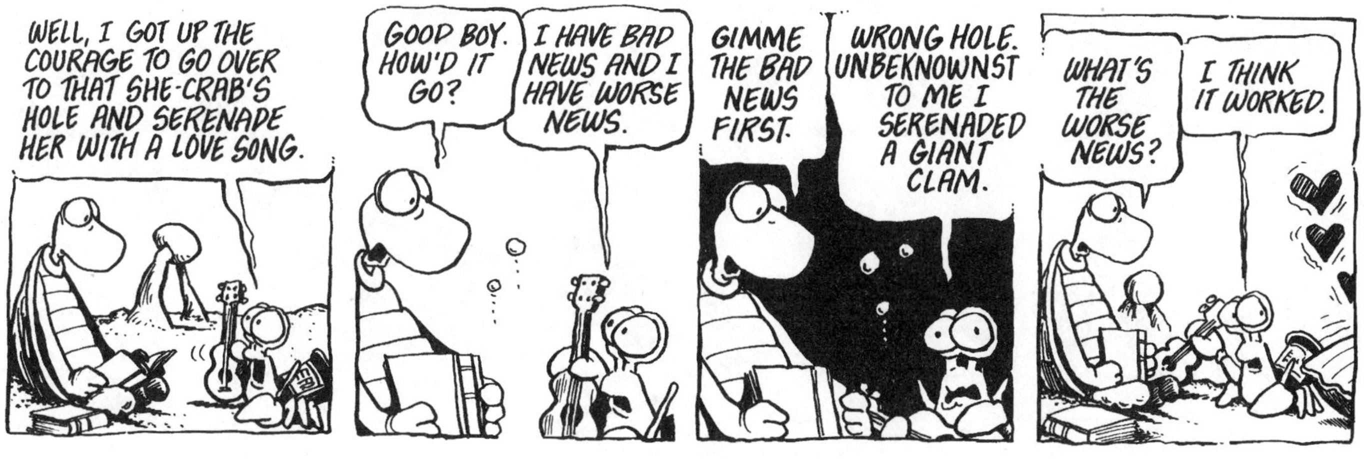
WELL, I GOT UP THE COURAGE TO GO OVER TO THAT SHE-CRAB'S HOLE AND SERENADE HER WITH A LOVE SONG.
GOOD BOY. HOW'D IT GO?
I HAVE BAD NEWS AND I HAVE WORSE NEWS.
GIMME THE BAD NEWS FIRST.
WRONG HOLE. UNBEKNOWNST TO ME I SERENADED A GIANT CLAM.
WHAT'S THE WORSE NEWS?
I THINK IT WORKED.

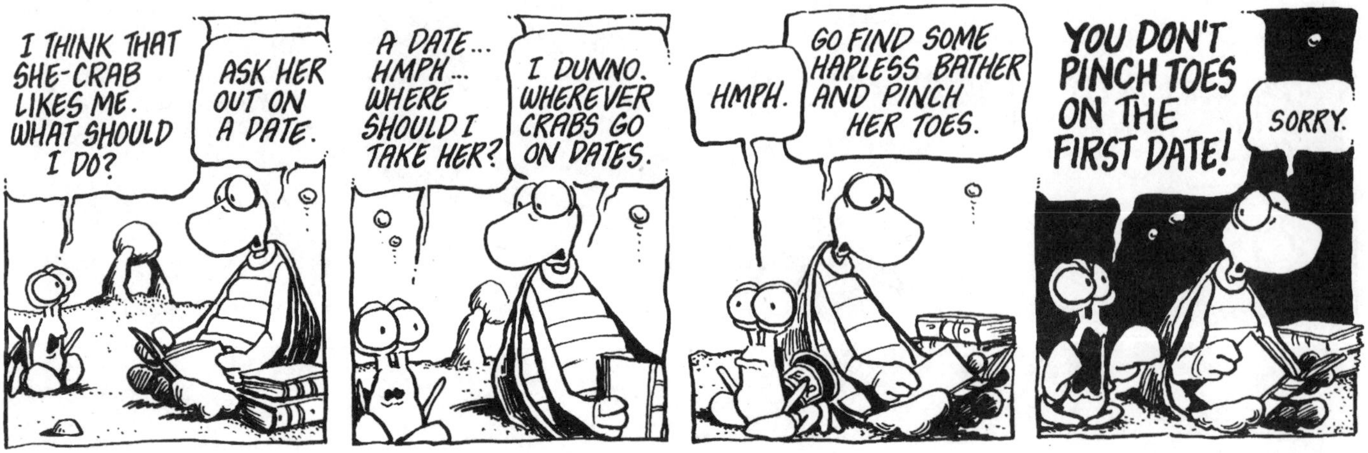
I THINK THAT SHE-CRAB LIKES ME. WHAT SHOULD I DO?
ASK HER OUT ON A DATE.
A DATE... HMPH... WHERE SHOULD I TAKE HER?
I DUNNO. WHEREVER CRABS GO ON DATES.
HMPH.
GO FIND SOME HAPLESS BATHER AND PINCH HER TOES.
YOU DON'T PINCH TOES ON THE FIRST DATE!
SORRY.

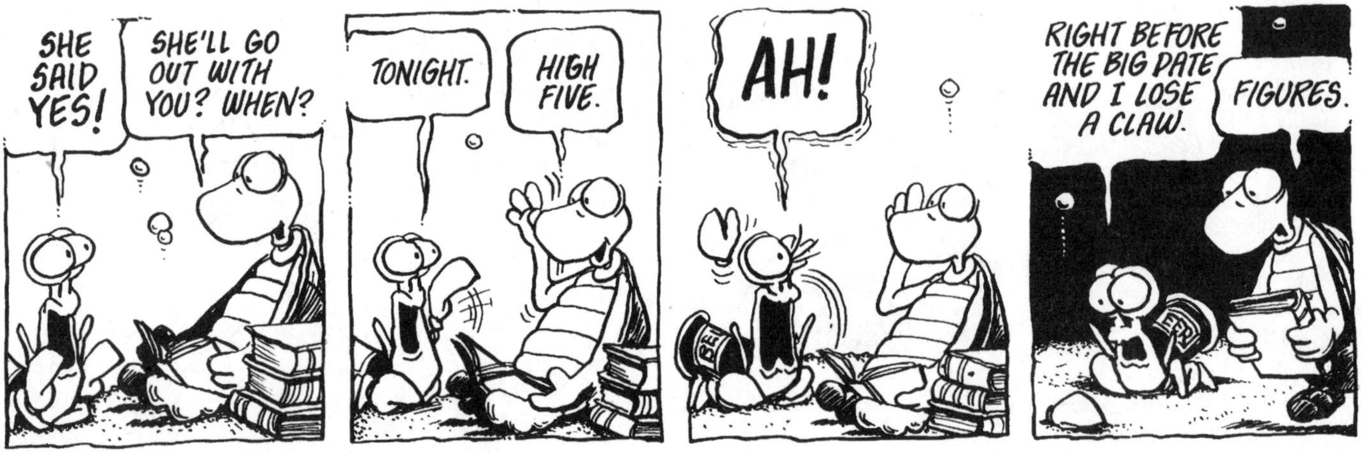
SHE SAID YES!
SHE'LL GO OUT WITH YOU? WHEN?
TONIGHT.
HIGH FIVE.
AH!
RIGHT BEFORE THE BIG DATE AND I LOSE A CLAW.
FIGURES.

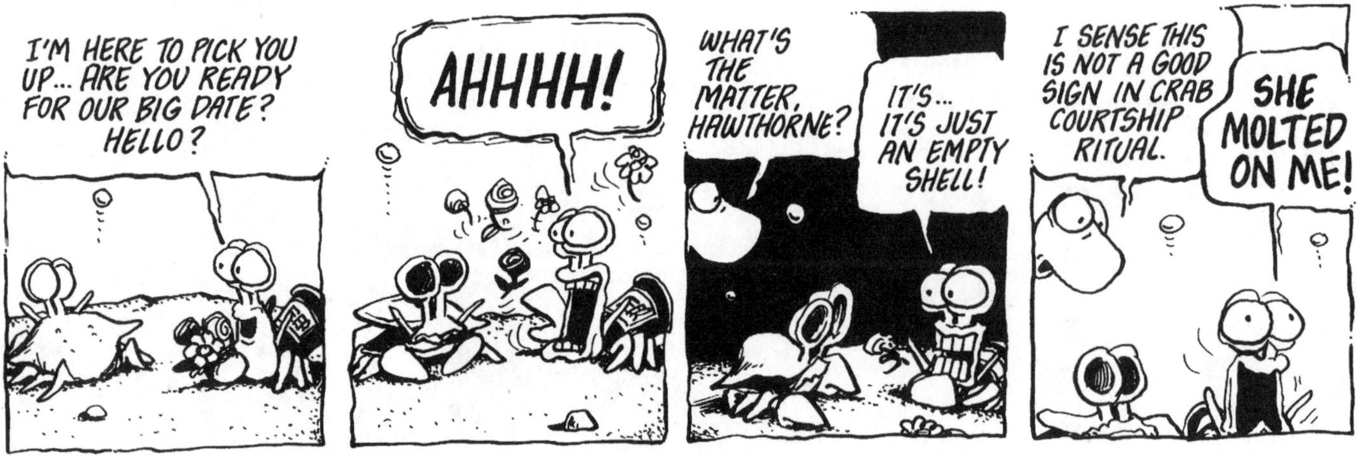
I'M HERE TO PICK YOU UP... ARE YOU READY FOR OUR BIG DATE? HELLO?
AHHHH!
WHAT'S THE MATTER, HAWTHORNE?
IT'S... IT'S JUST AN EMPTY SHELL!
I SENSE THIS IS NOT A GOOD SIGN IN CRAB COURTSHIP RITUAL.
SHE MOLTED ON ME!

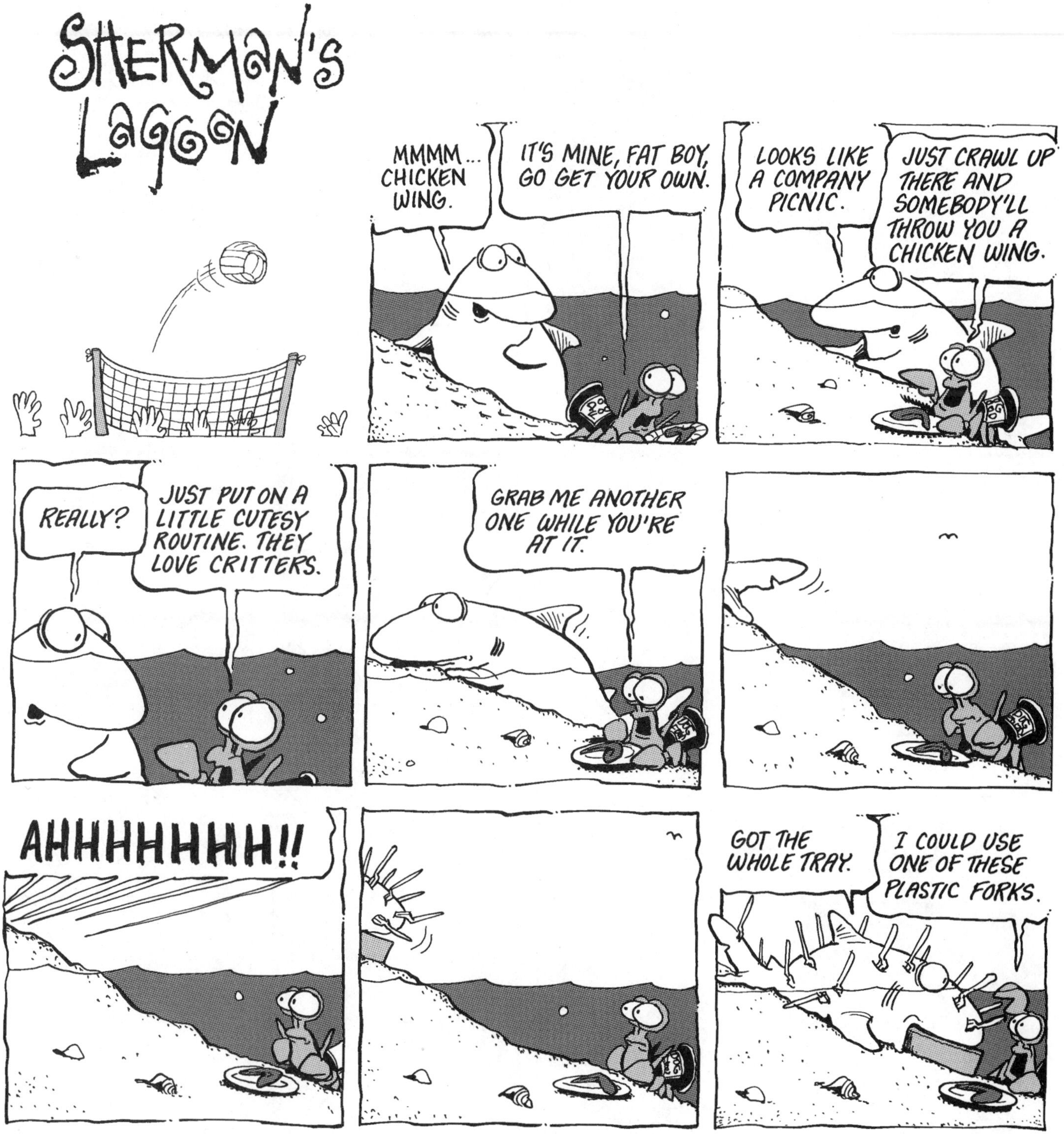
SHERMAN'S LAGOON
MMMM... CHICKEN WING.
IT'S MINE, FAT BOY, GO GET YOUR OWN.
LOOKS LIKE A COMPANY PICNIC.
JUST CRAWL UP THERE AND SOMEBODY'LL THROW YOU A CHICKEN WING.
REALLY?
JUST PUT ON A LITTLE CUTESY ROUTINE. THEY LOVE CRITTERS.
GRAB ME ANOTHER ONE WHILE YOU'RE AT IT.
AHHHHHHH!!
GOT THE WHOLE TRAY.
I COULD USE ONE OF THESE PLASTIC FORKS.

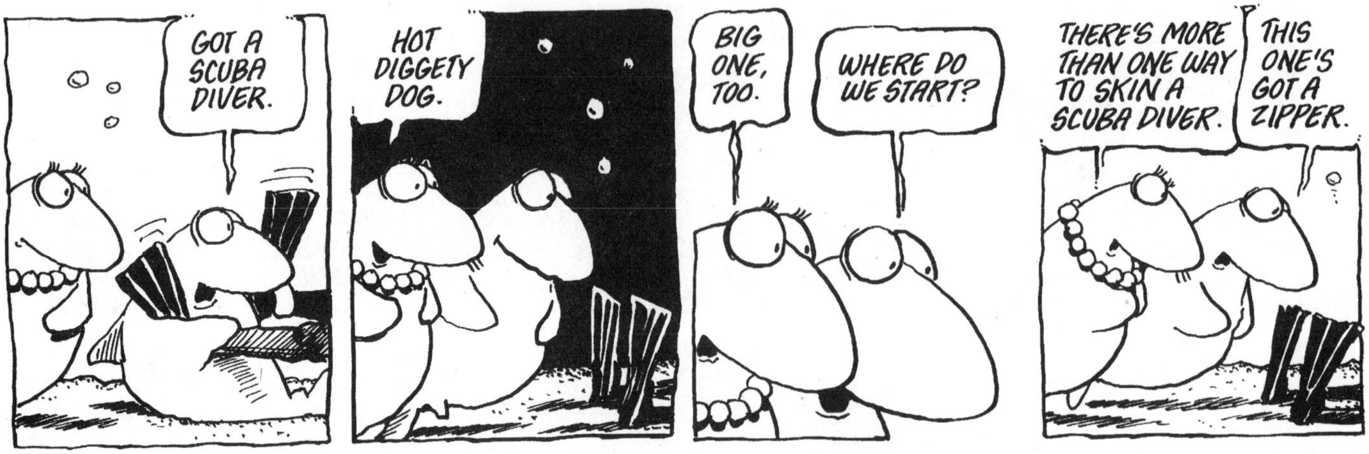
GOT A SCUBA DIVER.
HOT DIGGETY DOG.
BIG ONE, TOO.
WHERE DO WE START?
THERE'S MORE THAN ONE WAY TO SKIN A SCUBA DIVER.
THIS ONE'S GOT A ZIPPER.

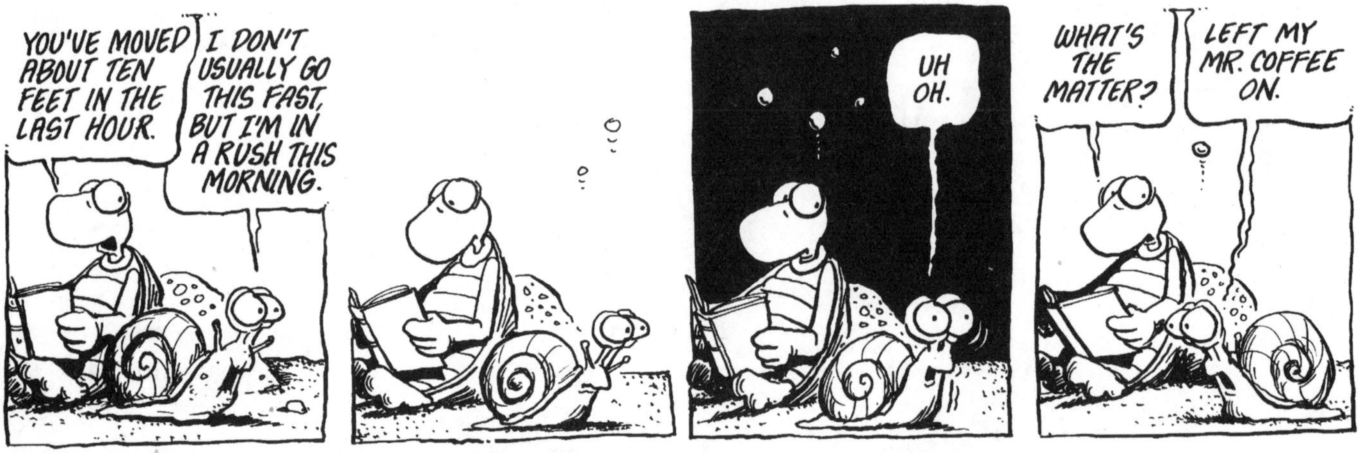
YOU'VE MOVED ABOUT TEN FEET IN THE LAST HOUR.
I DON'T USUALLY GO THIS FAST, BUT I'M IN A RUSH THIS MORNING.
UH OH.
WHAT'S THE MATTER?
LEFT MY MR. COFFEE ON.

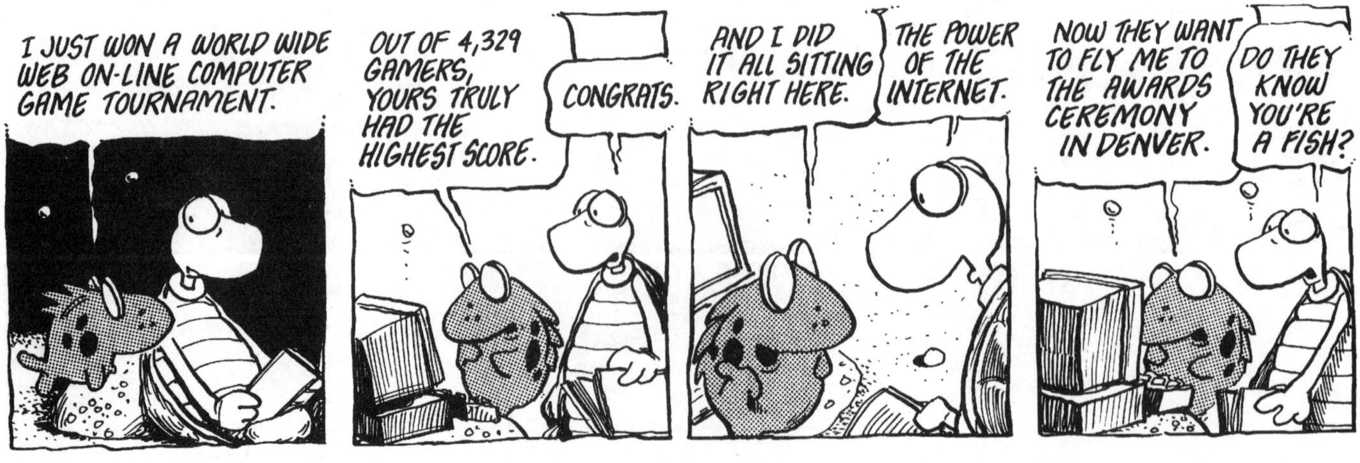
I JUST WON A WORLD WIDE WEB ON-LINE COMPUTER GAME TOURNAMENT.
OUT OF 4,329 GAMERS, YOURS TRULY HAD THE HIGHEST SCORE.
CONGRATS.
AND I DID IT ALL SITTING RIGHT HERE.
THE POWER OF THE INTERNET.
NOW THEY WANT TO FLY ME TO THE AWARDS CEREMONY IN DENVER.
DO THEY KNOW YOU'RE A FISH?

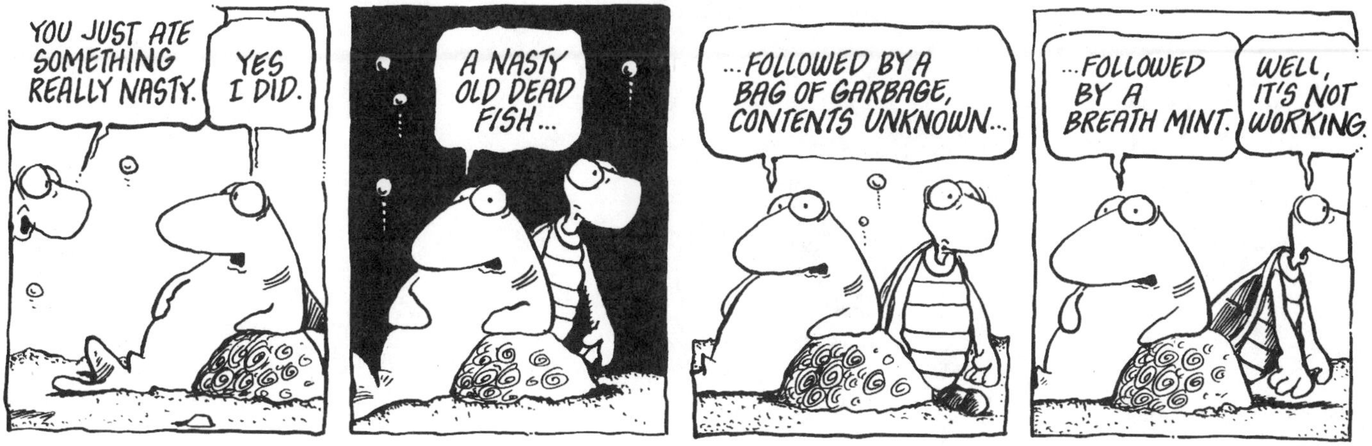
YOU JUST ATE SOMETHING REALLY NASTY.
YES. I DID.
A NASTY OLD DEAD FISH...
...FOLLOWED BY A BAG OF GARBAGE, CONTENTS UNKNOWN...
...FOLLOWED BY A BREATH MINT.
WELL, IT'S NOT WORKING.

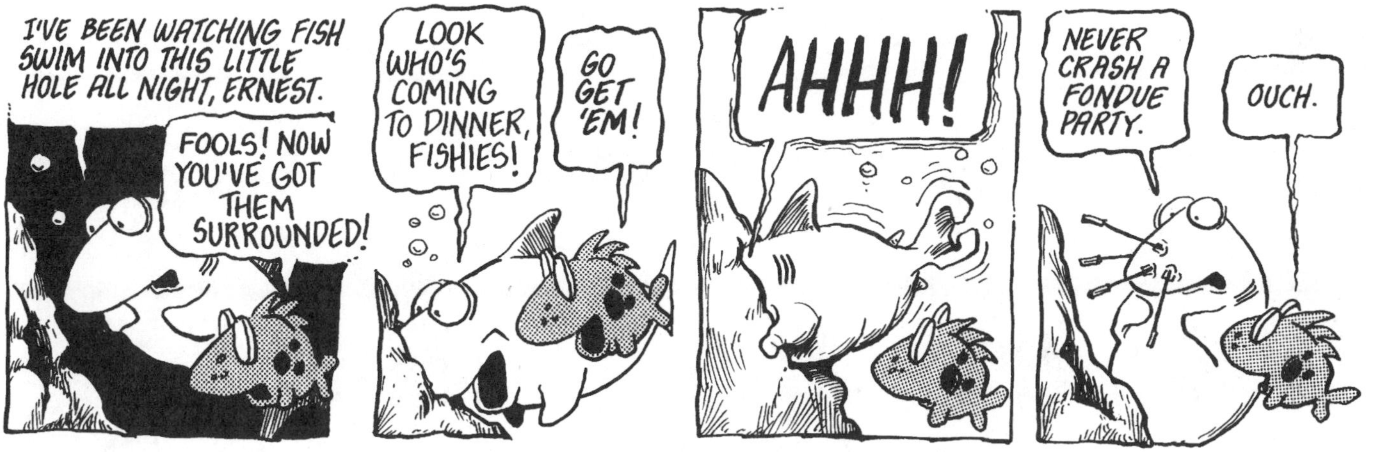
I'VE BEEN WATCHING FISH SWIM INTO THIS LITTLE HOLE ALL NIGHT, ERNEST.
FOOLS! NOW YOU'VE GOT THEM SURROUNDED!
LOOK WHO'S COMING TO DINNER, FISHIES!
GO GET 'EM!
AHHH!
NEVER CRASH A FONDUE PARTY.
OUCH.

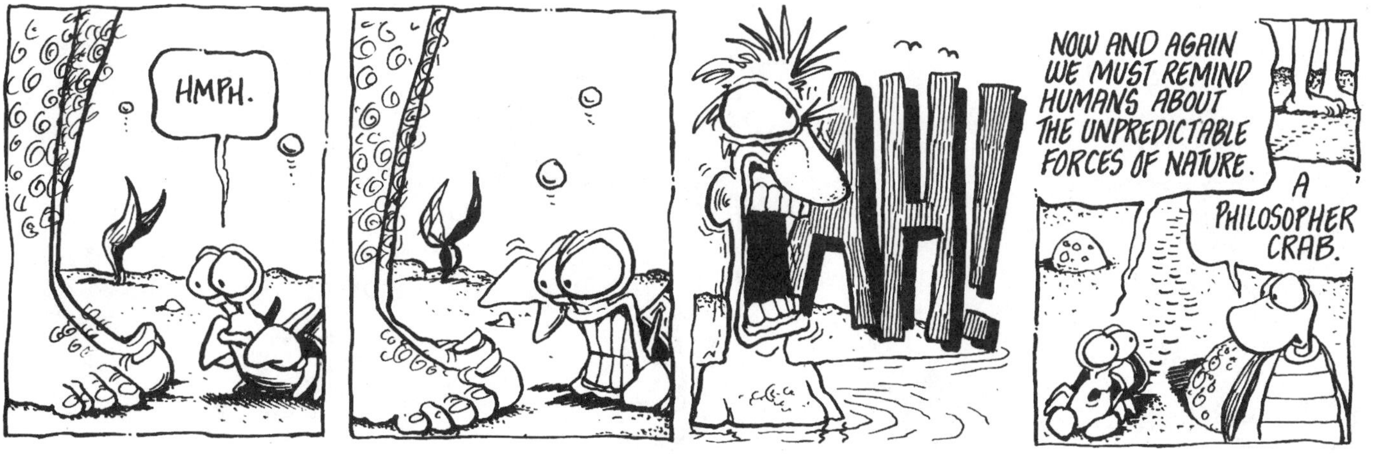
HMPH.
AHH!!
NOW AND AGAIN WE MUST REMIND HUMANS ABOUT THE UNPREDICTABLE FORCES OF NATURE.
A PHILOSOPHER CRAB.

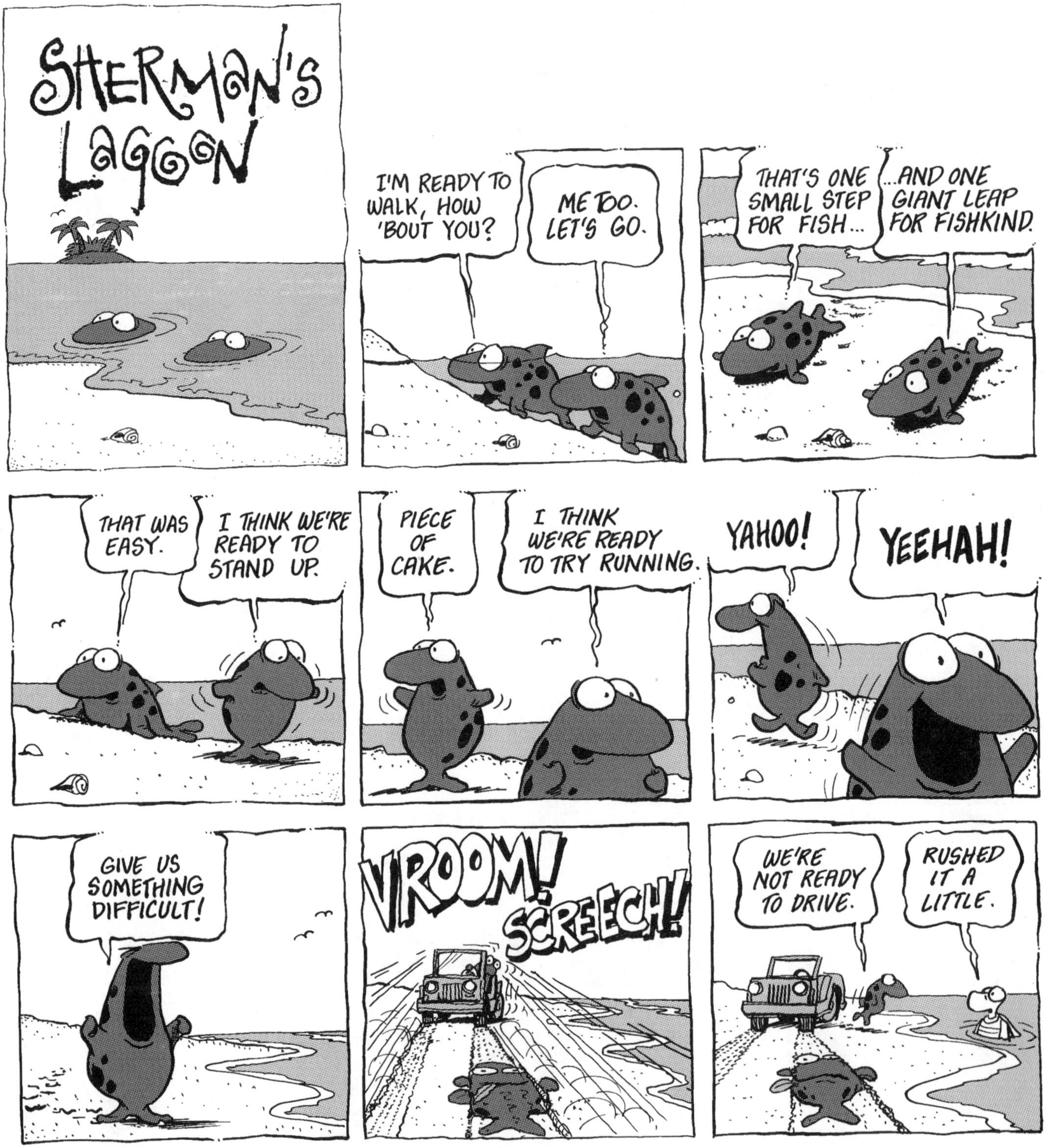
SHERMAN'S LAGOON
I'M READY TO WALK, HOW 'BOUT YOU?
ME TOO. LET'S GO.
THAT'S ONE SMALL STEP FOR FISH...
...AND ONE GIANT LEAP FOR FISHKIND.
THAT WAS EASY.
I THINK WE'RE READY TO STAND UP.
PIECE OF CAKE.
I THINK WE'RE READY TO TRY RUNNING.
YAHOO!
YEEHAH!
GIVE US SOMETHING DIFFICULT!
VROOM!
SCREECH!
WE'RE NOT READY TO DRIVE.
RUSHED IT A LITTLE.

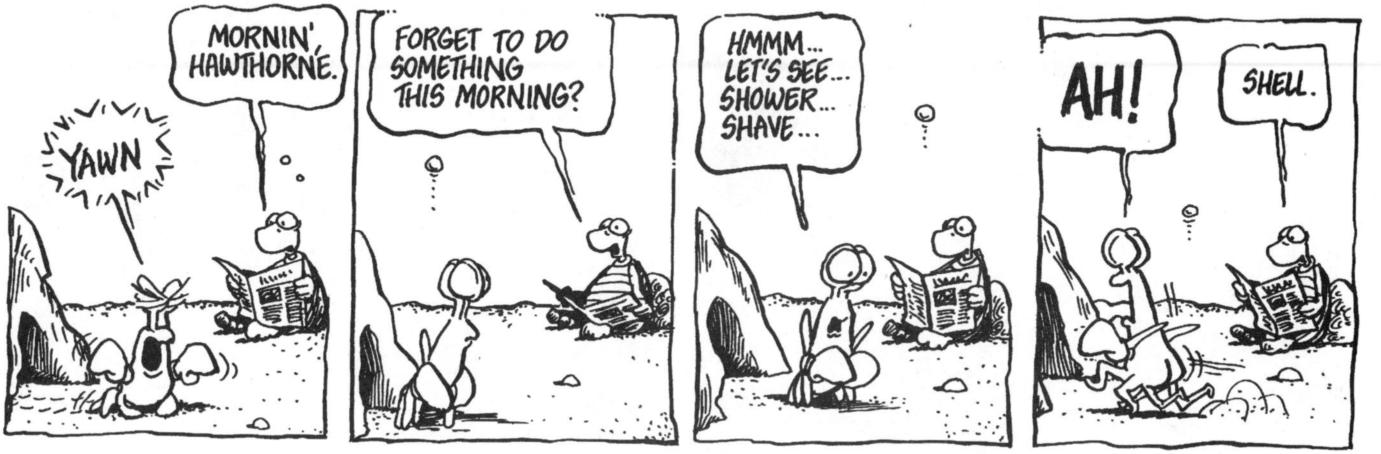
YAWN
MORNIN', HAWTHORNE.
FORGET TO DO SOMETHING THIS MORNING?
HMMM... LET'S SEE... SHOWER... SHAVE...
AH!
SHELL.

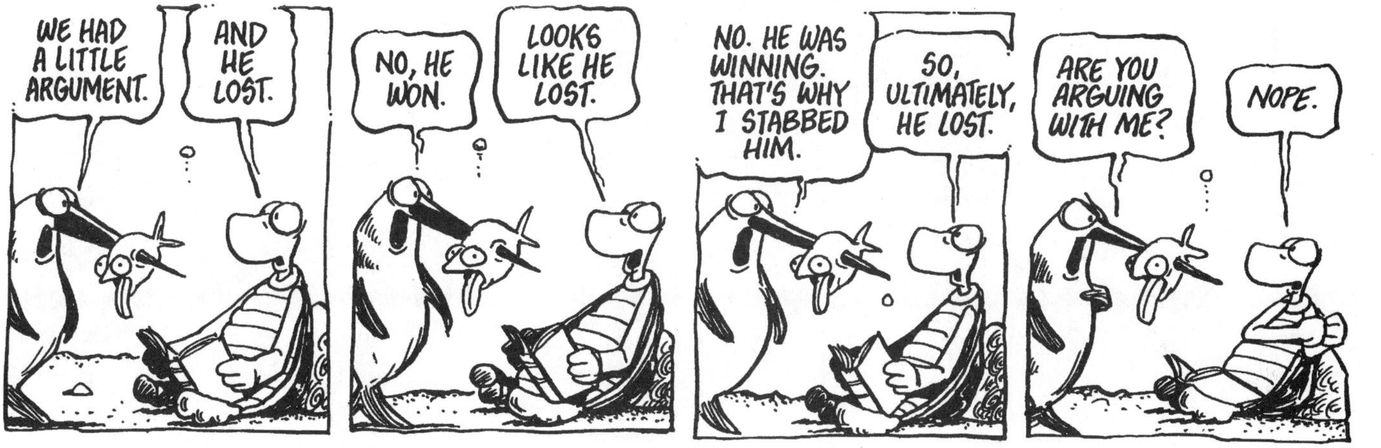
WE HAD A LITTLE ARGUMENT.
AND HE LOST.
NO, HE WON.
LOOKS LIKE HE LOST.
NO. HE WAS WINNING. THAT'S WHY I STABBED HIM.
SO, ULTIMATELY, HE LOST.
ARE YOU ARGUING WITH ME?
NOPE.

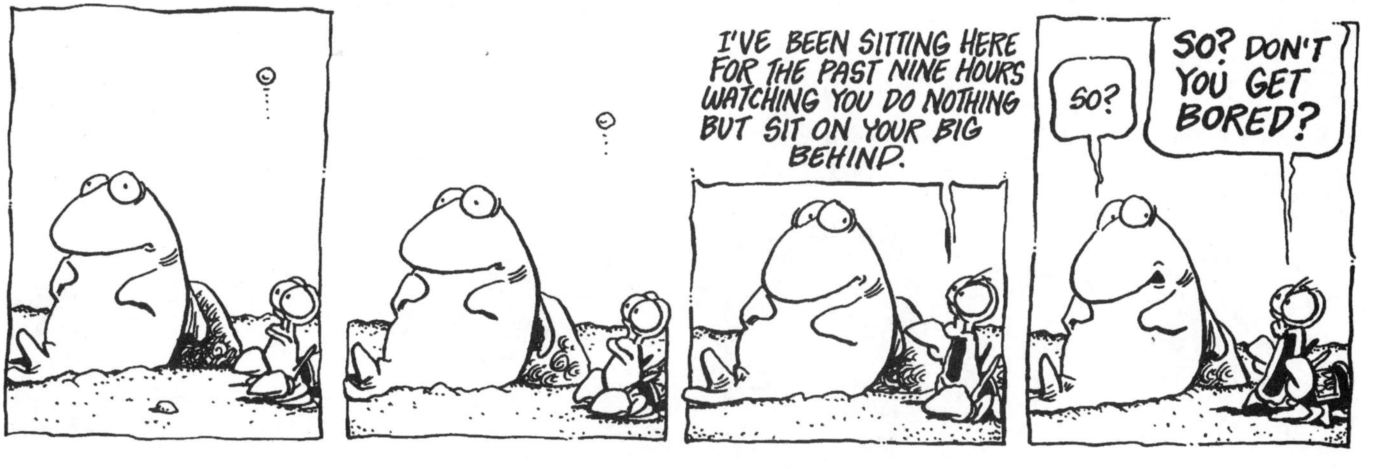
I'VE BEEN SITTING HERE FOR THE PAST NINE HOURS WATCHING YOU DO NOTHING BUT SIT ON YOUR BIG BEHIND.
SO?
SO? DON'T YOU GET BORED?

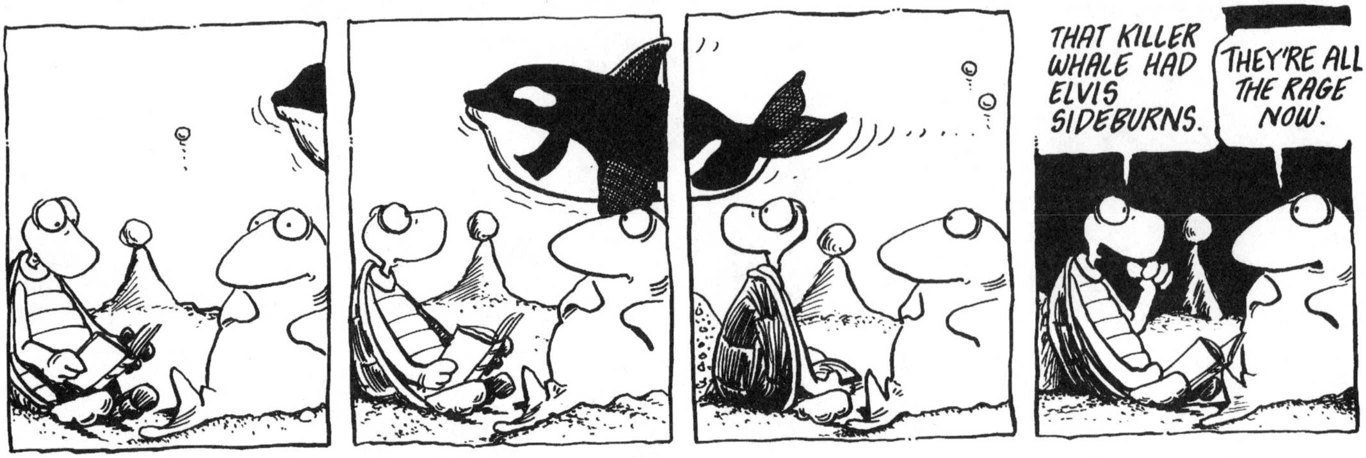
THAT KILLER WHALE HAD ELVIS SIDEBURNS.
THEY'RE ALL THE RAGE NOW.

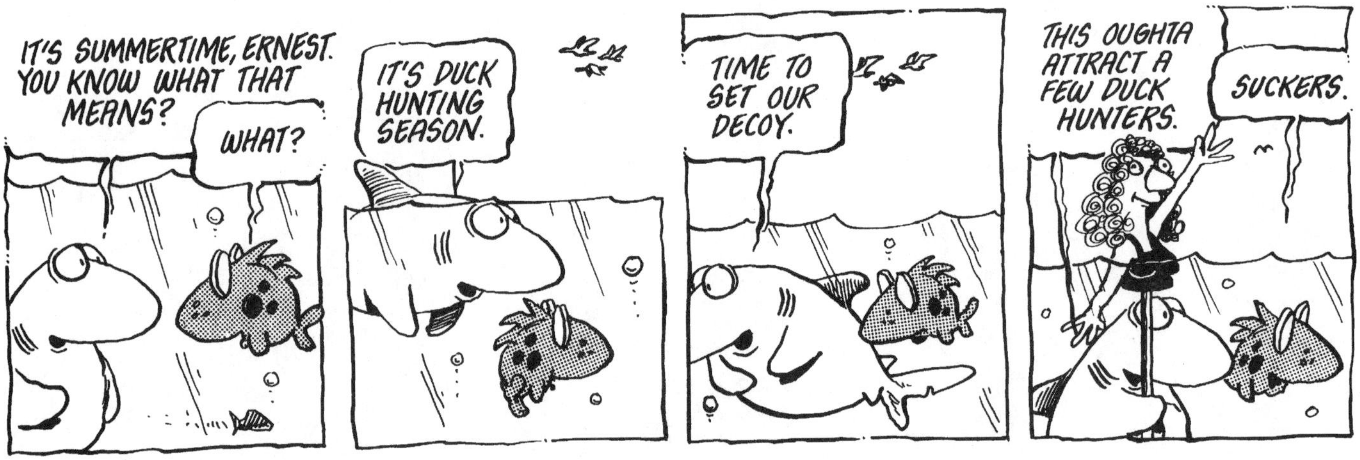
IT'S SUMMERTIME, ERNEST. YOU KNOW WHAT THAT MEANS?
WHAT?
IT'S DUCK HUNTING SEASON.
TIME TO SET OUR DECOY.
THIS OUGHTA ATTRACT A FEW DUCK HUNTERS.
SUCKERS.

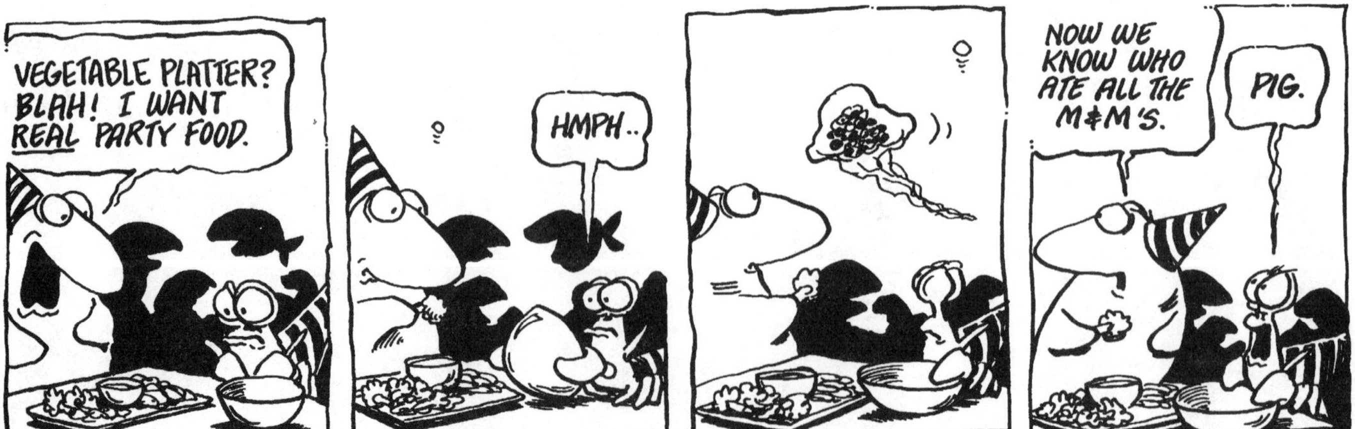
VEGETABLE PLATTER? BLAH! I WANT REAL PARTY FOOD.
HMPH..
NOW WE KNOW WHO ATE ALL THE M&M'S.
PIG.

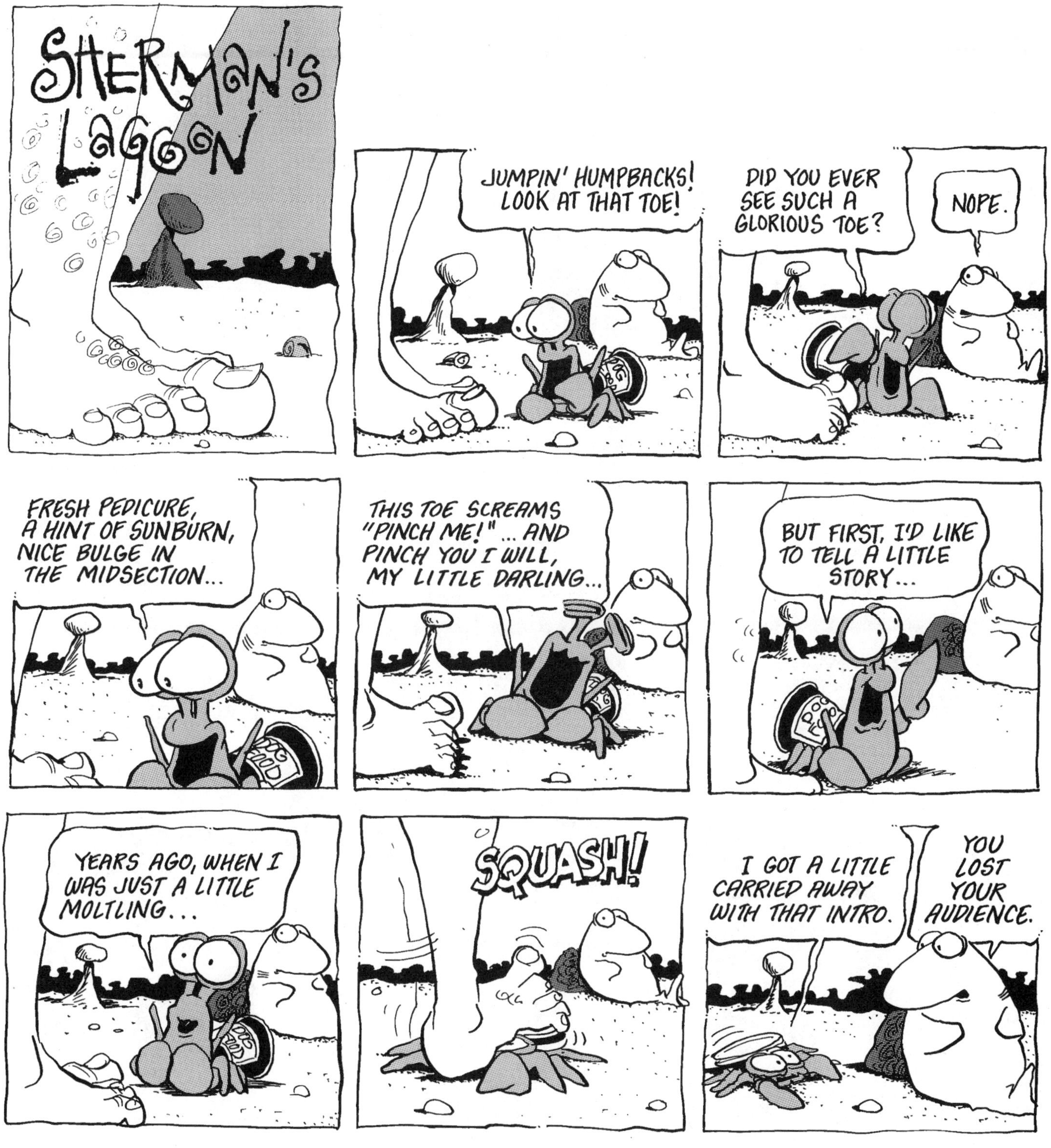
SHERMAN'S LAGOON
JUMPIN' HUMPBACKS! LOOK AT THAT TOE!
DID YOU EVER SEE SUCH A GLORIOUS TOE?
NOPE.
FRESH PEDICURE, A HINT OF SUNBURN, NICE BULGE IN THE MIDSECTION...
THIS TOE SCREAMS "PINCH ME!" ... AND PINCH YOU I WILL, MY LITTLE DARLING...
BUT FIRST, I'D LIKE TO TELL A LITTLE STORY...
YEARS AGO, WHEN I WAS JUST A LITTLE MOLTLING...
SQUASH!
I GOT A LITTLE CARRIED AWAY WITH THAT INTRO.
YOU LOST YOUR AUDIENCE.

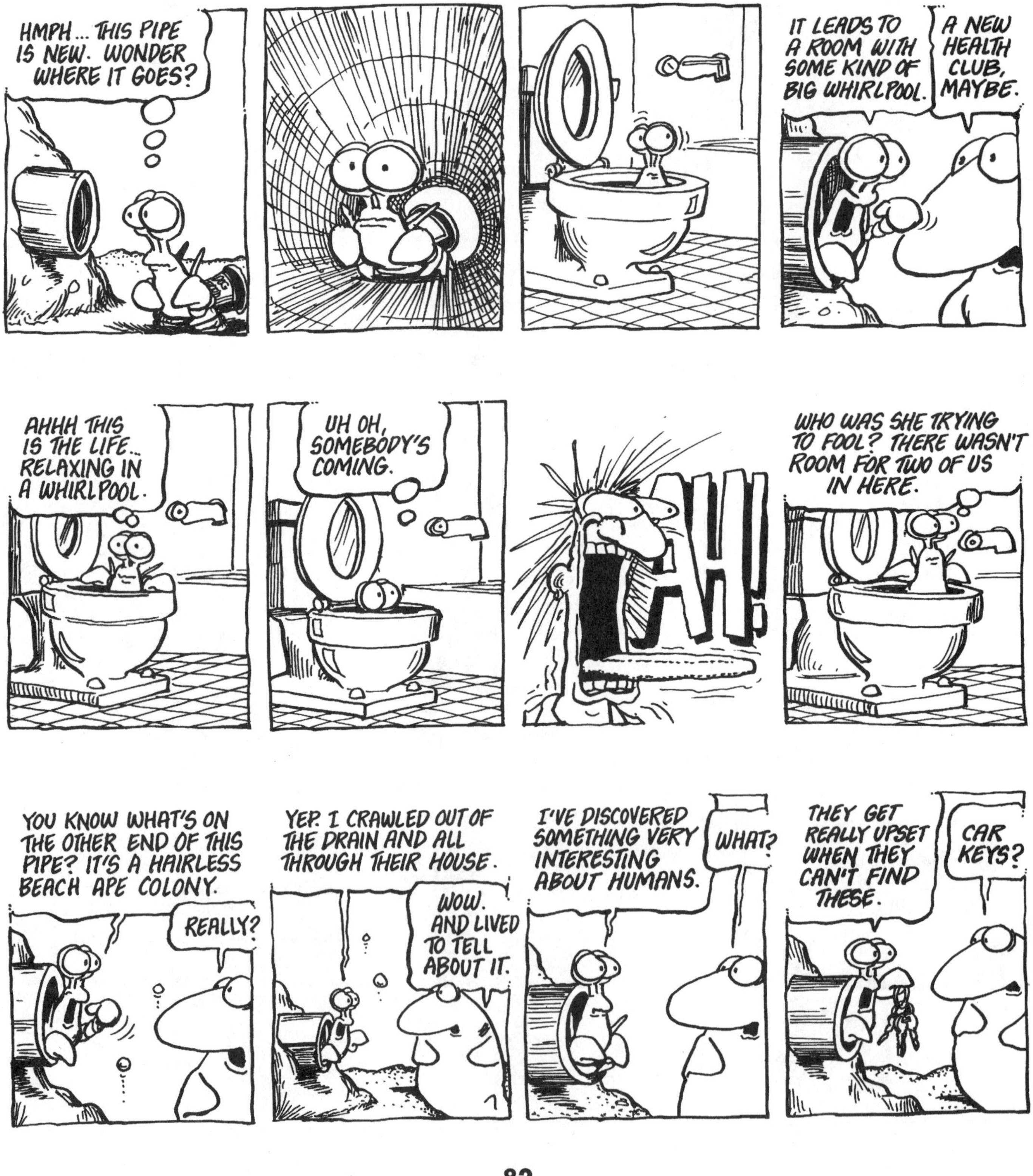
HMPH... THIS PIPE IS NEW. WONDER WHERE IT GOES?
IT LEADS TO A ROOM WITH SOME KIND OF BIG WHIRLPOOL.
A NEW HEALTH CLUB, MAYBE.
AHHH THIS IS THE LIFE... RELAXING IN A WHIRLPOOL.
UH OH, SOMEBODY'S COMING.
AH!
WHO WAS SHE TRYING TO FOOL? THERE WASN'T ROOM FOR TWO OF US IN HERE.
YOU KNOW WHAT'S ON THE OTHER END OF THIS PIPE? IT'S A HAIRLESS BEACH APE COLONY.
REALLY?
YEP. I CRAWLED OUT OF THE DRAIN AND ALL THROUGH THEIR HOUSE.
WOW. AND LIVED TO TELL ABOUT IT.
I'VE DISCOVERED SOMETHING VERY INTERESTING ABOUT HUMANS.
WHAT?
THEY GET REALLY UPSET WHEN THEY CAN'T FIND THESE.
CAR KEYS?

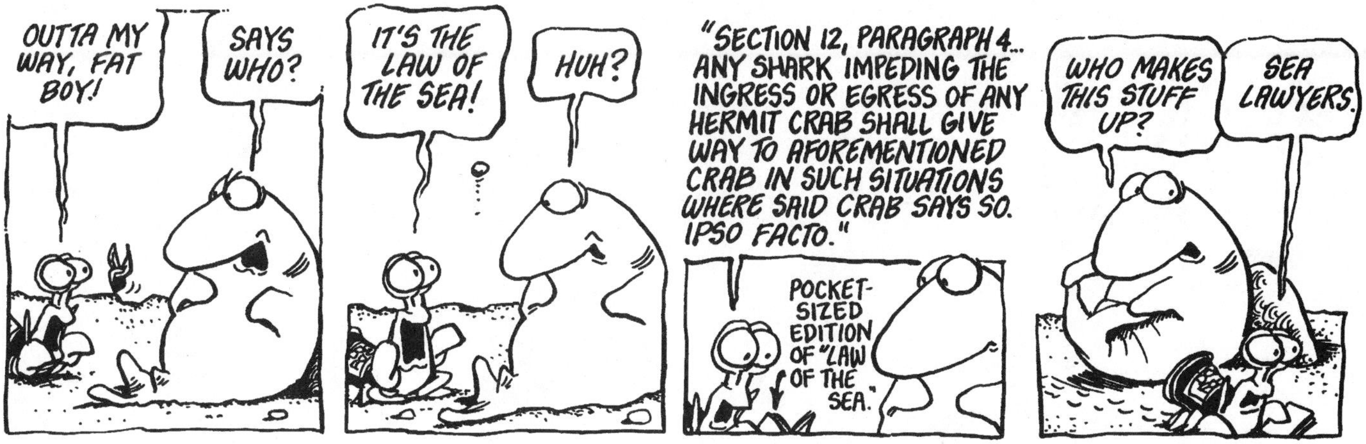
OUTTA MY WAY, FAT BOY!
SAYS WHO?
IT'S THE LAW OF THE SEA!
HUH?
"SECTION 12, PARAGRAPH 4... ANY SHARK IMPEDING THE INGRESS OR EGRESS OF ANY HERMIT CRAB SHALL GIVE WAY TO AFOREMENTIONED CRAB IN SUCH SITUATIONS WHERE SAID CRAB SAYS SO. IPSO FACTO."
POCKET-SIZED EDITION OF "LAW OF THE SEA."
WHO MAKES THIS STUFF UP?
SEA LAWYERS.

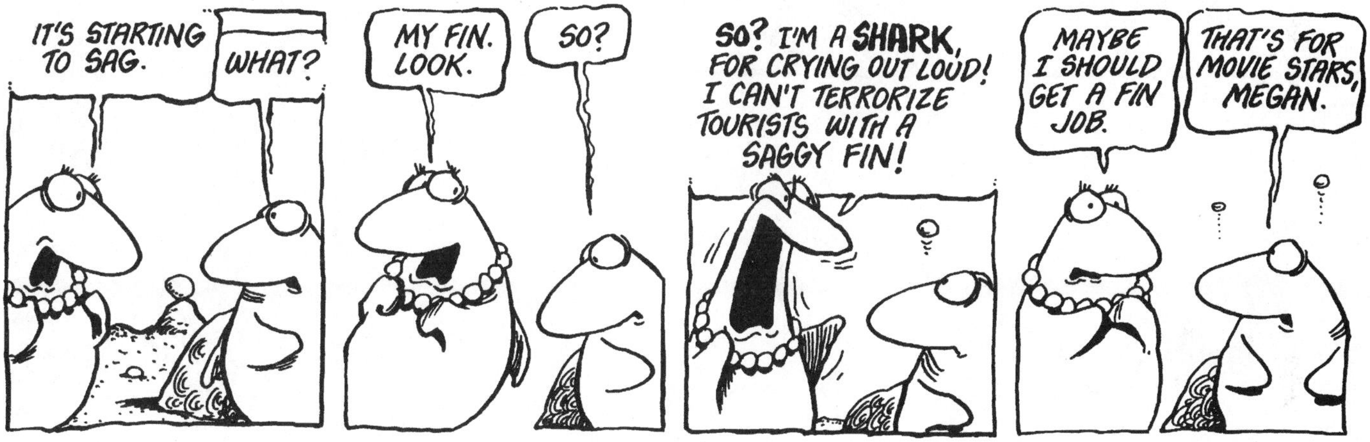
IT'S STARTING TO SAG.
WHAT?
MY FIN. LOOK.
SO?
SO? I'M A SHARK, FOR CRYING OUT LOUD! I CAN'T TERRORIZE TOURISTS WITH A SAGGY FIN!
MAYBE I SHOULD GET A FIN JOB.
THAT'S FOR MOVIE STARS, MEGAN.

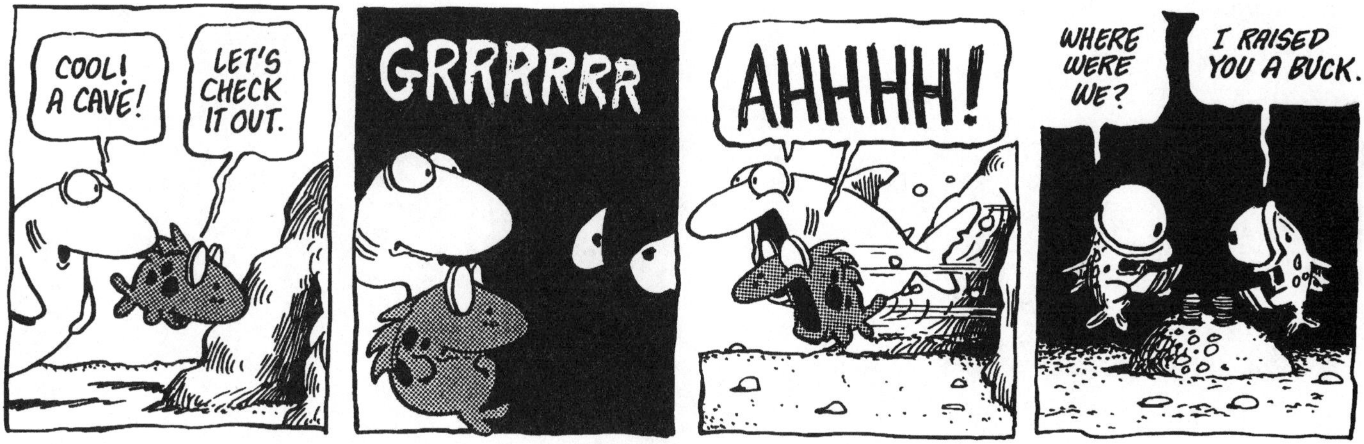
COOL! A CAVE!
LET'S CHECK IT OUT.
GRRRRRR
AHHHH!
WHERE WERE WE?
I RAISED YOU A BUCK.

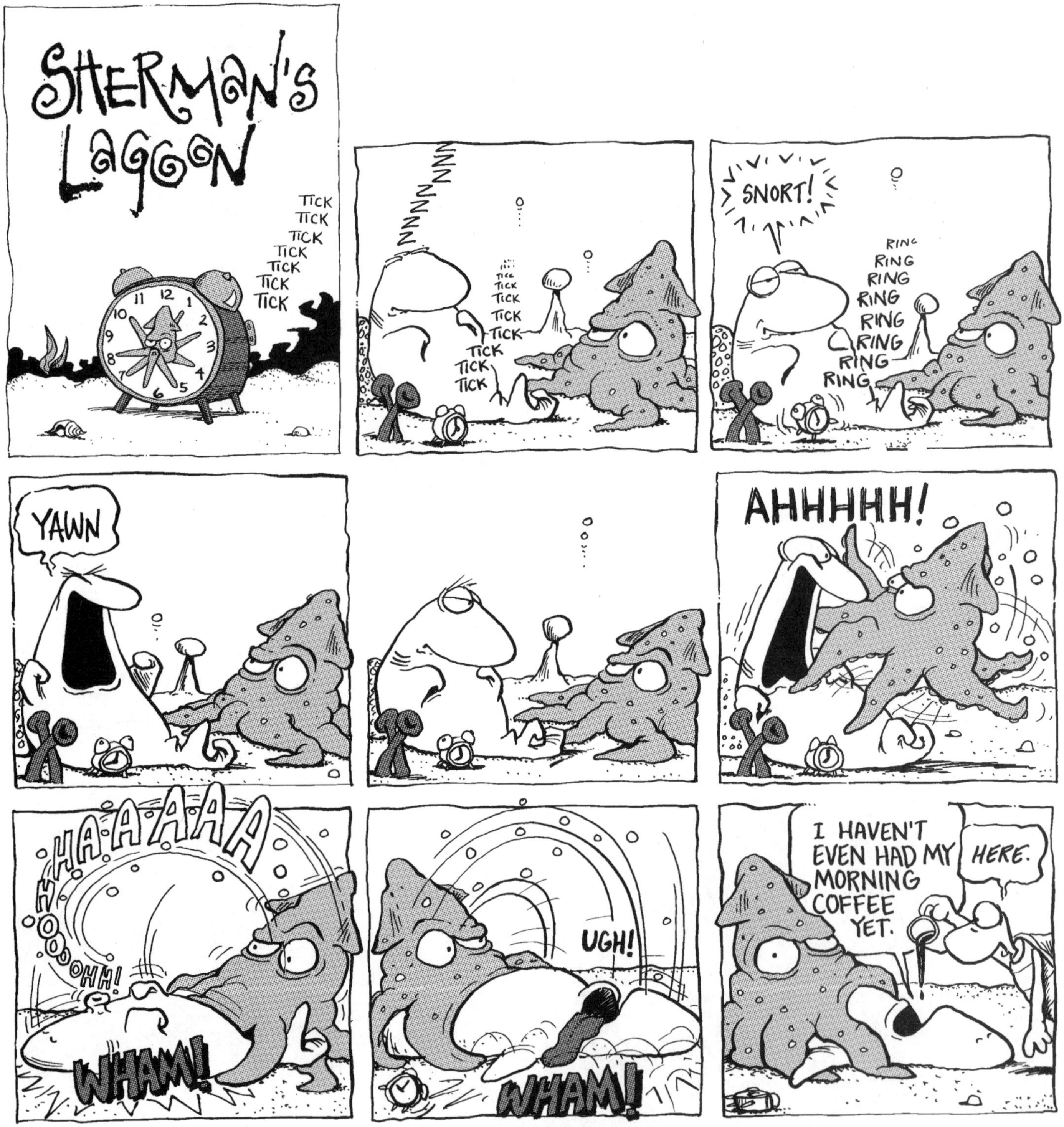
SHERMAN'S LAGOON
TICK TICK TICK TICK TICK TICK TICK
TICK TICK TICK TICK TICK TICK TICK
SNORT!
RING RING RING RING RING RING RING RING
YAWN
AHHHHH!
HAAAAAA HOOOOOHH!
WHAM!
UGH!
WHAM!
I HAVEN'T EVEN HAD MY MORNING COFFEE YET.
HERE.

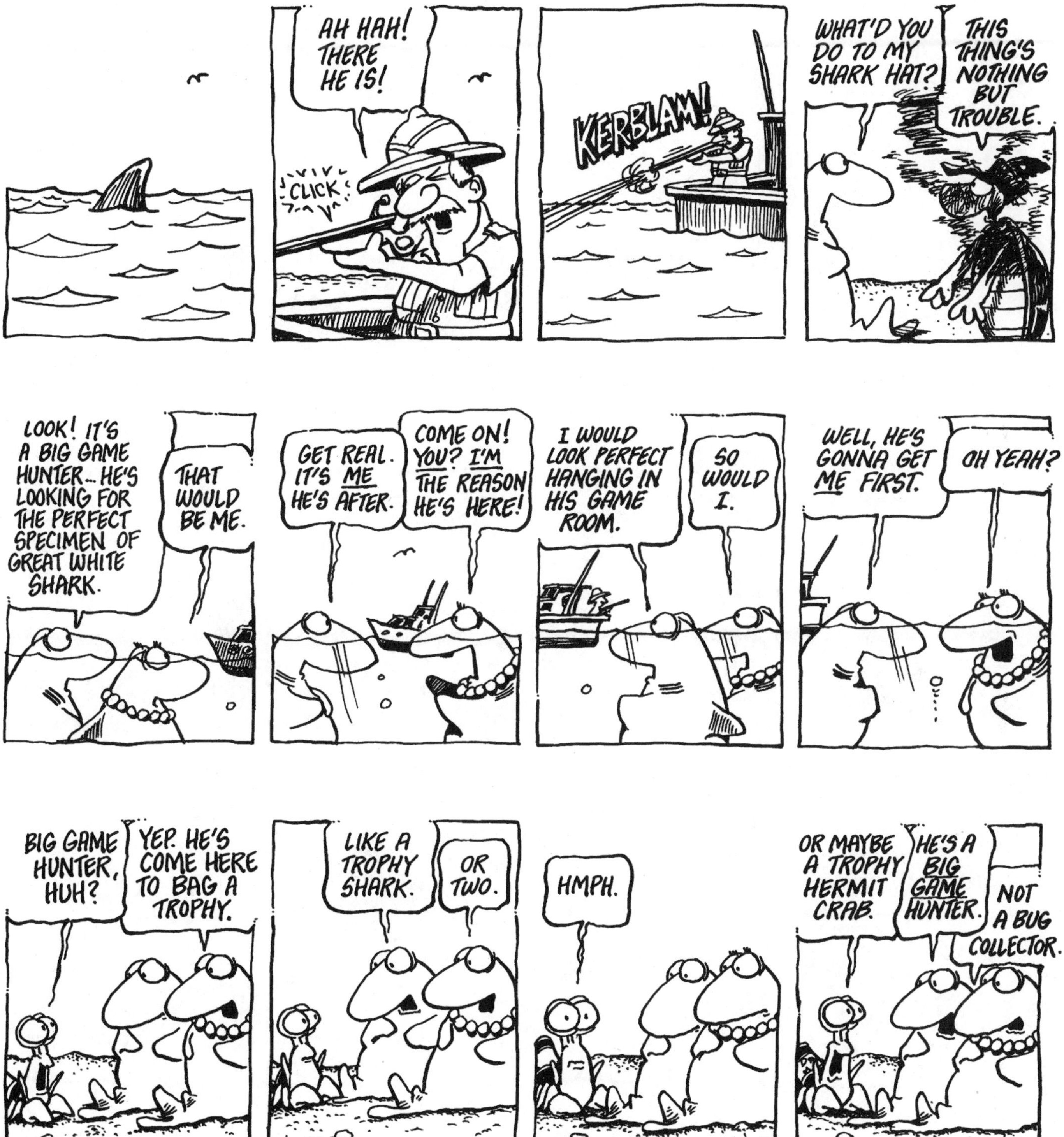
AH HAH! THERE HE IS!
CLICK
KERBLAM!
WHAT'D YOU DO TO MY SHARK HAT?
THIS THING'S NOTHING BUT TROUBLE.
LOOK! IT'S A BIG GAME HUNTER... HE'S LOOKING FOR THE PERFECT SPECIMEN OF GREAT WHITE SHARK.
THAT WOULD BE ME.
GET REAL. IT'S ME HE'S AFTER.
COME ON! YOU? I'M THE REASON HE'S HERE!
I WOULD LOOK PERFECT HANGING IN HIS GAME ROOM.
SO WOULD I.
WELL, HE'S GONNA GET ME FIRST.
OH YEAH?
BIG GAME HUNTER, HUH?
YEP. HE'S COME HERE TO BAG A TROPHY.
LIKE A TROPHY SHARK.
OR TWO.
HMPH.
OR MAYBE A TROPHY HERMIT CRAB.
HE'S A BIG GAME HUNTER.
NOT A BUG COLLECTOR.

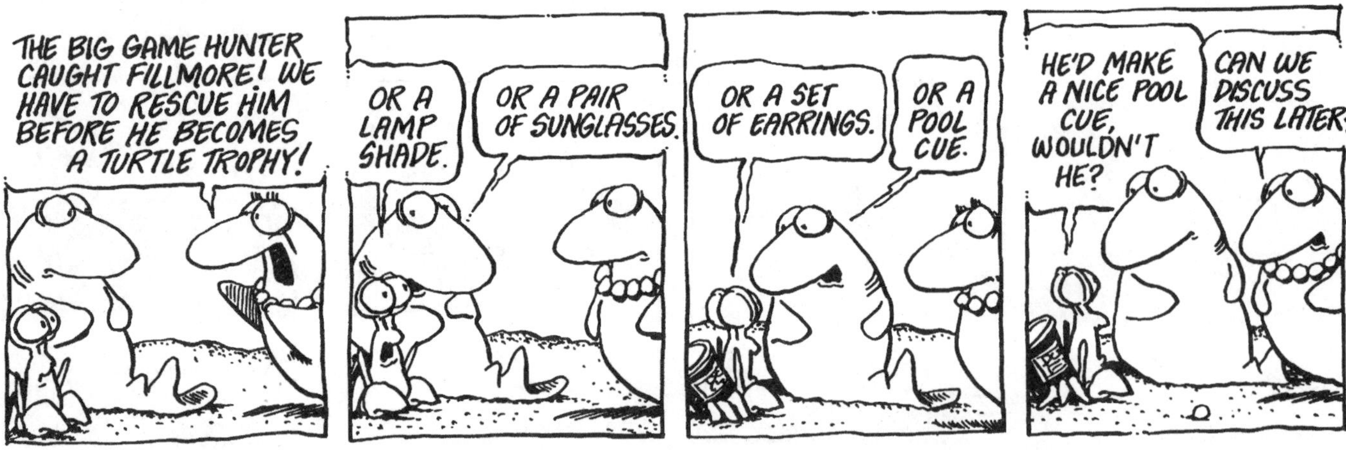
THE BIG GAME HUNTER CAUGHT FILLMORE! WE HAVE TO RESCUE HIM BEFORE HE BECOMES A TURTLE TROPHY!
OR A LAMP SHADE.
OR A PAIR OF SUNGLASSES.
OR A SET OF EARRINGS.
OR A POOL CUE.
HE'D MAKE A NICE POOL CUE, WOULDN'T HE?
CAN WE DISCUSS THIS LATER?

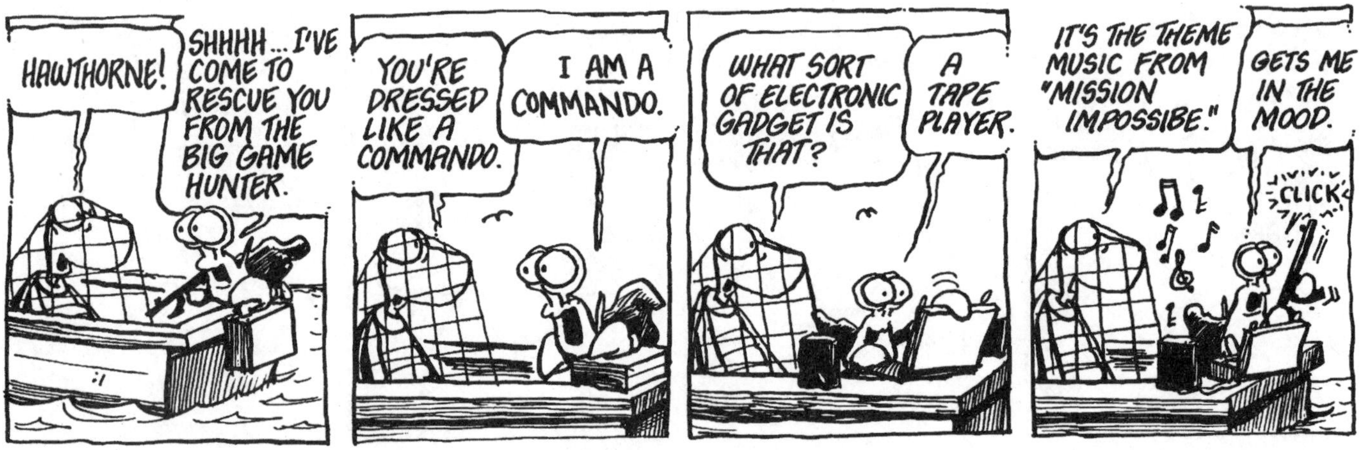
HAWTHORNE!
SHHHH... I'VE COME TO RESCUE YOU FROM THE BIG GAME HUNTER.
YOU'RE DRESSED LIKE A COMMANDO.
I AM A COMMANDO.
WHAT SORT OF ELECTRONIC GADGET IS THAT?
A TAPE PLAYER.
IT'S THE THEME MUSIC FROM "MISSION IMPOSSIBE."
GETS ME IN THE MOOD.
CLICK

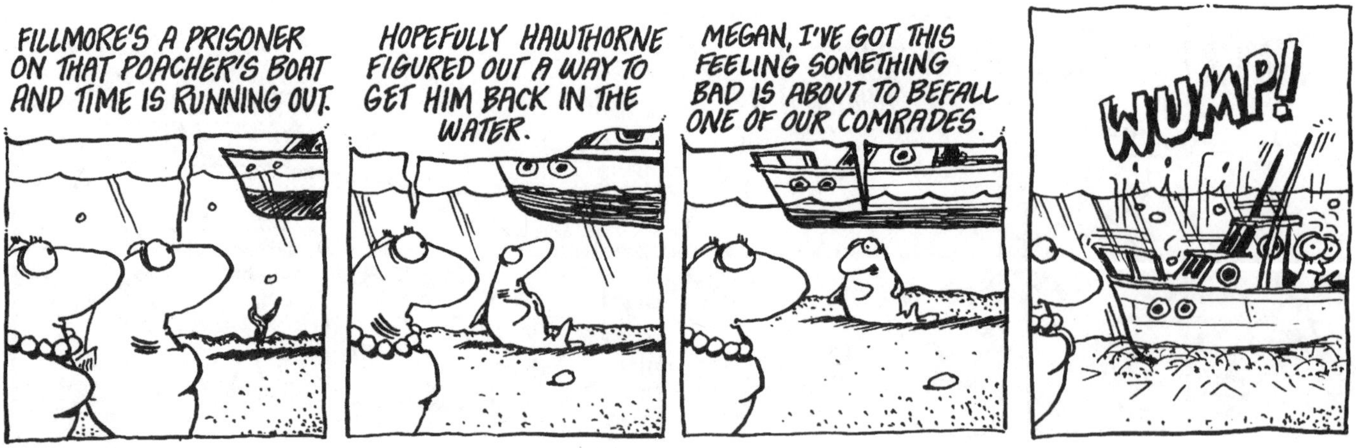
FILLMORE'S A PRISONER ON THAT POACHER'S BOAT AND TIME IS RUNNING OUT.
HOPEFULLY HAWTHORNE FIGURED OUT A WAY TO GET HIM BACK IN THE WATER.
MEGAN, I'VE GOT THIS FEELING SOMETHING BAD IS ABOUT TO BEFALL ONE OF OUR COMRADES.
WUMP!

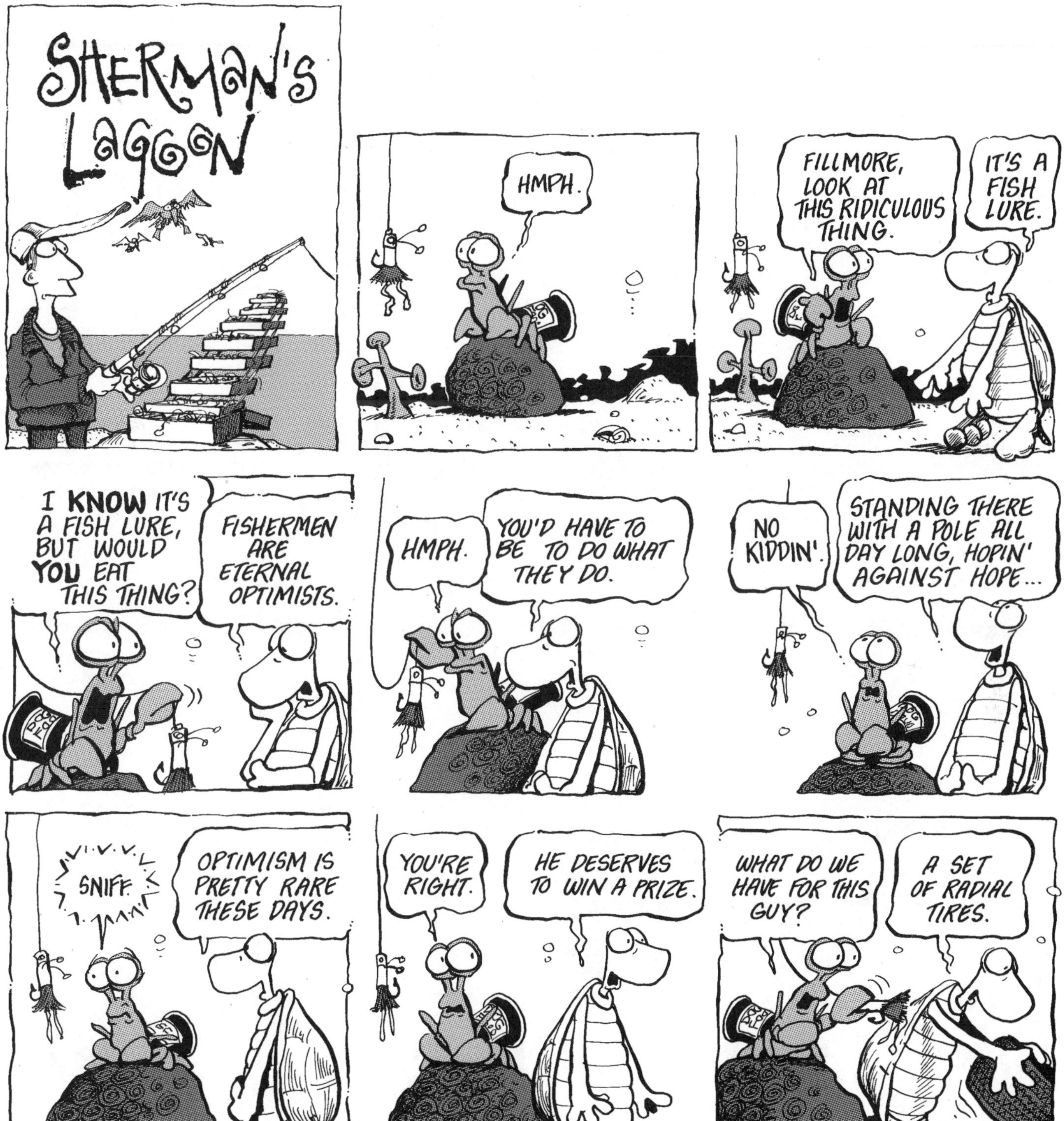
SHERMAN'S LAGOON
HMPH.
FILLMORE, LOOK AT THIS RIDICULOUS THING.
IT'S A FISH LURE.
I KNOW IT'S A FISH LURE, BUT WOULD YOU EAT THIS THING?
FISHERMEN ARE ETERNAL OPTIMISTS.
HMPH.
YOU'D HAVE TO BE TO DO WHAT THEY DO.
NO KIDDIN'.
STANDING THERE WITH A POLE ALL DAY LONG, HOPIN' AGAINST HOPE...
SNIFF.
OPTIMISM IS PRETTY RARE THESE DAYS.
YOU'RE RIGHT.
HE DESERVES TO WIN A PRIZE.
WHAT DO WE HAVE FOR THIS GUY?
A SET OF RADIAL TIRES.

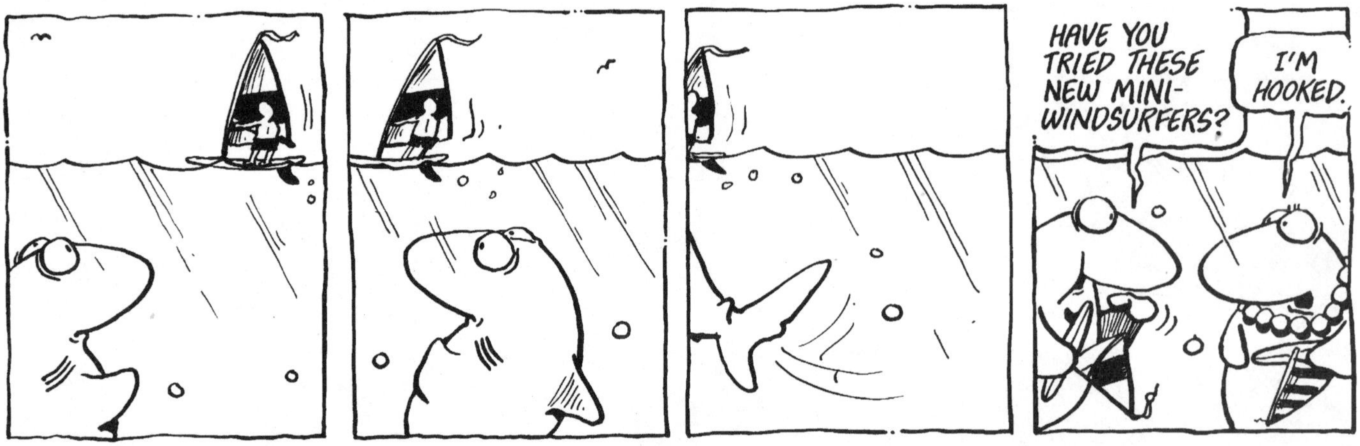
HAVE YOU TRIED THESE NEW MINI-WINDSURFERS?
I'M HOOKED.

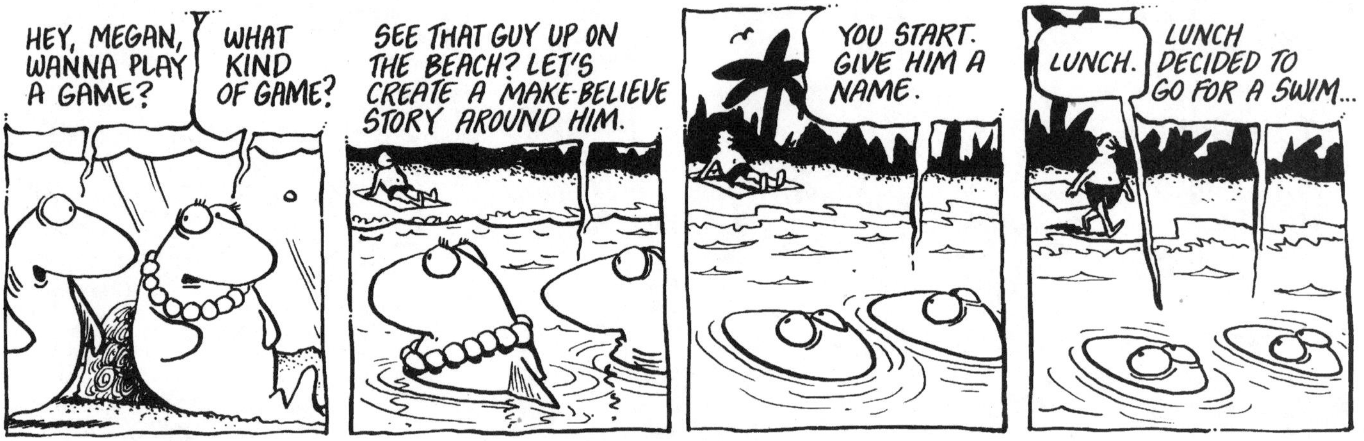
HEY, MEGAN, WANNA PLAY A GAME?
WHAT KIND OF GAME?
SEE THAT GUY UP ON THE BEACH? LET'S CREATE A MAKE-BELIEVE STORY AROUND HIM.
YOU START. GIVE HIM A NAME.
LUNCH.
LUNCH DECIDED TO GO FOR A SWIM...

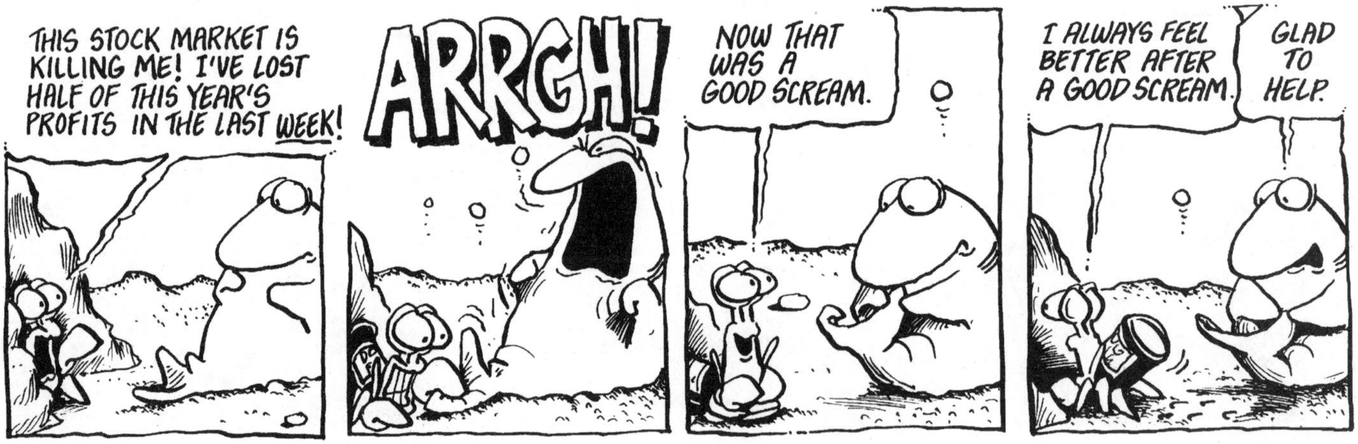
THIS STOCK MARKET IS KILLING ME! I'VE LOST HALF OF THIS YEAR'S PROFITS IN THE LAST WEEK!
ARRGH!
NOW THAT WAS A GOOD SCREAM.
I ALWAYS FEEL BETTER AFTER A GOOD SCREAM.
GLAD TO HELP.

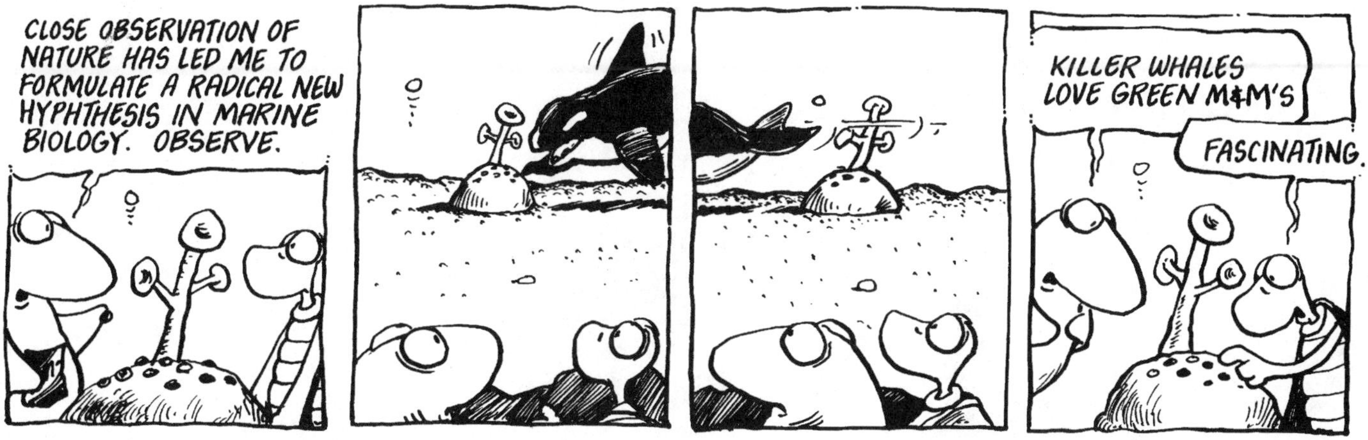
CLOSE OBSERVATION OF NATURE HAS LED ME TO FORMULATE A RADICAL NEW HYPHTHESIS IN MARINE BIOLOGY. OBSERVE.
KILLER WHALES LOVE GREEN M&M'S
FASCINATING.

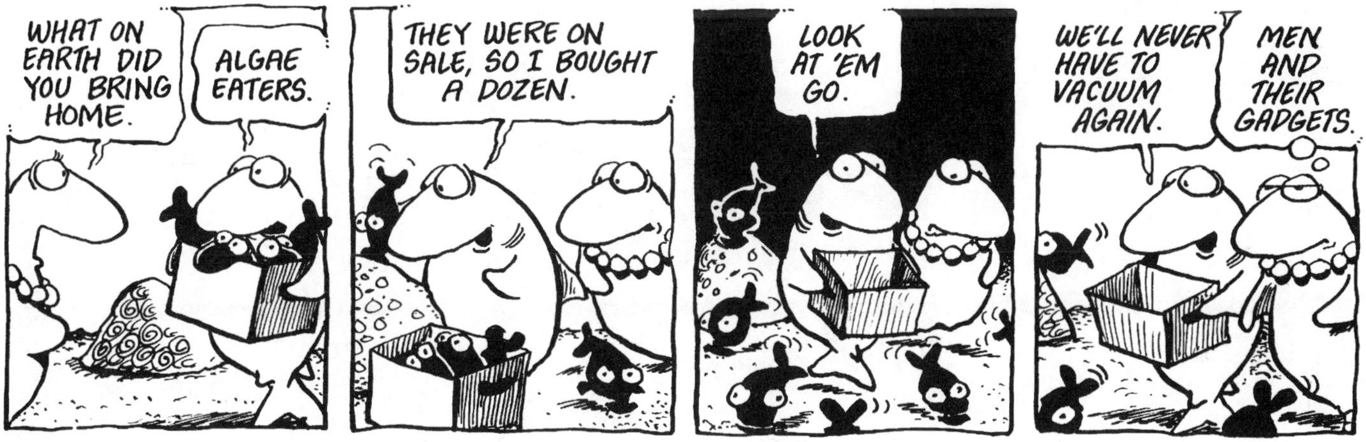
WHAT ON EARTH DID YOU BRING HOME.
ALGAE EATERS.
THEY WERE ON SALE, SO I BOUGHT A DOZEN.
LOOK AT 'EM GO.
WE'LL NEVER HAVE TO VACUUM AGAIN.
MEN AND THEIR GADGETS.

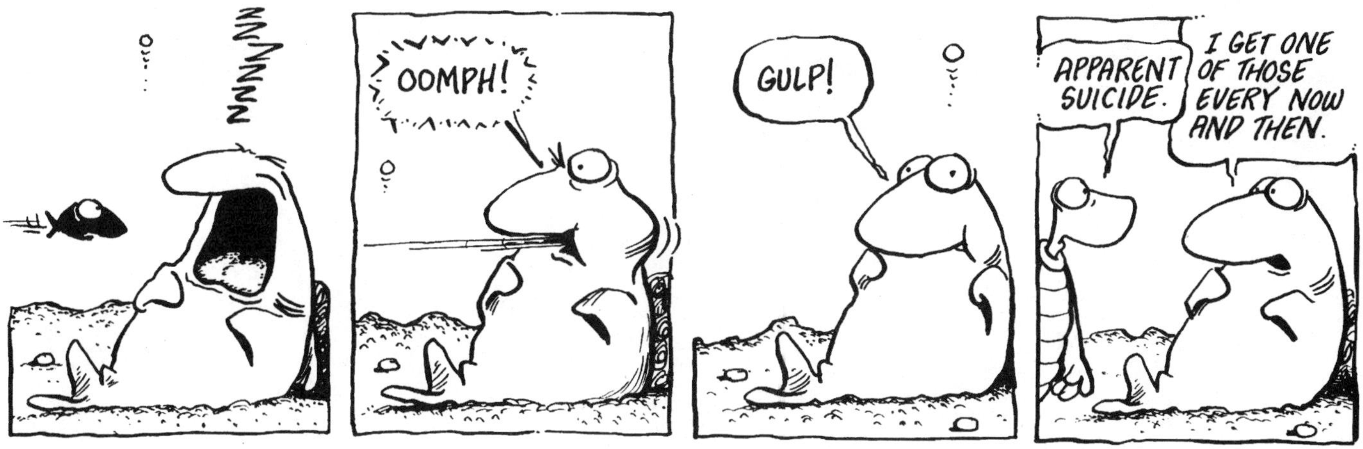
OOMPH!
GULP!
APPARENT SUICIDE.
I GET ONE OF THOSE EVERY NOW AND THEN.

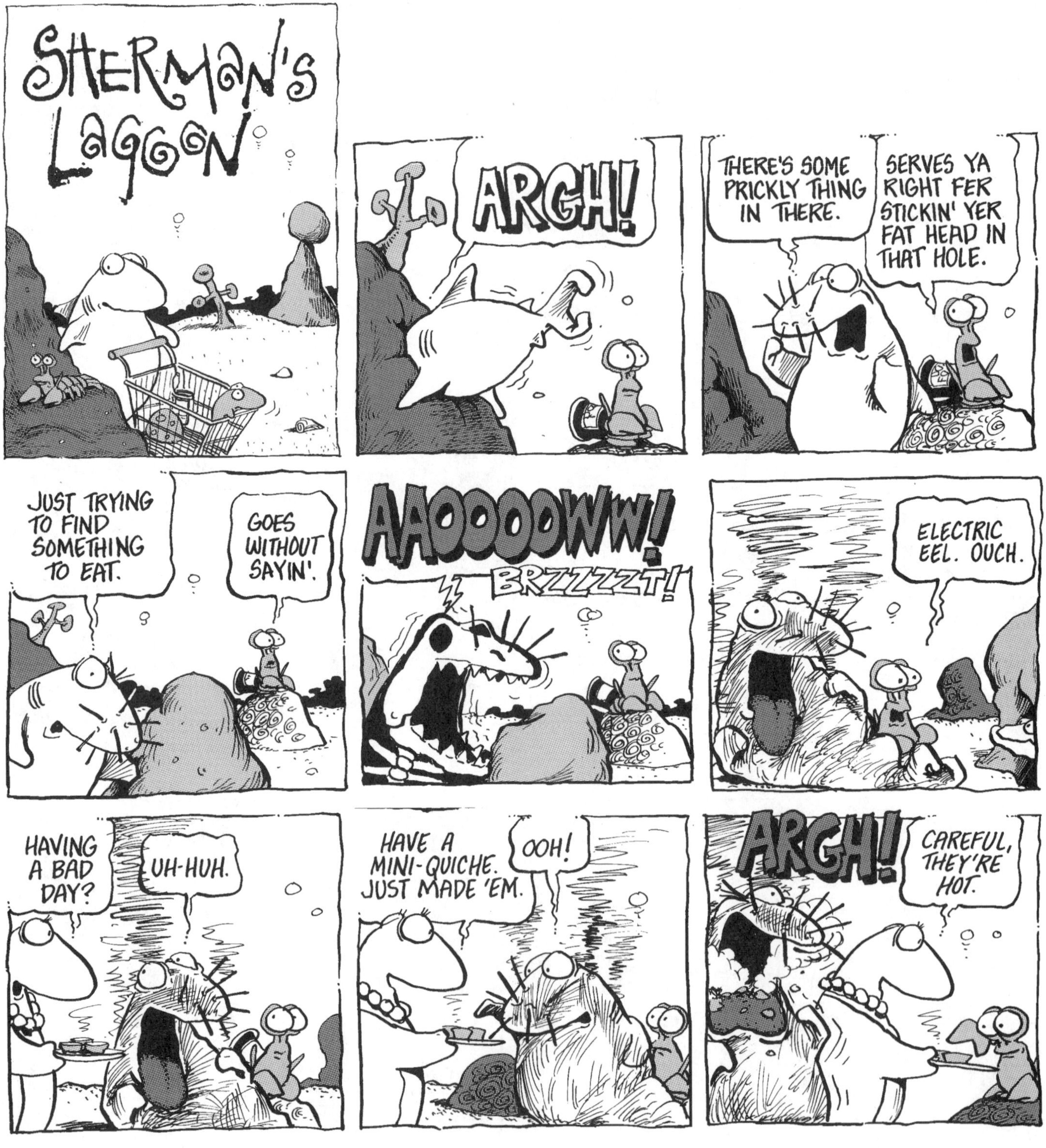
SHERMAN'S LAGOON
ARGH!
THERE'S SOME PRICKLY THING IN THERE.
SERVES YA RIGHT FER STICKIN' YER FAT HEAD IN THAT HOLE.
JUST TRYING TO FIND SOMETHING TO EAT.
GOES WITHOUT SAYIN'.
AAOOOOWW!
BRZZZZZT!
ELECTRIC EEL. OUCH.
HAVING A BAD DAY?
UH-HUH.
HAVE A MINI-QUICHE. JUST MADE 'EM.
OOH!
ARGH!
CAREFUL, THEY'RE HOT.

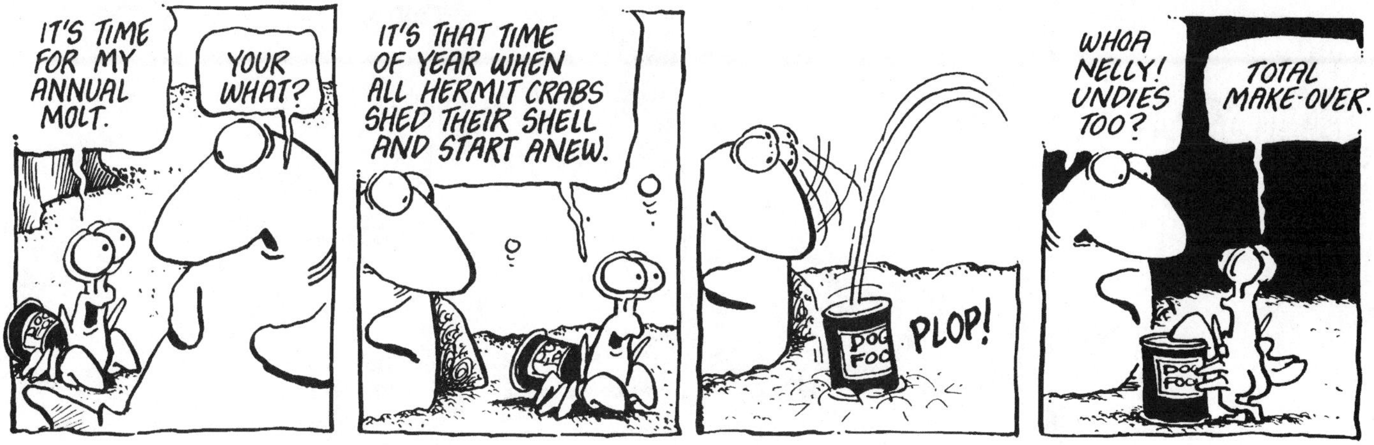
IT'S TIME FOR MY ANNUAL MOLT.
YOUR WHAT?
IT'S THAT TIME OF YEAR WHEN ALL HERMIT CRABS SHED THEIR SHELL AND START ANEW.
PLOP!
WHOA NELLY! UNDIES TOO?
TOTAL MAKE-OVER.

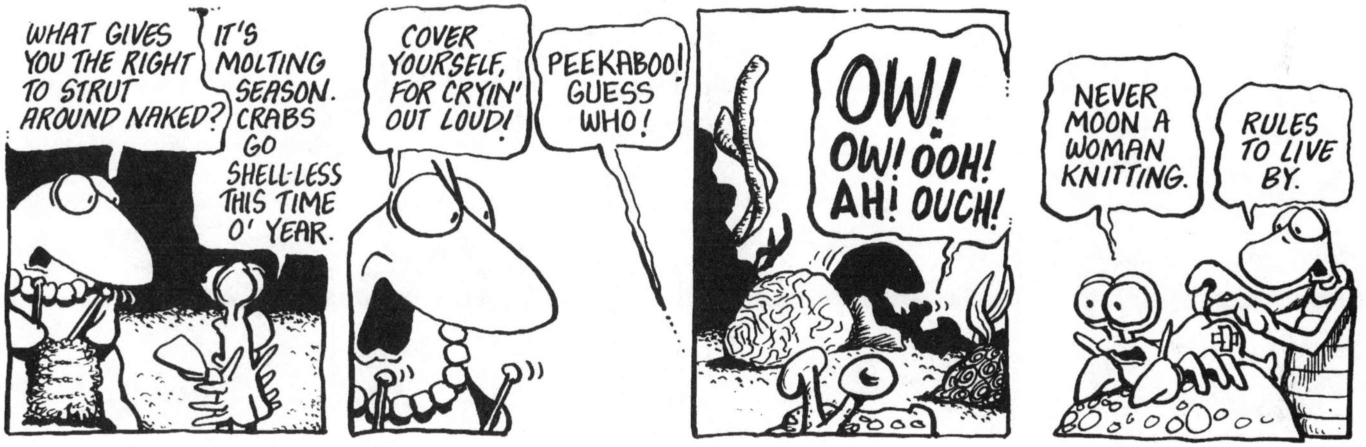
WHAT GIVES YOU THE RIGHT TO STRUT AROUND NAKED?
IT'S MOLTING SEASON. CRABS GO SHELL-LESS THIS TIME O' YEAR.
COVER YOURSELF, FOR CRYIN' OUT LOUD!
PEEKABOO! GUESS WHO!
OW! OW! OOH! AH! OUCH!
NEVER MOON A WOMAN KNITTING.
RULES TO LIVE BY.

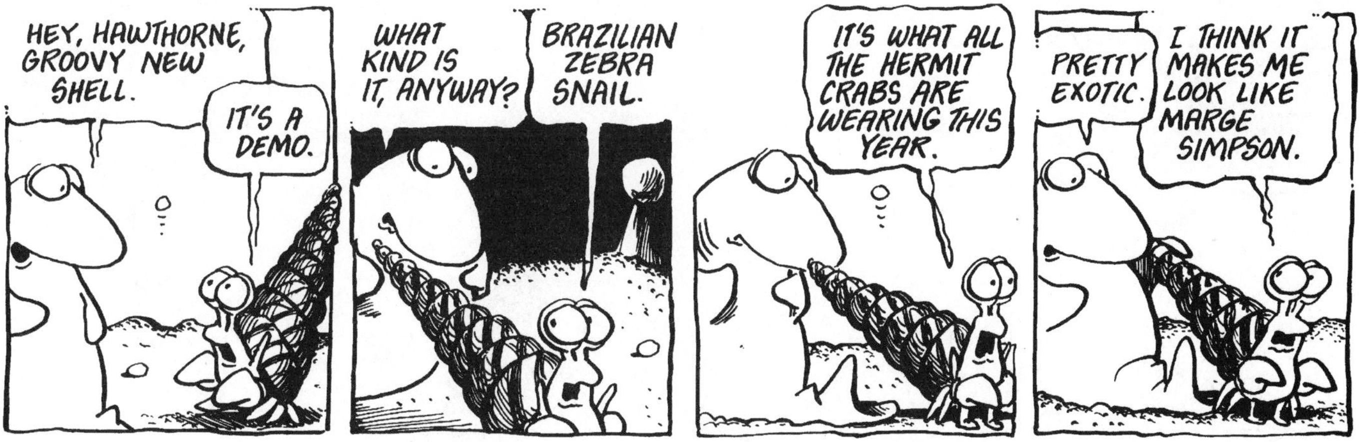
HEY, HAWTHORNE, GROOVY NEW SHELL.
IT'S A DEMO.
WHAT KIND IS IT, ANYWAY?
BRAZILIAN ZEBRA SNAIL.
IT'S WHAT ALL THE HERMIT CRABS ARE WEARING THIS YEAR.
PRETTY EXOTIC.
I THINK IT MAKES ME LOOK LIKE MARGE SIMPSON.

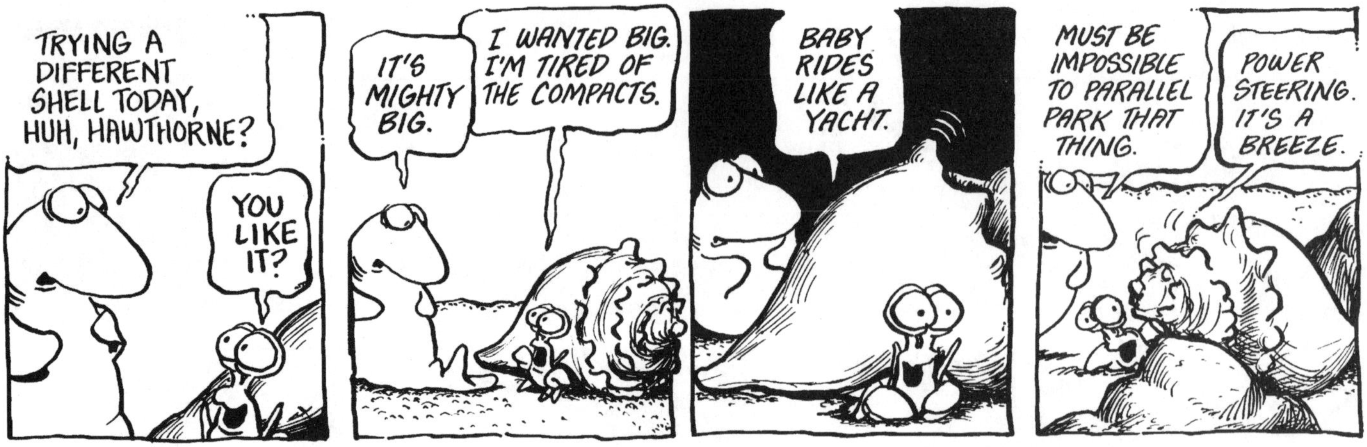
TRYING A DIFFERENT SHELL TODAY, HUH, HAWTHORNE?
YOU LIKE IT?
IT'S MIGHTY BIG.
I WANTED BIG. I'M TIRED OF THE COMPACTS.
BABY RIDES LIKE A YACHT.
MUST BE IMPOSSIBLE TO PARALLEL PARK THAT THING.
POWER STEERING. IT'S A BREEZE.

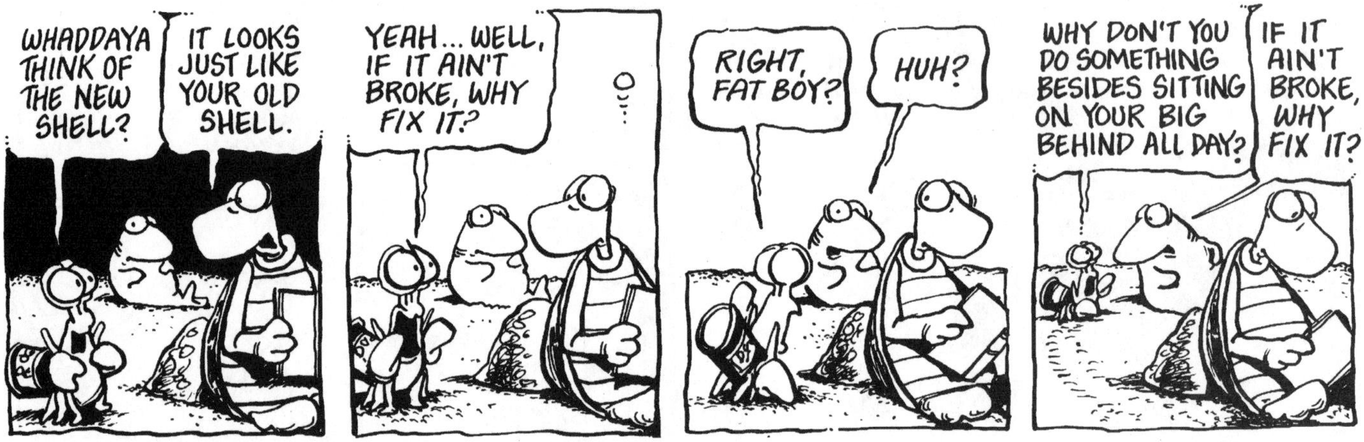
WHADDAYA THINK OF THE NEW SHELL?
IT LOOKS JUST LIKE YOUR OLD SHELL.
YEAH... WELL, IF IT AIN'T BROKE, WHY FIX IT?
RIGHT, FAT BOY?
HUH?
WHY DON'T YOU DO SOMETHING BESIDES SITTING ON YOUR BIG BEHIND ALL DAY?
IF IT AIN'T BROKE, WHY FIX IT?

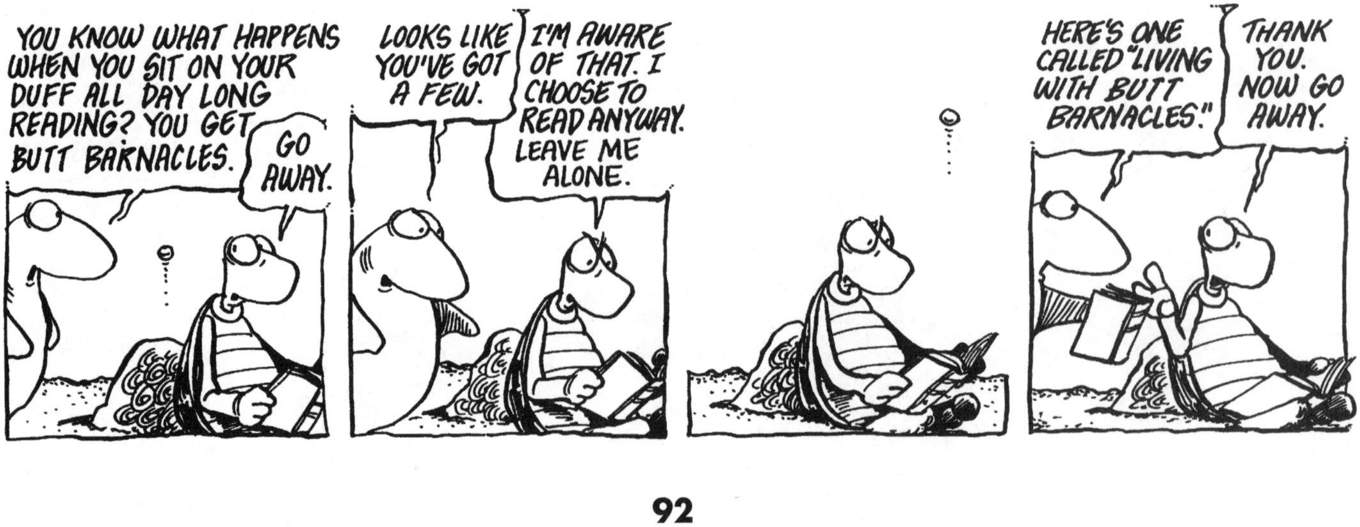
YOU KNOW WHAT HAPPENS WHEN YOU SIT ON YOUR DUFF ALL DAY LONG READING? YOU GET BUTT BARNACLES.
GO AWAY.
LOOKS LIKE YOU'VE GOT A FEW.
I'M AWARE OF THAT. I CHOOSE TO READ ANYWAY. LEAVE ME ALONE.
HERE'S ONE CALLED "LIVING WITH BUTT BARNACLES."
THANK YOU. NOW GO AWAY.

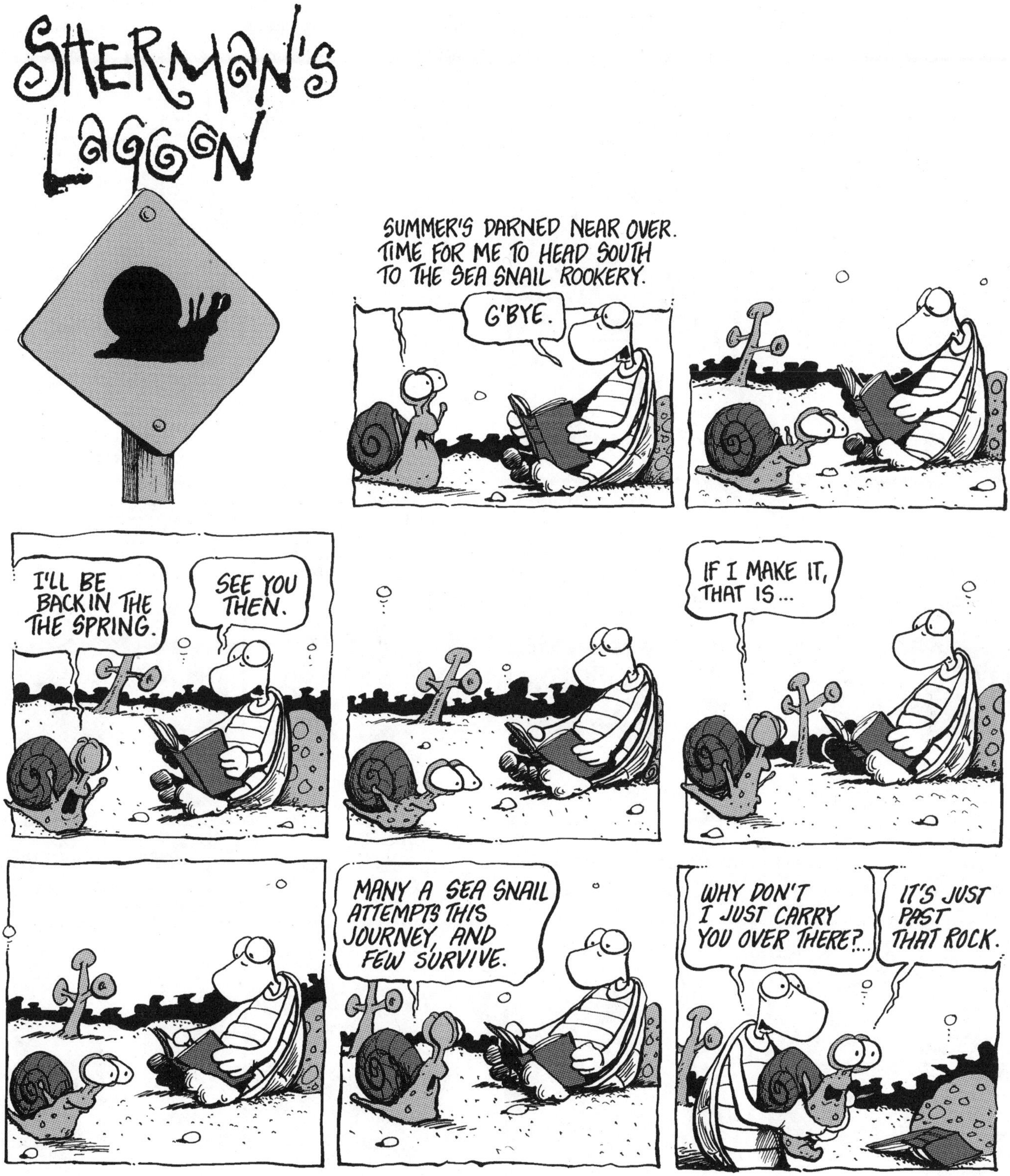
SHERMAN'S LAGOON
SUMMER'S DARNED NEAR OVER. TIME FOR ME TO HEAD SOUTH TO THE SEA SNAIL ROOKERY.
G'BYE.
I'LL BE BACK IN THE THE SPRING.
SEE YOU THEN.
IF I MAKE IT, THAT IS...
MANY A SEA SNAIL ATTEMPTS THIS JOURNEY, AND FEW SURVIVE.
WHY DON'T I JUST CARRY YOU OVER THERE?...
IT'S JUST PAST THAT ROCK.

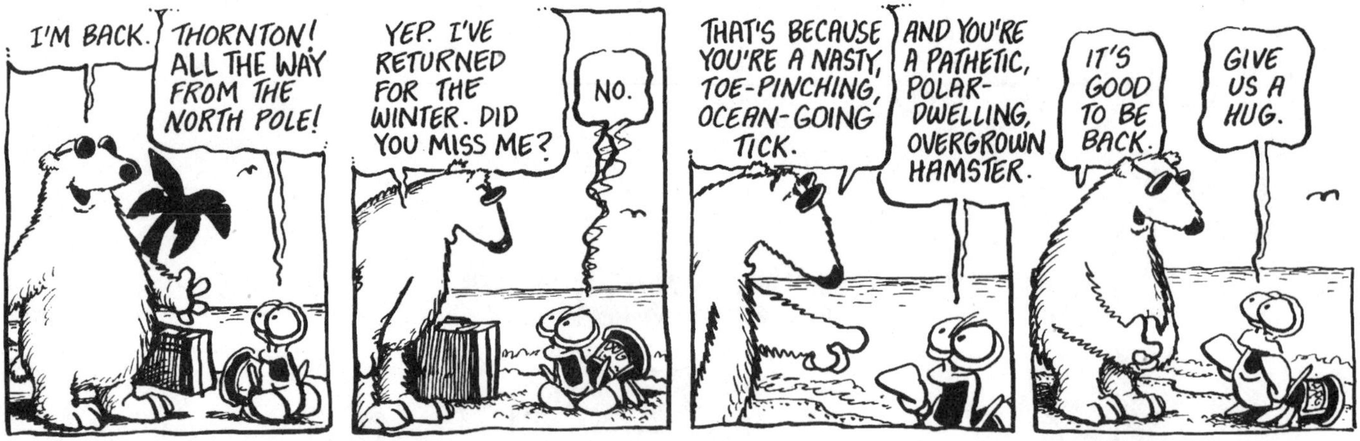
I'M BACK.
THORNTON! ALL THE WAY FROM THE NORTH POLE!
YEP. I'VE RETURNED FOR THE WINTER. DID YOU MISS ME?
NO.
THAT'S BECAUSE YOU'RE A NASTY, TOE-PINCHING, OCEAN-GOING TICK.
AND YOU'RE A PATHETIC, POLAR-DWELLING, OVERGROWN HAMSTER.
IT'S GOOD TO BE BACK.
GIVE US A HUG.

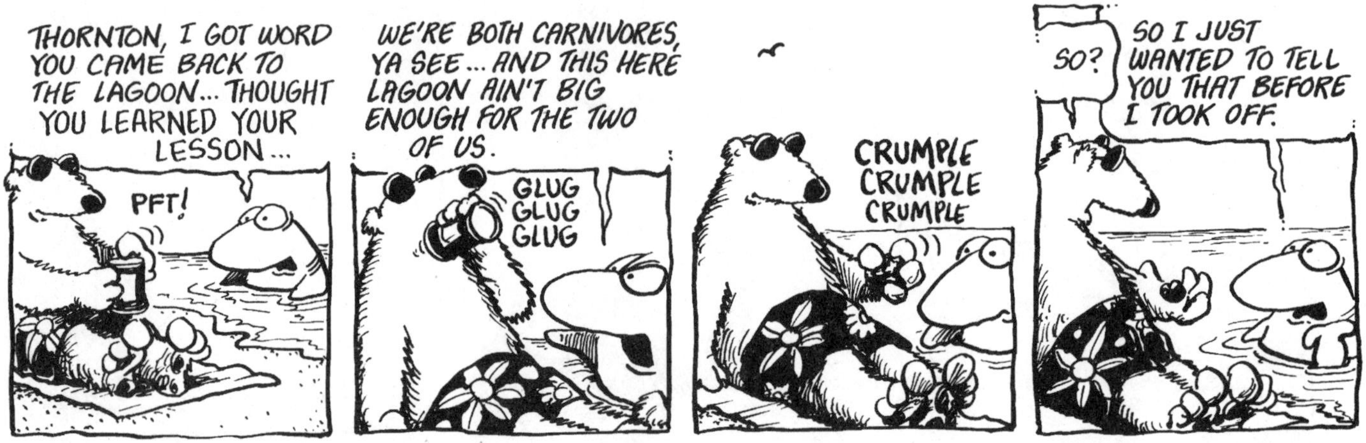
THORNTON, I GOT WORD YOU CAME BACK TO THE LAGOON... THOUGHT YOU LEARNED YOUR LESSON...
PFT!
WE'RE BOTH CARNIVORES, YA SEE... AND THIS HERE LAGOON AIN'T BIG ENOUGH FOR THE TWO OF US.
GLUG GLUG GLUG
CRUMPLE CRUMPLE CRUMPLE
SO?
SO I JUST WANTED TO TELL YOU THAT BEFORE I TOOK OFF.

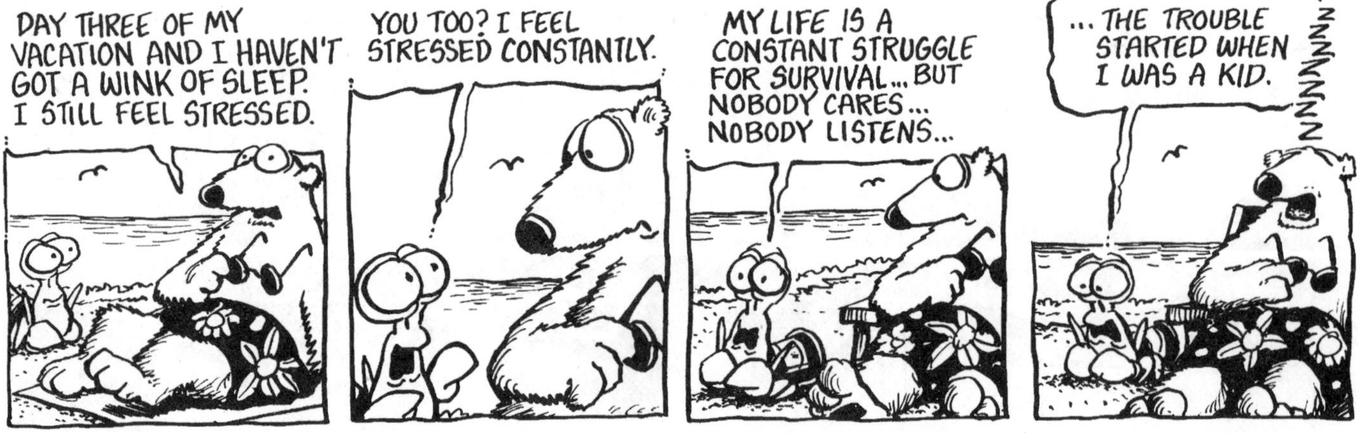
DAY THREE OF MY VACATION AND I HAVEN'T GOT A WINK OF SLEEP. I STILL FEEL STRESSED.
YOU TOO? I FEEL STRESSED CONSTANTLY.
MY LIFE IS A CONSTANT STRUGGLE FOR SURVIVAL... BUT NOBODY CARES... NOBODY LISTENS...
...THE TROUBLE STARTED WHEN I WAS A KID.
ZZZZZZZ

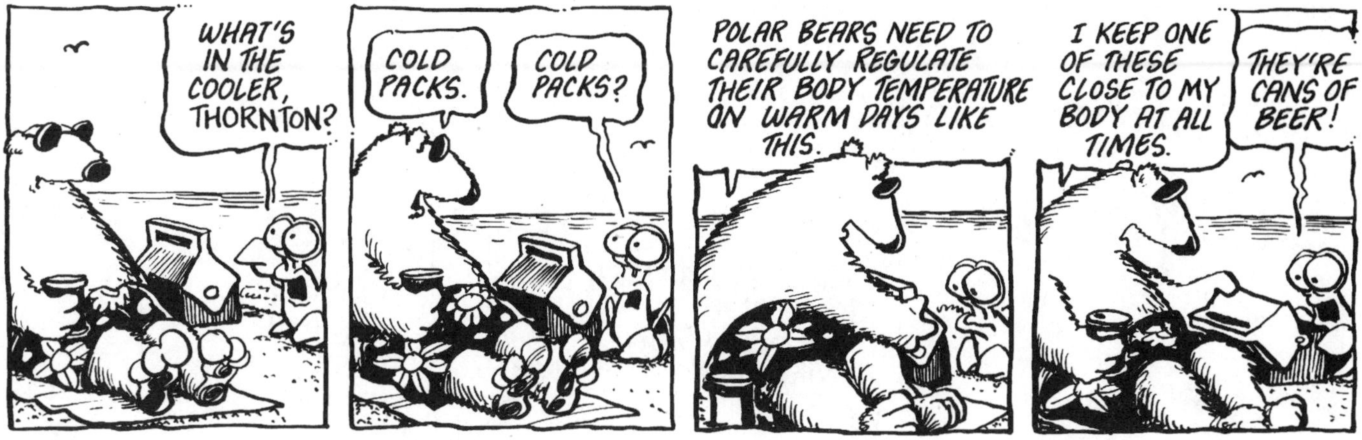
WHAT'S IN THE COOLER, THORNTON?
COLD PACKS.
COLD PACKS?
POLAR BEARS NEED TO CAREFULLY REGULATE THEIR BODY TEMPERATURE ON WARM DAYS LIKE THIS.
I KEEP ONE OF THESE CLOSE TO MY BODY AT ALL TIMES.
THEY'RE CANS OF BEER!

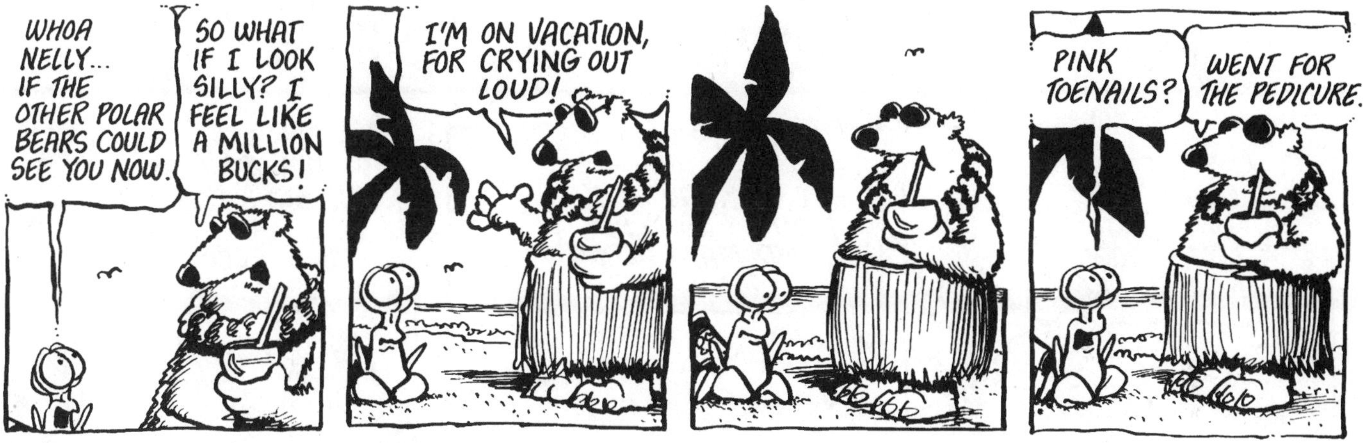
WHOA NELLY... IF THE OTHER POLAR BEARS COULD SEE YOU NOW.
SO WHAT IF I LOOK SILLY? I FEEL LIKE A MILLION BUCKS!
I'M ON VACATION, FOR CRYING OUT LOUD!
PINK TOENAILS?
WENT FOR THE PEDICURE.

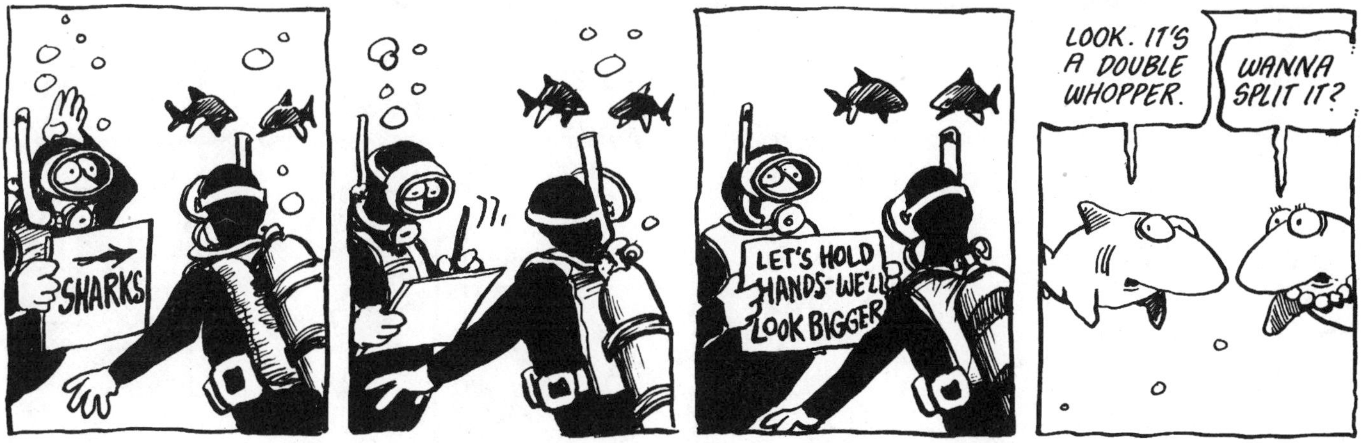
SHARKS
LET'S HOLD HANDS-WE'LL LOOK BIGGER
LOOK. IT'S A DOUBLE WHOPPER.
WANNA SPLIT IT?

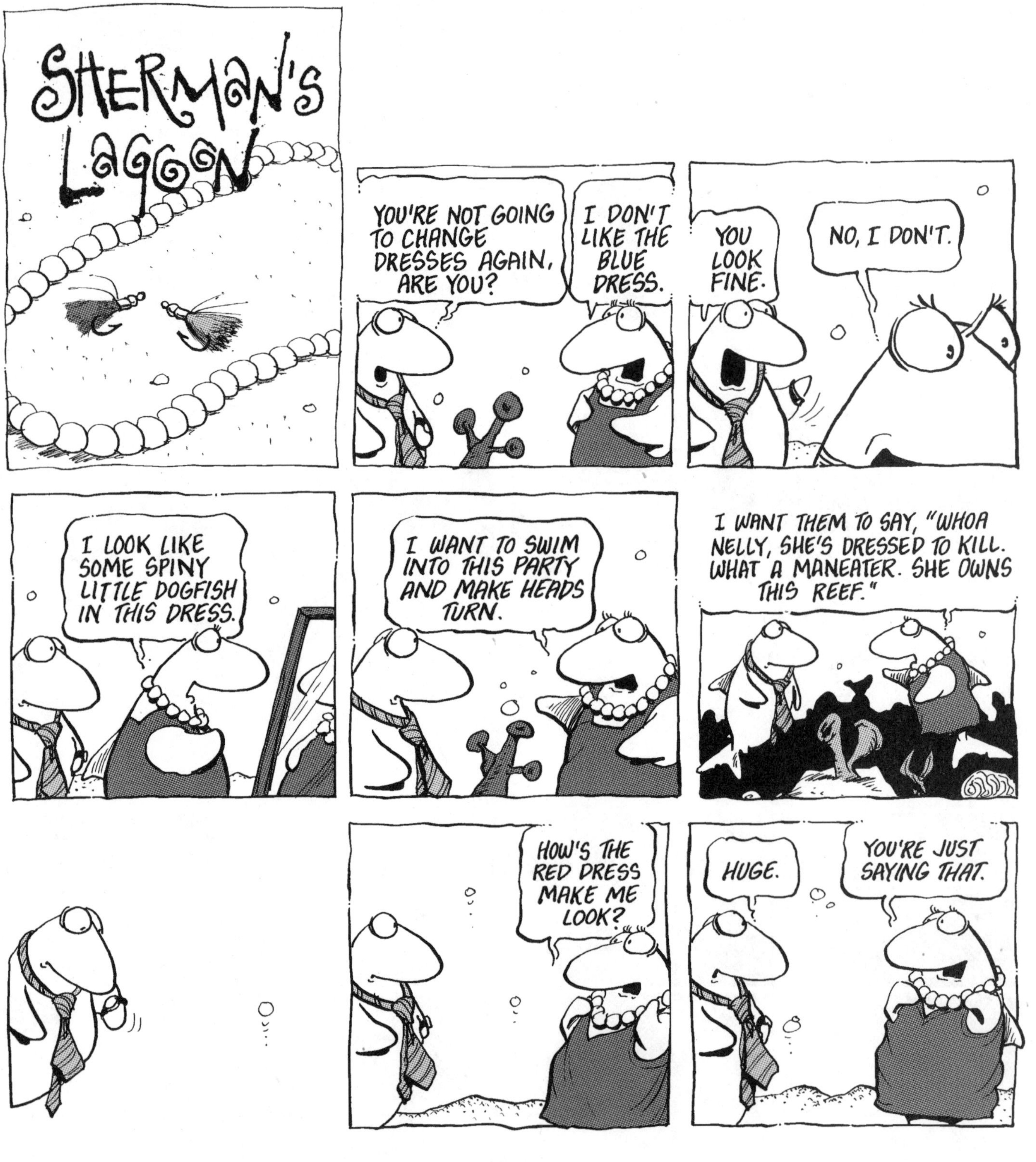
SHERMAN'S LAGOON
YOU'RE NOT GOING TO CHANGE DRESSES AGAIN, ARE YOU?
I DON'T LIKE THE BLUE DRESS.
YOU LOOK FINE.
NO, I DON'T.
I LOOK LIKE SOME SPINY LITTLE DOGFISH IN THIS DRESS.
I WANT TO SWIM INTO THIS PARTY AND MAKE HEADS TURN.
I WANT THEM TO SAY, "WHOA NELLY, SHE'S DRESSED TO KILL. WHAT A MANEATER. SHE OWNS THIS REEF."
HOW'S THE RED DRESS MAKE ME LOOK?
HUGE.
YOU'RE JUST SAYING THAT.

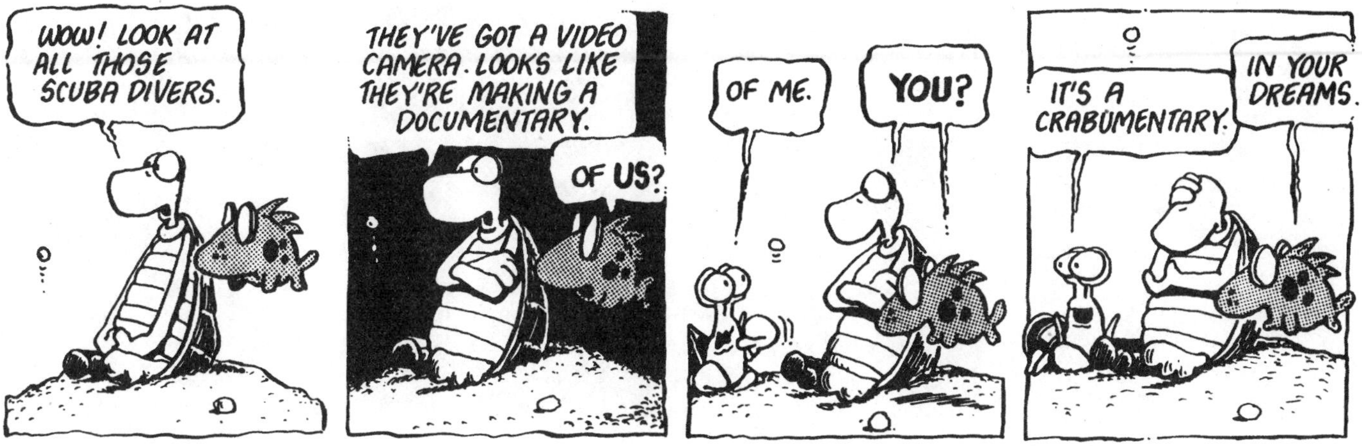
WOW! LOOK AT ALL THOSE SCUBA DIVERS.
THEY'VE GOT A VIDEO CAMERA. LOOKS LIKE THEY'RE MAKING A DOCUMENTARY.
OF US?
OF ME.
YOU?
IT'S A CRABUMENTARY.
IN YOUR DREAMS.

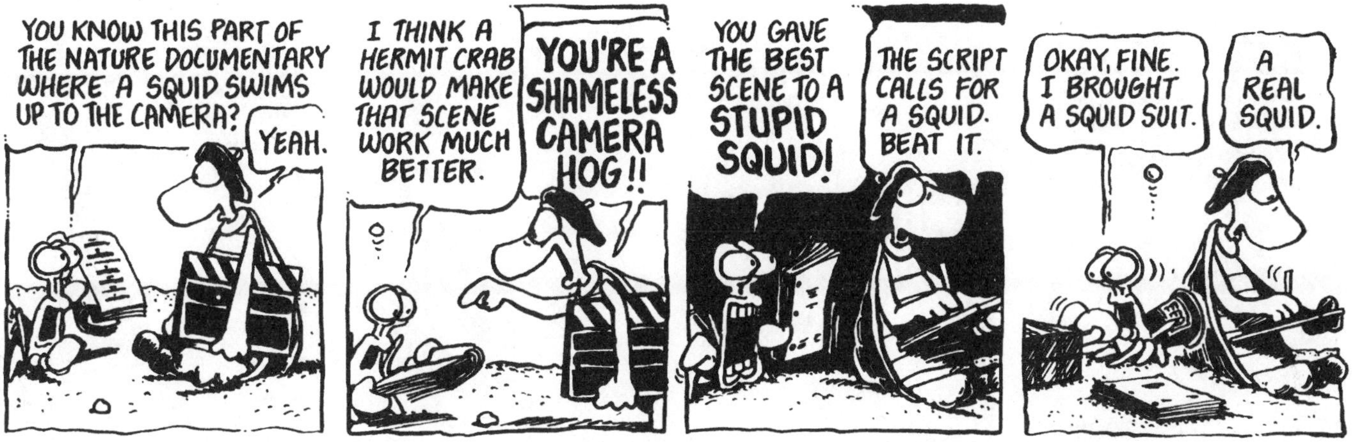
YOU KNOW THIS PART OF THE NATURE DOCUMENTARY WHERE A SQUID SWIMS UP TO THE CAMERA?
YEAH.
I THINK A HERMIT CRAB WOULD MAKE THAT SCENE WORK MUCH BETTER.
YOU'RE A SHAMELESS CAMERA HOG!!
YOU GAVE THE BEST SCENE TO A STUPID SQUID!
THE SCRIPT CALLS FOR A SQUID. BEAT IT.
OKAY, FINE. I BROUGHT A SQUID SUIT.
A REAL SQUID.

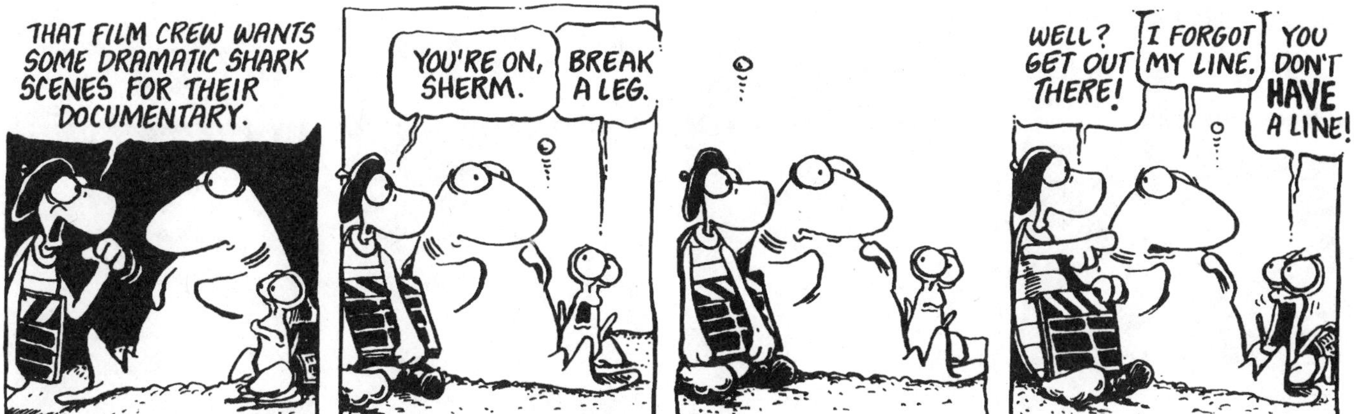
THAT FILM CREW WANTS SOME DRAMATIC SHARK SCENES FOR THEIR DOCUMENTARY.
YOU'RE ON, SHERM.
BREAK A LEG.
WELL? GET OUT THERE!
I FORGOT MY LINE.
YOU DON'T HAVE A LINE!

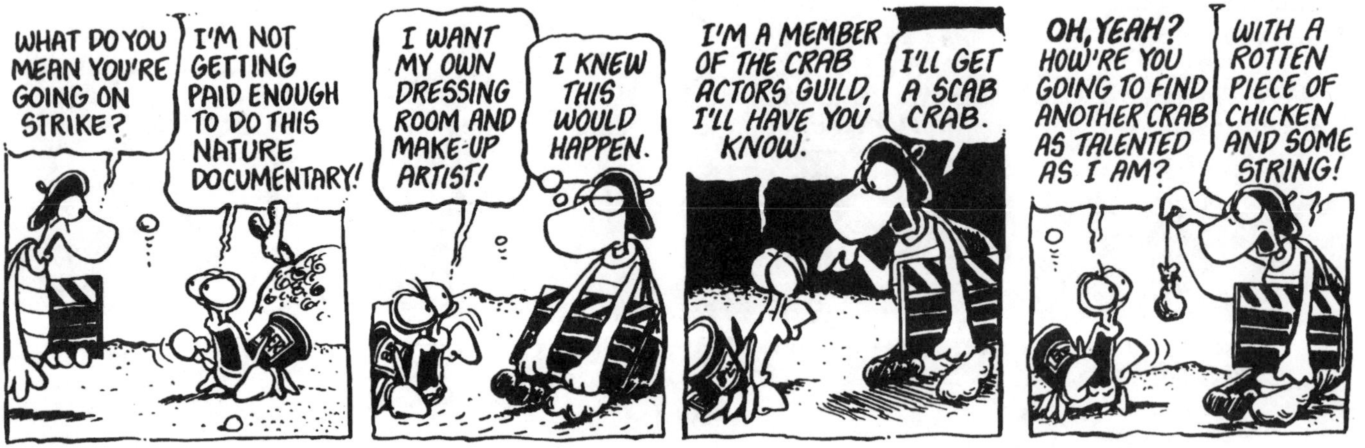
WHAT DO YOU MEAN YOU'RE GOING ON STRIKE?
I'M NOT GETTING PAID ENOUGH TO DO THIS NATURE DOCUMENTARY!
I WANT MY OWN DRESSING ROOM AND MAKE-UP ARTIST!
I KNEW THIS WOULD HAPPEN.
I'M A MEMBER OF THE CRAB ACTORS GUILD, I'LL HAVE YOU KNOW.
I'LL GET A SCAB CRAB.
OH, YEAH? HOW'RE YOU GOING TO FIND ANOTHER CRAB AS TALENTED AS I AM?
WITH A ROTTEN PIECE OF CHICKEN AND SOME STRING!

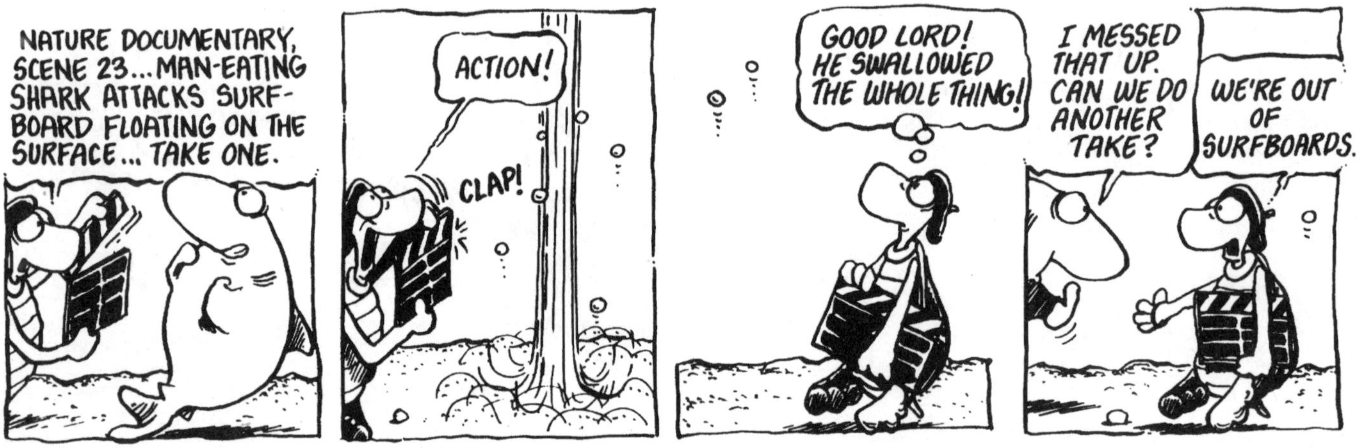
NATURE DOCUMENTARY, SCENE 23... MAN-EATING SHARK ATTACKS SURF-BOARD FLOATING ON THE SURFACE... TAKE ONE.
ACTION!
CLAP!
GOOD LORD! HE SWALLOWED THE WHOLE THING!
I MESSED THAT UP. CAN WE DO ANOTHER TAKE?
WE'RE OUT OF SURFBOARDS.

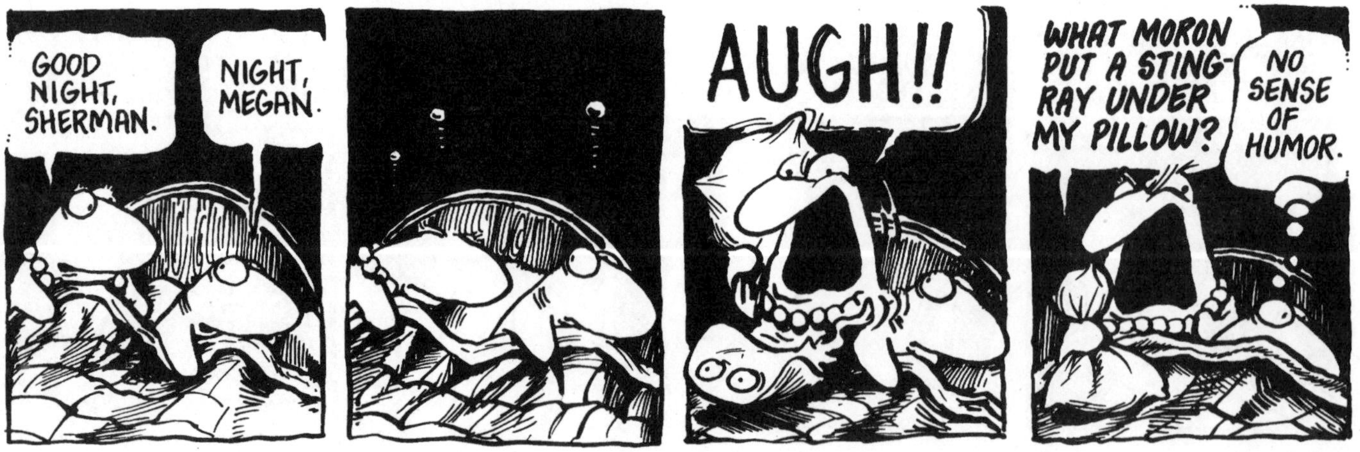
GOOD NIGHT, SHERMAN.
NIGHT, MEGAN.
AUGH!!
WHAT MORON PUT A STING-RAY UNDER MY PILLOW?
NO SENSE OF HUMOR.

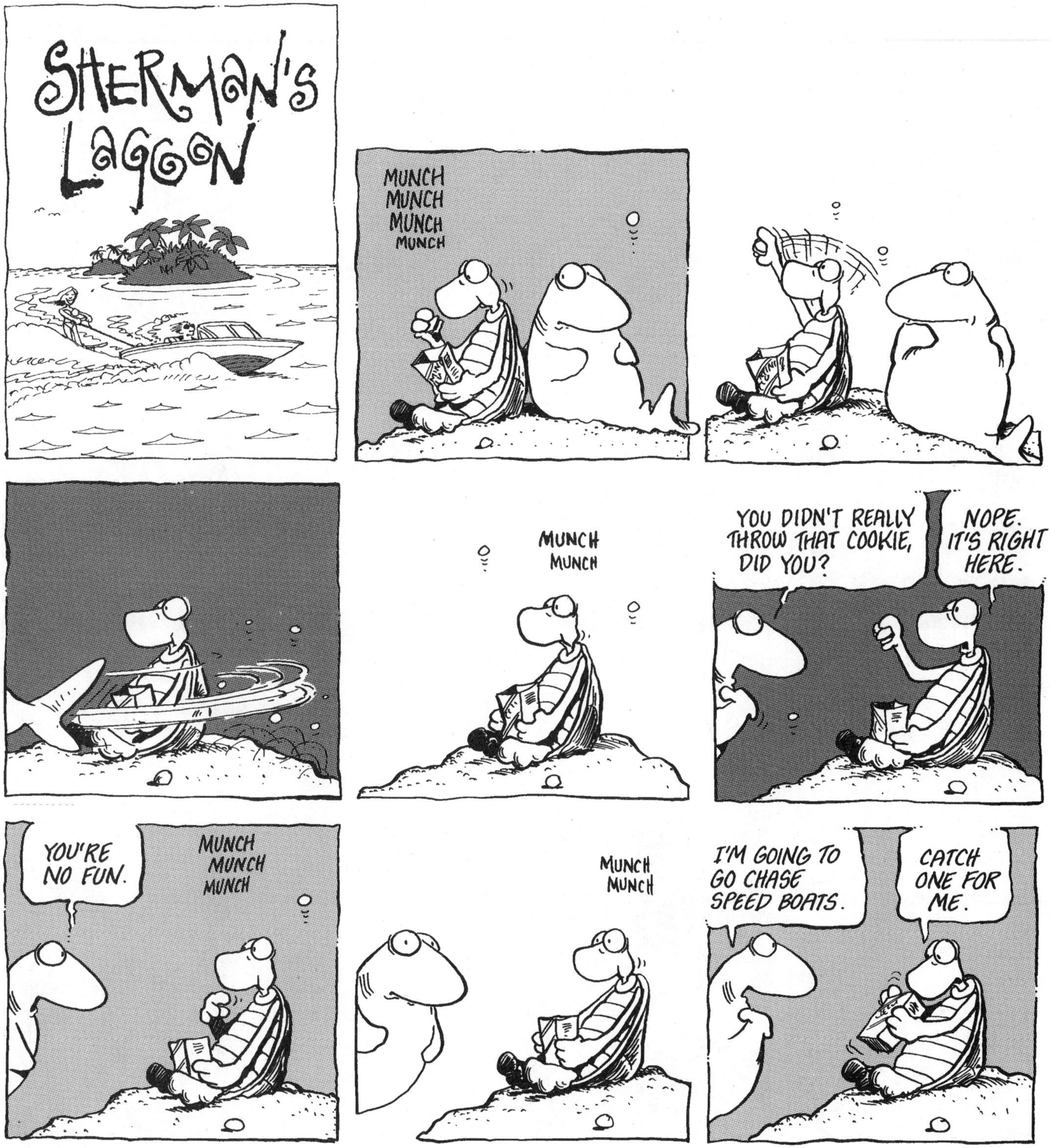
SHERMAN'S LAGOON
MUNCH MUNCH MUNCH MUNCH
MUNCH MUNCH
YOU DIDN'T REALLY THROW THAT COOKIE, DID YOU?
NOPE. IT'S RIGHT HERE.
YOU'RE NO FUN.
MUNCH MUNCH MUNCH
MUNCH MUNCH
I'M GOING TO GO CHASE SPEED BOATS.
CATCH ONE FOR ME.

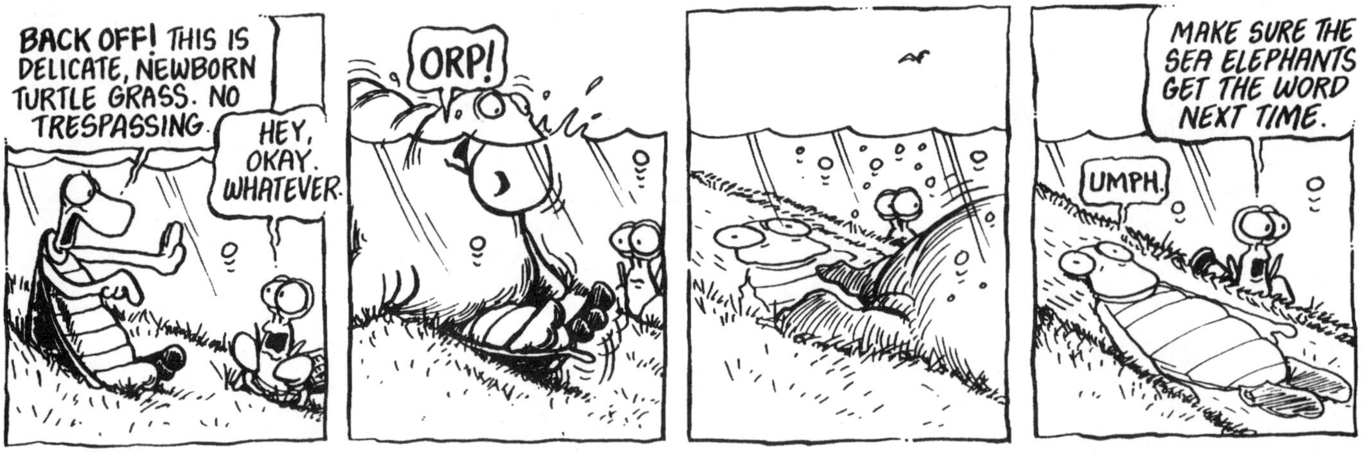
BACK OFF! THIS IS DELICATE, NEWBORN TURTLE GRASS. NO TRESPASSING.
HEY, OKAY. WHATEVER.
ORP!
MAKE SURE THE SEA ELEPHANTS GET THE WORD NEXT TIME.
UMPH.

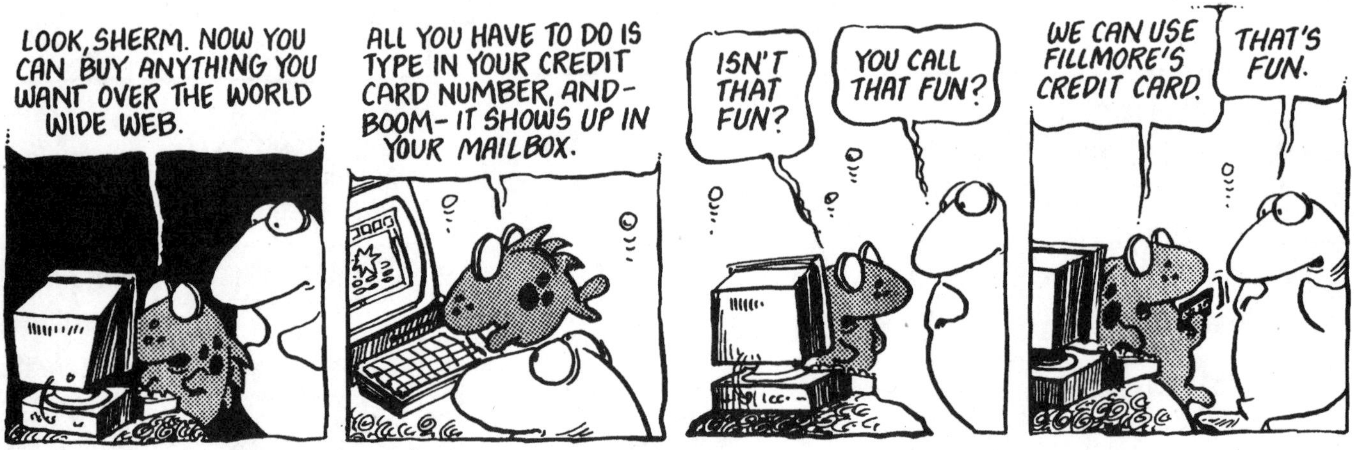
LOOK, SHERM. NOW YOU CAN BUY ANYTHING YOU WANT OVER THE WORLD WIDE WEB.
ALL YOU HAVE TO DO IS TYPE IN YOUR CREDIT CARD NUMBER, AND- BOOM- IT SHOWS UP IN YOUR MAILBOX.
ISN'T THAT FUN?
YOU CALL THAT FUN?
WE CAN USE FILLMORE'S CREDIT CARD.
THAT'S FUN.

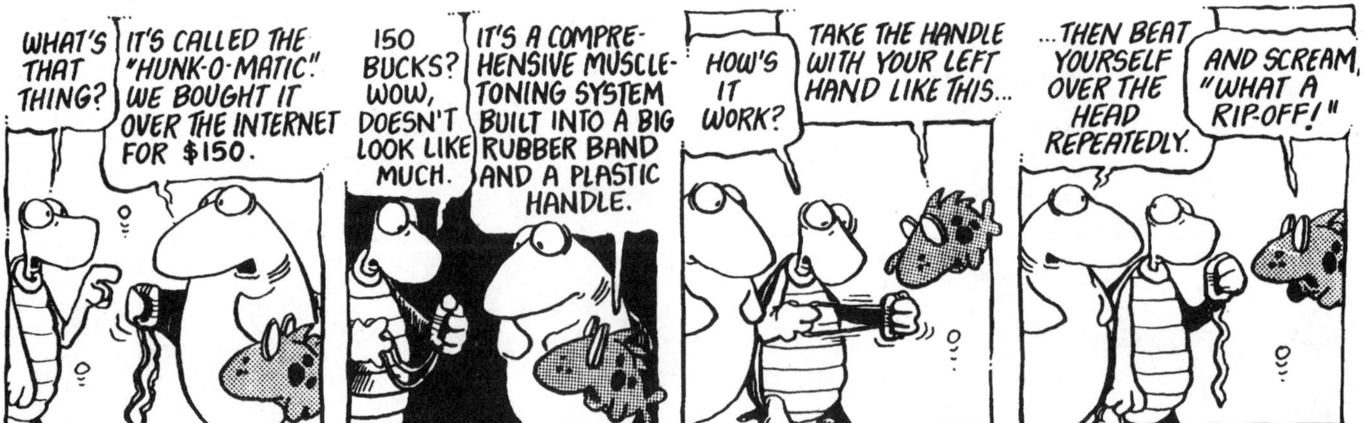
WHAT'S THAT THING?
IT'S CALLED THE "HUNK-O-MATIC." WE BOUGHT IT OVER THE INTERNET FOR $150.
150 BUCKS? WOW, DOESN'T LOOK LIKE MUCH.
IT'S A COMPREHENSIVE MUSCLE-TONING SYSTEM BUILT INTO A BIG RUBBER BAND AND A PLASTIC HANDLE.
HOW'S IT WORK?
TAKE THE HANDLE WITH YOUR LEFT HAND LIKE THIS...
...THEN BEAT YOURSELF OVER THE HEAD REPEATEDLY.
AND SCREAM, "WHAT A RIP-OFF!"

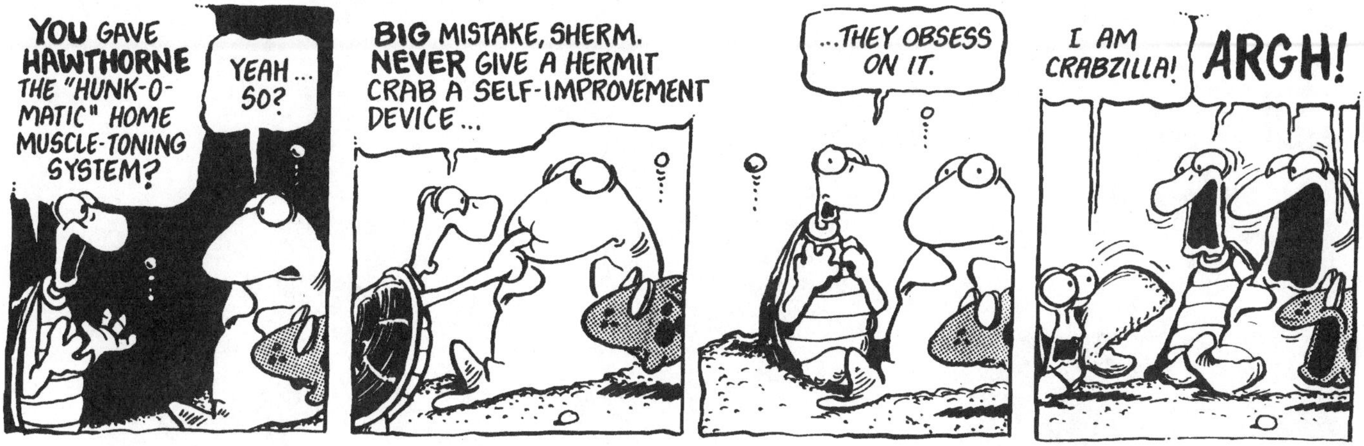
YOU GAVE HAWTHORNE THE "HUNK-O-MATIC" HOME MUSCLE-TONING SYSTEM?
YEAH... SO?
BIG MISTAKE, SHERM. NEVER GIVE A HERMIT CRAB A SELF-IMPROVEMENT DEVICE...
...THEY OBSESS ON IT.
I AM CRABZILLA!
ARGH!

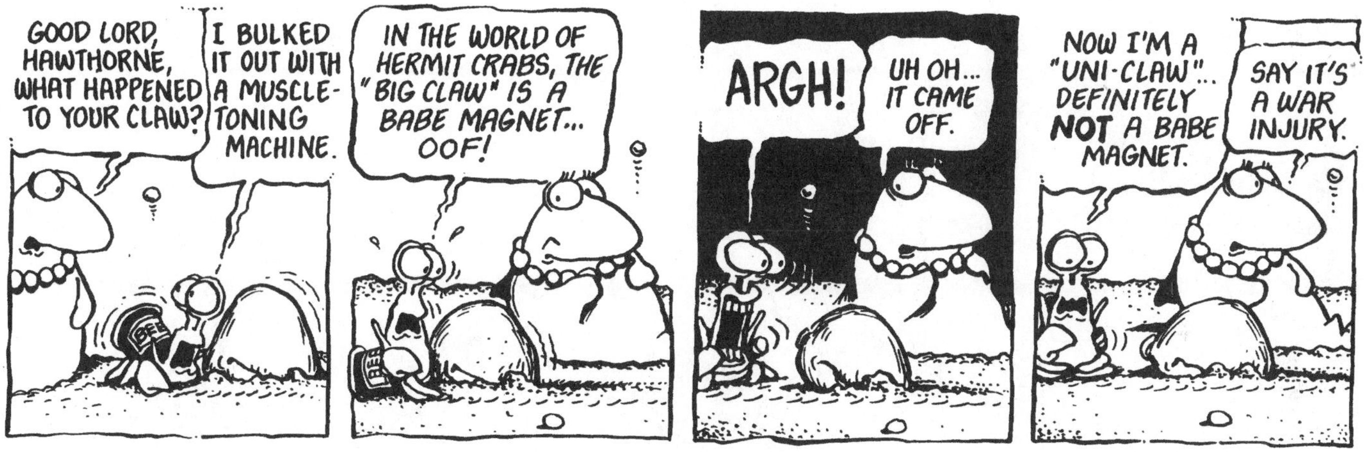
GOOD LORD, HAWTHORNE, WHAT HAPPENED TO YOUR CLAW?
I BULKED IT OUT WITH A MUSCLE-TONING MACHINE.
IN THE WORLD OF HERMIT CRABS, THE "BIG CLAW" IS A BABE MAGNET... OOF!
ARGH!
UH OH... IT CAME OFF.
NOW I'M A "UNI-CLAW"... DEFINITELY NOT A BABE MAGNET.
SAY IT'S A WAR INJURY.

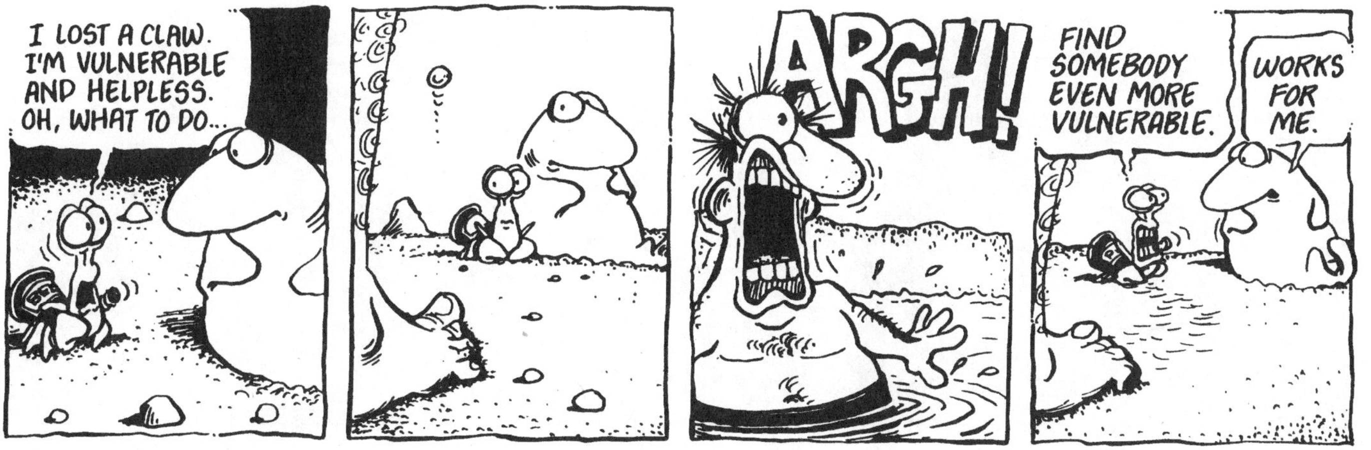
I LOST A CLAW. I'M VULNERABLE AND HELPLESS. OH, WHAT TO DO...
ARGH!
FIND SOMEBODY EVEN MORE VULNERABLE.
WORKS FOR ME.

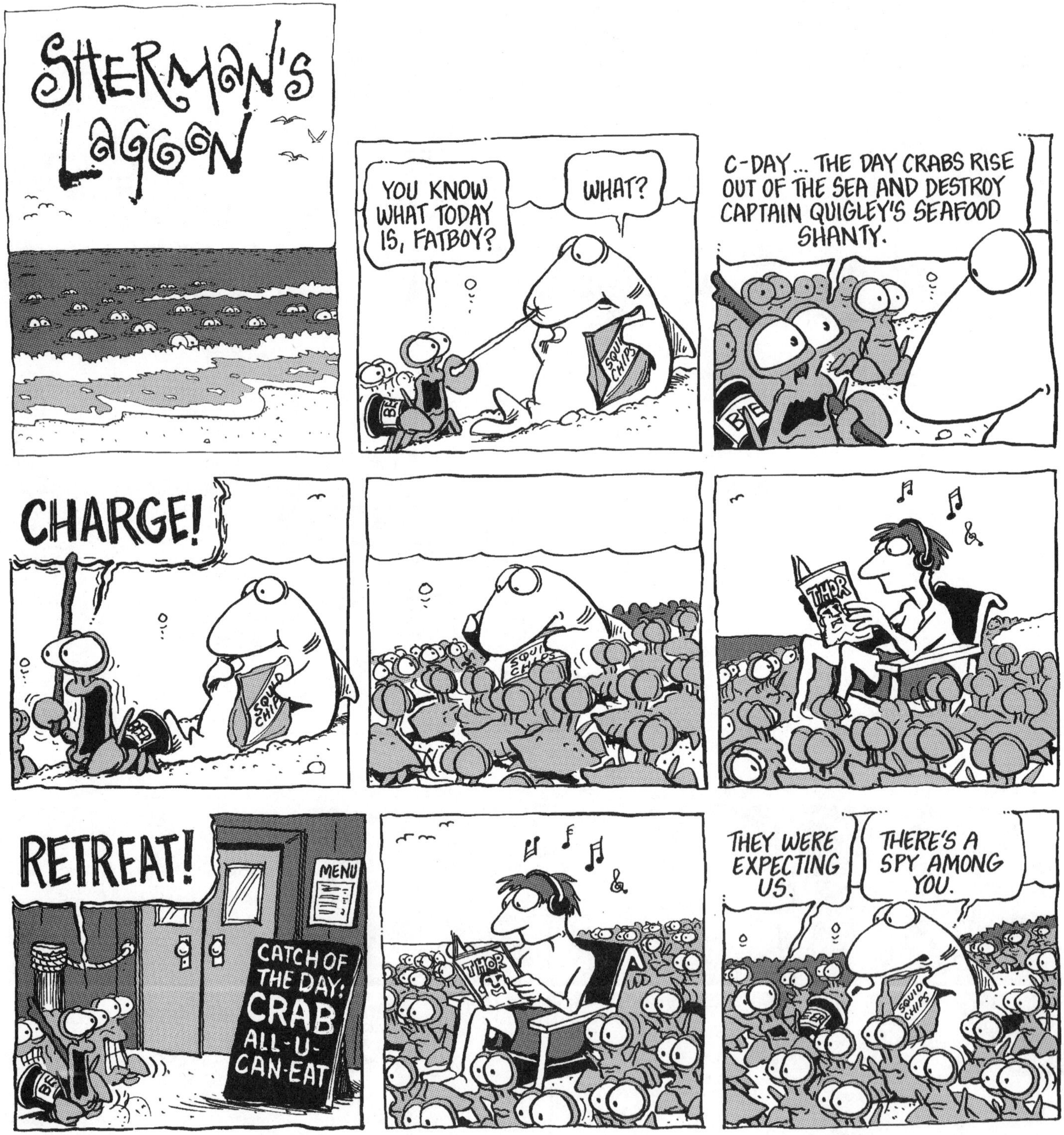
SHERMAN'S LAGOON
YOU KNOW WHAT TODAY IS, FATBOY?
WHAT?
C-DAY... THE DAY CRABS RISE OUT OF THE SEA AND DESTROY CAPTAIN QUIGLEY'S SEAFOOD SHANTY.
CHARGE!
RETREAT!
MENU
CATCH OF THE DAY: CRAB ALL-U-CAN-EAT
THEY WERE EXPECTING US.
THERE'S A SPY AMONG YOU.

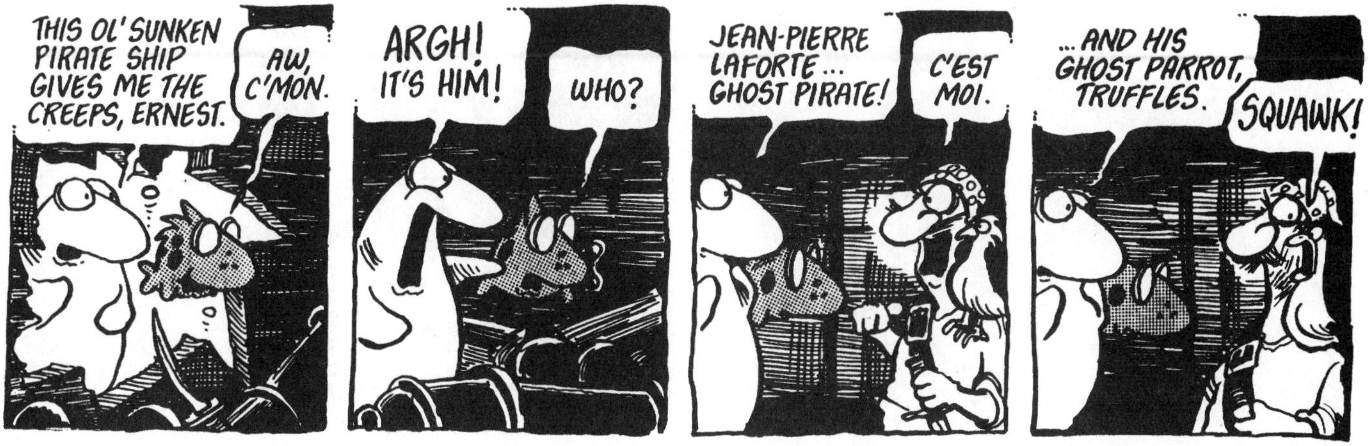
THIS OL' SUNKEN PIRATE SHIP GIVES ME THE CREEPS, ERNEST.
AW, C'MON.
ARGH! IT'S HIM!
WHO?
JEAN-PIERRE LAFORTE... GHOST PIRATE!
C'EST MOI.
...AND HIS GHOST PARROT, TRUFFLES.
SQUAWK!

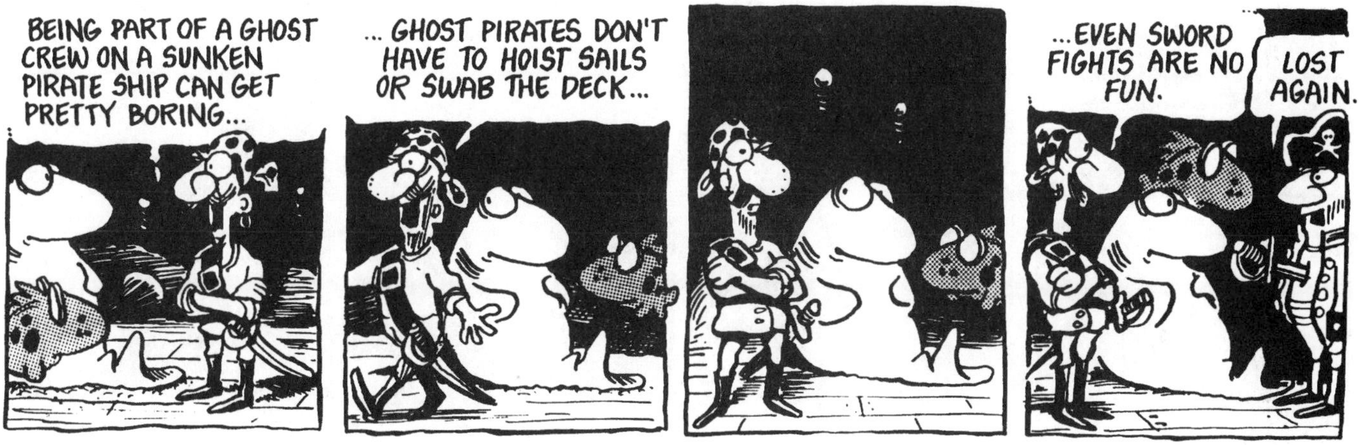
BEING PART OF A GHOST CREW ON A SUNKEN PIRATE SHIP CAN GET PRETTY BORING...
... GHOST PIRATES DON'T HAVE TO HOIST SAILS OR SWAB THE DECK...
...EVEN SWORD FIGHTS ARE NO FUN.
LOST AGAIN.

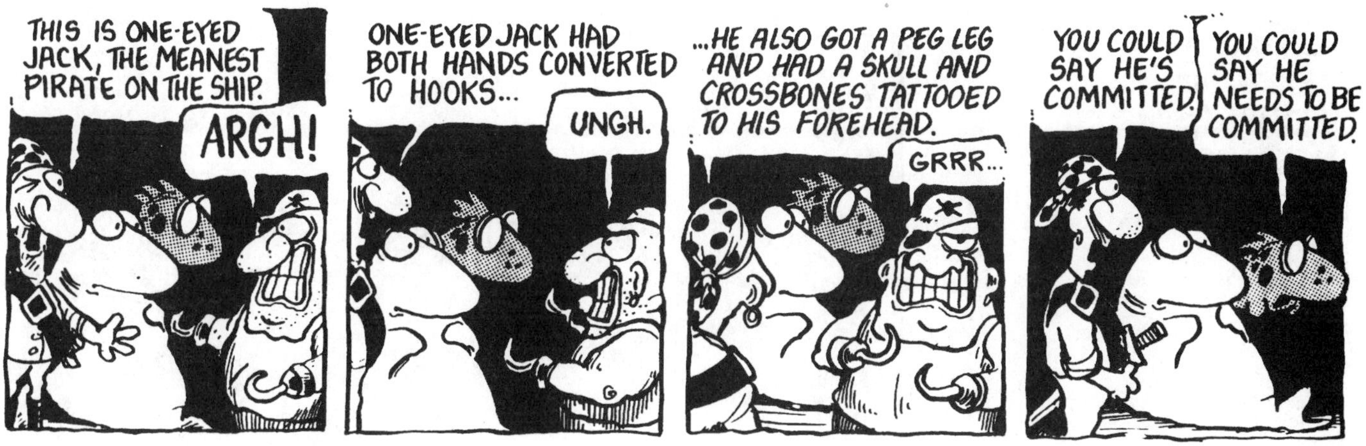
THIS IS ONE-EYED JACK, THE MEANEST PIRATE ON THE SHIP.
ARGH!
ONE-EYED JACK HAD BOTH HANDS CONVERTED TO HOOKS...
UNGH.
...HE ALSO GOT A PEG LEG AND HAD A SKULL AND CROSSBONES TATTOOED TO HIS FOREHEAD.
GRRR...
YOU COULD SAY HE'S COMMITTED.
YOU COULD SAY HE NEEDS TO BE COMMITTED.

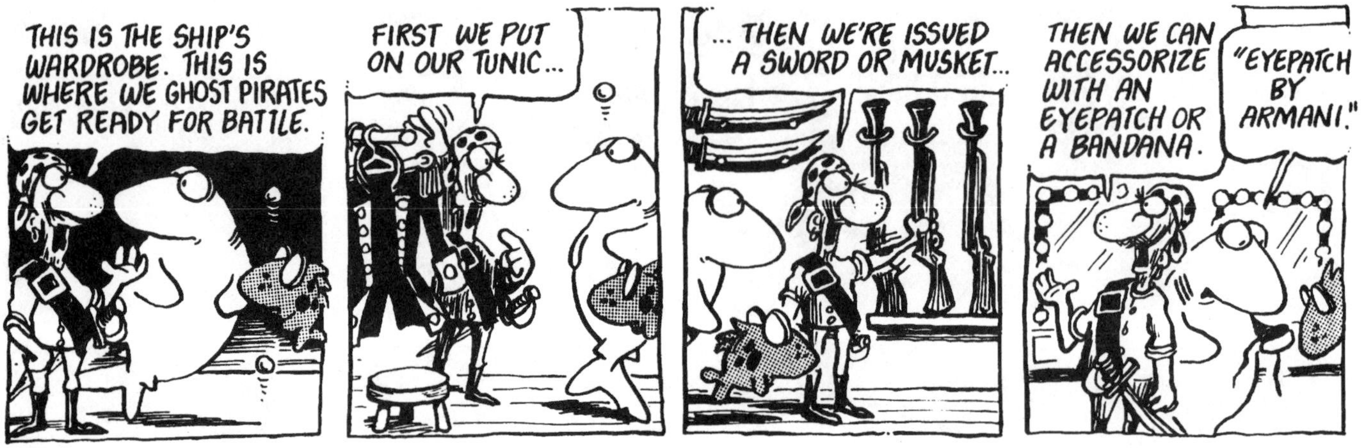
THIS IS THE SHIP'S WARDROBE. THIS IS WHERE WE GHOST PIRATES GET READY FOR BATTLE.
FIRST WE PUT ON OUR TUNIC...
... THEN WE'RE ISSUED A SWORD OR MUSKET...
THEN WE CAN ACCESSORIZE WITH AN EYEPATCH OR A BANDANA.
"EYEPATCH BY ARMANI."

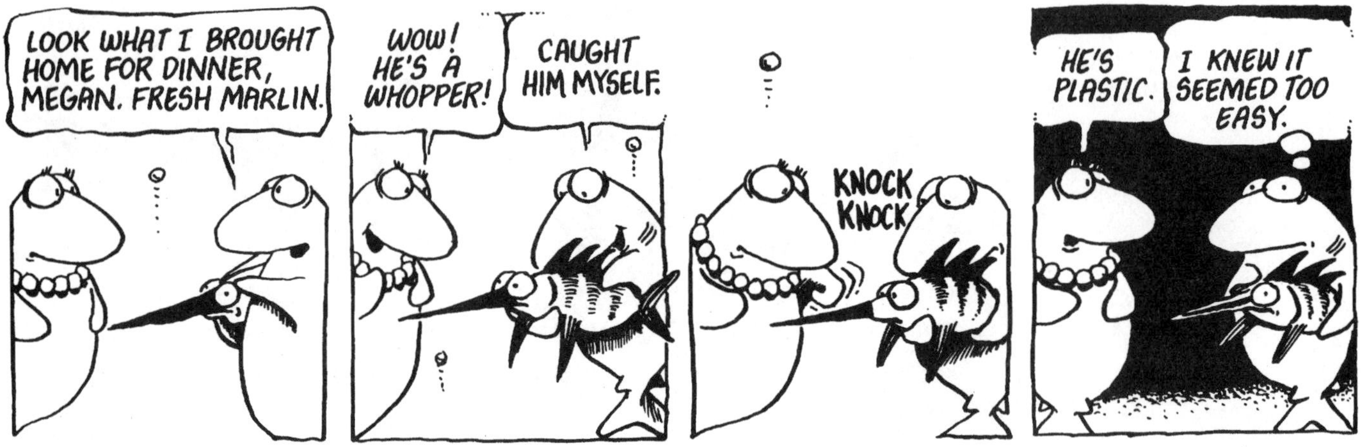
LOOK WHAT I BROUGHT HOME FOR DINNER, MEGAN. FRESH MARLIN.
WOW! HE'S A WHOPPER!
CAUGHT HIM MYSELF.
KNOCK KNOCK
HE'S PLASTIC.
I KNEW IT SEEMED TOO EASY.

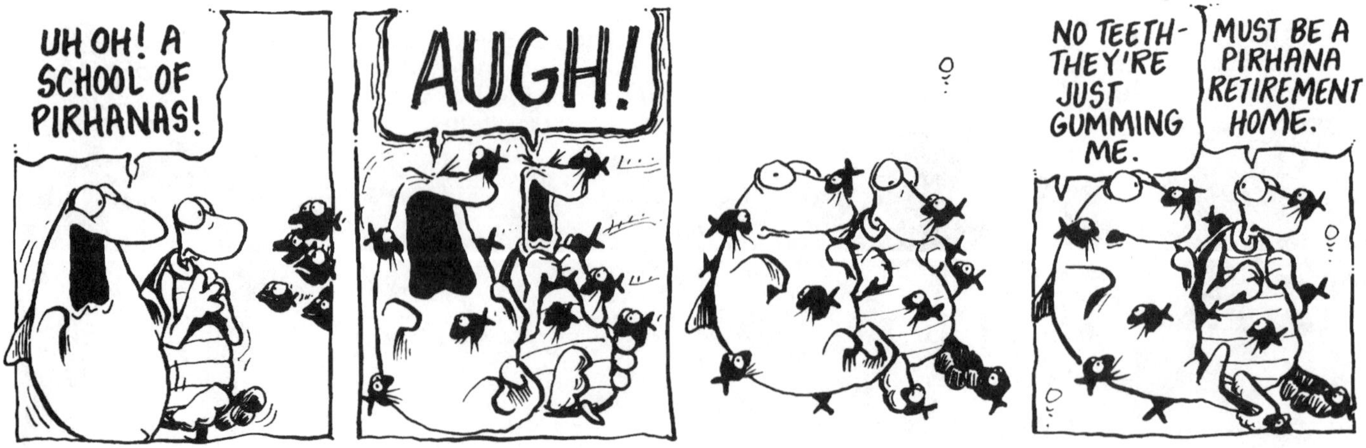
UH OH! A SCHOOL OF PIRHANAS!
AUGH!
NO TEETH- THEY'RE JUST GUMMING ME.
MUST BE A PIRHANA RETIREMENT HOME.

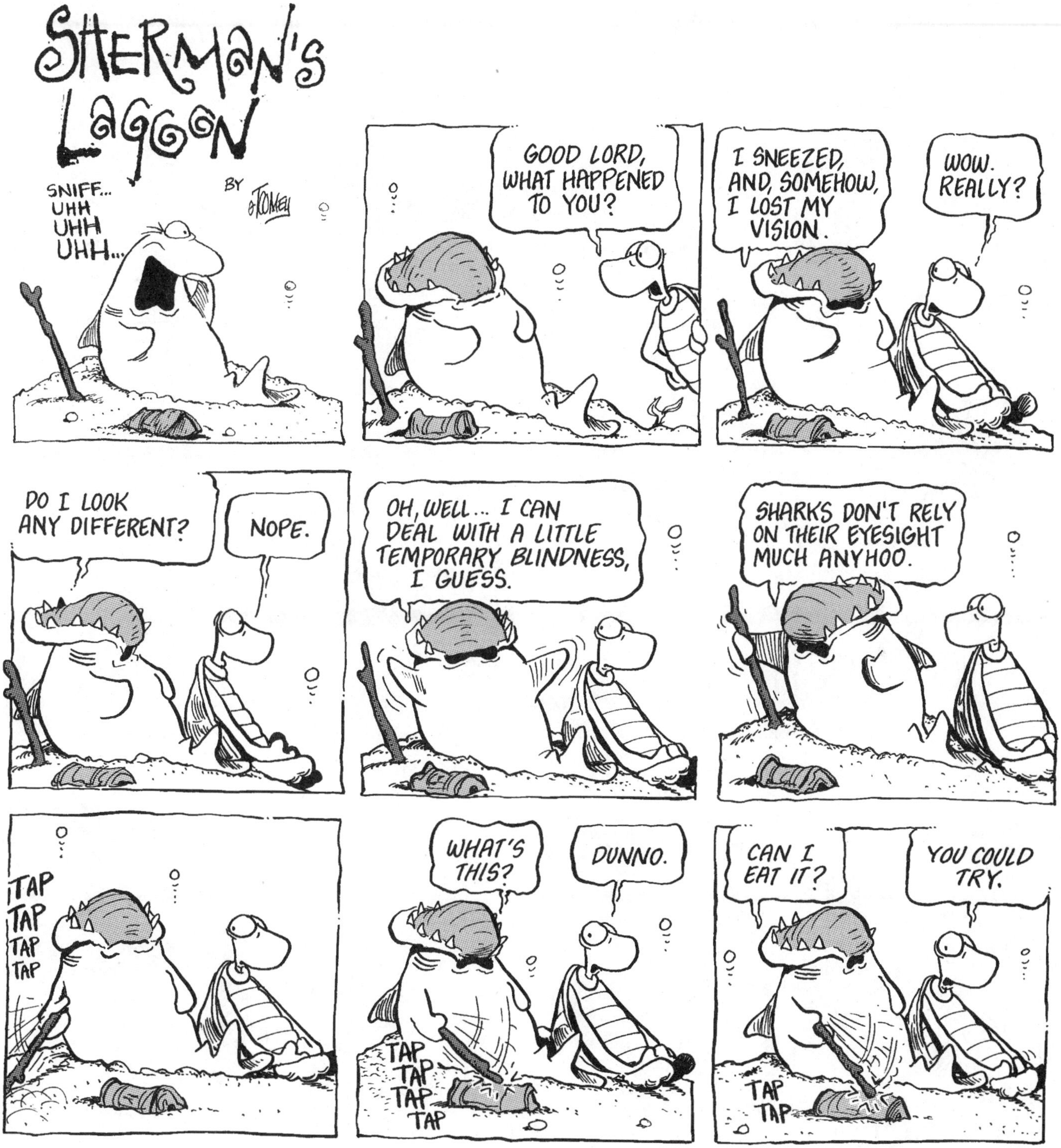
SHERMAN'S LAGOON
BY TOOMEY
SNIFF... UHH UHH UHH...
GOOD LORD, WHAT HAPPENED TO YOU?
I SNEEZED, AND, SOMEHOW, I LOST MY VISION.
WOW. REALLY?
DO I LOOK ANY DIFFERENT?
NOPE.
OH, WELL... I CAN DEAL WITH A LITTLE TEMPORARY BLINDNESS, I GUESS.
SHARKS DON'T RELY ON THEIR EYESIGHT MUCH ANYHOO.
TAP TAP TAP TAP
WHAT'S THIS?
DUNNO.
TAP TAP TAP TAP
CAN I EAT IT?
YOU COULD TRY.
TAP TAP

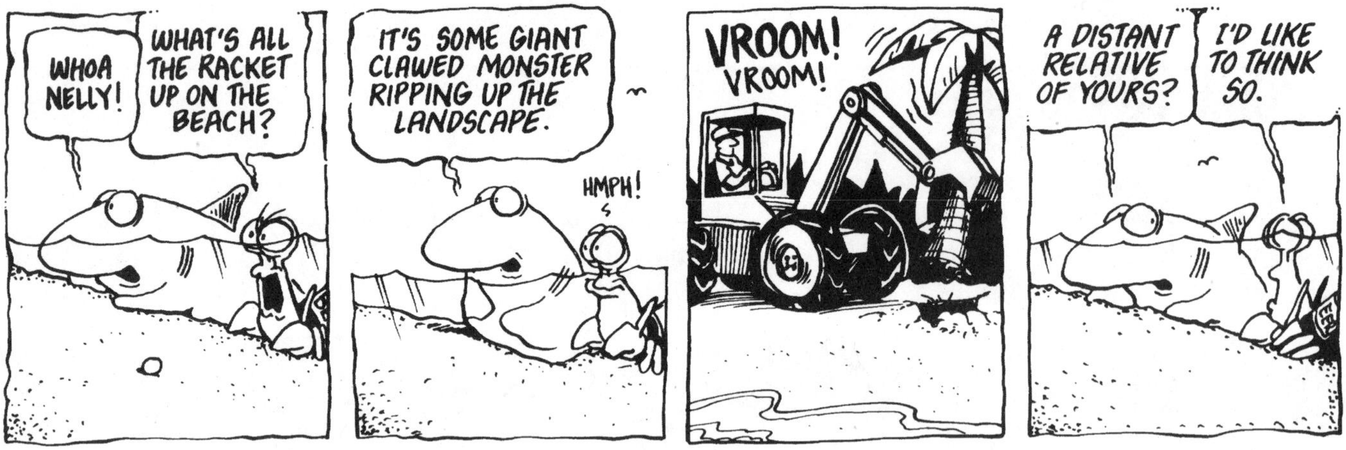
WHOA NELLY!
WHAT'S ALL THE RACKET UP ON THE BEACH?
IT'S SOME GIANT CLAWED MONSTER RIPPING UP THE LANDSCAPE.
HMPH!
VROOM! VROOM!
A DISTANT RELATIVE OF YOURS?
I'D LIKE TO THINK SO.

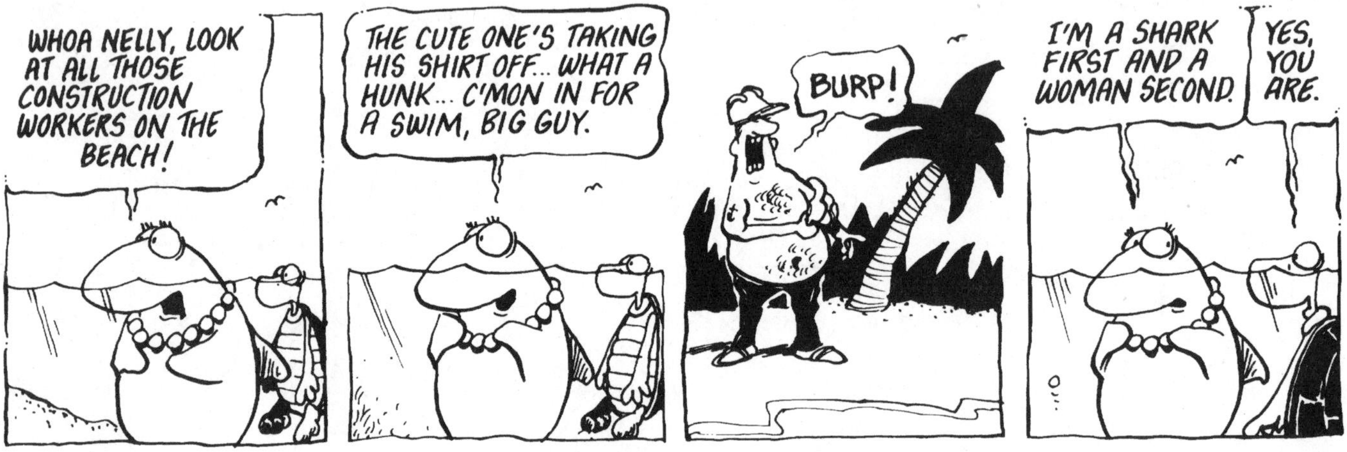
WHOA NELLY, LOOK AT ALL THOSE CONSTRUCTION WORKERS ON THE BEACH!
THE CUTE ONE'S TAKING HIS SHIRT OFF... WHAT A HUNK... C'MON IN FOR A SWIM, BIG GUY.
BURP!
I'M A SHARK FIRST AND A WOMAN SECOND.
YES, YOU ARE.

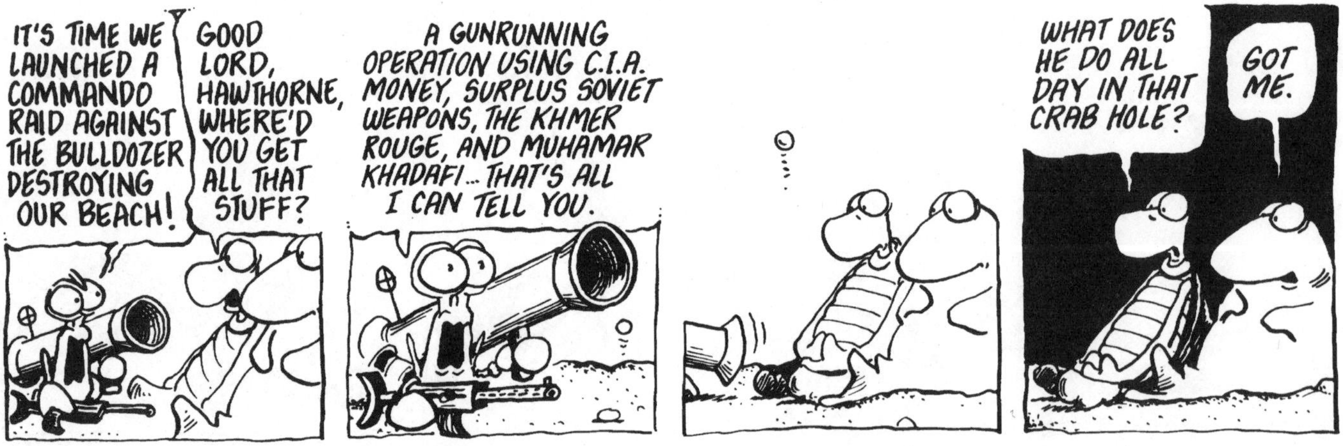
IT'S TIME WE LAUNCHED A COMMANDO RAID AGAINST THE BULLDOZER DESTROYING OUR BEACH!
GOOD LORD, HAWTHORNE, WHERE'D YOU GET ALL THAT STUFF?
A GUNRUNNING OPERATION USING C.I.A. MONEY, SURPLUS SOVIET WEAPONS, THE KHMER ROUGE, AND MUHAMAR KHADAFI... THAT'S ALL I CAN TELL YOU.
WHAT DOES HE DO ALL DAY IN THAT CRAB HOLE?
GOT ME.

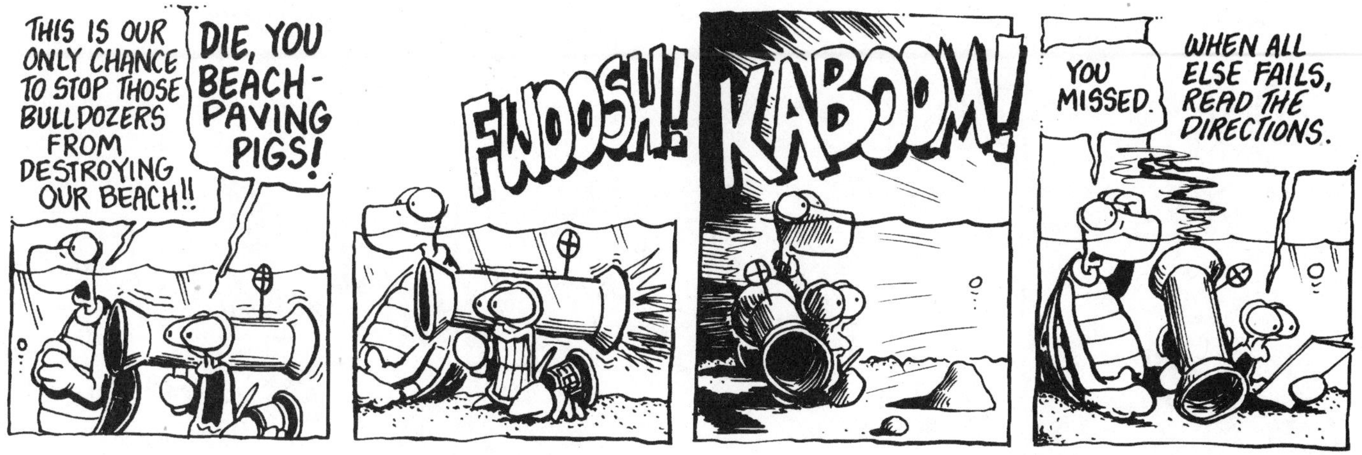
THIS IS OUR ONLY CHANCE TO STOP THOSE BULLDOZERS FROM DESTROYING OUR BEACH!!
DIE, YOU BEACH-PAVING PIGS!
FWOOSH!
KABOOM!
YOU MISSED.
WHEN ALL ELSE FAILS, READ THE DIRECTIONS.

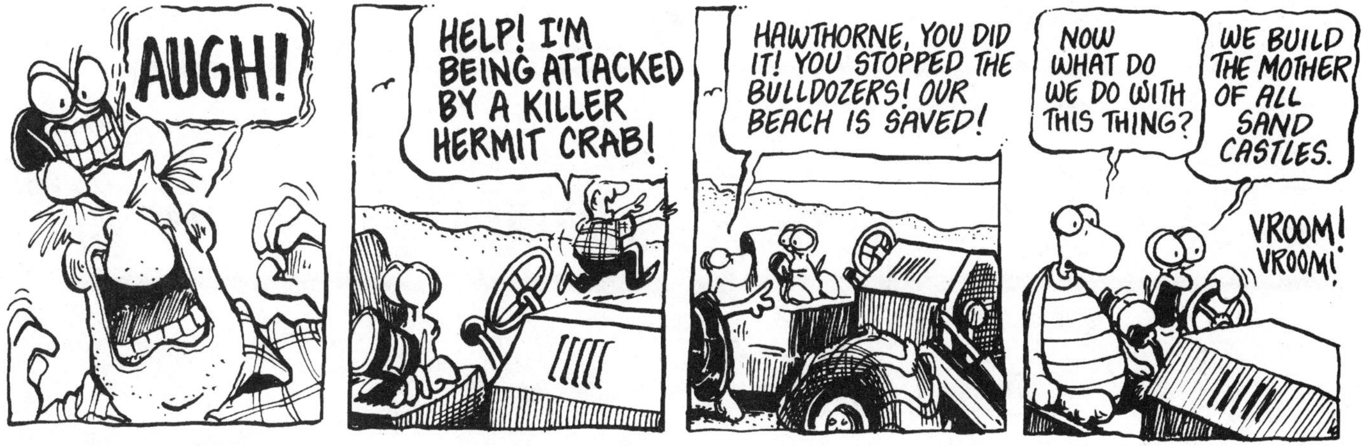
AUGH!
HELP! I'M BEING ATTACKED BY A KILLER HERMIT CRAB!
HAWTHORNE, YOU DID IT! YOU STOPPED THE BULLDOZERS! OUR BEACH IS SAVED!
NOW WHAT DO WE DO WITH THIS THING?
WE BUILD THE MOTHER OF ALL SAND CASTLES.
VROOM! VROOM!

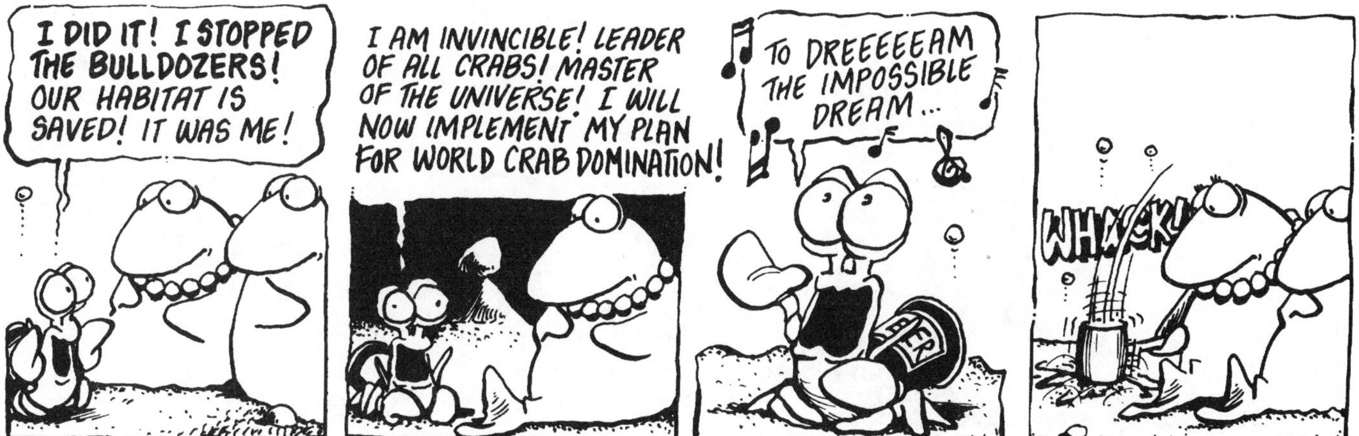
I DID IT! I STOPPED THE BULLDOZERS! OUR HABITAT IS SAVED! IT WAS ME!
I AM INVINCIBLE! LEADER OF ALL CRABS! MASTER OF THE UNIVERSE! I WILL NOW IMPLEMENT MY PLAN FOR WORLD CRAB DOMINATION!
TO DREEEEEAM THE IMPOSSIBLE DREAM...

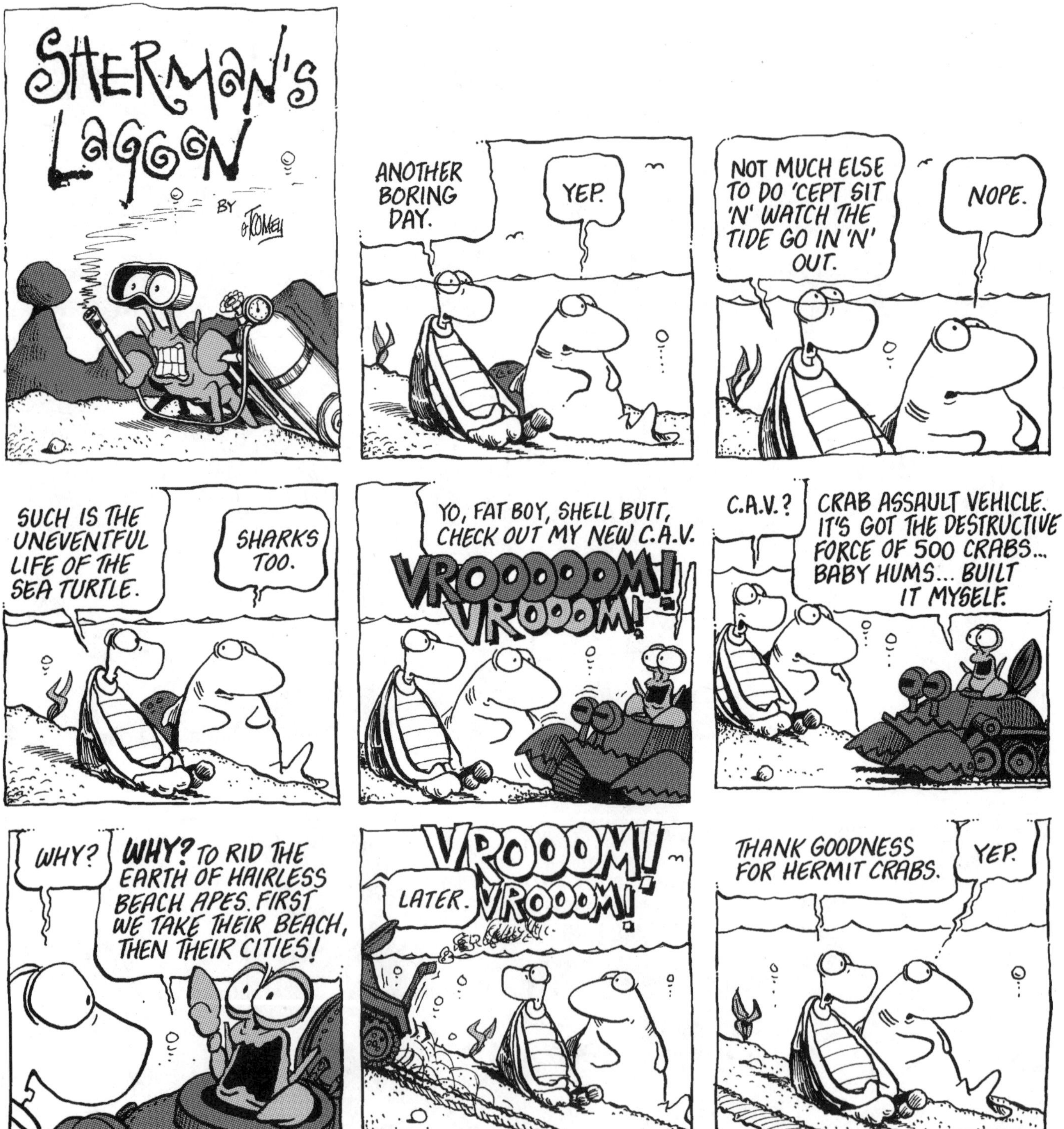
SHERMAN'S LAGOON
BY TOMEY
ANOTHER BORING DAY.
YEP.
NOT MUCH ELSE TO DO 'CEPT SIT 'N' WATCH THE TIDE GO IN 'N' OUT.
NOPE.
SUCH IS THE UNEVENTFUL LIFE OF THE SEA TURTLE.
SHARKS TOO.
YO, FAT BOY, SHELL BUTT, CHECK OUT MY NEW C.A.V.
VROOOOOM! VROOOM!
C.A.V.?
CRAB ASSAULT VEHICLE. IT'S GOT THE DESTRUCTIVE FORCE OF 500 CRABS... BABY HUMS... BUILT IT MYSELF.
WHY?
WHY? TO RID THE EARTH OF HAIRLESS BEACH APES. FIRST WE TAKE THEIR BEACH, THEN THEIR CITIES!
VROOOOM! VROOOM!
LATER.
THANK GOODNESS FOR HERMIT CRABS.
YEP.

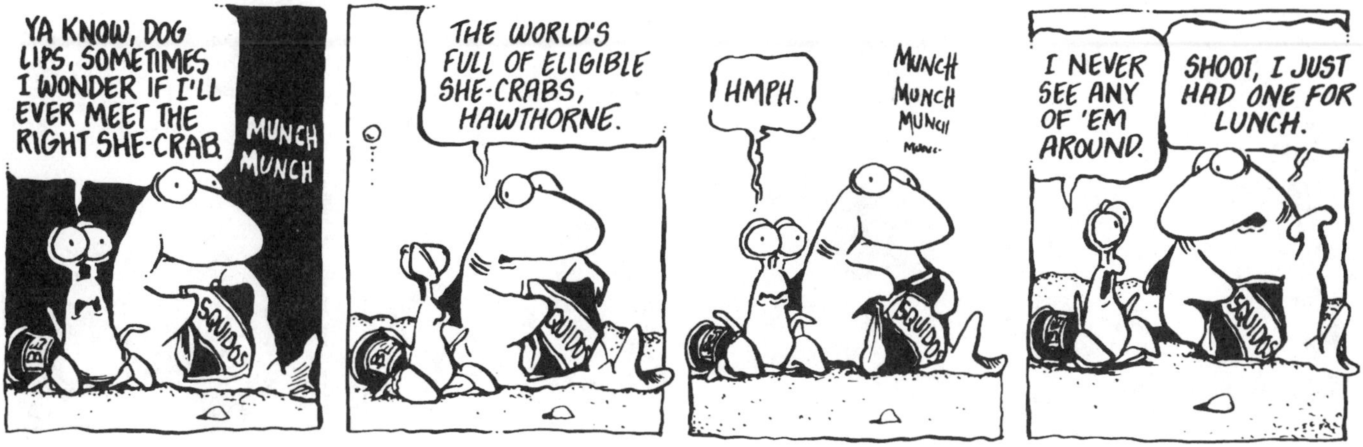
YA KNOW, DOG LIPS, SOMETIMES I WONDER IF I'LL EVER MEET THE RIGHT SHE-CRAB.
MUNCH MUNCH
SQUIDOS
THE WORLD'S FULL OF ELIGIBLE SHE-CRABS, HAWTHORNE.
HMPH.
MUNCH MUNCH MUNCH
I NEVER SEE ANY OF 'EM AROUND.
SHOOT, I JUST HAD ONE FOR LUNCH.

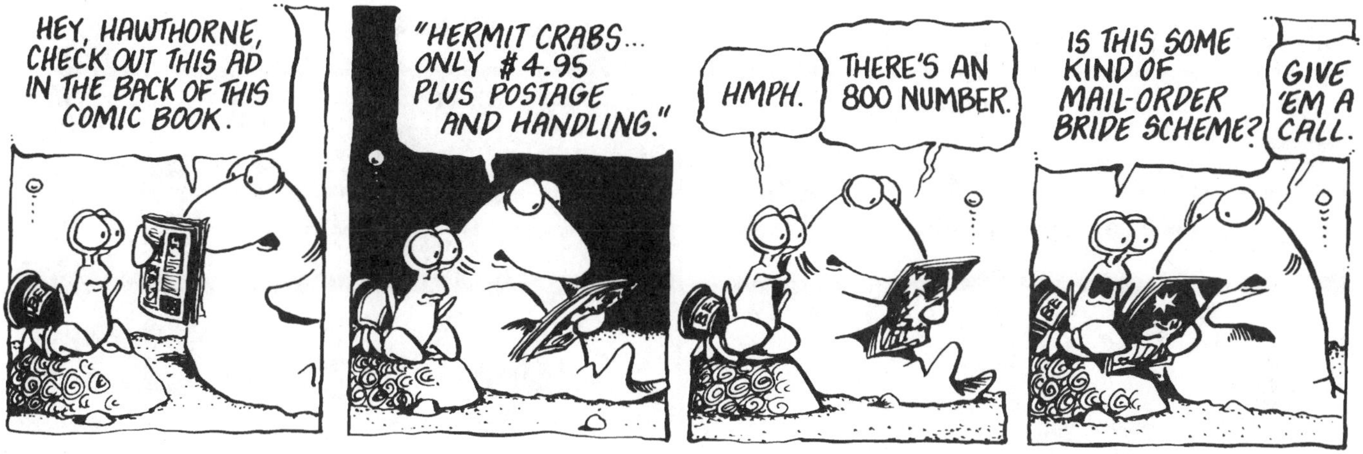
HEY, HAWTHORNE, CHECK OUT THIS AD IN THE BACK OF THIS COMIC BOOK.
"HERMIT CRABS... ONLY #4.95 PLUS POSTAGE AND HANDLING."
HMPH.
THERE'S AN 800 NUMBER.
IS THIS SOME KIND OF MAIL-ORDER BRIDE SCHEME?
GIVE 'EM A CALL.

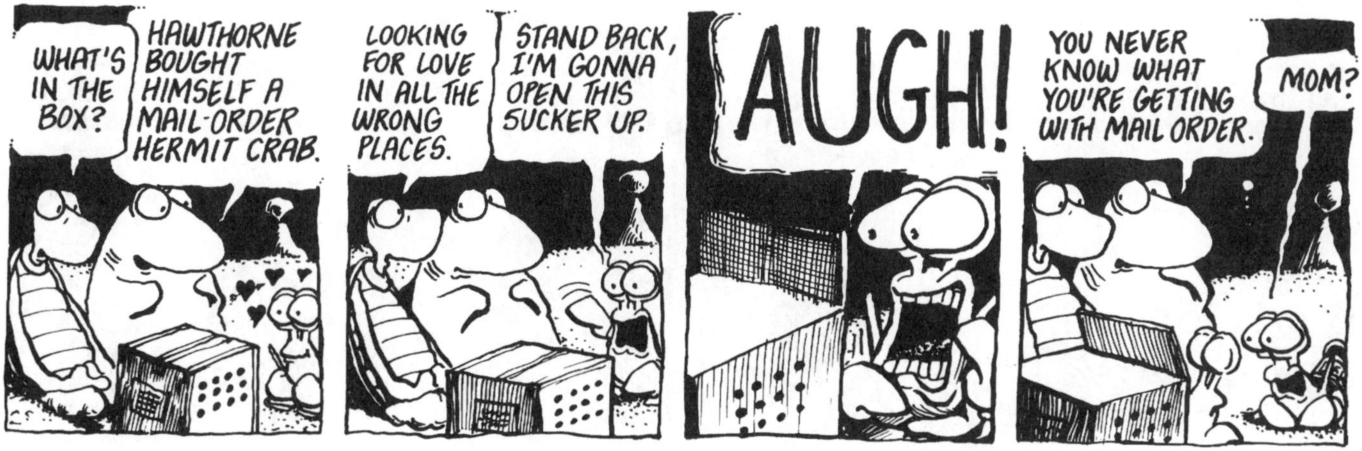
WHAT'S IN THE BOX?
HAWTHORNE BOUGHT HIMSELF A MAIL-ORDER HERMIT CRAB.
LOOKING FOR LOVE IN ALL THE WRONG PLACES.
STAND BACK, I'M GONNA OPEN THIS SUCKER UP.
AUGH!
YOU NEVER KNOW WHAT YOU'RE GETTING WITH MAIL ORDER.
MOM?

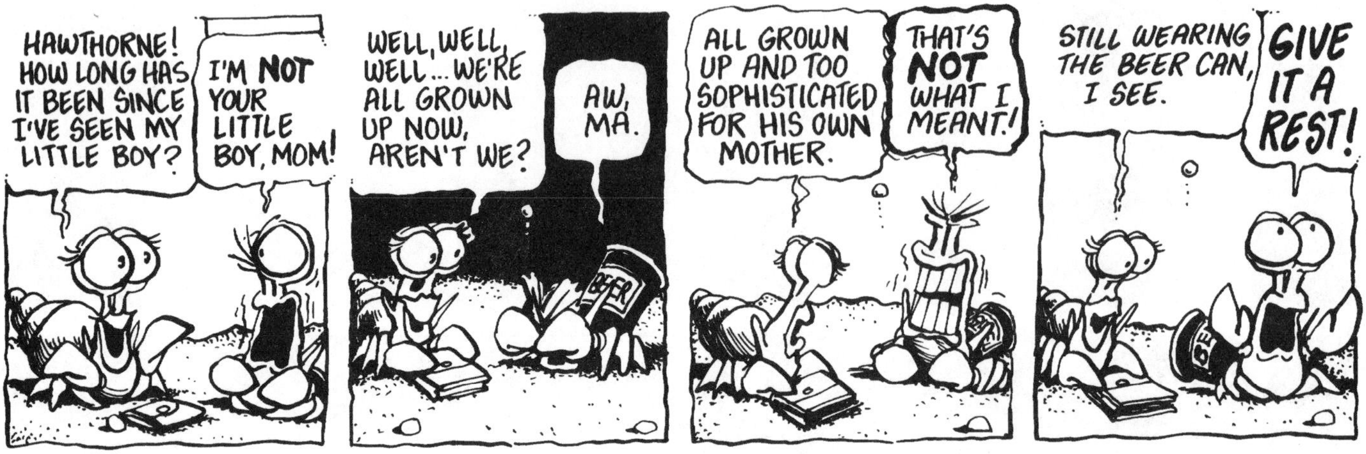
HAWTHORNE! HOW LONG HAS IT BEEN SINCE I'VE SEEN MY LITTLE BOY?
I'M NOT YOUR LITTLE BOY, MOM!
WELL, WELL, WELL... WE'RE ALL GROWN UP NOW, AREN'T WE?
AW, MA.
BEER
ALL GROWN UP AND TOO SOPHISTICATED FOR HIS OWN MOTHER.
THAT'S NOT WHAT I MEANT!
STILL WEARING THE BEER CAN, I SEE.
GIVE IT A REST!

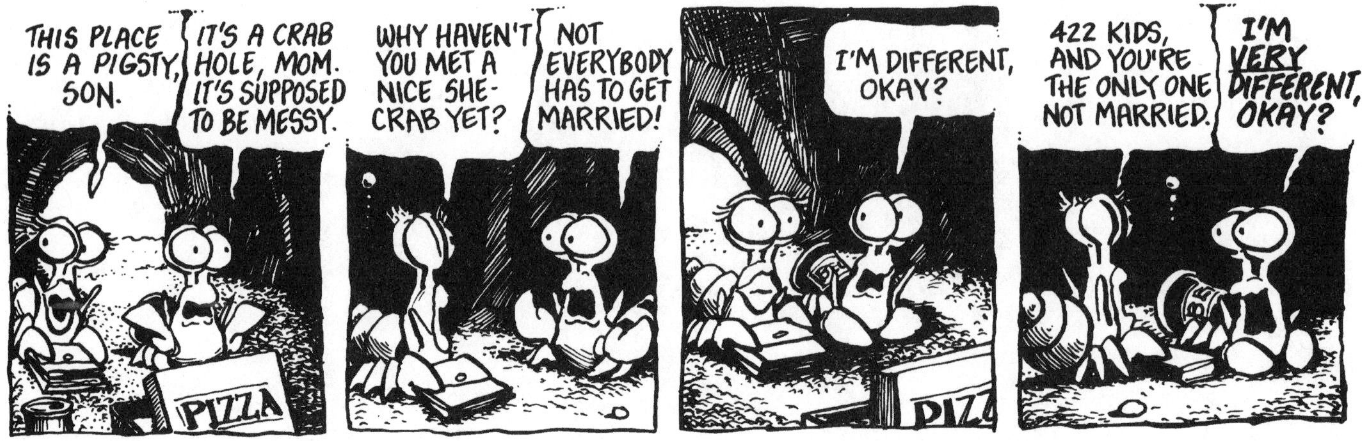
THIS PLACE IS A PIGSTY, SON.
IT'S A CRAB HOLE, MOM. IT'S SUPPOSED TO BE MESSY.
PIZZA
WHY HAVEN'T YOU MET A NICE SHE-CRAB YET?
NOT EVERYBODY HAS TO GET MARRIED!
I'M DIFFERENT, OKAY?
422 KIDS, AND YOU'RE THE ONLY ONE NOT MARRIED.
I'M VERY DIFFERENT, OKAY?

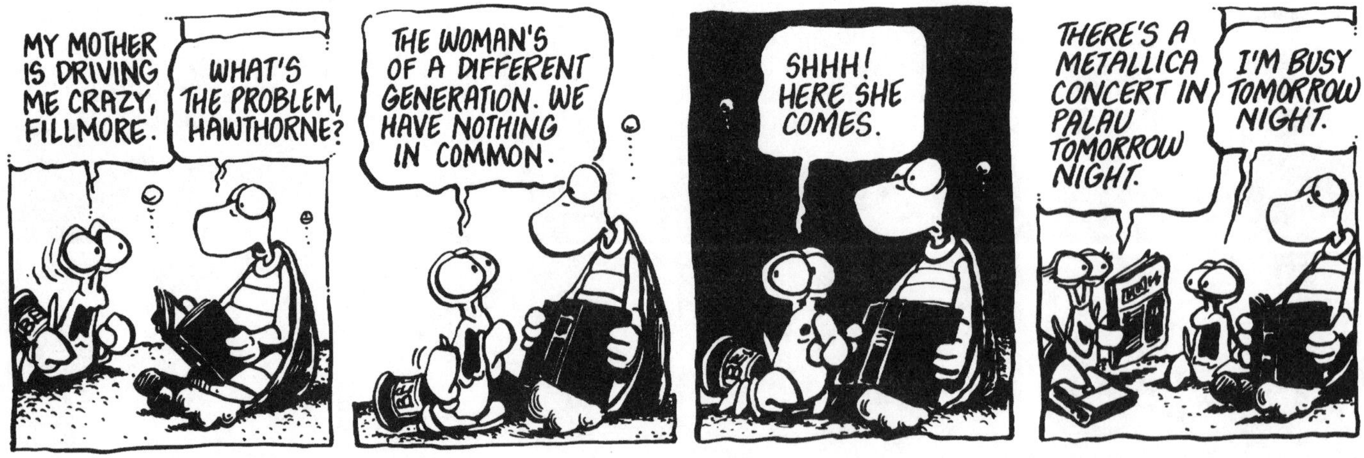
MY MOTHER IS DRIVING ME CRAZY, FILLMORE.
WHAT'S THE PROBLEM, HAWTHORNE?
THE WOMAN'S OF A DIFFERENT GENERATION. WE HAVE NOTHING IN COMMON.
SHHH! HERE SHE COMES.
THERE'S A METALLICA CONCERT IN PALAU TOMORROW NIGHT.
I'M BUSY TOMORROW NIGHT.

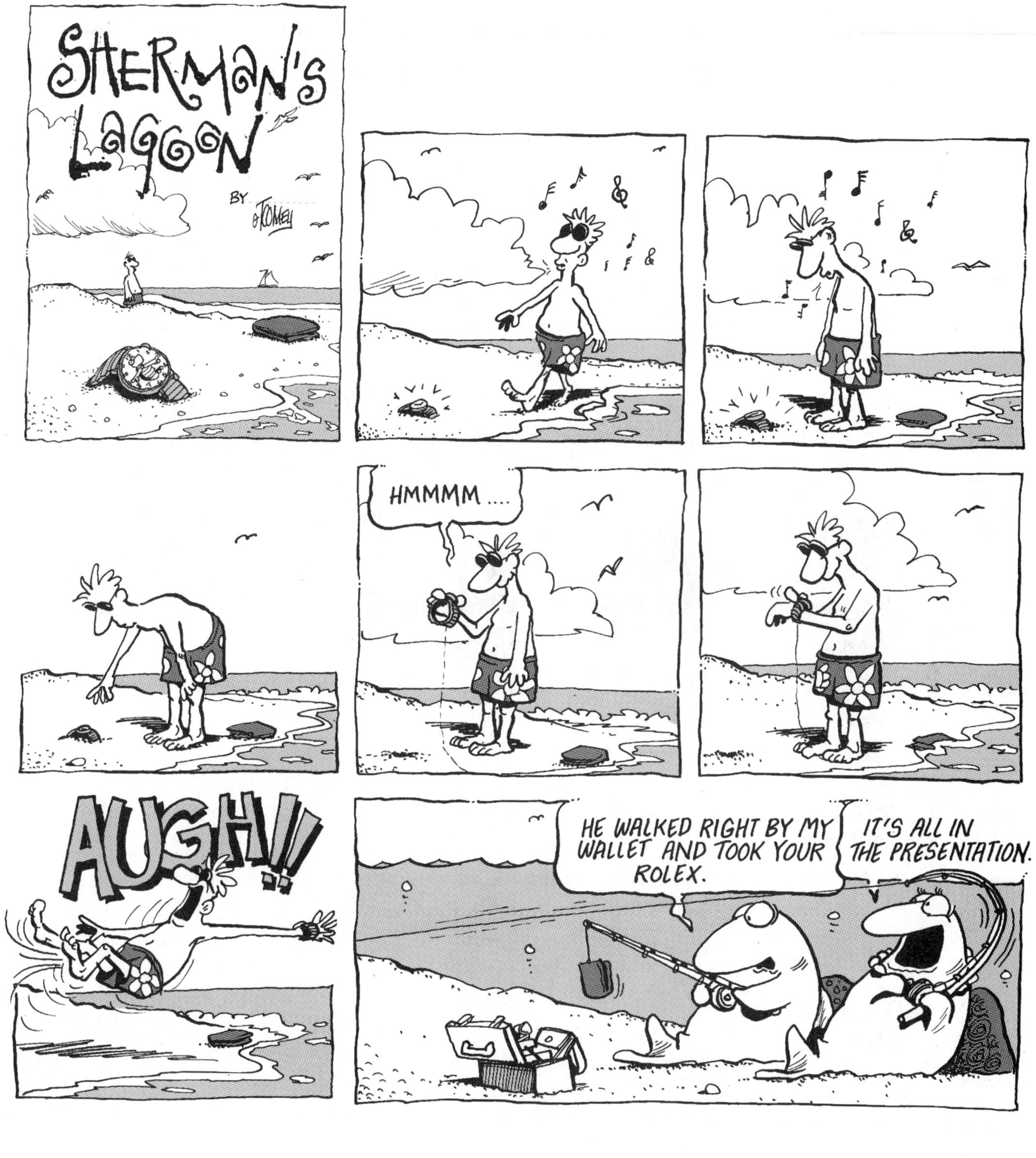
SHERMAN'S LAGOON
BY TOOMEY
HMMMM....
AUGH!!!
HE WALKED RIGHT BY MY WALLET AND TOOK YOUR ROLEX.
IT'S ALL IN THE PRESENTATION.

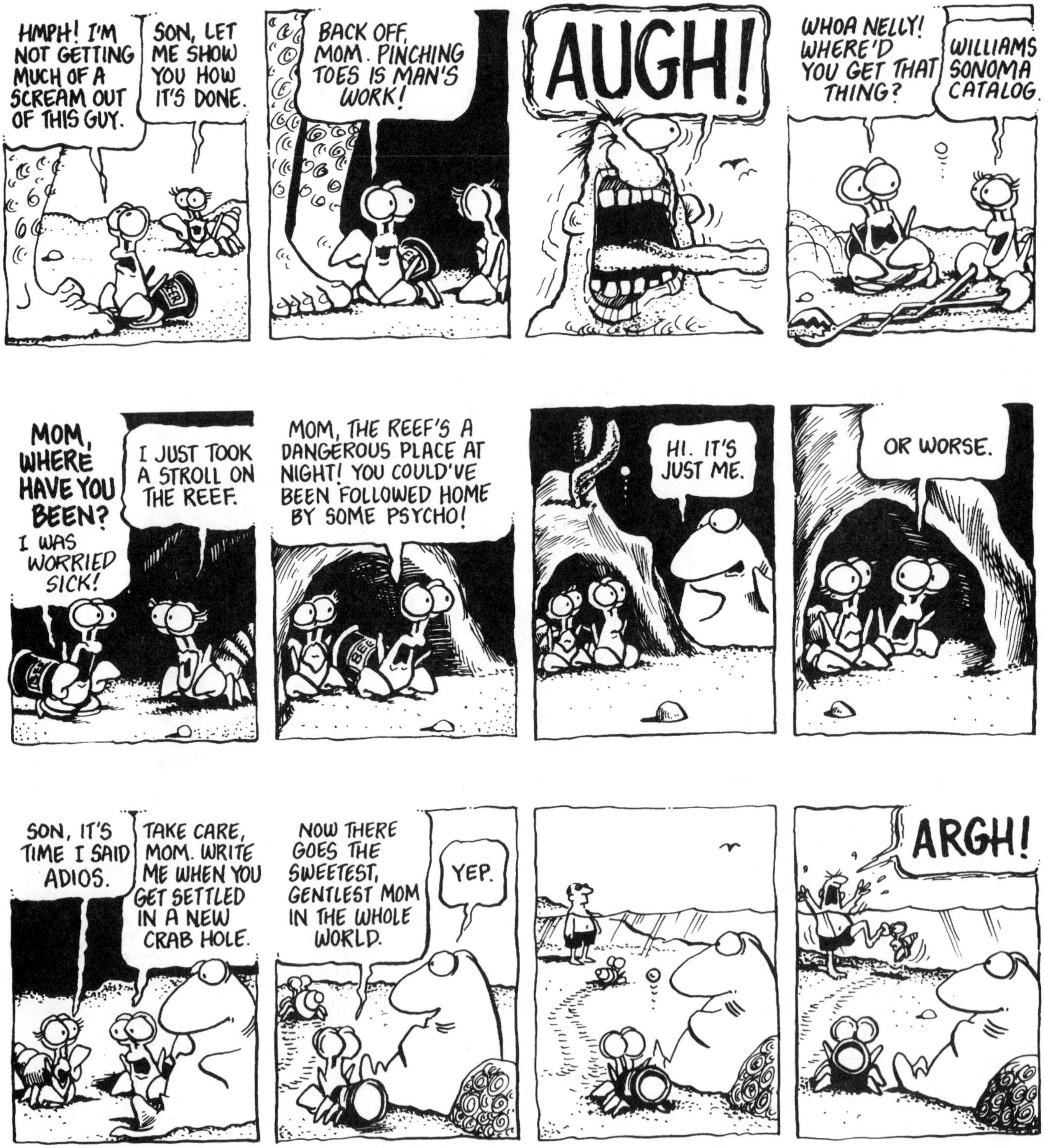
HMPH! I'M NOT GETTING MUCH OF A SCREAM OUT OF THIS GUY.
SON, LET ME SHOW YOU HOW IT'S DONE.
BACK OFF, MOM. PINCHING TOES IS MAN'S WORK!
AUGH!
WHOA NELLY! WHERE'D YOU GET THAT THING?
WILLIAMS SONOMA CATALOG.
MOM, WHERE HAVE YOU BEEN? I WAS WORRIED SICK!
I JUST TOOK A STROLL ON THE REEF.
MOM, THE REEF'S A DANGEROUS PLACE AT NIGHT! YOU COULD'VE BEEN FOLLOWED HOME BY SOME PSYCHO!
HI. IT'S JUST ME.
OR WORSE.
SON, IT'S TIME I SAID ADIOS.
TAKE CARE, MOM. WRITE ME WHEN YOU GET SETTLED IN A NEW CRAB HOLE.
NOW THERE GOES THE SWEETEST, GENTLEST MOM IN THE WHOLE WORLD.
YEP.
ARGH!

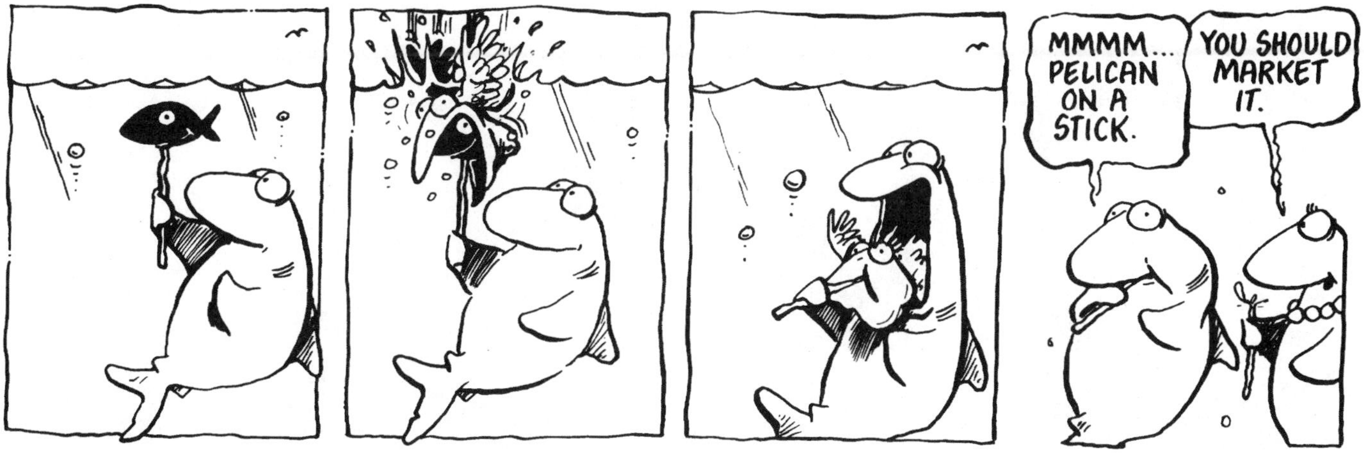
MMMM... PELICAN ON A STICK.
YOU SHOULD MARKET IT.

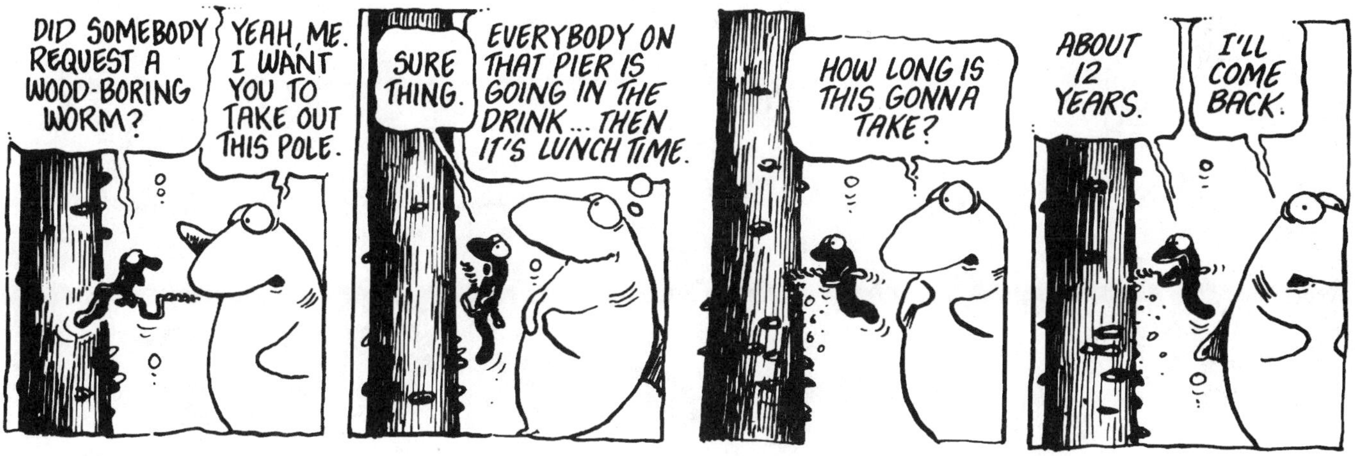
DID SOMEBODY REQUEST A WOOD-BORING WORM?
YEAH, ME. I WANT YOU TO TAKE OUT THIS POLE.
SURE THING.
EVERYBODY ON THAT PIER IS GOING IN THE DRINK... THEN IT'S LUNCH TIME.
HOW LONG IS THIS GONNA TAKE?
ABOUT 12 YEARS.
I'LL COME BACK.

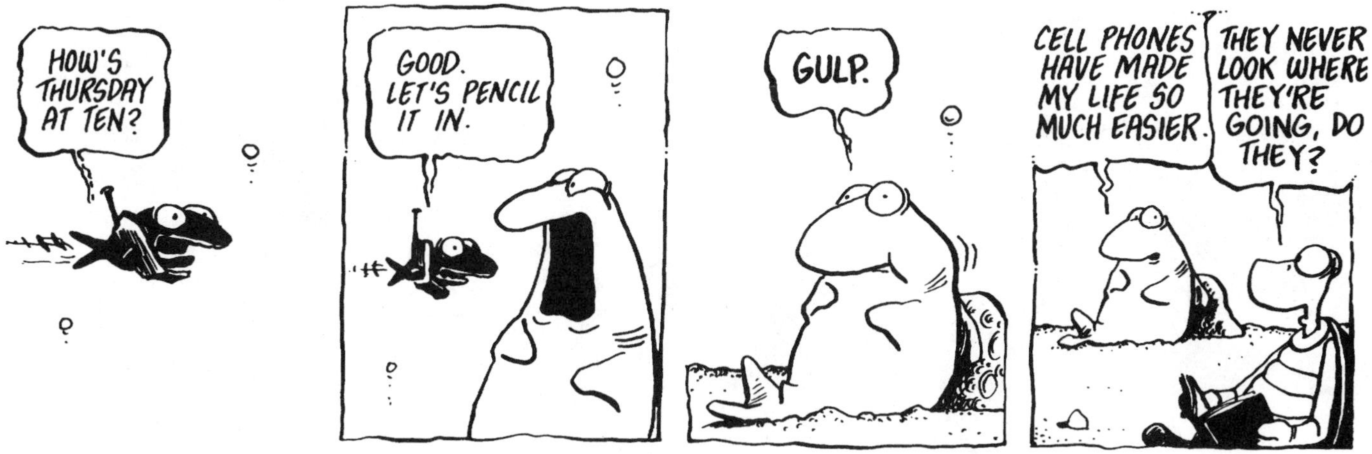
HOW'S THURSDAY AT TEN?
GOOD. LET'S PENCIL IT IN.
GULP.
CELL PHONES HAVE MADE MY LIFE SO MUCH EASIER.
THEY NEVER LOOK WHERE THEY'RE GOING, DO THEY?

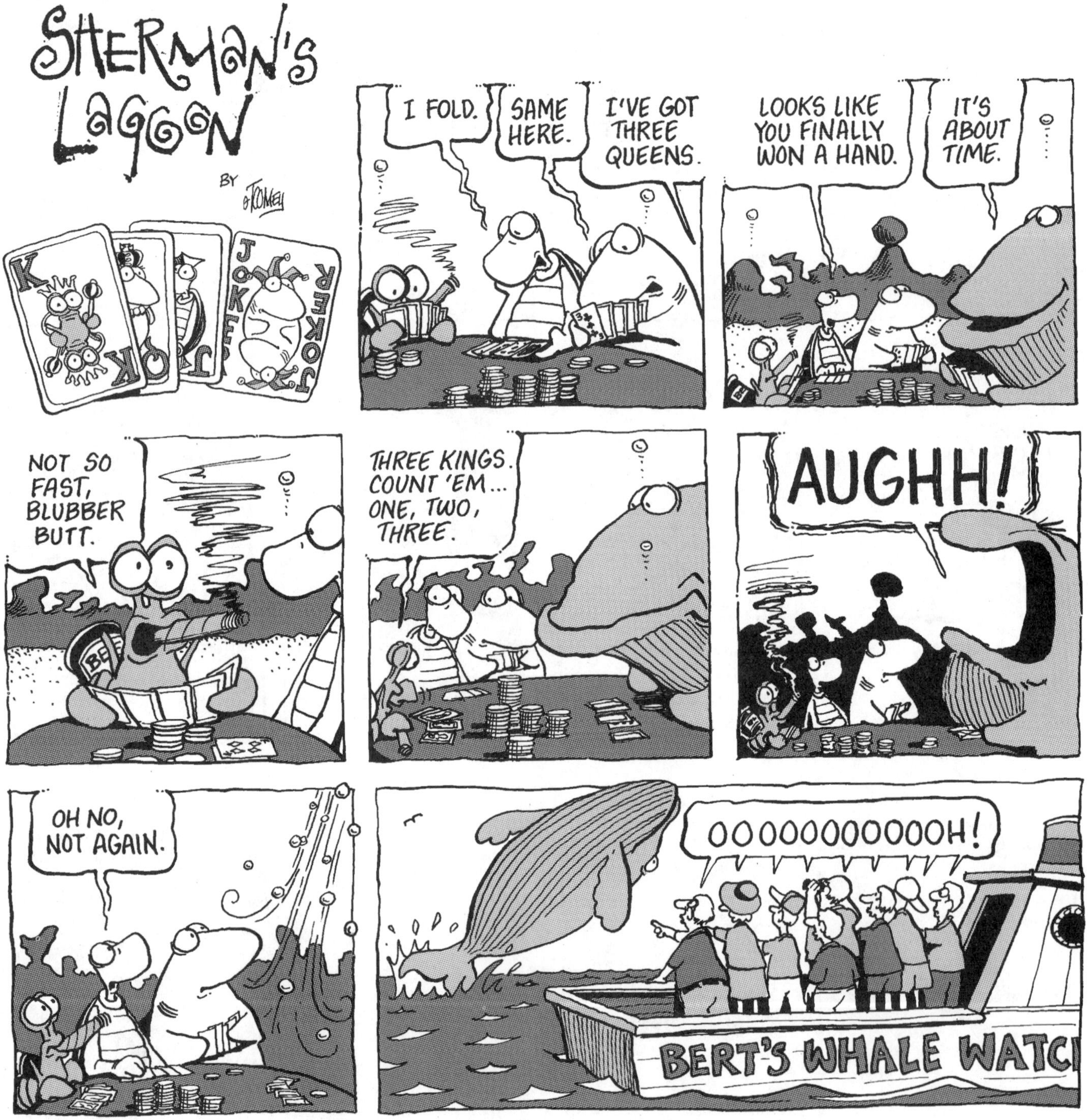
SHERMAN'S LAGOON
BY TOOMEY
I FOLD.
SAME HERE.
I'VE GOT THREE QUEENS.
LOOKS LIKE YOU FINALLY WON A HAND.
IT'S ABOUT TIME.
NOT SO FAST, BLUBBER BUTT.
THREE KINGS. COUNT 'EM... ONE, TWO, THREE.
AUGHH!
OH NO, NOT AGAIN.
OOOOOOOOOOOOH!
BERT'S WHALE WATCH

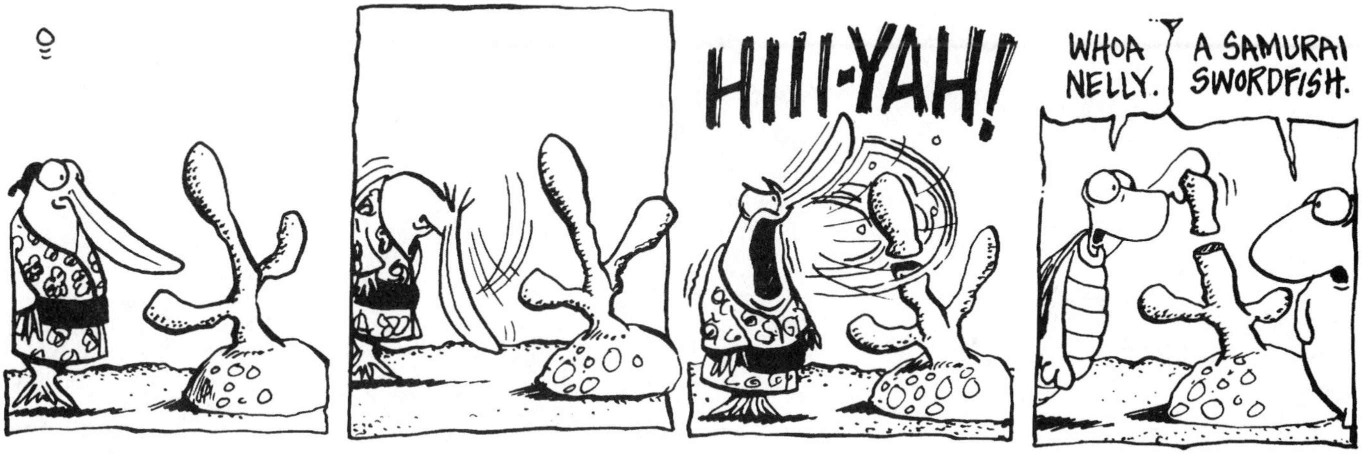
HIII-YAH!
WHOA NELLY.
A SAMURAI SWORDFISH.

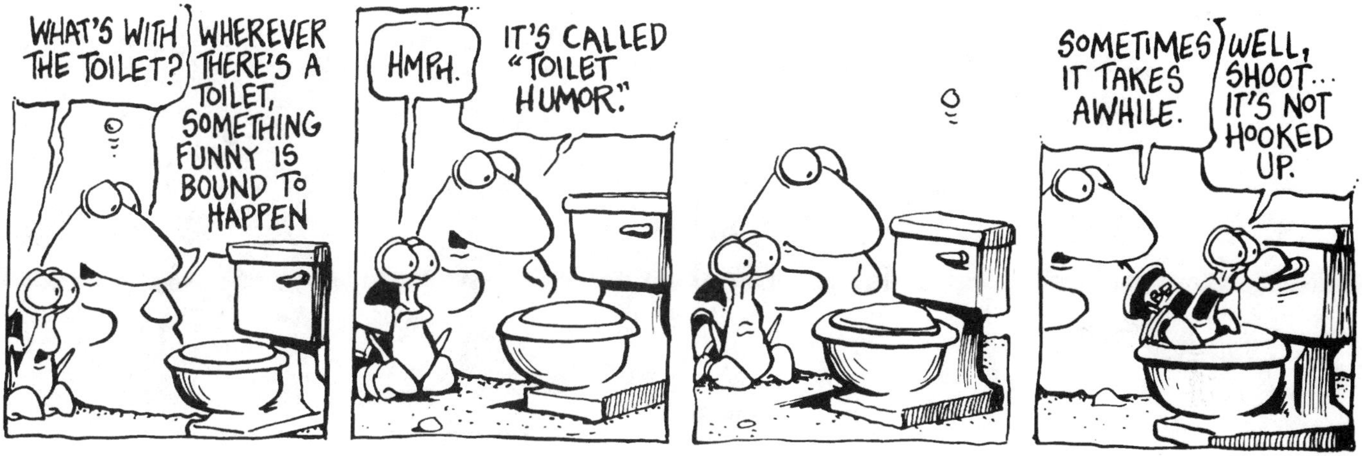
WHAT'S WITH THE TOILET?
WHEREVER THERE'S A TOILET, SOMETHING FUNNY IS BOUND TO HAPPEN
HMPH.
IT'S CALLED "TOILET HUMOR."
SOMETIMES IT TAKES AWHILE.
WELL, SHOOT... IT'S NOT HOOKED UP.

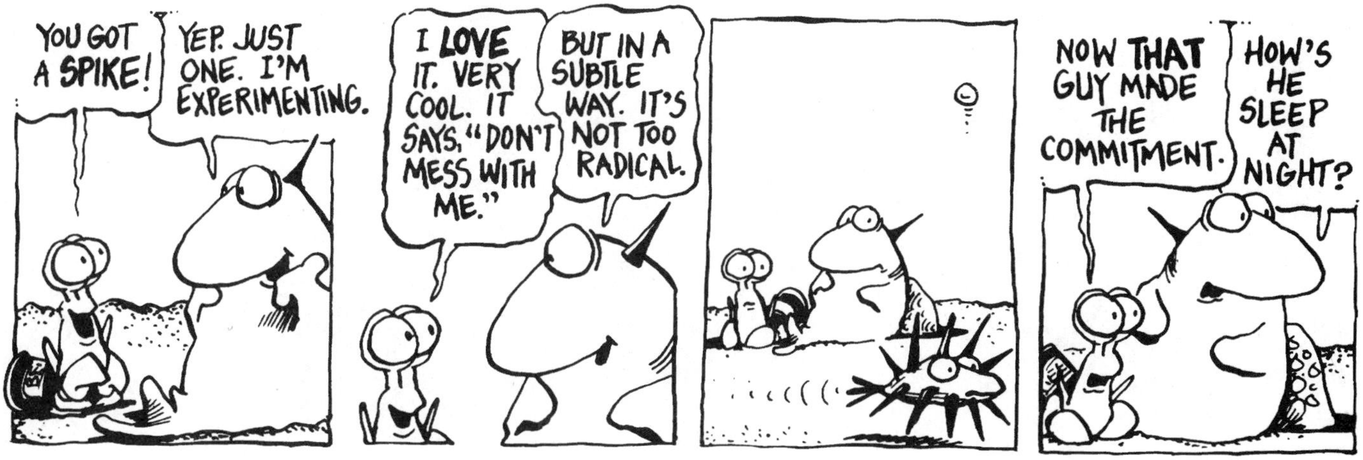
YOU GOT A SPIKE!
YEP. JUST ONE. I'M EXPERIMENTING.
I LOVE IT. VERY COOL. IT SAYS, "DON'T MESS WITH ME."
BUT IN A SUBTLE WAY. IT'S NOT TOO RADICAL.
NOW THAT GUY MADE THE COMMITMENT.
HOW'S HE SLEEP AT NIGHT?

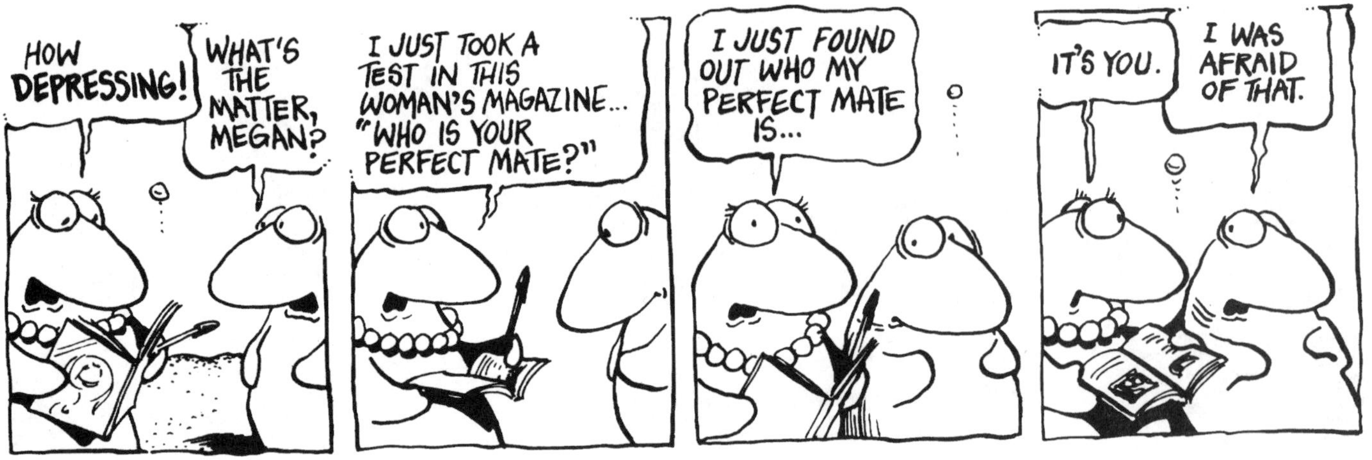
HOW DEPRESSING!
WHAT'S THE MATTER, MEGAN?
I JUST TOOK A TEST IN THIS WOMAN'S MAGAZINE... "WHO IS YOUR PERFECT MATE?"
I JUST FOUND OUT WHO MY PERFECT MATE IS...
IT'S YOU.
I WAS AFRAID OF THAT.

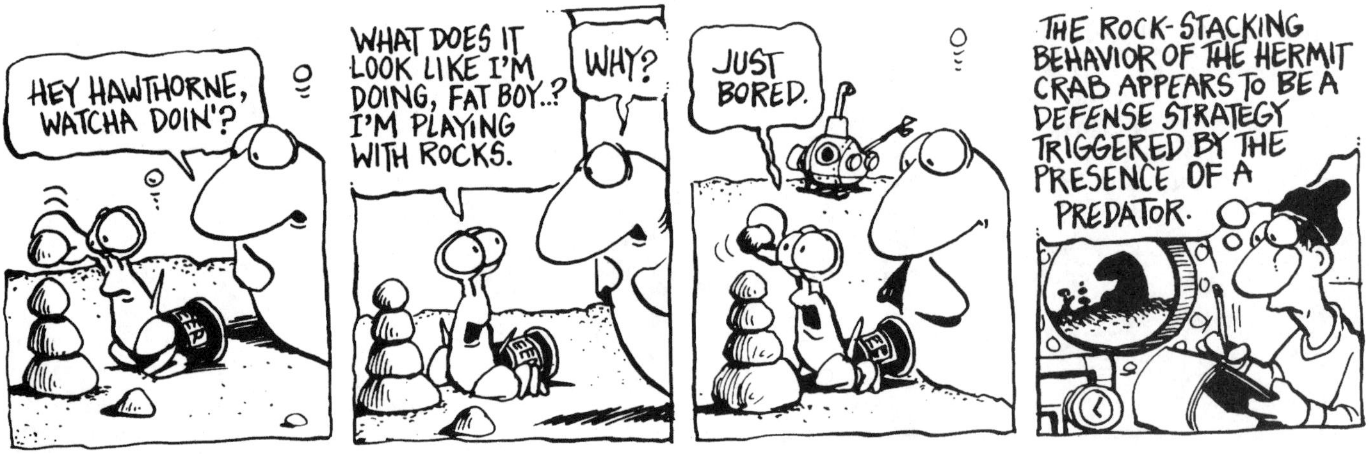
HEY HAWTHORNE, WATCHA DOIN'?
WHAT DOES IT LOOK LIKE I'M DOING, FAT BOY..? I'M PLAYING WITH ROCKS.
WHY?
JUST BORED.
THE ROCK-STACKING BEHAVIOR OF THE HERMIT CRAB APPEARS TO BE A DEFENSE STRATEGY TRIGGERED BY THE PRESENCE OF A PREDATOR.

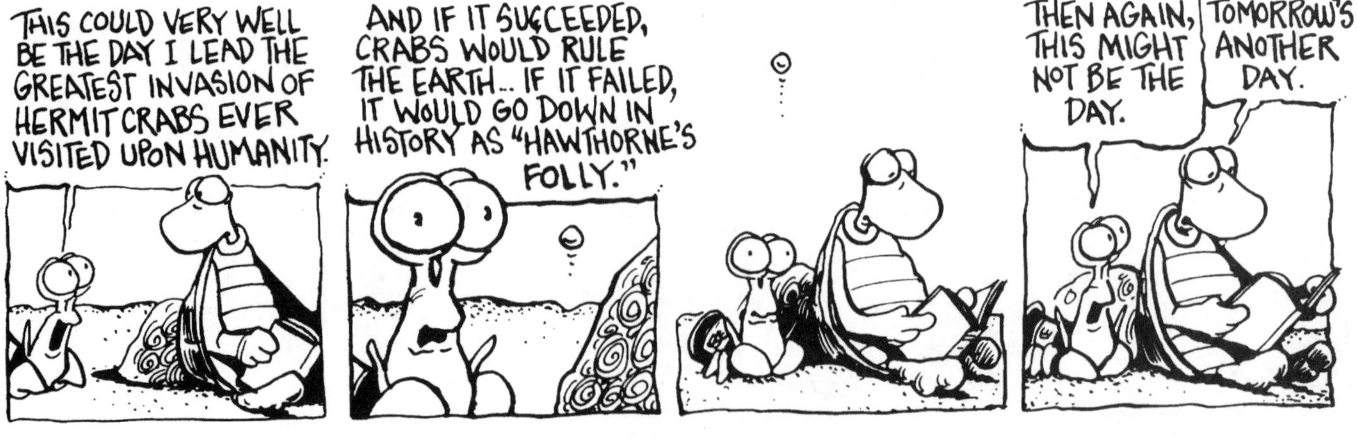
THIS COULD VERY WELL BE THE DAY I LEAD THE GREATEST INVASION OF HERMIT CRABS EVER VISITED UPON HUMANITY.
AND IF IT SUCCEEDED, CRABS WOULD RULE THE EARTH... IF IT FAILED, IT WOULD GO DOWN IN HISTORY AS "HAWTHORNE'S FOLLY."
THEN AGAIN, THIS MIGHT NOT BE THE DAY.
TOMORROW'S ANOTHER DAY.

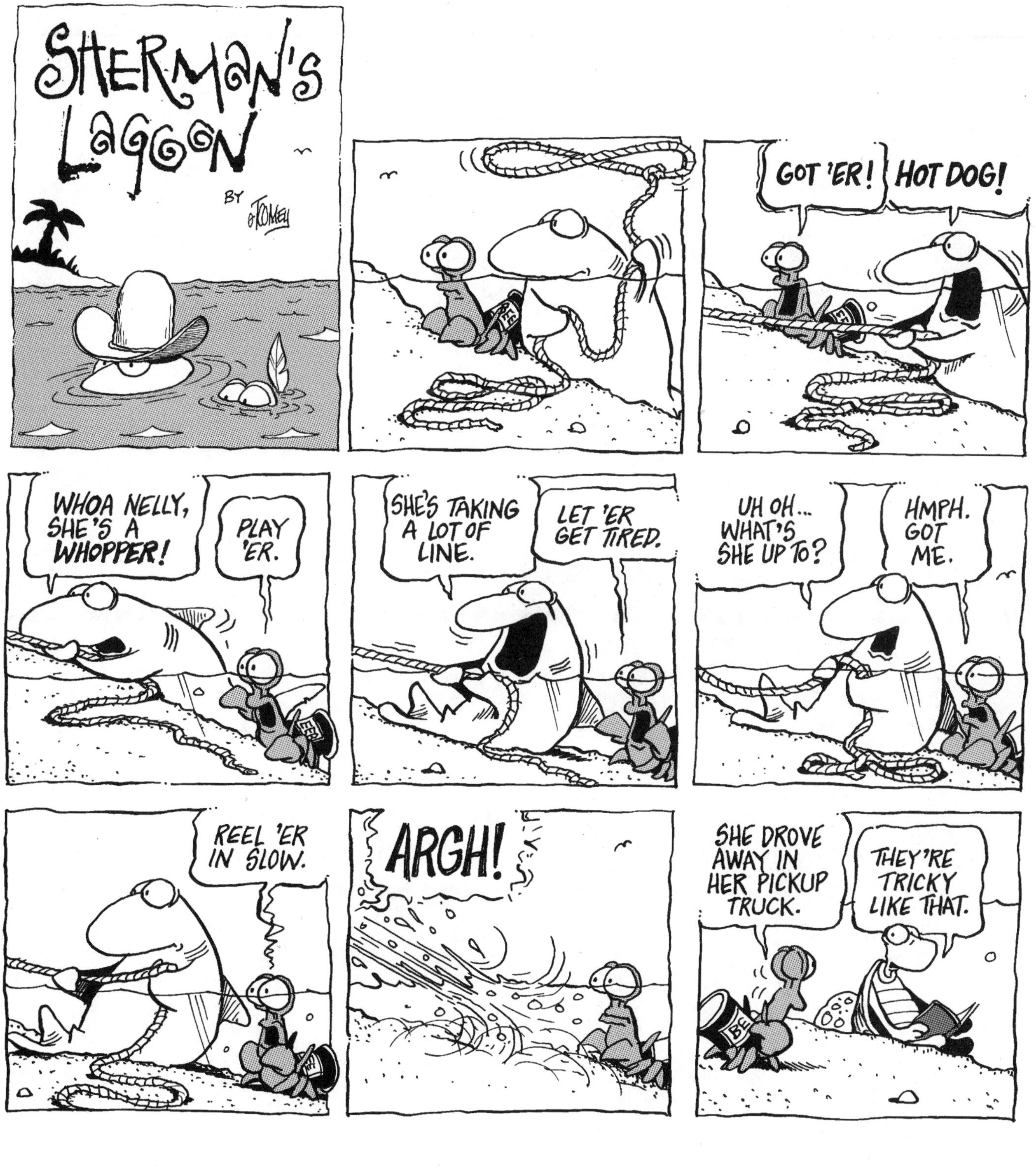
SHERMAN'S LAGOON
BY TOOMEY
GOT 'ER!
HOT DOG!
WHOA NELLY, SHE'S A WHOPPER!
PLAY 'ER.
SHE'S TAKING A LOT OF LINE.
LET 'ER GET TIRED.
UH OH... WHAT'S SHE UP TO?
HMPH. GOT ME.
REEL 'ER IN SLOW.
ARGH!
SHE DROVE AWAY IN HER PICKUP TRUCK.
THEY'RE TRICKY LIKE THAT.

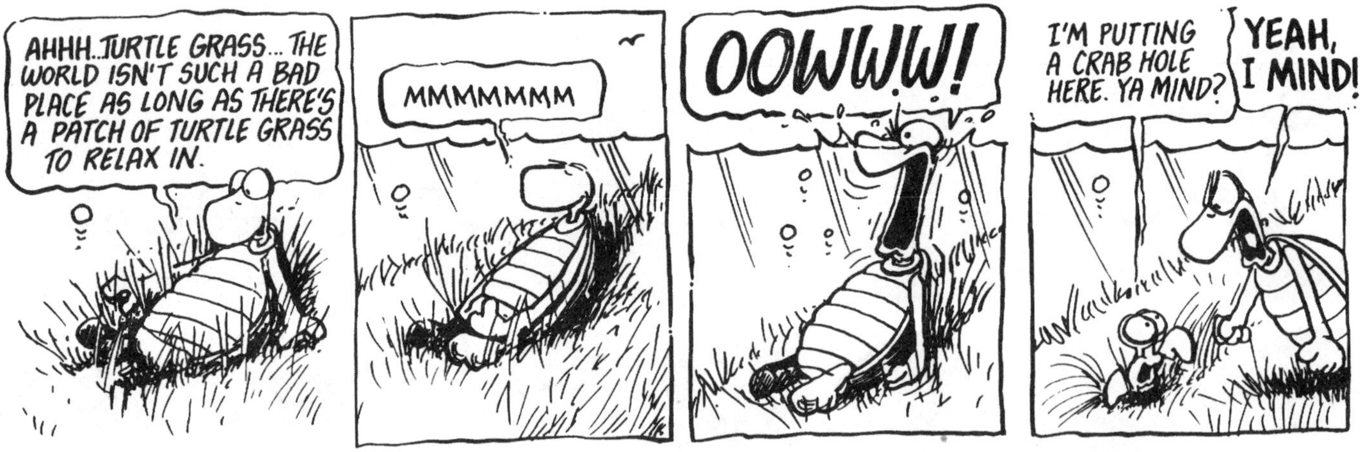
AHHH...TURTLE GRASS... THE WORLD ISN'T SUCH A BAD PLACE AS LONG AS THERE'S A PATCH OF TURTLE GRASS TO RELAX IN.
MMMMMMM
OOWWW!
I'M PUTTING A CRAB HOLE HERE. YA MIND?
YEAH, I MIND!

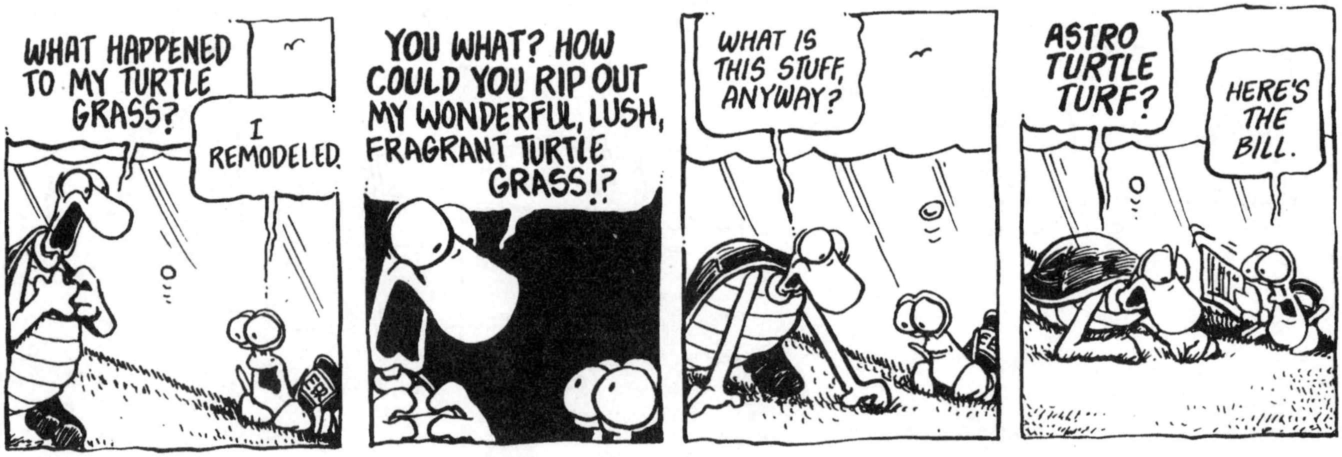
WHAT HAPPENED TO MY TURTLE GRASS?
I REMODELED.
YOU WHAT? HOW COULD YOU RIP OUT MY WONDERFUL, LUSH, FRAGRANT TURTLE GRASS!?
WHAT IS THIS STUFF, ANYWAY?
ASTRO TURTLE TURF?
HERE'S THE BILL.

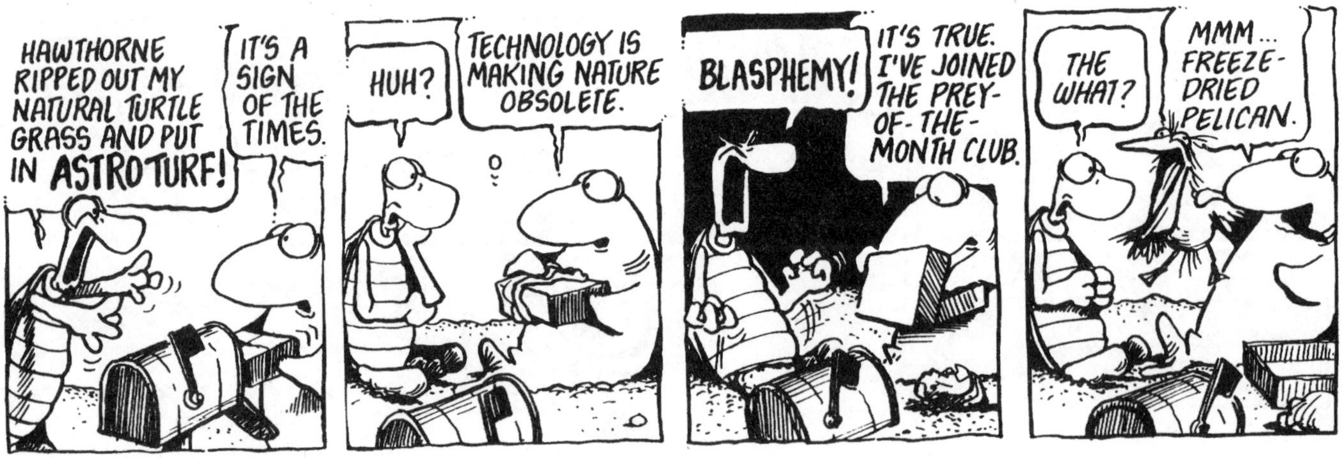
HAWTHORNE RIPPED OUT MY NATURAL TURTLE GRASS AND PUT IN ASTROTURF!
IT'S A SIGN OF THE TIMES.
HUH?
TECHNOLOGY IS MAKING NATURE OBSOLETE.
BLASPHEMY!
IT'S TRUE. I'VE JOINED THE PREY-OF-THE-MONTH CLUB.
THE WHAT?
MMM... FREEZE-DRIED PELICAN.

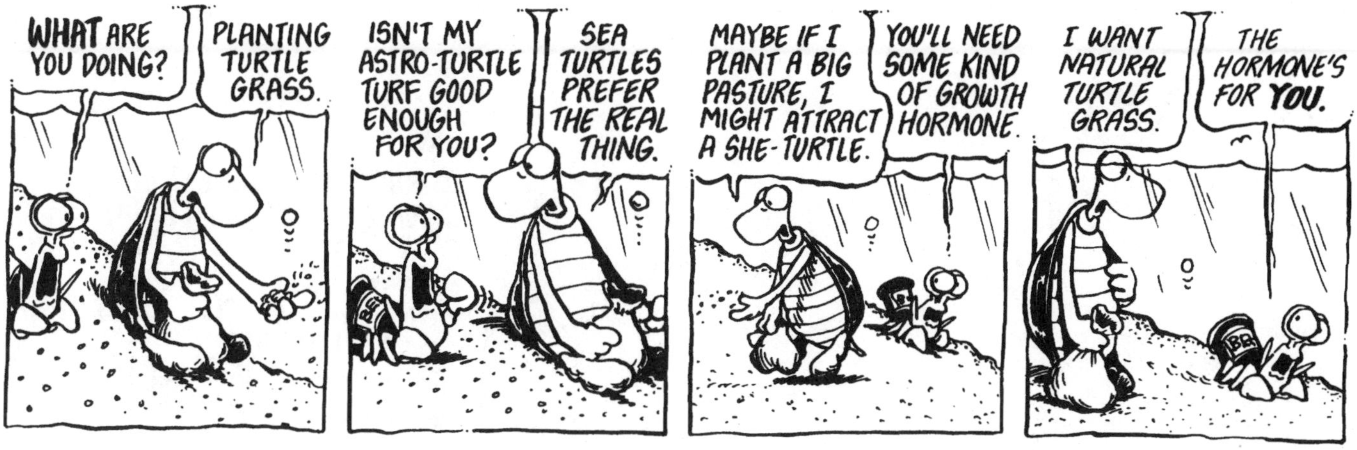
WHAT ARE YOU DOING?
PLANTING TURTLE GRASS.
ISN'T MY ASTRO-TURTLE TURF GOOD ENOUGH FOR YOU?
SEA TURTLES PREFER THE REAL THING.
MAYBE IF I PLANT A BIG PASTURE, I MIGHT ATTRACT A SHE-TURTLE.
YOU'LL NEED SOME KIND OF GROWTH HORMONE.
I WANT NATURAL TURTLE GRASS.
THE HORMONE'S FOR YOU.

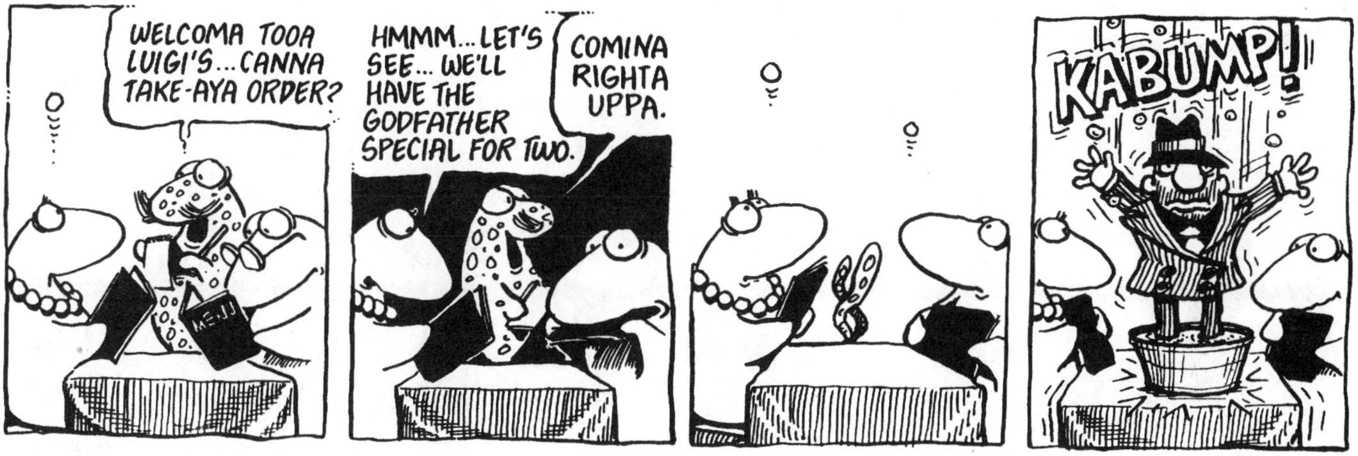
WELCOMA TOOA LUIGI'S...CANNA TAKE-AYA ORDER?
MENU
HMMM...LET'S SEE... WE'LL HAVE THE GODFATHER SPECIAL FOR TWO.
COMINA RIGHTA UPPA.
KABUMP!

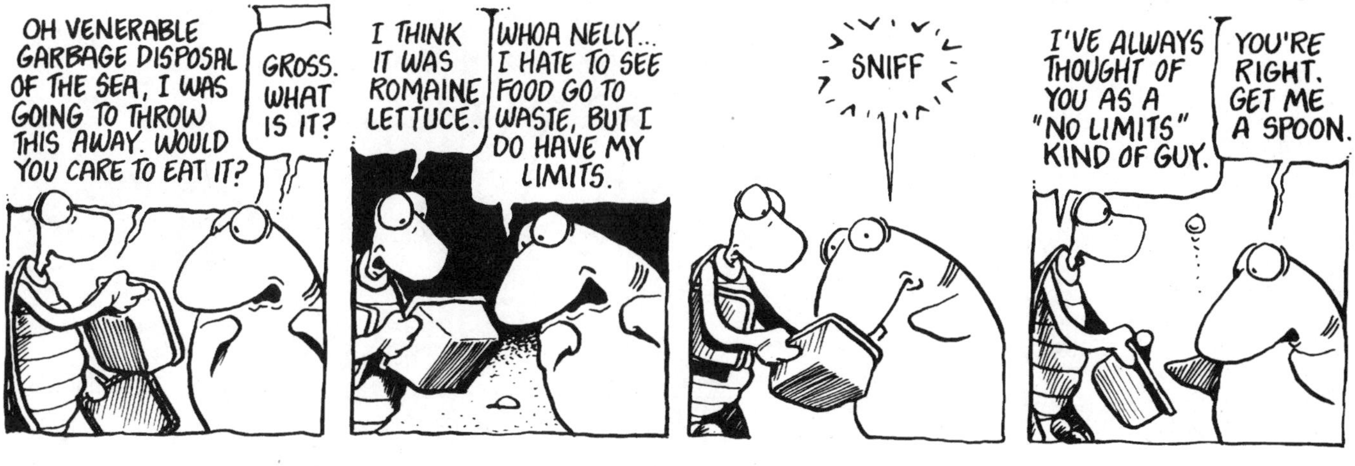
OH VENERABLE GARBAGE DISPOSAL OF THE SEA, I WAS GOING TO THROW THIS AWAY. WOULD YOU CARE TO EAT IT?
GROSS. WHAT IS IT?
I THINK IT WAS ROMAINE LETTUCE.
WHOA NELLY... I HATE TO SEE FOOD GO TO WASTE, BUT I DO HAVE MY LIMITS.
SNIFF
I'VE ALWAYS THOUGHT OF YOU AS A "NO LIMITS" KIND OF GUY.
YOU'RE RIGHT. GET ME A SPOON.

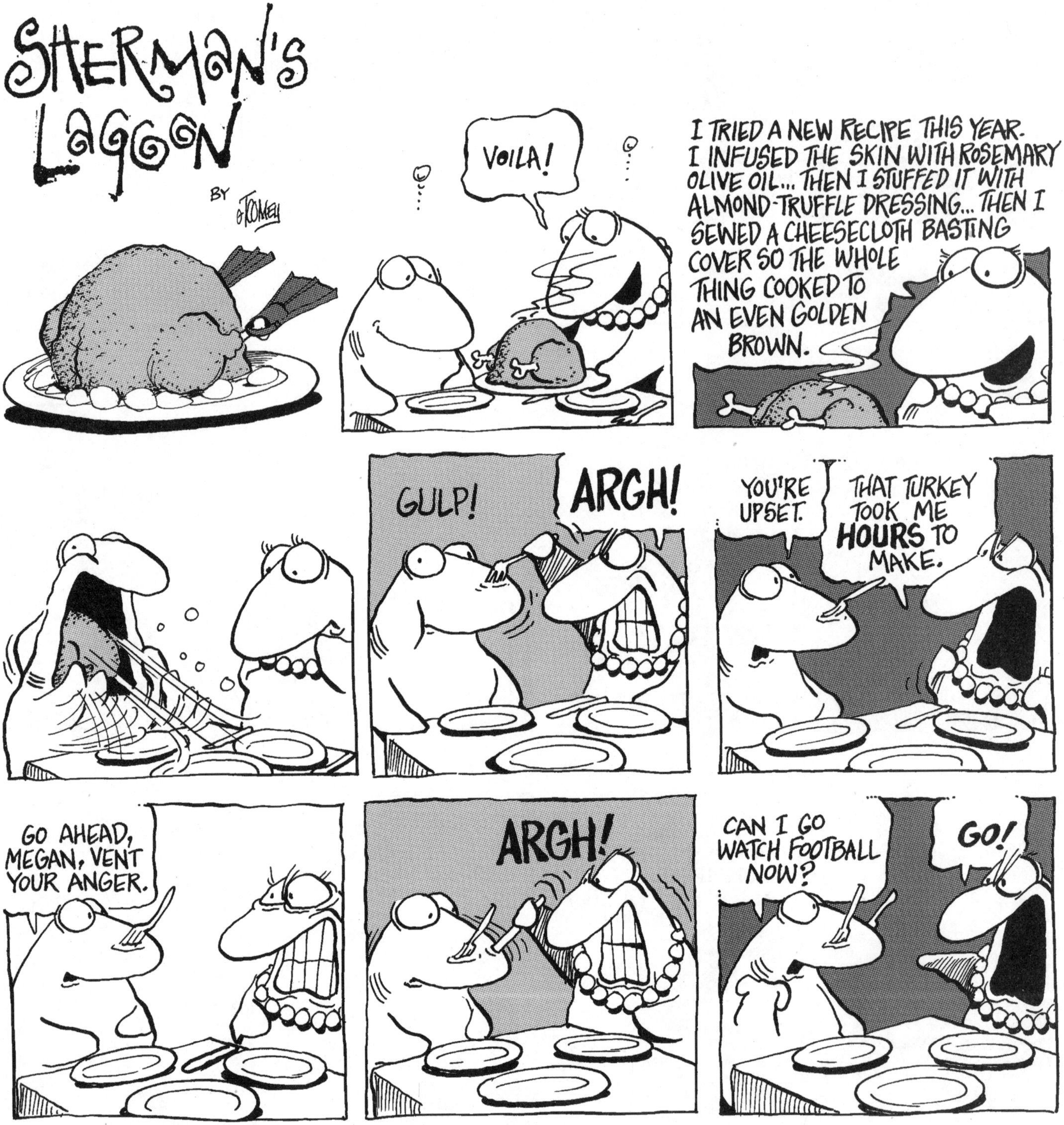
SHERMAN'S LAGOON
BY TOOMEY
VOILA!
I TRIED A NEW RECIPE THIS YEAR. I INFUSED THE SKIN WITH ROSEMARY OLIVE OIL... THEN I STUFFED IT WITH ALMOND-TRUFFLE DRESSING... THEN I SEWED A CHEESECLOTH BASTING COVER SO THE WHOLE THING COOKED TO AN EVEN GOLDEN BROWN.
GULP!
ARGH!
YOU'RE UPSET.
THAT TURKEY TOOK ME HOURS TO MAKE.
GO AHEAD, MEGAN, VENT YOUR ANGER.
ARGH!
CAN I GO WATCH FOOTBALL NOW?
GO!

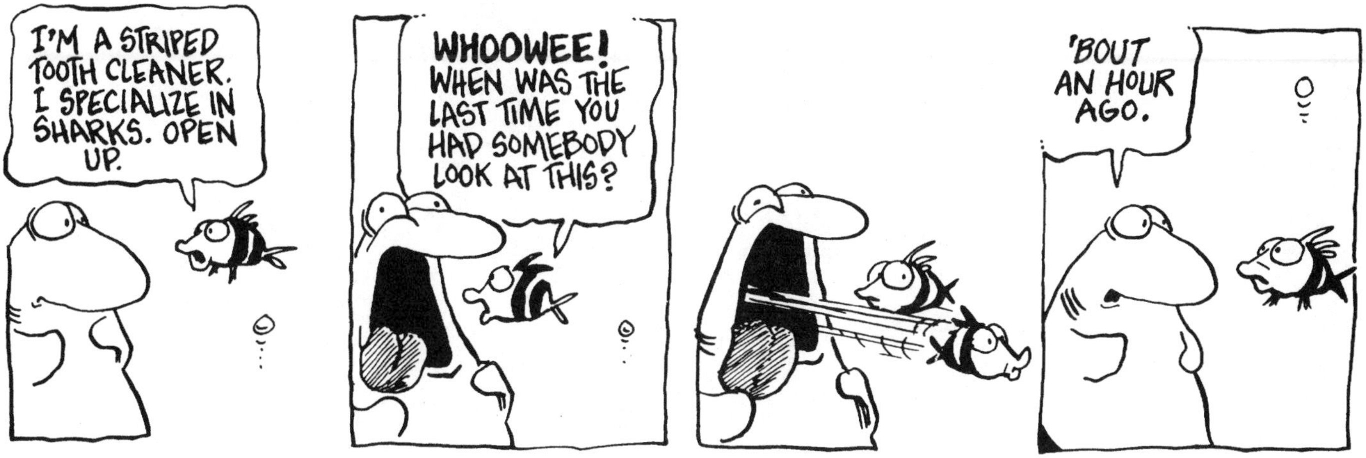
I'M A STRIPED TOOTH CLEANER. I SPECIALIZE IN SHARKS. OPEN UP.
WHOOWEE! WHEN WAS THE LAST TIME YOU HAD SOMEBODY LOOK AT THIS?
'BOUT AN HOUR AGO.

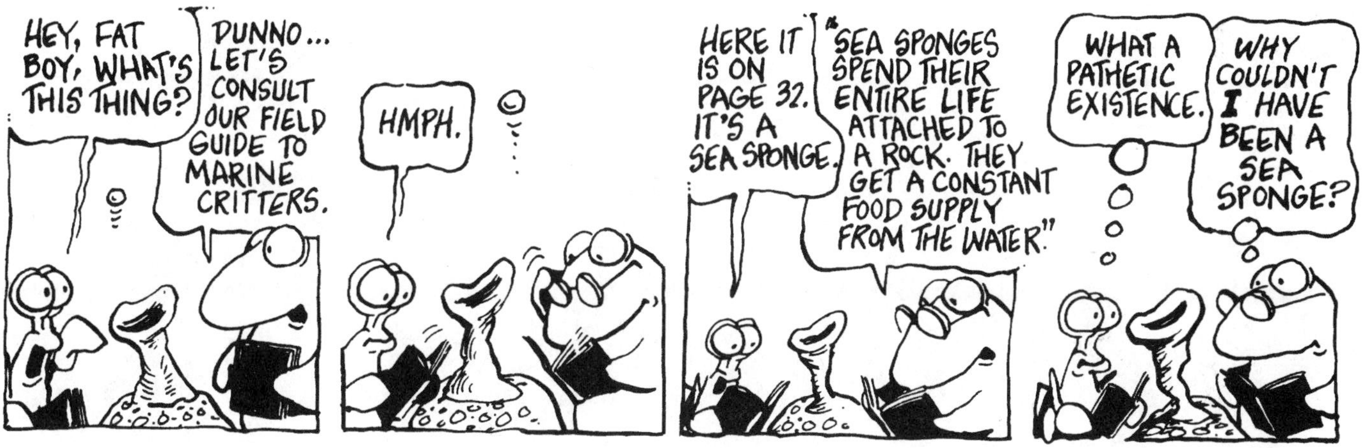
HEY, FAT BOY, WHAT'S THIS THING?
DUNNO... LET'S CONSULT OUR FIELD GUIDE TO MARINE CRITTERS.
HMPH.
HERE IT IS ON PAGE 32. IT'S A SEA SPONGE.
"SEA SPONGES SPEND THEIR ENTIRE LIFE ATTACHED TO A ROCK. THEY GET A CONSTANT FOOD SUPPLY FROM THE WATER."
WHAT A PATHETIC EXISTENCE.
WHY COULDN'T I HAVE BEEN A SEA SPONGE?

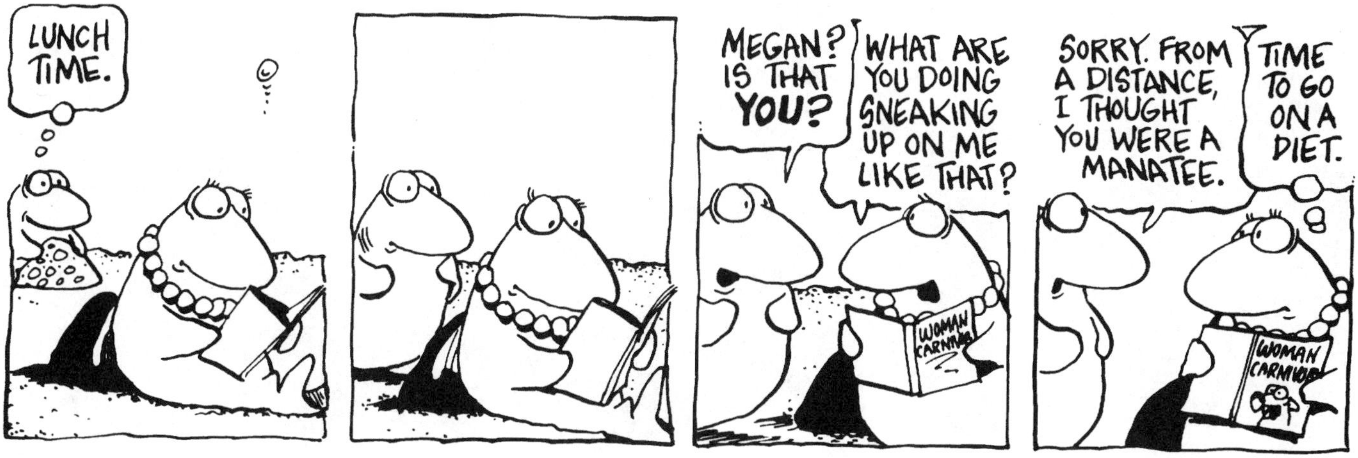
LUNCH TIME.
MEGAN? IS THAT YOU?
WHAT ARE YOU DOING SNEAKING UP ON ME LIKE THAT?
WOMAN CARNIVORE
SORRY. FROM A DISTANCE, I THOUGHT YOU WERE A MANATEE.
TIME TO GO ON A DIET.
WOMAN CARNIVORE

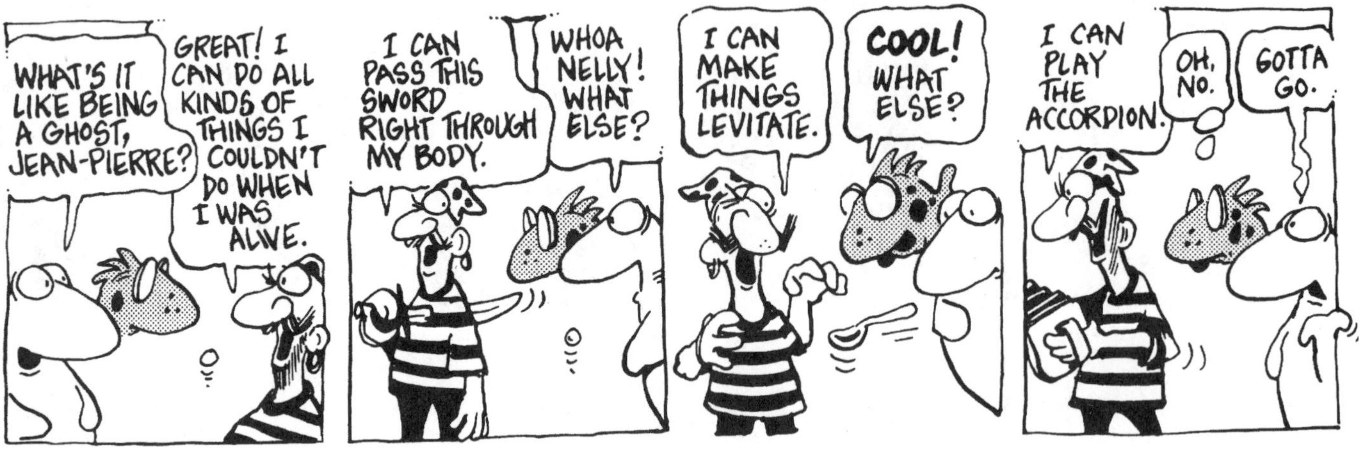
WHAT'S IT LIKE BEING A GHOST, JEAN-PIERRE?
GREAT! I CAN DO ALL KINDS OF THINGS I COULDN'T DO WHEN I WAS ALIVE.
I CAN PASS THIS SWORD RIGHT THROUGH MY BODY.
WHOA NELLY! WHAT ELSE?
I CAN MAKE THINGS LEVITATE.
COOL! WHAT ELSE?
I CAN PLAY THE ACCORDION.
OH, NO.
GOTTA GO.

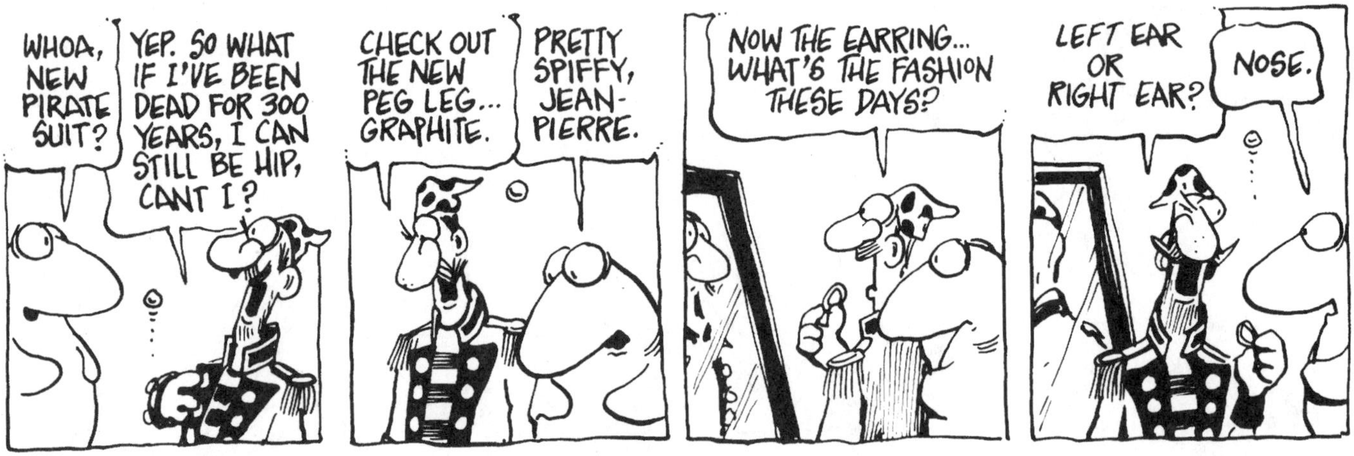
WHOA, NEW PIRATE SUIT?
YEP. SO WHAT IF I'VE BEEN DEAD FOR 300 YEARS, I CAN STILL BE HIP, CANT I?
CHECK OUT THE NEW PEG LEG... GRAPHITE.
PRETTY SPIFFY, JEAN-PIERRE.
NOW THE EARRING... WHAT'S THE FASHION THESE DAYS?
LEFT EAR OR RIGHT EAR?
NOSE.

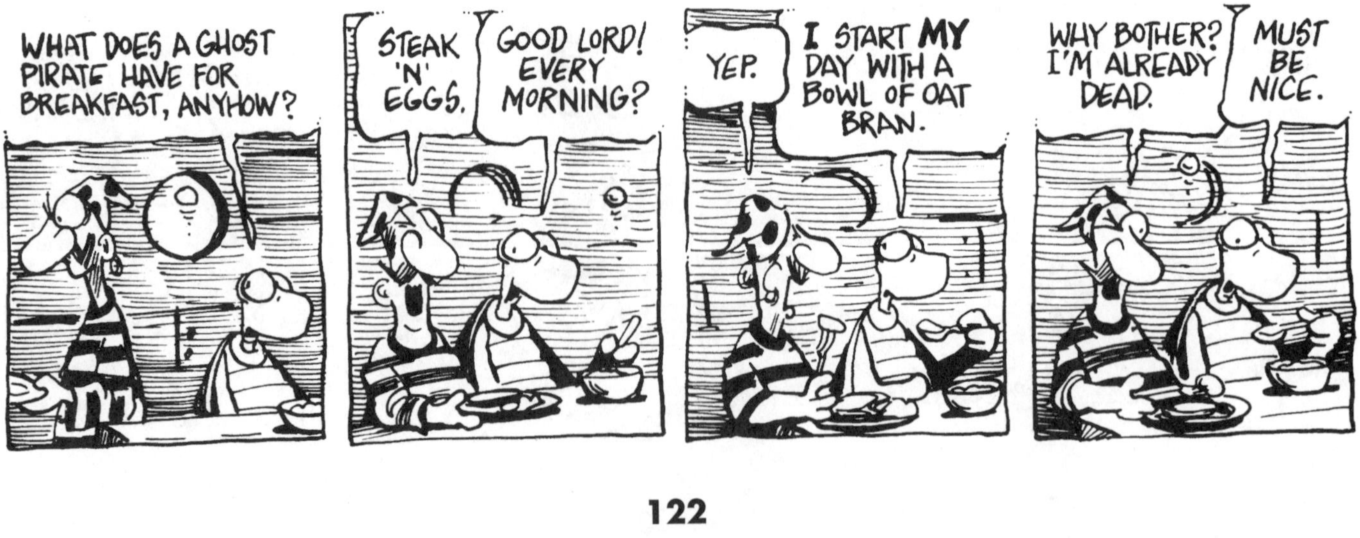
WHAT DOES A GHOST PIRATE HAVE FOR BREAKFAST, ANYHOW?
STEAK 'N' EGGS.
GOOD LORD! EVERY MORNING?
YEP.
I START MY DAY WITH A BOWL OF OAT BRAN.
WHY BOTHER? I'M ALREADY DEAD.
MUST BE NICE.

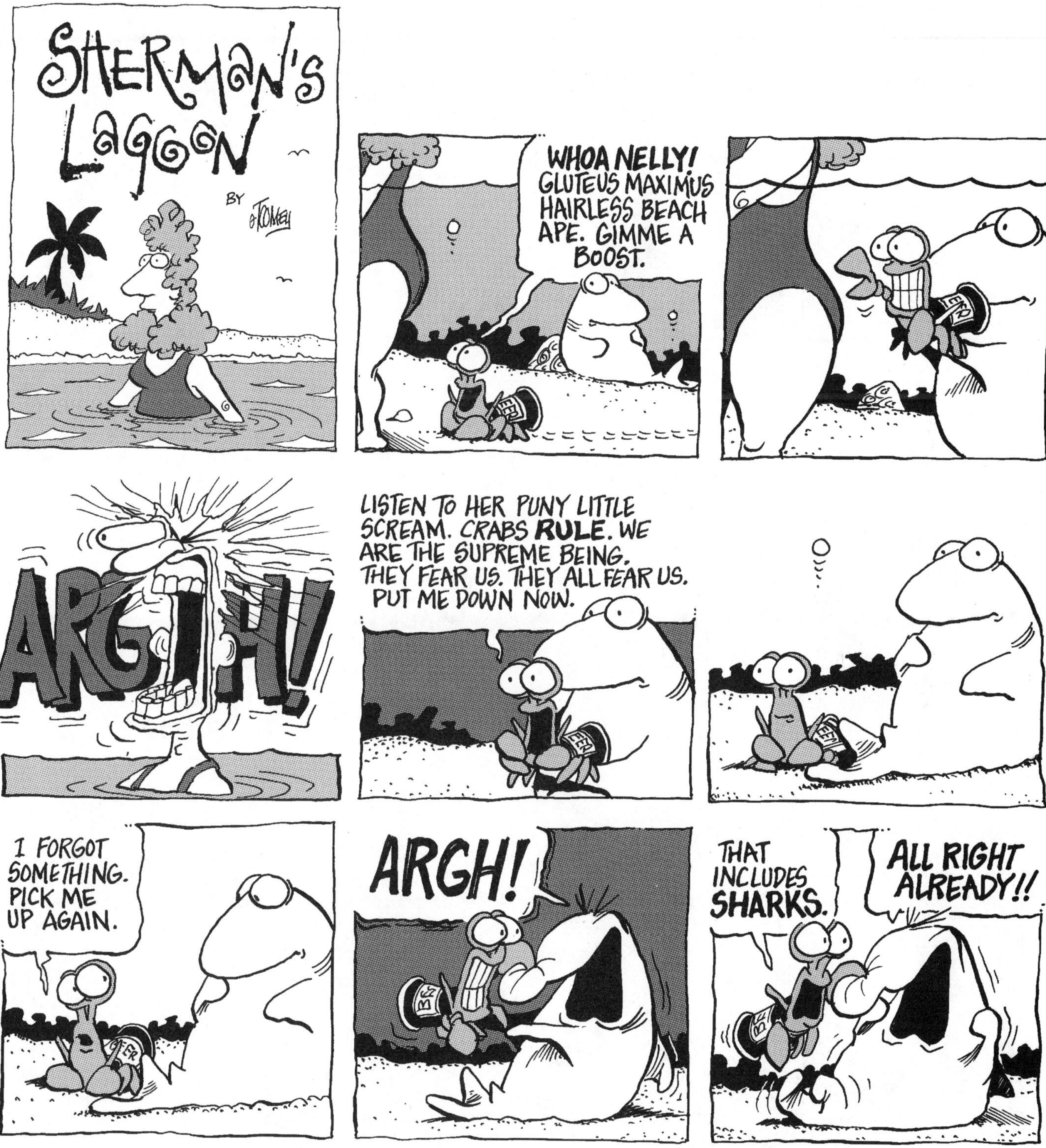
SHERMAN'S LAGOON
BY TOOMEY
WHOA NELLY! GLUTEUS MAXIMUS HAIRLESS BEACH APE. GIMME A BOOST.
ARGH!
LISTEN TO HER PUNY LITTLE SCREAM. CRABS RULE. WE ARE THE SUPREME BEING. THEY FEAR US. THEY ALL FEAR US. PUT ME DOWN NOW.
I FORGOT SOMETHING. PICK ME UP AGAIN.
ARGH!
THAT INCLUDES SHARKS.
ALL RIGHT ALREADY!!

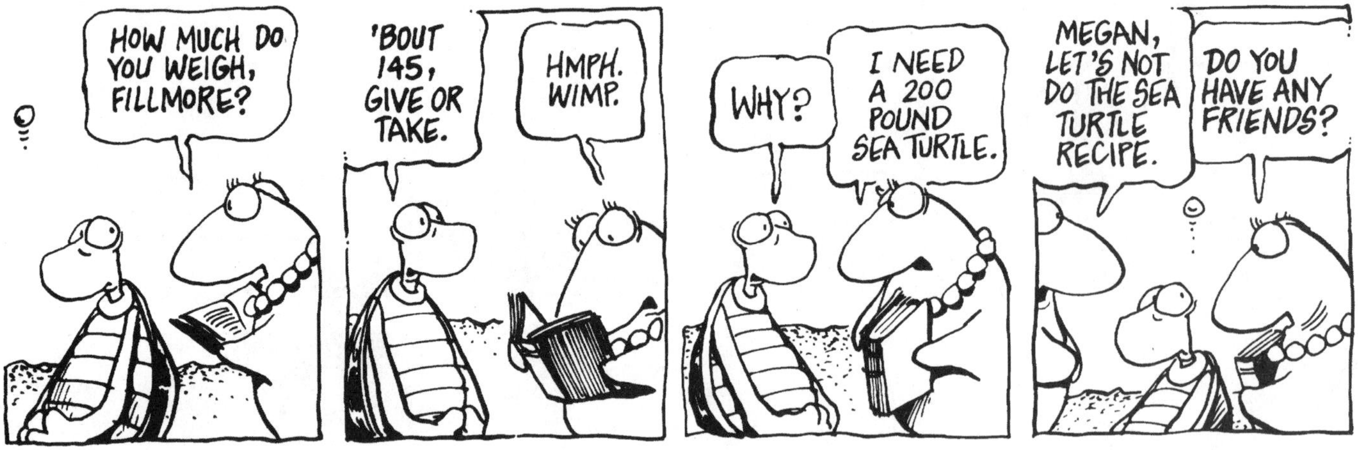
HOW MUCH DO YOU WEIGH, FILLMORE?
'BOUT 145, GIVE OR TAKE.
HMPH. WIMP.
WHY?
I NEED A 200 POUND SEA TURTLE.
MEGAN, LET'S NOT DO THE SEA TURTLE RECIPE.
DO YOU HAVE ANY FRIENDS?

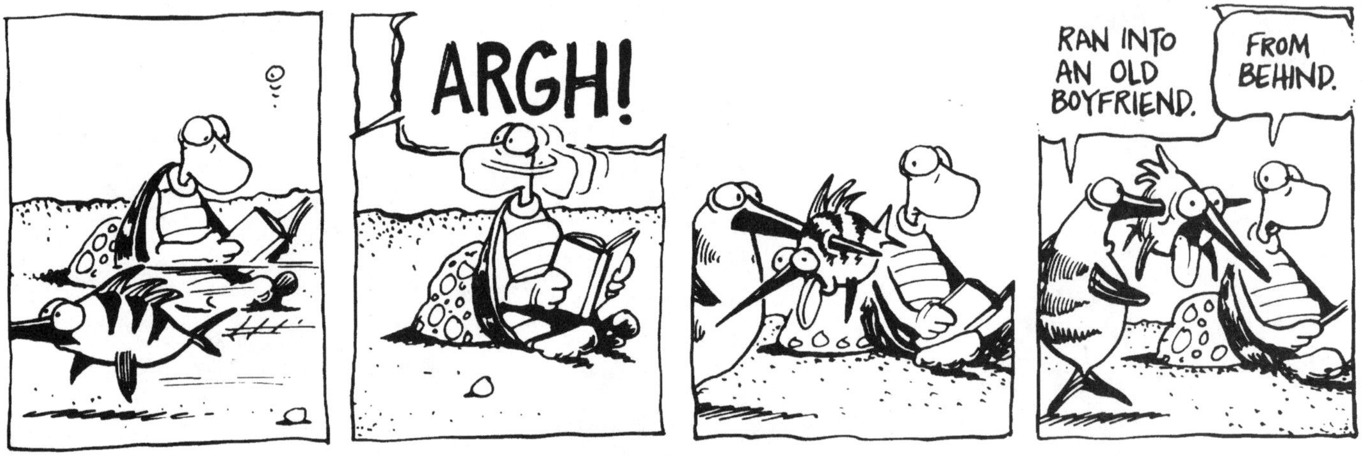
ARGH!
RAN INTO AN OLD BOYFRIEND.
FROM BEHIND.

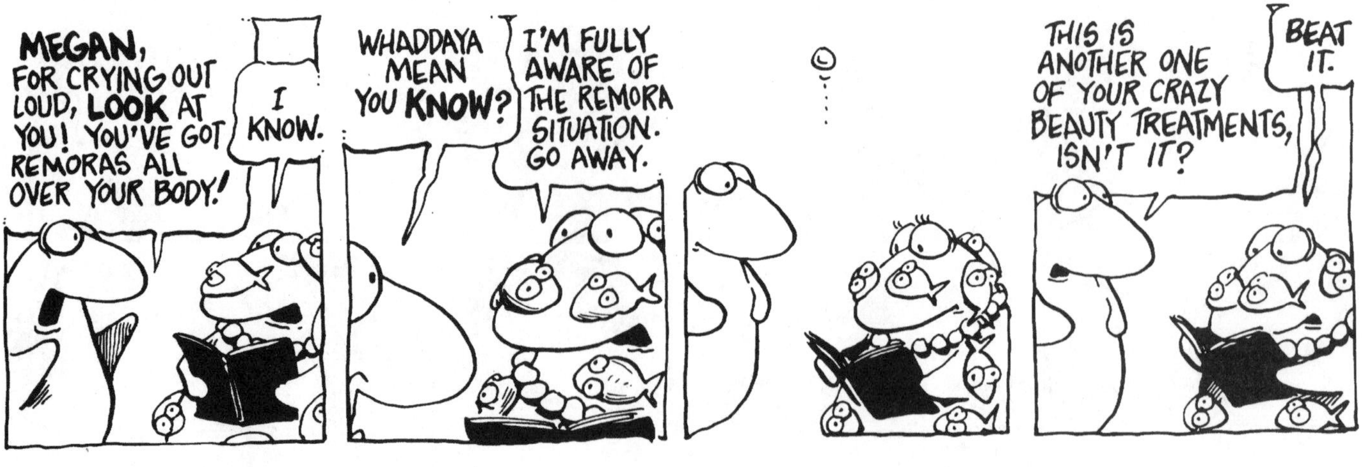
MEGAN, FOR CRYING OUT LOUD, LOOK AT YOU! YOU'VE GOT REMORAS ALL OVER YOUR BODY!
I KNOW.
WHADDAYA MEAN YOU KNOW?
I'M FULLY AWARE OF THE REMORA SITUATION. GO AWAY.
THIS IS ANOTHER ONE OF YOUR CRAZY BEAUTY TREATMENTS, ISN'T IT?
BEAT IT.

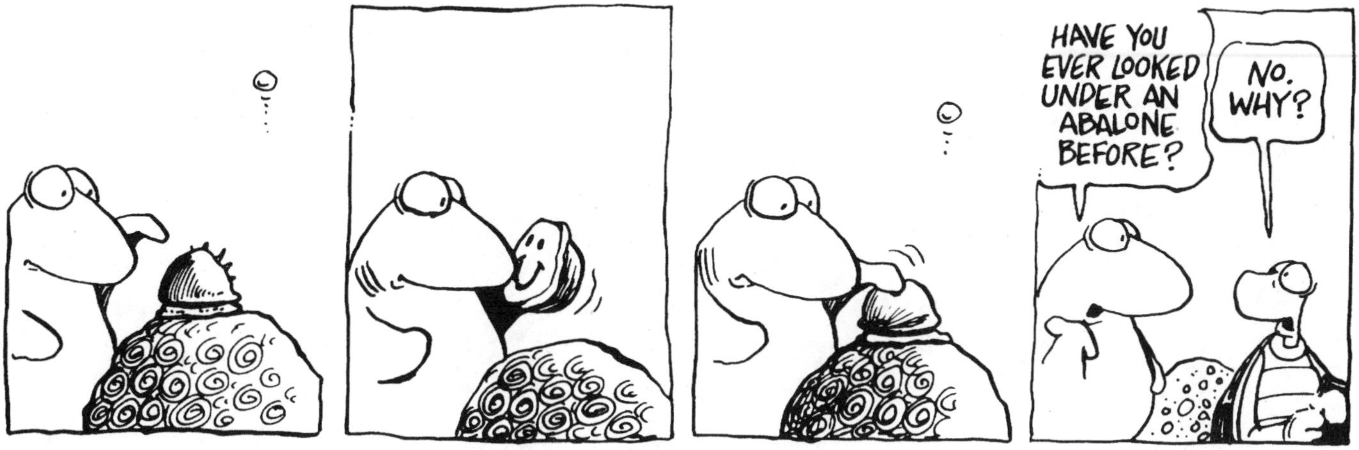
HAVE YOU EVER LOOKED UNDER AN ABALONE BEFORE?
NO. WHY?

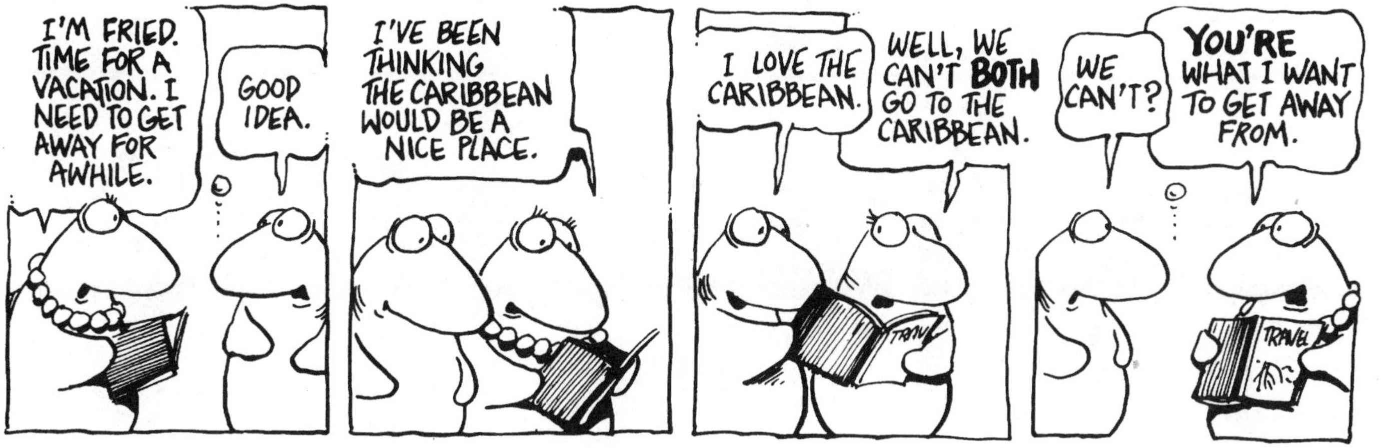
I'M FRIED. TIME FOR A VACATION. I NEED TO GET AWAY FOR AWHILE.
GOOD IDEA.
I'VE BEEN THINKING THE CARIBBEAN WOULD BE A NICE PLACE.
I LOVE THE CARIBBEAN.
WELL, WE CAN'T **BOTH** GO TO THE CARIBBEAN.
TRAVEL
WE CAN'T?
YOU'RE WHAT I WANT TO GET AWAY FROM.
TRAVEL

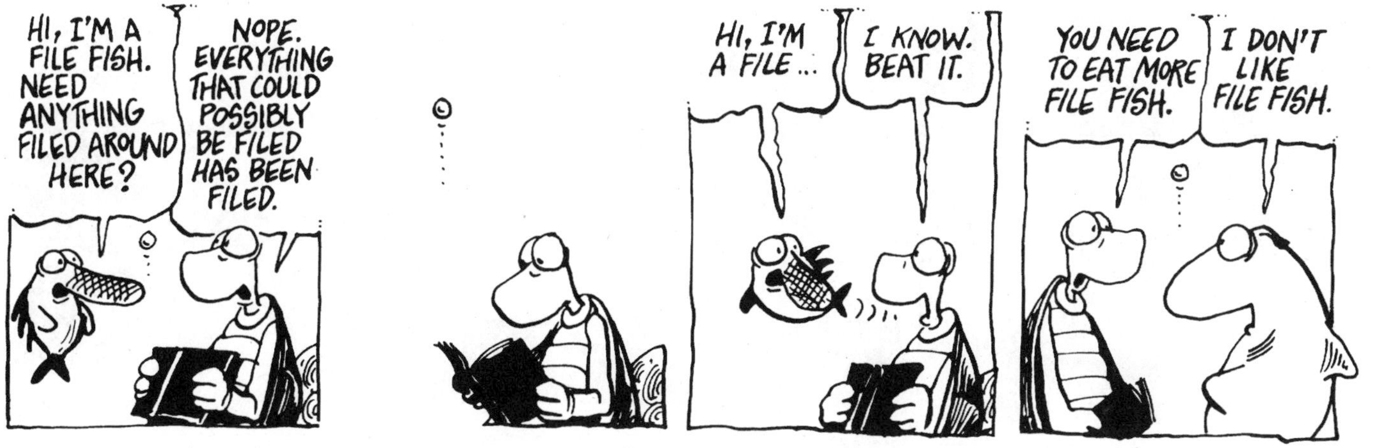
HI, I'M A FILE FISH. NEED ANYTHING FILED AROUND HERE?
NOPE. EVERYTHING THAT COULD POSSIBLY BE FILED HAS BEEN FILED.
HI, I'M A FILE...
I KNOW. BEAT IT.
YOU NEED TO EAT MORE FILE FISH.
I DON'T LIKE FILE FISH.

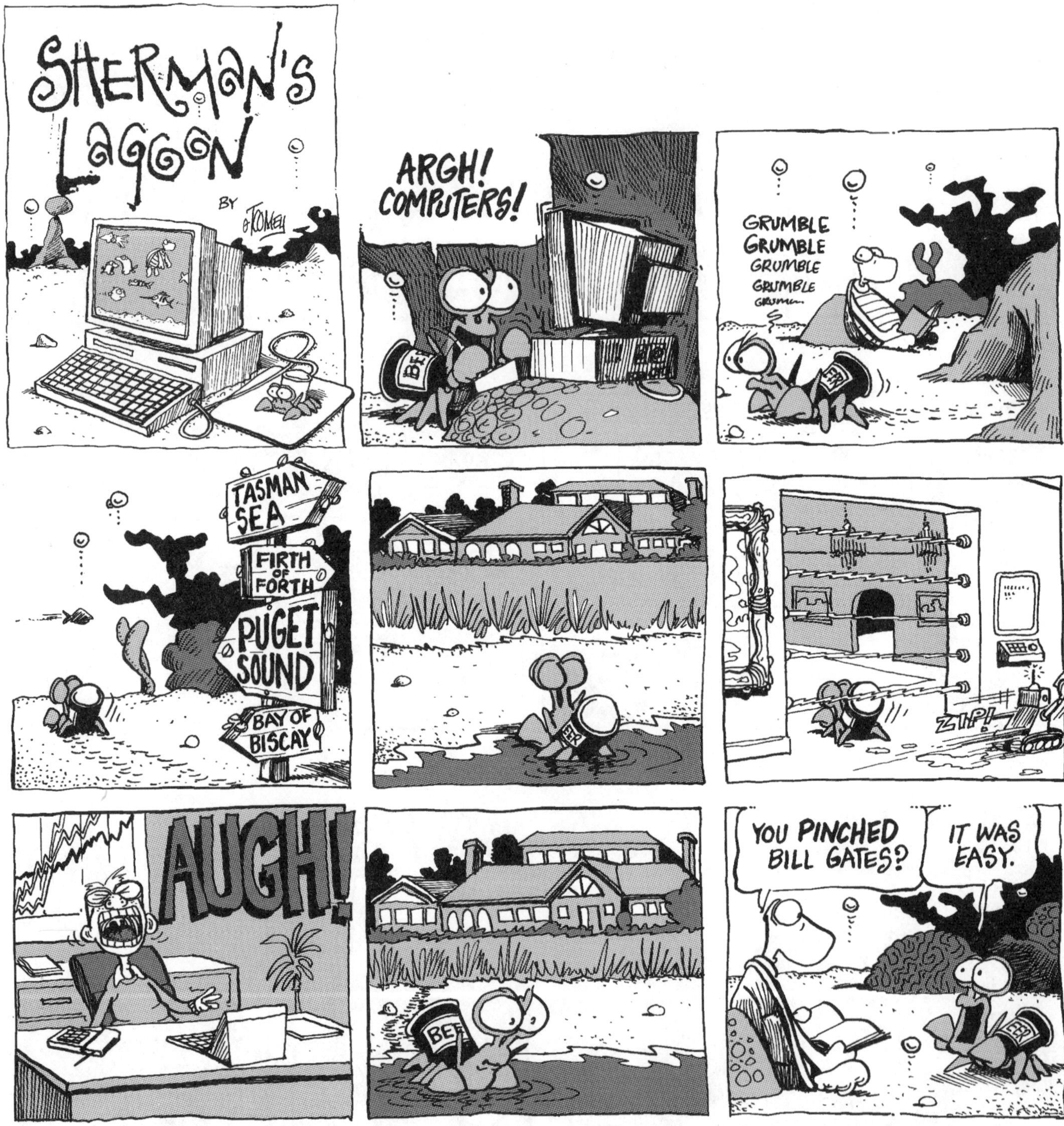
SHERMAN'S LAGOON
BY TOOMEY
ARGH! COMPUTERS!
BEER
GRUMBLE GRUMBLE GRUMBLE GRUMBLE GRUMBLE
BEER
TASMAN SEA
FIRTH OF FORTH
PUGET SOUND
BAY OF BISCAY
EER
ZIP!
AUGH!
BEE
YOU PINCHED BILL GATES?
IT WAS EASY.
EER

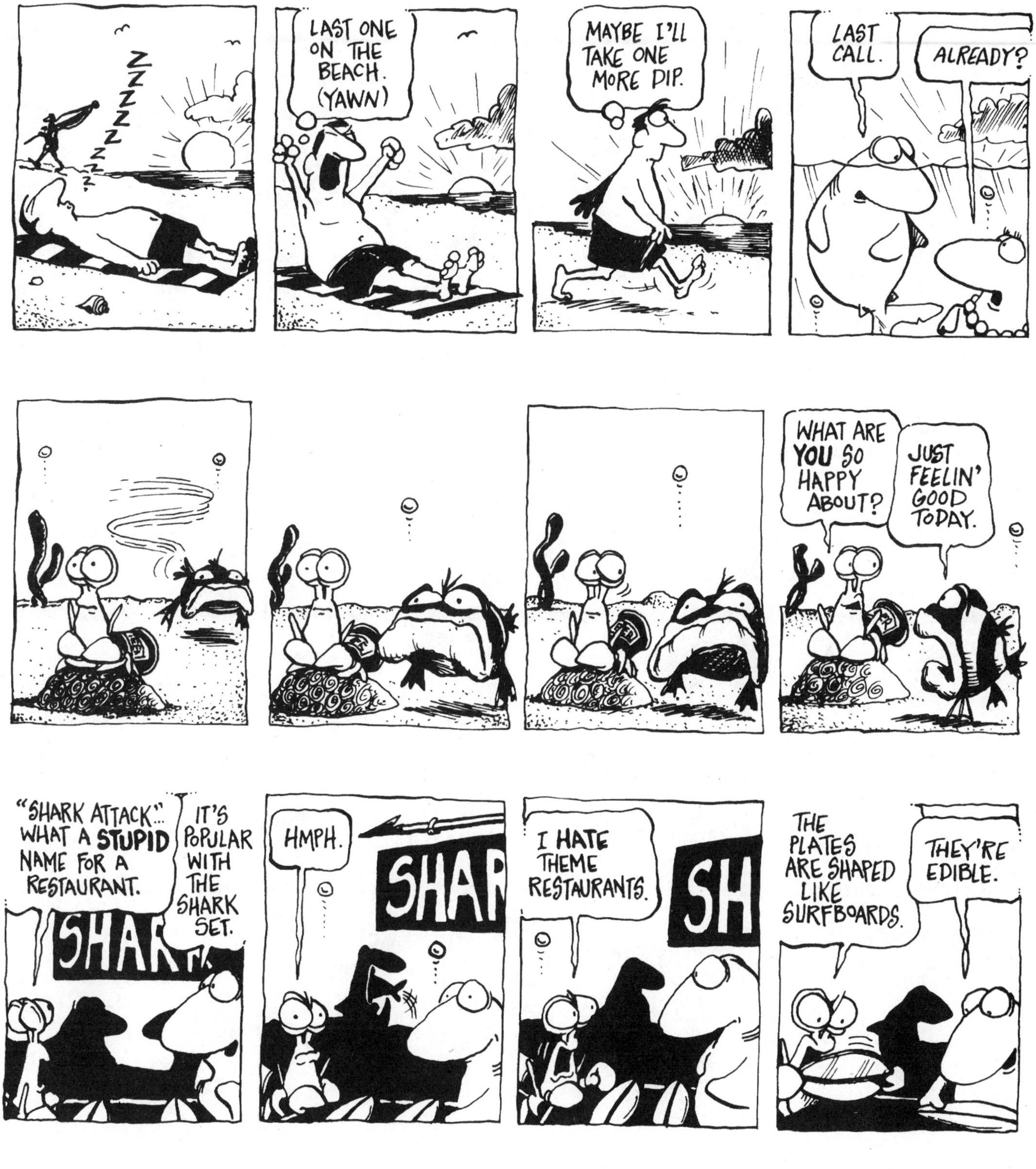
ZZZZZZZZ
LAST ONE ON THE BEACH. (YAWN)
MAYBE I'LL TAKE ONE MORE DIP.
LAST CALL.
ALREADY?
WHAT ARE YOU SO HAPPY ABOUT?
JUST FEELIN' GOOD TODAY.
"SHARK ATTACK"... WHAT A STUPID NAME FOR A RESTAURANT.
IT'S POPULAR WITH THE SHARK SET.
SHAR
HMPH.
SHAR
I HATE THEME RESTAURANTS.
SH
THE PLATES ARE SHAPED LIKE SURFBOARDS.
THEY'RE EDIBLE.

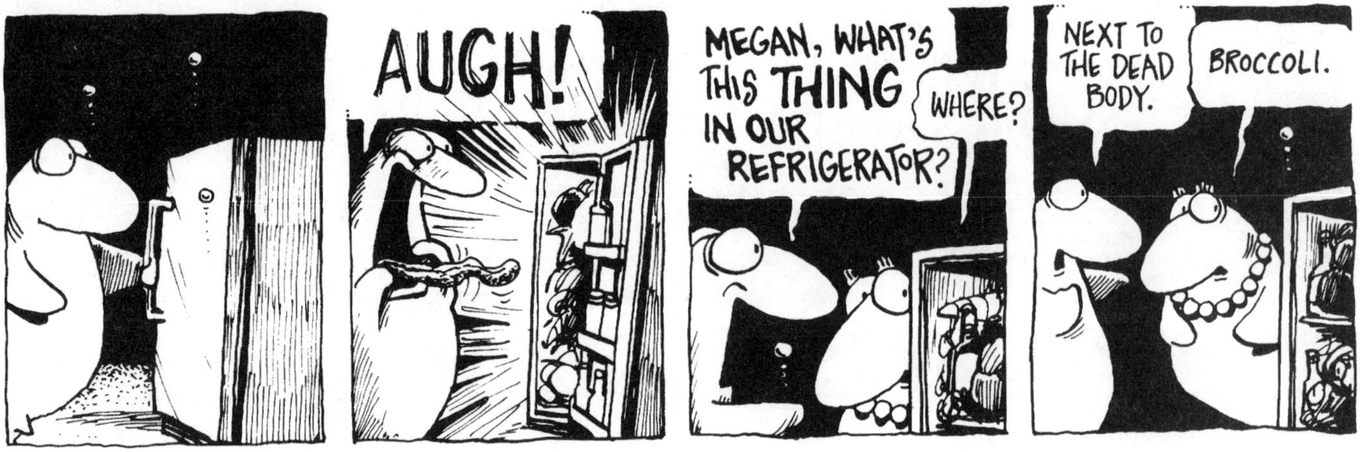
AUGH!
MEGAN, WHAT'S THIS THING IN OUR REFRIGERATOR?
WHERE?
NEXT TO THE DEAD BODY.
BROCCOLI.

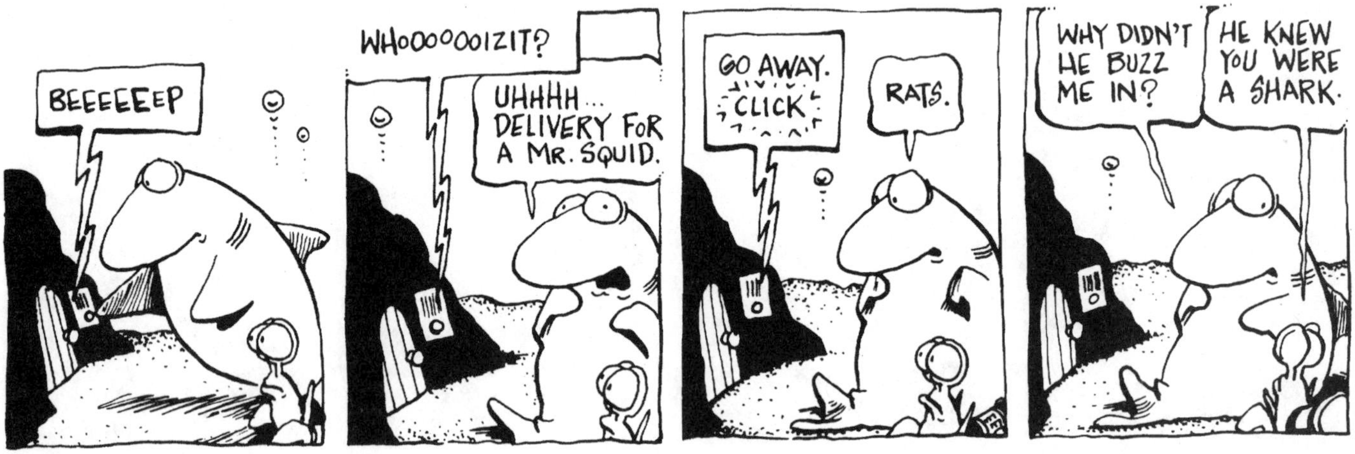
BEEEEEEP
WHOOOOOOIZIT?
UHHHH... DELIVERY FOR A MR. SQUID.
GO AWAY.
CLICK
RATS.
WHY DIDN'T HE BUZZ ME IN?
HE KNEW YOU WERE A SHARK.

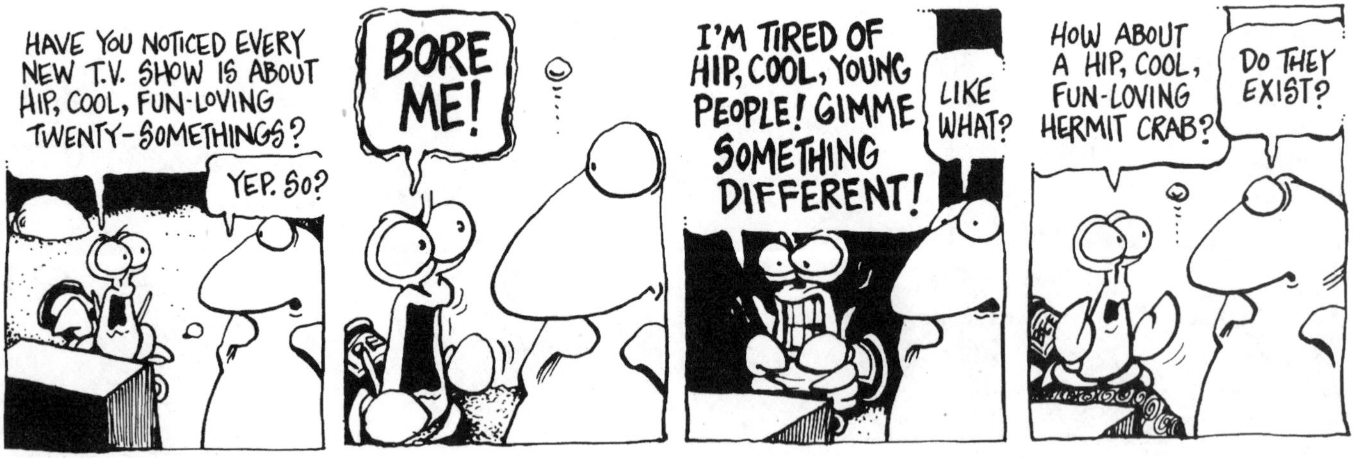
HAVE YOU NOTICED EVERY NEW T.V. SHOW IS ABOUT HIP, COOL, FUN-LOVING TWENTY-SOMETHINGS?
YEP. SO?
BORE ME!
I'M TIRED OF HIP, COOL, YOUNG PEOPLE! GIMME SOMETHING DIFFERENT!
LIKE WHAT?
HOW ABOUT A HIP, COOL, FUN-LOVING HERMIT CRAB?
DO THEY EXIST?